Girls Who Like Boys Who Like Boys

CW01082418

Lucy Neville

Girls Who Like Boys Who Like Boys

Women and Gay Male Pornography and Erotica

Lucy Neville
University of Leicester
Leicester, UK

ISBN 978-3-319-69133-6 (hardcover)   ISBN 978-3-319-69134-3 (eBook)
ISBN 978-3-030-01296-0 (softcover)
https://doi.org/10.1007/978-3-319-69134-3

Library of Congress Control Number: 2018932586

Cover design by Jenny Vong

Printed on acid-free paper

This Palgrave Macmillan imprint is published by Springer Nature
The registered company is Springer International Publishing AG
The registered company address is: Gewerbestrasse 11, 6330 Cham, Switzerland

To Anna Damski: you have been, and always shall be, my friend.

Foreword

This Girl Who Likes Boys: A Personal History

My sister had a Take That video with the boys on tour. There was a scene with them in a jacuzzi, naked. I was about 9, and fascinated with the human body—so often clothed and hidden—unveiled, be it strapping young men or my elderly grandma. But for once I wasn't that interested in the nudity *per se*, I was preoccupied by the way they were with each other, the intimacy, the *flirting*. *Look at how they touch each other.*

Cut to doing GCSEs at school. At house parties, the boys would ask us girls to make out with each other while they watched. My stock reply was, 'only if you do the same'. I think maybe some of my girlfriends were more amused by the politics of this response than intrigued to see its outcome, but none of them ever objected to this deal. The boys did object. However, they also often conceded. I was fascinated by watching them kiss. It was different from watching these very same boys get off with girls. They were softer, more vulnerable somehow. The kiss was para-doxically often more gentle than the snogs I saw so often between boys and girls. Hesitant, uncertain. They were beginning to get stubble, and the contrast of the masculinity of the hair alongside the softness of their mouths—for boys' mouths were soft, I noted, and often just as plush and plump as girls'—had a kind of erotic hypnosis over me.

Cut to university. 2001. Watching *Top Gun* in the common room. Ice Man biting his teeth at Maverick, an exaggerated signal of—*what?*—sexual desire, surely? Going back to my dorm, thinking—we have the internet now. Someone, somewhere, must have *done* something with this. Finding a story where they were lovers as well as rivals. Brutal, angry sex, but it was right somehow, not about gender or politics, but a perfectly enclosed bubble of their relationship, the two of them, not the rest of the world. And *hot.* After that, seeing more and more films through a queer lens. McManus and Fenster. They must be doing it, surely? The film barely even tries to *hide* the fact they're a couple. There must be something about that on the internet, too? There was. It was *good*, got me off quickly, like only the very best heterosexual porn could.

Rediscovering these stories many years later, but this time finding there's whole websites dedicated to m/m pairings. Reading, and reading. Watching the few het porn videos saved on my laptop less and less, preferring to use the gay sites.

Remembering how I always liked this.

Wondering why.

Leicester, UK   Lucy Neville

Acknowledgements

This book would not have happened without the tremendous generosity of participants, friends, colleagues, academics, fangirls, and slashers (not all mutually exclusive categories!) who have: taken part in the research, helped me to recruit for surveys and interviews, called me out on any lingering vestiges of heteronormative indoctrination, granted me a sabbatical to write the damn thing, taken over my teaching during said sabbatical, and read and commented on work—not to mention, in some cases, listened to me drunkenly rambling about gay porn at dinner parties and conferences. I am hugely indebted.

Particular thanks to: Mostest Beautifulest Interdisciplinariest Dr Erin Sanders-McDonagh, my #workwife, Elaine to my Masha, Ilana to my Abbi; Dr Simon Harding, my office husband (a girl needs both) and survey checker; the lovely&amazing Professor Feona Attwood, the most truly feminist and inclusionary scholar I have ever had the good fortune to meet; Sue Joyce for facilitating the zillions and squillions of inter-library loans I've requested these past few years; the indomitable Professor Clarissa Smith; various other sexademics (© Dr Paul Maginn) I have fangirled over at various events: Dr Nathan Rambukkana—so smart! Professor John Mercer—so gracious!; all the folks at *Transformative Works and Cultures* who are so generous with their time and expertise, as well as being best practice AF when it comes to publishing models; Dr Laura Helen Marks, the fiercest porn scholar of them all, tireless promoter of my work, sweetheart, fellow Jezebel #NTBC; Dr Nicki Smith, academic writing coach extraordinaire; Dr Jodi McAlister and Dr Brian Kavanagh for scholarly tips on (respectively) romance and barebacking; Professor Louise Ryan for demonstrating how to be a badass woman in the academy—a brilliant mentor (and the superlative Professor Teela Sanders for taking over this mantle); obviously the students—funny and bright and open (special props to my all-time teacher's pet, Anna Segal, and my horrifically talented PhD student, Patricia MacLeod); King DoP; Mogs; DP; JDogg; Carly; Showgirl; Mia; Queen B; Johan; the awesome Nancy Mendoza for Queer Anxieties Counselling; Caren, Jane, Zoe, Tif, Ami, and countless other slasher visionaries.

Thanks to the School of Law at Middlesex University for their support of this project; in particular, thanks to my former dean, Professor Joshua Castellino.

Thanks to my editors at Palgrave for their patience in the face of my extreme tardiness.

Thanks to Clémence Brousse for her stunning cover mock-ups.

Thanks to the first fandom I wrote in (Esca/Marcus forever!) for getting me started down this strange and beautiful pathway. I ♥ you bbs.

Thanks to my family for creating this little weirdo: Pappy, Sally, Sister Kate, Twin ('I mean I wouldn't *choose* to read it—I'd rather read your *Star Trek* porn—but it's interesting, I guess'), collected horrified grandparents, Bustopher Jones, Pretty Boy Floyd, FGMY, Henry, Double Godsister, and Willis.

Thanks to Dan for general wonderfulness and being the best cheerleader a girl could hope for.

Contents

Contents

List of Figures

List of Tables

1

Welcome to the Freak Show

A good friend of mine talks about what she calls 'the dinner party test'. The idea behind the dinner party test is this: if you can't sum up what you do in a brief, pithy, engaging sentence or two that will be easily understood by everyone at the party, then maybe you don't really understand what you're doing. I've never had a problem passing the dinner party test in real life.

'I'm a lecturer,' I say, 'in Criminology.'

Then, 'I study women who like gay male porn.'

There you go. Brief. Pithy. Engaging.

Men tend to tilt their heads quizzically to one side. 'Really?' they ask. 'Is that a *thing*?' Sometimes they'll add '*Oh*, like when guys like lesbian porn' (more on that later). Other times they'll look at me askance, 'that's … just *weird*'.

Women tend to respond a little differently. Either with happy affirmations of their own interest in m/m erotica, or with intrigue and a desire to know more. Often they'll launch into an enthusiastic story of how hot it was when Jason and Eric made out in *True Blood,* or how much they enjoyed Anthony Kedis and Dave Navarro snogging in The Red Hot Chilli Peppers' *Warped* video.

© The Author(s) 2018
L. Neville, *Girls Who Like Boys Who Like Boys*,
https://doi.org/10.1007/978-3-319-69134-3_1

It's not just that I go to progressive dinner parties, either. In recent years the TV series *Game of Thrones* has become as notorious for its racy sex scenes as it has for its gripping storylines. However, despite the near ubiquitous sexuality, it appears some viewers feel like they're not being catered for. Speaking at the Edinburgh Literary Festival in 2014, the series' author, G. R. R. Martin, discussed how he received numerous letters from fans asking for more explicit gay male sex scenes to be included, and that 'most of the[se] letters come from women' (in Furness, 2014). Certainly Martin isn't the first author or producer to realise that women might be interested in the representation of m/m sex. The m/m romance in *Brokeback Mountain* proved phenomenally successful with female audiences—as Michael Jensen observes 'women [took] to *Brokeback* like flies to over-salted peanuts' (Jensen, in Nayar, 2011, p. 235). Since then we have seen the increasing inclusion of gay male love scenes in TV shows with a large female viewership (e.g. *The Carrie Diaries, The Following, Teen Wolf*). Reviewing this phenomenon has led eminent transgender scholar Bobby Noble (2007, p. 154) to conclude that 'women constitute a powerful emerging demographic as consumers of sexualised images of men—even, or perhaps especially, queer men—in popular culture'.

Female passion for m/m sex is not limited only to popular culture and the written word, but extends into erotica and hardcore pornography as well. Acknowledging that more women than men had bought his first m/m erotic novel, gay fiction author James Lear observed that women 'fancy men, they're turned on by men and so they're *even more* turned on by men with men—it's like "man squared"' (in *The Metro*, 2008). In the realm of visual pornography, analysis of billions of hits to the PornHub site (one of the largest online porn sites in the world) shows that gay male porn has been the second most popular choice for women porn users out of 25+ possible genre choices for two years running (PornHub, 2014, 2015). Pornhub estimates that women make up 37 per cent of its m/m porn viewers (Pornhub, 2015), suggesting that women represent viable secondary consumers of m/m porn. Anecdotal data supports these figures. George Alvin, a performer in The Cocky Boys, a troupe of gay male porn stars, notes that women make up 'at least 80 percent' of the fans present at the troupe's frequent meet-and-greets, adding 'if it wasn't for our women fans, I don't think we would have the level of exposure that we've had. They are the ones that create the conversation and support the work' (in Wischhover, 2016).

However, despite the emergence of porn studies as an area of interest, to date there has been little exploration as to the nature or prevalence of female interest in m/m sex, nor of what this might have to say about female audiences, female desire, and the female gaze. There are few academic data on how widespread the practice of watching gay male pornography is within the female population, as the majority of surveys exploring women's engagement with porn have not asked this question. In McKee, Albury and Lumby's (2008, p. 117) comprehensive account of their study of over 1000 porn users, the idea that images produced 'by men, for men' might appeal to women too warrants only one brief sentence. Of course, it could be that the women I've spoken with when writing this book represent only a tiny outlier group, although the PornHub (2014, 2015) data would suggest this is not the case. Viewing these data alongside the popularity of m/m sex in visual cultural products targeted at a largely female audience, the prevalence of m/m sex in women's sexual fantasies (Nicholas, 2004), numerous anecdotal references in the literature to women in focus groups responding positively to gay male sex scenes (see Gunn, 1993), and the burgeoning popularity of writing featuring explicit m/m sex amongst women of all ages and sexual orientations (Green, Jenkins, & Jenkins, 1998; Jamison, 2013), it would appear that engaging with m/m content is not an unusual practice among women who consume erotic material—from hardcore visual pornography to erotic romance novels.

Through an analysis of the responses given by over 500 (self-identified) women who engage with m/m sexually explicit media [SEM] as to what they enjoy about it, I hope to provide a deeper insight into how and why these women engage with this type of erotica. Although consumers may not be conscious of all their reasons for enjoying a genre, it is still important to examine the reasons that they give for their enjoyment.

Women Watching Pornography

The paucity of research into women who watch m/m pornography may be partly explained by the fact that for much of the twentieth century the common assumption within the academic literature was that women were not aroused by *any* porn (Carter, 1977). Many researchers have observed that it is possible that this perception arose because porn seemed to be about sexual imagery made public, and women had been taught that public displays of sexuality were negatively valued in social terms—'we have learned that to engage in public displays of sexuality is to be defined as a slut. Where boys learn that sex makes them powerful, we learn that it makes us powerful and bad' (Diamond, 1985, p. 50). Being a human who is sexual—who is *allowed* to be sexual—appears to be a freedom much more readily afforded by society to males than females. It is perhaps not surprising, then, that up until the mid-1990s research on porn found that men tended to hold more permissive attitudes towards porn and were the predominant consumers when compared with women (Laumann, Gagnon, Michael, & Michaels, 1994). However, more recent studies suggest gender disparity in accessing porn may be narrowing in the age of the internet. A cross-sectional online probability survey of 2021 adults found that 82 per cent of males reported accessing porn online, as did 60 per cent of females (Herbenick et al., 2010). There has also been a growing acknowledgement that women may like similar kinds of porn to men. Mackinnon (1997, p. 120) argues that the rise of 'female'-produced hardcore heterosexual porn and lesbian S&M fantasy porn make it 'far more difficult to maintain the distinctions between male-orientated pornography and female-orientated erotica', the latter being historically regarded as 'soft, tender, non-explicit' (Williams, 1990, p. 231). Nevertheless, female interest in pornography has been less well explored than male interest, with Ciclitira (2004, p. 286, emphasis added) noting that 'there has been little empirical work which has elicited women's own accounts about *their* experiences of pornography'.

Women Watching m/m Pornography

There has been even less empirical work looking at women's experiences of gay male pornography. In her seminal work, *Hard Core: Power, Pleasure and the 'Frenzy of the Visible'* Linda Williams (1990, p. 7) implies that m/m porn is of little interest to women, when she states that she is not going to include gay male pornography in her study of hardcore porn on the grounds that it could not appeal to *her* as a heterosexual woman; 'lesbian and gay pornography do not address me personally'. While Schauer (2005, pp. 54, 58) observes that there is a large number of scenes of lesbian sex distributed across heterosexual male porn sites, noting 'the 'discovery' of lesbian 'pleasures' among the female population is virtually *de rigueur* here', she believes that in 'women's porno … nowhere is man-to-man sex symbolically or otherwise evident'.

However, even if certain areas of the social sciences have been slow to explore and understand this phenomenon, the psychological sciences have noted for some time that many women respond, physiologically at least, to m/m sexual images. Meredith Chivers, who has looked extensively into the nature of female sexual response to pornographic imagery (see, e.g., Chivers & Bailey, 2005; Chivers, Rieger, Latty, & Bailey, 2004) has run a number of studies where women have been shown a variety of sexual films: including lesbian porn, gay male porn, heterosexual porn, and monkeys having sex. She and her colleagues have observed that, with respect to genital arousal, most women show a 'strikingly flat profile' (Bailey, 2008, p. 55)—that is, they appear at a physiological level to find gay male sex as arousing as heterosexual sex. The journalist and writer Caitlin Moran acknowledges the omnivorous nature of female sexual tastes, joking that the best things about masturbation are that 'it doesn't cost anything, it doesn't make you fat, [and] you can knock it off in five minutes flat if you think about Han Solo, or some monkeys "doing it" on an Attenborough documentary' (Moran, 2016). This is not to say that most women *consciously* feel equally as aroused by all visual representations of sex. Vaginal 'arousal' does not always tally with self-reported arousal scores (where women tend to rate films that concur with their sexual orientation as more arousing than those which do not), leading

Chivers, Seto, Lalumière, Laan, and Grimbos (2010, p. 48) to conclude that 'a woman's genital responding might reveal little about her sexual interests'.[1] Chivers et al. (2010) also speculate that, for women, based on observations of higher levels of female consumption of nonvisual forms of erotic literature (see Malamuth, 1996 for a review), concordance between physiological and self-reported arousal would be greater when assessed using nonvisual modalities of erotic stimuli. However, it should be noted that, much the same as men, women have more genital arousal while watching sexually explicit videos than they do reading erotic stories or engaging in erotic fantasy (Van Dam, Honnebier, van Zelinge, & Barendregt, 1976), and that romantic content does not enhance genital arousal (Heiman, 1977). It would seem that women respond to the same explicit content that men do, and, not only that, they respond to a greater variety of content too.

So, while the work of Chivers and her colleagues may well suggest a dissociation between mind and body in women's arousal—and I'm certainly not suggesting that a woman's vaginal lubrication is a good predictor of what she's actually feeling—it may also suggest that women have a more fluid sexual response than men. In her work on sexual fluidity, Lisa Diamond (2008) identifies two different types of sexual desire: *proceptivity*, that is lust or libido, and *arousability*, the capacity to become aroused once certain cues are encountered. She observes that as female proceptivity is a lot less constant than men's, and only peaks for a few days at a time in-line with ovulation, a woman's sexual desire is therefore primarily driven by arousability. Diamond (2008, pp. 210–212) adds that proceptivity is essentially heterosexual in so much as it is geared around reproductive sexual activity. However arousability is not intrinsically oriented and therefore does not need to be 'gender targeted', leading Diamond to conclude 'if the majority of women's day-to-day desires are governed by arousability, and if arousability is a 'gender-neutral' system, then … women … are [more] likely to have … "cross-orientation" desires [than men]'. Diamond here is discussing women's greater propensity towards same-sex attractions, and a fluid sense of sexual orientation. However, there is no reason that her theory could not also explain why women might find m/m sex arousing. Taken with the work of Chivers and her colleagues, and viewed in the light of the recent 'discovery' by the media that women might like watching men have sex with each other, it may well be that women enjoying watching m/m pornography is not particularly surprising.

Women and Slash

One dimension of female interest in m/m eroticism which has been more thoroughly explored is the area of slash fiction (and, to a lesser extent, slash videos [slash vids]). Slash[2] is a genre of fan fiction that focuses on interpersonal attraction and sexual relationships between fictional characters of the same sex, believed to have originated in the 1970s when female fans started to compose stories based around *Star Trek* where Kirk and Spock had a romantic—and often sexual—relationship. Much of the academic research on slash fiction has come from the areas of media studies and cultural studies, with 'the former tending to emphasize the pornographic aspects of slash, the latter its romantic aspects' (Salmon & Symons, 2001, p. 74). Hayes and Ball (2009, p. 222) observe that 'by far the most popular stories have sex scenes between the two main male characters, which are graphically depicted in detail with the explicit aim of titillating the reader' (see also Bruner, 2013). The more sexually explicit genres within slash have (not without controversy) been characterised as 'porn' by some scholars (Russ, 1985). Paasonen (2010, p. 139) agrees that these sorts of texts can certainly be classified as pornographic, describing the tendency to understand pornography purely in terms of the visual as problematic, particularly considering 'the history of pornography has largely been one concerning the written word'. To this extent explicit online slash texts can be viewed as a form of pornography for women. However, it should be noted that slash fiction is about far more than sex. Lothian, Busse and Reid (2007, p. 103, emphasis added) maintain that online slash fandoms 'can induct us into new and unusual narratives of identity and sexuality, calling into question familiar identifications and assumptions' and that as such 'slash fandom's discursive sphere has been termed *queer female space* by some who inhabit and study it'. Catherine Driscoll (2006, p. 91) also notes that, as one of the few forms of pornography mainly produced and consumed by women, slash fiction is important for what it says about the gendering of porn.

The concept of 'slashing' male characters in films, TV shows, and books is increasingly spilling over into the mainstream. In May 2016 the hashtag #GiveCaptainAmericaABoyfriend trended on Twitter, with thousands of social media users taking to the site to campaign for Marvel to include a same-sex love story for Captain America in his next film outing. Tweets not only pointed to the existing romantic tension between the character and his 'BFF', James Buchanan 'Bucky' Barnes, but also highlighted how positive it would be for younger members of the LGBTQ+ community to have a non-heterosexual superhero to look up to on the big screen. However, despite the growing awareness and popularity of slash fic (Jamison, 2013), research in media and cultural studies tends to view slashing as a somewhat isolated phenomenon. Indeed, in her influential chapter on women's involvement in slash, Bacon-Smith (1992, p. 248) talks about how 'only a very small number' of female slash writers and readers have any interest in gay literature or pornography more generally; and the possibility of slashers having a broader interest in m/m SEM is not often discussed in more recent analyses of slash. In terms of why women are drawn to slash, CarrieLynn Reinhard (2009) notes that explanations for this behaviour have typically consisted of theorists discussing *their* ideas of why women slash, and there has been less work grounding these ideas in conversations with slashers, using their interpretative stance to develop theories.

Women and Boys' Love Manga

Boys' Love [BL], and its more explicit subgenre *yaoi*,[3] are usually defined as same-sex male romances or erotica written 'by women for women' (Meyer, 2010). Much like slash, BL developed from (primarily) women taking manga intended for male consumption and rewriting them to accommodate their own desires and interests. However, while there are many similarities between BL and slash, BL is produced in comic book or graphic novel format. Slash often includes illustrations, but the artwork is not an essential part of the narrative. In this respect, Pagliassotti (2010, p. 74) argues that 'sexually explicit BL manga may more closely resemble Western pornography than it does Western romance or erotica'. There is the same emphasis on the aesthetic of maximum visibility that we see in video pornography. Nagaike (2003) has therefore suggested that it can be productive to analyse BL as pornography that reflects women's sexual desires. Insofar as readers consume such texts as a medium through which they satisfy at least some of their sexual appetites, we can define these texts as pornographic.

BL has proved incredibly popular with women, both in Japan, where the genre originates, and worldwide. Part of this may well be down to the fact that, unlike slash, which is beset by issues with copyright regarding who owns the characters and their universes, BL has enjoyed commercial success, with Japanese publishing companies publishing work by amateur *yaoi* artists. Commercially produced *yaoi* in Japan is now a big business, and 'has generated enough jobs for hundreds of women to be economically independent by providing products to female customers' (Mizoguchi, 2003, p. 66). It may also be because the concept of women appreciating m/m sex and gay culture is regarded as less unusual in Japan than in the West. As journalist Richard McGregor states, 'in Japan almost anything homosexual can attract an all-female audience' (1996, p. 229). Lesbian activist Sarah Schulman reported being astonished to discover in Tokyo in 1992 that a lesbian and gay film festival was being held in a popular shopping mall and that 'the audience was 80 per cent straight women' (1994, p. 245).

Much like with slash, there is a preponderance of interesting theoretical work on women and BL. A lot of this analysis tends to treat the genre as problematic, and attempts to explain the sexist features of Japanese society that drive Japanese women to fantasise about homosexual, not heterosexual, romance (McLelland, 2000). Within this outlook, m/m content is only consumed because it offers a form of escapism from women's confined roles within heterosexual erotica, presenting women with the sort of equal relationship they could never hope to achieve with a man themselves (Buruma, 1984; Suzuki, 1998). Moreover, some critics believe the men and boys featured in BL are simply the women's displaced selves, citing the androgynous appearance of male characters in many comics (Matsui, 1993). Meyer (2010, p. 237) agrees that BL is about equality, but not just women wanting equal relationships with men, rather the equality here is 'more literal and physical. It is about the availability of both sexual roles for women and men, not just euphemistically 'active' and 'passive' roles, but about who penetrates and who gets penetrated'. Others have argued that, far from being a simple expression of sexual fantasy, BL offers a space where readers and creators can think through transforming social ideologies around gender and sexuality (Martin, 2012). Mizoguchi (2011, p. 164) describes the BL fan community in Japan as an 'unprecedented, effective political arena for women with the potential for [feminist and/or queer] activism'.

Thorn (2004, p. 173) observes that the independent rise of 'identical' m/m genres in Japan and the English speaking world is a 'striking coincidence', adding, 'clearly there is something about this formula that pushes the buttons, so to speak, of a certain demographic of women throughout much of the industrialised world'. However, once again, while the theoretical work is rich and complex, there has been far less empirical research done asking creators and consumers of BL what they like about the genre, and what, if any, impact it has on their lives and politics. Dru Pagliassotti (2010), who *has* carried out extensive survey work with BL fans, notes that the growing popularity of m/m romance—not only in the form of BL, but also slash and original fiction—requires further consideration and analysis.

'Good, Old-Fashioned Girl-on-Girl Action': Men and f/f Porn

Here we return to the comparison I hear a lot when discussing my research: that perhaps we shouldn't be surprised that women like m/m porn when we all know that men like 'lesbian' porn. And we do 'know' this. Countless popular texts are littered with references to this normal facet of heterosexual male desire. In an often-screened *Friends* episode, 'The One With The Sharks', one of the show's central characters, Monica Geller, catches her husband Chandler masturbating while apparently watching a shark documentary. Monica attempts to reconcile herself to the idea that her husband is secretly into 'shark porn', even going as far as to put footage of sharks on as a prelude to the pair having sex. When he discovers her mistake, Chandler is quick to reassure her that he had actually just changed the channel when she came into the room, and had originally been getting off to 'some regular … good, old fashioned, American, girl-on-girl action'. Bauer (2012, p. 1) comments on how this scene is endemic of what she describes as 'the naturalisation of straight men watching "lesbian" porn'. By contrasting the viewing of 'girl-on-girl action' with what Monica sees as the 'weird' notion of being turned on by 'angry' fish, *Friends* portrays the idea of men watching f/f porn as not only acceptable, but 'regular'.

It is certainly the case that porn marketed for straight men often involves women having sex with women. Linda Williams (1992, p. 253) notes how this kind of 'lesbian number' has often been presented for the gaze of the male voyeur in straight pornography, so that it is 'constrained and consumed by masculine heterosexual frames'. Heather Butler (2004, p. 253) discusses how lesbian sex in straight pornography is often presented as a warm-up for sex between a man and a woman, or as "lesbo-jelly' in the hetero-donut'. Even though feminist scholars such as Adrienne Rich and Barbara Smith have criticised ersatz 'lesbian' pornography from as long ago as the 1980s, pointing out that the majority of 'girl-on-girl' pornography was produced for 'the male voyeuristic eye' (Rich, 1980, p. 234) to the detriment of real homosexual women, the tendency to portray this potentially queer phenomenon as a 'normal' part of 'regular' male heterosexuality has seldom been questioned. Williams (2005, p. 206) mentions the 'strangeness' of this 'widely accepted form' of 'male heterosexual titillation', but in general the straight-male erotic fascination with 'lesbianism' is universalised and naturalised within an academic context. Bauer (2012, p. 2) describes this as 'one of *the* unquestioned clichés within U.S. popular culture *and* academic culture'.

Mark McLelland, who has carried out extensive research in the area of women's engagement with BL manga, asks whether we actually *need* to better understand why women might like m/m sex, and what they might like about it.

> Why should men's interest in 'lesbianism' be taken for granted, whereas women's interest in male homosexuality is somehow in need of interpretation?… If heterosexual men enjoy the idea of two women getting it on, why should heterosexual women not enjoy the idea of two men

bonking?... [There is a supposition here that] in a non-sexist world women would 'naturally' choose heterosexual fantasy, itself a sexist assumption. (McLelland, 2001, pp. 6, 1)

While this is true, there is something, I would argue, different and interesting happening here. Male interest in lesbianism, while certainly undertheorised, is in-keeping with many previous explanations of how and why men view and consume pornographic content (Attwood, 2005). Female interest in watching the visual portrayal of m/m sex is challenging, in so much as it raises questions about the ways in which women can, and do, engage with pornography, and the existence (or not) of the female gaze.

Asking Women What They Like and Why They Like It

In her seminal work, *At Home With Pornography*, Jane Juffer (1998) argues that scholars need to develop a better understanding of how women have 'domesticated' pornography, that is, brought it into their own lives on their own terms. In today's world, where access to the internet is widespread and has served to democratise access to porn (McNair, 2013), this call to understanding remains as pertinent as ever. However, little work has been carried out that sheds light on the ways in which porn is 'used, worked on, elaborated, remembered, fantasised about by its subjects' (Wicke, 1993, p. 70), and even less work has been carried out looking at the ways *women* in particular interact with sexually explicit media. Karen Ciclitira (2004, p. 293, emphasis added) points out that 'the feminist debate about how women *should* respond to pornography is bedevilled by an ignorance of how they actually *do*'. Just as most porn is created with a male spectator in mind, thus creating objectivity for women and subjectivity for men, much of the scholarship about porn has been logical-positivist 'effects'-based studies (Gunter, 2002) of whether exposure to porn has negative effects on men, especially with regards to their views on women (e.g. Morrison, Ellis, Morrison, Bearden, & Harriman, 2006). Ironically, this paradigm positions women as passive objects to be reacted to by men and, in doing so, 'reflexively replicates and applies to the *study* of pornography the same exploitative motive that anti-pornography feminists … apply to creating and consuming pornography itself' (Beggan & Allison, 2009, p. 447). Susan Shaw (1999, p. 200) therefore highlights the importance of looking at individual women's meanings and interpretations of pornography, while Mowlabocus and Wood (2015, p. 120) assert that a more nuanced understanding of women's porn consumption is imperative if we are to 'make an intervention into the ongoing discussions of pornography use and effect'.

Despite the growing awareness of the need to solicit women's accounts of their interactions with sexually explicit media, it has only been in the past few years that any work has emerged that has asked women about their experiences with m/m pornography (McCutcheon & Bishop, 2015; Neville, 2015; Ramsay, 2017). Blair (2010, p. 111) notes that most researchers approach the question of why women like m/m erotic content 'by theorising rather than by asking readers [or watchers] for their reasons'. Green et al. (1998) similarly critique theories about slash fic for failing to take account of fans' own ideas about what they enjoy about the genre, even though fans themselves tend to be highly self-reflexive, questioning why they are drawn to slash. They also criticise academic accounts for their desire to find a univocal explanation for women's interest in m/m sex, noting that, in stark contrast, the women themselves are often 'interested in exploring the multiple and differing—sometimes even contradictory—motivations that led them to this genre' (Green et al., 1998, p. 12).

It is for reasons such as this that reception researchers originally turned away from critical traditions in cultural studies, as they found theoretical models to be too abstract and streamlined to reflect the complexities of lived relations. The 'speculative' approach whereby scholars simply try to imagine the possible implications of how and why a reader or spectator identifies with a text can lead to 'universalisations' of analysis, which can turn out to be based on little more than assumption (Morley, 1989). There isn't one unequivocal reason why women like m/m sexually explicit media, and this book isn't trying to present a unified theory. I feel any attempt to do so is doomed to be partial, incomplete, lacking in some way. I want to centre women's own accounts of their pleasures and interpretive practices, but I am less concerned with synthesising the content of participants' 'micro-theories' into a 'macro-theory' capable of taking into account a range of different perspectives, than I am in exploring the *processes* interlinking the field of discourse and practices around women engaging with m/m erotica. In giving voice to such women, this book aims to explore their multiple and differing motivations, and look at how they tie in with other aspects of these women's experiences of, and attitudes towards, sex, gender, and sexuality.

Some of the reasons women give for why they like m/m pornography and erotica are perhaps unsurprising. The reason m/m author James Lear gives, that women are turned on by seeing or thinking about two attractive men together—'boys are hot!' as one of my participants puts it—is the most common response. Others' reasons are perhaps less self-evident. Some participants give harrowing accounts of abuse they suffered as children or young adults, experiences that left them feeling so alienated from the female body and female sexuality that they can't 'get off' on any sexual fantasy scenario featuring women. Many respondents mention how they feel m/m porn is more 'authentic', insomuch as there is visual proof of both arousal (in the form of erections) and what they see as pleasure (in the form of ejaculation). There is awareness that things are not always as they seem; one participant notes 'a good [gay male] friend of mine … started to burst my bubble about gay porn. Because he's saying, 'You know that these guys are all given Viagra? And the bottoms…' [winces]. And he starts… And I thought: shut up, shut up, shut up!… I don't want to know… I need some fantasies' (Italian/British, 45–54, married, heterosexual). However, overall many participants feel male performers are more likely to enjoy the erotic labour they are performing, and, moreover, that unlike female performers they have the economic and social capital to be able to quit porn if they want.

Asking women about their relationship with erotic content is also likely to be hampered by a reluctance to take part in such studies. A number of women expressed concern at taking part in research that examined what could be viewed as a contentious issue—non-normative female desire. One participant memorably speaks about previous research on the topic treating women who engage with m/m SEM as being part of a 'freak show' (American, 35–44, single, demisexual/lesbian)—something to be fetishised and marvelled at. Another observes that 'we have been burnt before by people peering under the rock of [slash] fandom and finding it fascinating in a condescending and offensive way' (British, 35–44, married, heterosexual). To be a good researcher one must be respectful of participants who may be dissuaded from taking part based on previous experiences and/or typical representations of their community in the academic or popular press. Previous researchers have noted that slashers are understandably wary of engaging in research about their fandom and fanshipping[4] due to the traditional portrayal of such fans as socially deviant (Jenkins, 1992; Penley, 1991), while academics, operating from positions of intellectual elitism, have been sceptical of porn watchers' abilities to know and represent themselves.

It is telling that 73 per cent of the women who took part in this research feel that my position as a community insider (a fan, a watcher, a reader, a writer) affected their decision to be involved in some way (n = 508). There is considerable wariness expressed by participants as to the outcome of taking part in research that isn't being conducted by someone who is involved in m/m sexually explicit media themselves. 'I would worry that you would portray us as sexual deviants or in a negative light,' one respondent writes, 'I wouldn't feel as forthcoming or trustful' (American, 18–24, single, bisexual). Another notes, 'I think it looks weird from the outside, at least where I am [from] it's not commonly discussed that women masturbate or have sexual fantasies, never mind [that] their fantasies involve two men… I think you kind of need to know and understand the appeal to even ask the right questions and understand people's answers' (American, 25–34, single, asexual). This kind of wariness is particularly prevalent from respondents who are involved in slash fandom, with one stating 'people who don't have a vested interest in the community all too often have a skewed perspective or want to present fannish activity as a sort of freak-show. If you're 'one of us' so to speak, I have less fear of that' (American, 18–24, single, bisexual), and another adding 'I know I wouldn't be answering this if you weren't one of 'us" (Chilean, 25–34, single, heterosexual).

Comments such as these help to shed light on why my involvement in the community would affect participant decisions to participate in research around women and m/m SEM, given both the sensitive nature of the subject, and the uneasy—and, at times, downright tempestuous—history of research within both women's sexual desire and women's involvement in m/m fandoms. It is to this history that I now want to turn, in order to better illustrate the concerns felt by many women in taking part in research looking at their engagement with m/m sexually explicit media.

Bad Girls: A Brief History of Researching Women Who Like m/m SEM

There has been a long history of viewing women who are vocal about their sexual desire, or who are proactively involved in the sex industry, as unfeminine, weird, or abnormal in some way. This has led to a pathologising of such women, and has meant that they are often viewed with a mixture of distaste and fascination. This is not a view taken exclusively within popular discourse or the media, but one that has been replicated within the academy itself. In her book *Exposure*, which details her observational research within the pornography industry, Chauntelle Tibbals describes the time she met an academic who works in feminist media studies at a birthday party. The academic suggested they all go to a Vegas show so '[they could] go and watch the porn people and laugh at them!' (Tibbals, 2015, p. 152). Tibbals continues:

'Laugh at them?' I asked. 'Do you mean laugh at the people working, or do you mean laugh at the people who go to the show? Or everyone? We could laugh at all 'those' people. Maybe that would be fun?' I suggested, laying on the sarcasm thick.
'God, yes!' she squealed. 'What a bunch of freaks!'
'Freaks' worthy only of mockery—this was the unfiltered response from a person who described her work as 'feminist media studies'. (Tibbals, 2015, pp. 152–153)

John Sutherland (2006), a professor emeritus of Modern English Literature at UCL, takes a similar view of slash writers in his piece for *The Telegraph*. He claims that an hour spent sampling slash fic sites is instructive to the uninitiated, 'it offers the pleasures of a trip to the ... zoo: one gawps at the exotic specimens', adding that the women who write such m/m erotic stories are motivated by 'irrational … emotions'. 'Alas,' he laments, '…a pity it's not more readable'.

My participants are highly attuned to the historic representation of them both inside and outside the academy. As one notes, 'so far, the way the outside world has treated slash has been incredibly shitty. Outsiders are drawn to misrepresenting us, to asserting things for us rather than letting us speak for ourselves. They don't want to understand; they want to mock. I don't have patience for that. I mean, I would have filled this survey out no matter who was asking for answers, but I trust the data analysis and conclusions of someone acclimated to slash more than that of someone who isn't' (American, 18–24, in a relationship, heterosexual).

Crazy Fangirls

In both scholarly work and popular culture the notion of the 'crazy fan' is well established (Evans & Stasi, 2014; Webb, 2012). Overly-obsessive, hormonal, and nearly always female, the crazy fan is mocked or repudiated for their interest in something that society deems they probably shouldn't be interested in. The term has been liberally applied to women within slash fandoms. Athena Bellas (2015) feels this is part of a larger issue whereby women are called 'crazy' or 'embarrassing' for simply expressing their desire. Where male fans and fandoms are viewed as passionate and committed, female fans and fandoms are seen as deviant, over-the-top and illogical. Bellas (2015) states that, in her opinion, 'this condemnation has little to do with the content of [women's] fantasy scenario[s], and more to do with the fact that they are unashamedly, and often quite explicitly and loudly, demanding a space to declare their desires'. She feels this policing of female desire is particularly prevalent in fandom, where women's fantasies are often met with 'derision and depreciation'—which has 'everything to do with cultural anxieties about women's desire and pleasure' (Bellas, 2015).

In an interview with *Out Magazine*'s Aaron Hicklin, Benedict Cumberbatch, star of the BBC show *Sherlock* which has an avid slash fan following, agrees with Hicklin that a primary motivation for writing Holmes and Watson as gay might be to 'remove other women from the picture' (Hicklin, 2014). Hicklin writes that Cumberbatch 'enthusiastically' concurred with this analysis, adding 'I think it's about burgeoning sexuality in adolescence, because you don't necessarily know how to operate that. And I think it's a way of neutralising the threat, so this person is sort of removed from them as somebody who could break their heart'. Hicklin goes on to call Cumberbatch's female fans 'rabid', and describes slash writers as 'rapacious'—women who have wilfully misinterpreted the tone of the show in order to turn Cumberbatch's 'distinctly asexual' Sherlock into 'a lustful cock monster'. Commenting on this story in *The New Statesmen*, Elizabeth Minkel describes such a response as patronising, claiming that what Hicklin and Cumberbatch are doing here is 'gawk[ing] at … female fans and their funny ways, and … belittle[ing] them' (Minkel, 2014). She feels this is a classic example of how female desires and female fan practices are unduly misunderstood and mocked, and adds that while it doesn't particularly matter what Benedict Cumberbatch thinks about slash fic, it does matter that 'two middle-aged men with very large platforms were sitting at a table pathologising teenage girls' sexuality—and making a whole load of potentially harmful assumptions about a topic they know literally nothing about'. This is an issue that came up frequently in the discussions I had with slashers:

T: I think still a lot of the time fandom, and slash fandom in particular, is, like, the kicking dog of a lot of actors, writers, journalists… [They] will be incredibly dismissive of something that's very important to a lot of people…. [The actor] Zachary Quinto has been *so* rude about people who write fanfic—as much as he ever is, because he's very media savvy—but he's very sneery. And I just think: well, who the hell's he when I've been in *Star Trek* fandom and know—

D: You know more about *Trek* than he does!

T: —I know Spock every bit as much as Zachary flippin' Quinto does, so who the hell is he to judge? But you know, it seems to be very much OK to sneer at slashers.

N: Yeah. So he can interpret the character but you can't interpret the character.

T: Exactly! I'm, you know—

N: A fellow artist.

T: Quite, quite. Well, *he* doesn't see it as art, he says people have too much time on their hands, which I don't, which is *so* rude!

N: And actually if it wasn't for our art he wouldn't have an art, without writers—

T: Yes, well, what's so important about being in adverts and stuff? Yes, all hail Zachary Quinto and his acting talent!

W: Have you seen *American Horror Story*?

N: No

W: OK. I think if he talks about art he needs to look at his work in that [laughs]

This isn't unique to slash either. While The Cocky Boys have responded positively to their female fans, other gay male porn stars have not. The well-known gay porn star Spencer Reed lashed out at his female fans on Twitter, ridiculing their interest in m/m porn and calling them 'cunts'.[5]

Given the often very gendered nature of this derision of women who are open about their interest in m/m sex, it is perhaps not surprising that a number of women who took part in this study state that an even bigger barrier to their decision to participate would have been me being a man: 'to be honest I'd have a greater issue with you doing this research if you were male. I feel that female sexuality has been misrepresented in the past because it's been examined from a male perspective and I would be wary of a man coming in [and] examining the community because I don't feel he would be able to experience something which I feel is so linked to the way *women* experience things of a sexual nature' (Australian, 25–34, single, heterosexual/borderline asexual).

Camille Bacon-Smith and the 'Fat Virgin' Hypothesis

Many of these general perceptions of female fans of m/m sex as being somehow abnormal or deviant can also be found in previous academic research focusing on slash. Despite identifying herself as a *Star Trek* fan, and a reader of its accompanying fan fiction, in her book *Enterprising*

Women (Bacon-Smith, 1992) Camille Bacon-Smith nevertheless takes a perspective that marks slash fans out as the 'other'. Writing about her 'discovery' of the existence of slash fic, she exclaims that she wanted to 'jump up and down and scream: "Look what I found!"' (1992, p. 3). Once again, we hear echoes of the desire to gawk at the freaks.

Based on her own observations at fan conventions, and survey data shared with her by fellow acafans[6] via personal communication, Bacon-Smith claims that slash fandom contains a high percentage of women who find men intimidating, and relationships with them 'simultaneously attractive and threatening' (1992, p. 246). For these women, she believes, homoerotic stories can serve to stimulate them sexually, while at the same time distancing them from the risks that sexual relationships with men represent in real life. She goes on to state:

> For most women [who write slash] … men are the alien, the other… A high percentage of the women … [are] not involved in relationships with men … and many consider themselves celibate. Some of these were divorced, or post-relationship, but others had never had long-term, loving, sexual relationships with men. A small but significant number of the women in media fandom suffer from extreme, health-threatening obesity, and that group tends to cluster in homoerotic genres. (Bacon-Smith, 1992, p. 247)

Bacon-Smith does not publish the survey upon which her observations were based (and does not provide a sample size), but it seems unlikely it contained questions asking 'Have you ever had a long-term, loving, sexual relationship with a man?' and 'Do you suffer from extreme, health-threatening obesity?' While *Enterprising Women* remains an important text which did a great deal to further understanding of women's involvement in media fandoms, Bauer (2012, p. 64) describes this 'reduction of slash fans to unattractive, divorced, or virginal "ladies"—who have no choice but to satisfy their desires this way' as not only a way of dismissing the force of the genre, but also as a continuation of Gayle Rubin's (1992, p. 278) assertion that female masturbation counts as an inferior replacement activity in the 'hierarchical valuation of sex acts'. The implication being, if only these women could meet a *real* man to give them *real* sexual satisfaction through heterosexual intercourse, they wouldn't need to be touching themselves to thoughts of Kirk kissing Spock. This perspective is not unique to slash; Ingulsrud and Allen (2009, p. 58) observe how *yaoi* fans have a reputation for being 'socially inept and incapable of securing a partner'. Evans and Stasi (2014, p. 13) warn that this psycho-analytical approach tends to view the slash fan as 'a damaged and tragic individual who lives through fantasy' and thus comes close to reinvesting heavily in the notions of pathological femininity and the public figure of the discursively produced 'crazy' fan. Participants from within slash fandom are often aware of this perception of them, with one commenting 'I think you'd have somewhat of a problem with getting responses from people who perceive you as an outsider, since fandom tends to be represented by outside sources as some collection of fat, crazy, hot and bothered freaks' (American, 25–34, single, bisexual).

Psychosexual Quirks

The study of female interest in m/m sex has also been investigated from within the field of evolutionary psychology. Evolutionary psychology has a chequered past with sex research. It purports to be able to present us with an all-encompassing understanding of our sexual selves, built on the sturdy foundations of Darwin's theory of evolution. However, it is incredibly difficult to discern which characteristics of our sexual behaviour are created by culture, and which are inherited through our chromosomes. Particularly with regards to women's sexuality and desire, what we end up with is a circular argument that posits that because women across most cultures are more sexually reserved and less sexually motivated than men, women must *be*, by their very nature, more sexually reserved and less sexually motivated than men. It often[7] overlooks the possibility that the shared worldwide value placed on female sexual modesty might have more to do with the world's span of male-dominated cultures and historic global suspicion of female sexuality than a biological absolute. Michel Foucault (1980) has argued that such cultural and historical factors do more than just heighten or dampen our biological sex drives, they actually constitute or construct sexual experience at a more basic level.

Foucault argued that conceptualisations of sexual desire as repressed 'essences' are *themselves* strategic social discourses that are crafted and deployed by those with power in the service of particular political and ideological ends. Such discourses are therefore usually not visible as such, rather they reflect what *appears* to be natural, factual, or objectively real. As Daniel Bergner (2013, p. 39) writes, 'the sexual insights of evolutionary psychology can sometimes seem nothing but a conservative fable, conservative inadvertently but nevertheless preservationist in spirit, protective of a sexual status quo. Women, the fable teaches us, are *naturally* the more restrained sex; this is the inborn norm; this is normal. And the normal always wields a self-confirming and self-perpetuating power. Because few people like to defy it, to stray from it'.

As one of the women in my study notes, the evolutionary psychological perspective has tended to view women's production of m/m erotic material as 'some kind of fetish' carried out by 'gay groupies' (Canadian, 18–24, single, bisexual). In the introduction to the book on slash fiction he co-authored with Catherine Salmon, the evolutionary psychologist Donald Symons remarks that 'what distinguishes slash fans from tens of millions of women who read mainstream romances … might conceivably be some sort of psychosexual quirk among the former—analogous, say, to male paraphiliacs (aka fetishists) who can be sexually aroused only by women's shoes or only by rubber clothing' (Symons, in Salmon & Symons, 2001, p. 6). He adds that on being introduced to slash fiction for the first time, 'consider[ing the stories] strictly as fiction I found them pretty tedious… Consider[ing them] as clues to women's mating psychology, however, I found them riveting… My reactions to reading … slash fiction may be a bit reminiscent of the reactions many women have when viewing porn videos, especially for the first time (Good grief, are men actually turned on by this? Can this possibly be what men want?)' (Symons, in Salmon & Symons, 2001, p. 3). While Salmon and Symons (2001, p. 79) later conclude that their 'psychosexual quirk' hypothesis is unlikely, the idea that all women respond to erotic content in a similar and innate way, and that anyone who deviates from this 'natural' response is some sort of weird anomaly remains prevalent. Beggan and Allison (2009, p. 456) comment that 'despite a current zeitgeist that emphasises both equality and the social construction of reality, beliefs about women's attitudes toward pornography is one area where essentialist views seem to hold'. A woman I spoke with comments on this perception: 'women's sexuality in general has been wilfully misunderstood and used to support misogyny and sexism. There is a long and terrible history of this in the social sciences, and it continues. There is an element of trust in belonging to the community, and I expect you'll have a better grip on the substance than an outsider, and [be] less likely to use our comments to paint all women with the same brush, or explain our inferiority or malleability or how to hack our brains' (American, 25–34, married, bisexual).

SurveyFail

An even more controversial study into women's interest in m/m sexually explicit media from within the field of evolutionary psychology took place in 2009. Calling their research 'The Cognitive Neuroscience of Fan Fiction', Ogi Ogas and Sai Gaddam, two researchers claiming affiliation with Boston University, posed their central research question as 'How is straight female interest in slash fiction like straight male interest in 'shemale' models? And why does this matter?' They then included a link to a survey they had constructed, and asked slashers to take part. Many slash fans reacted very negatively to how the survey was framed. They found Ogas and Gaddam's use of the term 'shemales'—in online posts related to the survey they also used the term 'trannies'—grossly offensive, and also objected to the underlying assumptions: that slash is written by and for *straight* women, and that straight women's interest in slash can be reasonably compared to straight men's interest in porn featuring transfolk. There was also a feeling among the slash community that the survey was badly designed—it was open to minors, participants were asked to pick between binary gender options, and were then asked about drug use, real-life sexual behaviour, personal kinks, masturbation habits, and rape fantasies in a way that many felt was inappropriate. Writing on their Dreamwidth blog, Tablesaw (2009) states that the survey, the academics' handling of the situation, and their interaction with fans and critics was 'both stupid and offensive… There are, essentially, two lines of outrage in this whole thing. There's the political outrage at the horribly sexist, heteronormative, transphobic attitudes of Ogas and Gaddam in their survey and their interactions. And there's the outrage about the horribly bad science—the lack of clear methodology, patently biased questions, an ignorance of previous research in the area, etc.' The situation deteriorated further after slashers contacted the researchers, on their public Livejournal blog pages, to address some of the issues they felt had been raised by the framing of the research project and the phrasing of the survey. As another Dreamwidth blogger, Jonquil (2009), explains:

> Dr. Ogas replied with condescension when he chose to reply at all—praising people for being, variously, published authors, scholars, and academics, and then carefully explaining topics that had nothing to do with their questions with handwavy references to 'culture' and the 'lizard brain' and the dreaded evolutionary psychology. He finally threw out a deliberate slur ... and disappeared in a cloud of f-lock.[8]

Several of the women who took part in this study referred back to the events of 2009, and commented on how what had transpired meant they were hesitant to participate in further research around slash fic, with one noting 'I think the community is, rightly, pretty wary of ... oh ... outside researchers who turn out to be evo-psychos with book deals' (American, 35–44, married, bisexual).

Reprise: Asking Women What They Like and Why They Like It

Given the chequered history of how academia and the media have treated women who have expressed non-normative sexual desire, particularly women who are interested in some aspect of m/m sexuality, it is not surprising that 73 per cent of the women who took part in this study felt that my position as a community insider influenced their decision to become involved. Discussing her survey with nearly 8000 fan fic readers and writers, most of whom were very actively involved with slash fic, Katherine Morrissey (2008, p. 55) writes that 'asking questions of a community which faces stigma for its activities and interests involves a great deal of trust on the part of that community'.

I was very fortunate insomuch as the fact that I write gay male erotica and slashfic meant that I was able to use my existing contacts (in real life and over the internet) to signal boost the call for participation, using a snowball sampling method. I also advertised the survey on a number of websites either affiliated with pornography and written erotica, or hosting discussion boards on related topics, such as reddit, literotica, justusboys.com, adultdvdtalk.com etc. At all stages during the recruitment process I was open with potential participants about my own position as a user and creator of m/m erotic content, and a member of several m/m slash fandoms. Not only did I clearly state this in the participant information sheet (displayed at the beginning of the survey and in the call for focus group participants), I also provided a link to my Livejournal homepage, where I indicated potential participants could read some of my erotic fiction.

The analysis of the data took a contextual thematic analysis approach. Thematic analysis is a method for identifying, analysing, and reporting patterns (themes) within data. While it is important to note that the active process of analysing data means that a researcher cannot simply 'give voice' (Fine, 2002) to their participants, I nevertheless was determined to foreground the reasons participants *themselves* gave for what they liked about sexually explicit m/m media and how it related to their feelings around pornography, romance, sex, gender, and sexuality more generally. As previously discussed, consumers of pornography have often been spoken *for* in academic works around media effects (e.g. Donnerstein & Malamuth, 1984)—as such I believe it is paramount to allow their voices to come through in the analysis of empirical data. Participants don't always agree with each other. They can, and do, have different reasons as to why they enjoy m/m erotic content. These reasons can all help to shed light on the nature of this phenomenon, even if they seem at times to contradict each other. This is why my analysis is contextualist: it acknowledges there are different realities—different ways of seeing and being—for different women. However, by representing the perspectives of respondents through basing findings in participants' actual descriptions, this book hopes to find some kind of grounding for results (Tindall, 1994).

Contextual analysis also acknowledges the inevitability of the researcher bringing their own personal and cultural baggage to bear on research (Madill, Jordan, & Shirley, 2000). I don't operate in a vacuum, I am part of these communities. The women I spoke with, and who filled in my survey, are part of the same chat forums as me, they are sometimes my readers (and sometimes I am theirs). Being an insider researcher has both its windfalls and its shortfalls. Greater familiarity with the matter under investigation can certainly lead to a loss of objectivity. Kanuha (2000, p. 444) notes that 'for each of the ways that being an insider researcher enhances the depth and breadth of understanding a population that may or may not be accessible to a non-native scientist, questions about objectivity, reflexivity, and authenticity of a research project are raised because perhaps one knows too much or is too close to the project and may be too similar to those being studied'. However, despite these drawbacks, my insider status also brings what Devereux (1967, p. 160) calls 'methodologically relevant empathy'. I care about these women, and I care about this work. The arenas of m/m erotica and slash fiction are not just my fields of research, they are also places where I have found a sense of personal belonging, kinship, and acceptance. I am, what Jodie Taylor (2011, p. 9) calls an 'intimate insider', a researcher who is not just part of the community under investigation, but 'is working, at the deepest level, within their own "backyard"'.

Madill et al. (2000, p. 10) note that a contextualist approach to thematic analysis acknowledges that the empathy provided by 'a shared humanity and common cultural understanding can be an important bridge between researcher and participant and a valuable analytic resource'. It was evident from responses I received that a number of the women who took part in this research shared this view, with one commenting 'I feel very confident telling you stuff because I know you get it… Because I "know" you—more so that I've read your stuff too—I care and want to help, and I know you want to get the nuances of the field, in all its glory' (English, 45–55, in a relationship, a little bent). Dwyer and Buckle (2009, p. 58) state that membership of the group under investigation is likely to be a benefit in terms of both recruitment and richness of data provided, claiming that participants often think 'you are one of us and it is us versus them (those on the outside who don't understand)'.

Even in cases where individual respondents weren't familiar with me or my work, my presence on chat forums and platforms such as AO3[9] still had a positive impact on respondents' decisions to participate. As one participant comments, 'some of my friends 'vetted' … you, which is why I responded; I suspect someone delved into … your background deeper than I knew before giving a stamp of approval' (American, 55–64, single, heterosexual).

I conducted my research in two phases. Phase one involved a number of focus groups and one-to-one interviews (both in-person and via Skype) with women who produced and/or consumed m/m SEM (n = 17). A rough interview guide was created, but rarely used—instead I encouraged participants to talk generally and openly, to free associate, and, in the case of focus groups, to interject to ask each other any questions they felt were pertinent or interesting, or even were just curious about. Once interviews and focus groups were recorded and transcribed verbatim, data were analysed using a largely inductive approach, in that instead of attempting to prove a preconceived idea or theory, individual cases or instances were studied from which abstract concepts were then eventually developed. Phase two involved the construction and launch of an online questionnaire (with open text boxes as well as closed questions) (n = 508). The inductive phase of the research project (interviews and focus groups) occurred before the questionnaire was created, so that themes that had been generated within the interview and focus group data were used to inform the design and construction of the questionnaire.

Both sets of data (interview/focus group and questionnaire) were then collated and were coded, producing a long list of different codes that I had identified across the data set. Codes were then sorted into potential themes, and relevant coded data extracts from within the identified themes were collected. Themes were then reviewed and refined, and sub-themes were created. This process followed the 'phases of thematic analysis' outlined by Braun and Clarke (2006). This book provides a general overview of the main thematic areas discussed by participants as to why they like m/m SEM, and what they get from producing and/or consuming it.

What About the Women Who Didn't Take Part?

During the research process, I kept open a post on my Livejournal page for people to comment and feedback on the survey. The survey was live for two years, and for the last 23 months of this period (wherein I received the vast majority of responses) not a single person commented on the discussion thread. However, the first few days of the survey going live saw a flurry of activity, with a number of posters stating their express intent *not* to take part in the survey. This was primarily down to the fact that the first call for participation originated from within slash fandom, but the survey explicitly focused on m/m erotic content, and not slash fiction *per se*. As such, I was not interested in exploring general [gen] slash fan fiction—that is, fanfic that may include reference to m/m pairings but is focussed on other story aspects, such as adventure or humour. Posters felt this was (yet again) misrepresenting slash fandom as being primarily sexual and about women getting off on m/m sex—ignoring the valuable opportunities fandom provides for creativity, universe building, paying homage to much loved TV shows and characters, support, developing a sense of community, and friendship (for further discussion of these aspects of fandom please see Chap. 3). Reid (2009, p. 465) points out that this is a common critique of work by academics on fan fiction: that 'scholars have privileged slash and ignored gen and het because ... of fascination with perceived perversity (women writing erotic/pornographic texts)'. She adds that many fans dislike the assumption that slash fics are by nature going to be adult themed/pornographic, when some contain only kissing or holding hands. Certainly, this is a valid concern, but it was never my intent to study fandom as a whole. There is much fantastic work in this area (see, e.g., Bury, 2005; Busse & Hellekson, 2006; Jenkins, 1992). The purpose of my study was to uncover more about women who are interested in m/m erotic content (including, but not limited to, slash fic) and how this fits in with their general attitudes towards sex and sexuality.

A proportion of participants who did choose to take part, nevertheless voiced their concerns about the nature of academic research in general, with one commenting 'academic research into people's lives and cultures in general is a crazy concept, [there is a] lot of potential [for it] to be fucked-up, appropriating, misrepresenting, disrespectful, exploitative.

That can all happen with a researcher from the community too of course. I think there are issues with you doing this research at all' (American, 18–24, single, queer). There are others who feel that while my insider status may make me more sensitive to the concerns of women who enjoy m/m erotic content, it could also cause me to view some respondents negatively if they did not fit within my worldview.

> Both [someone] sitting 'inside the community' and an outside researcher would approach this issue with bias. You, as someone on the inside, may be more inclined towards sympathy or empathy towards the issue, but that is still a bias. I can picture you reading the answers to this questionnaire and perhaps being judgmental towards the fact that I feel shame over my involvement in this form of erotica in the same way that I can picture someone outside the community feeling judgmental towards the fact that I'm involved at all. So, from my perspective, the 'issue' is there in either case. (American, 25–34, married, heterosexual)

Who's That Girl? Respondent Demographics

The 508 women who engage with m/m SEM who responded to my survey come from a wide range of backgrounds. Respondents consist of 40 different nationalities, with women participating from Europe, North America, South America, Asia, Australasia, and Africa. The majority of women who took part are from the USA (54 per cent), followed by the UK (13 per cent), Canada (6 per cent), Germany (6 per cent), Australia (5 per cent) and France (4 per cent). The remaining 12 per cent of respondents are spread across 34 countries. Given that the survey and call for participants were both in English, this bias towards English-speaking countries is to be expected. Certainly, there is ample room for more transnational work in this area.

Respondents were entirely free to self-define ethnicity, and the answers given are complex. However, approximately only 21 per cent of participants identify as women of colour. While gender equality in SEM has been put under the microscope, little frank discussion has been had surrounding racial equality. Racial stereotypes in pornography, including m/m pornography, remain popular (Fung, 1996; Williams, 2014). In

porn, race can often become a 'special object … of eroticisation as raced
… bodies are asked to confess their special discursive "truths"' (Williams,
2014, p. 27). Likewise, there has been little attention paid to race in fan
studies. As Wanzo (2015) argues, the continued and glaring absence of
race as an aspect of analysis in fan studies is not an oversight; but is pur-
posefully ignored because it 'troubles' some of the core assumptions
regarding slash fiction's subversive potential and inclusive ethos. White
characters predominate in slash fandom, and characters of colour are
often 'pushed to the side-lines or erased entirely' so that 'slash fandom's
obsession with white men can persist unrelentingly' (Fazekas, 2014,
pp. 2, 121). As Ann Jamison (2013, p. 342) explains, 'fanfic hasn't done
the kinds of deconstruction and reimagining of race and ethnicity that it's
done for gender and sexuality'. Fazekas (2014, p. 121) argues that women
of colour who point out the racism inherent in slash fandom are themselves often 'vilified, ignored and maligned in the service of white fans
retaining the supposed moral authority that comes with being a slash
fan'. Questions were not specifically asked about the intersections between
race and SEM consumption in this study, and it was not something that
was mentioned organically by my participants. However, it is important
to bear in mind the majority of the sample are white, and their views are
not representative of all women.

The age of respondents ranges from 18 to over 65 (see Table 1.1). The
fact that a high proportion of women involved in this study are well
beyond their teenaged years suggests this phenomenon is not simply an
adolescent phase carried out by 'experimenting' teenagers (Levi, 2009,
p. 148), but can remain an important part of older women's sexuality.

Sexual orientations and relationship statuses are diverse (see Tables 1.2
and 1.3).

Table 1.1 Table showing age range of respondents

Age range	n	Percentage
18–24	169	33
25–34	179	35
35–44	71	14
45–54	62	12
55–64	25	5
65–74	2	0.4

Table 1.2 Table showing sexual orientation of respondents

Sexual orientation	n	Percentage
Heterosexual	228	45
Bisexual	155	31
Pansexual	26	5
Asexual	24	5
Lesbian	21	4
Questioning sexuality	17	3
Queer	16	3
Demisexual	11	2
Prefer not to say	10	2

Table 1.3 Table showing relationship status of respondents

Relationship status	n	Percentage
Single (have had previous relationships)	169	33
Married/In a civil partnership	126	25
Single (have not had previous relationships)	95	19
In a non-marital relationship	91	18
In a polyamorous relationship	16	3
Casual/dating	6	1
Prefer not to say	5	1

The finding that the majority of women who took part in the survey do not identify as heterosexual goes some way to putting paid to the idea that m/m content is something that excites only 'straight' women (see Wischhover, 2016). This has also been a lingering misconception within slash fandom. While it might have been the case that it was straight women who were most visible inside slash fandoms in the 1980s and 1990s (see Bacon-Smith, 1992; Cicioni, 1998), it would appear that it certainly isn't the case today. Green et al. (1998, p. 11) maintain that lesbian and bisexual women have 'always' participated alongside heterosexual women in slash fandom, and 'people of all sexual orientations have found slash a place for exploring their differences and commonalities'. Falzone (2005, p. 246) notes that 'formal empirical survey proof does not exist' as evidence of the majority of slash producers being heterosexual women, and, indeed, much existing survey evidence finds figures broadly in line with my own respondents (Boyd, 2001; Busse, 2006; Fielding, 2013;

Hinton, 2006; LuLu, 2013; Morrissey, 2008). LuLu's (2013) analysis of AO3 census data for m/m fandoms (n = 8978) found that the largest group of women involved in slash fic identified as bi- or pan-sexual (38 per cent), followed by heterosexual (31 per cent), asexual spectrum (22 per cent), asexual (7 per cent) and homosexual (5 per cent). Morrissey (2008, p. 66) feels that the large population of bisexual readers within the slash fandom population 'suggests a more diverse, fluid approach to sexuality and attraction'.

The fact that only 19 per cent of respondents are single women who have never been involved in a romantic relationship also challenges the idea that women who engage with m/m SEM are socially awkward, virginal, and find it difficult to engage with men (or women) romantically in real-life situations. It should be noted that 58 per cent of the women who have not previously had romantic relationships are in the 18–24 age group, so even the overall figure of 19 per cent may well be an artefact of age. Put another way, 33 per cent of the 18–24 group have never had a romantic relationship, as opposed to 11 per cent of the respondent group aged 25 and above.

Of those in a relationship (n = 244), 87 per cent are involved with a man, 9 per cent with a woman, 2 per cent with a person who identifies as trans/genderqueer/gender fluid and 2 per cent with both a man and a woman.

Respondents tend to consume a variety of erotic texts in addition to m/m SEM, suggesting that when it comes to sexually explicit media

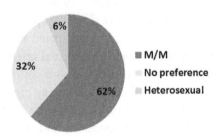

Fig. 1.1 If you read or watch both m/m and heterosexual pornography/erotica, which genre do you prefer?

women are not confined by their own sexual orientation. However, 62 per cent express a preference for m/m sexually explicit media over m/f SEM (Fig. 1.1).

Eighty four per cent of respondents state they use m/m sexually explicit media as a masturbatory aid ($n = 501$). Of these 420 women, 73 per cent also masturbate to m/f SEM, and 50 per cent to f/f SEM. The SEM most frequently used to accompany masturbatory activity is slash fiction (75 per cent of women), followed by pornographic videos (60 per cent of women), erotic fiction (38 per cent of women), and photographs or GIFs (27 per cent of women). It perhaps isn't surprising that the majority of the sample (in part) engage with m/m SEM in order to assist in arousal and orgasm—in fact, some readers may be more baffled by what the remaining 16 per cent are using it for! However, there has been a historical trend within the literature to downplay masturbation when discussing how women engage with SEM, from hardcore pornography through to erotic romance novels.

In her rich and nuanced account of porn for women, Clarissa Smith (2007, p. 45) complains that the process of using erotic material is often ignored: 'it [is] assumed that the intention in opening a porn magazine is to be aroused sexually, and, that once aroused, the reader will want and attempt sexual release'. She points out that when you look at the explanations of readers' relationships with specific magazines, physiological arousal is only possible if other interests, pleasures and activities have been acknowledged and addressed. While not in any way dismissing the validity of this observation, I would argue that the assumption within much of the literature actually seems to be that women *don't* use erotic material to get off on, regardless of the situation in which they find themselves. Talking about the nature of human sexuality, Abramson and Pinkerton (1995, p. 72) state that 'unlike pornographic books bought by men … [stories for women] are not intended to provoke, or accompany, female masturbation'. Ellis and Symons (1990, p. 545) agree, seeing the main purpose of male-orientated pornography as facilitating action, in the form of masturbation, whereas the main purpose of female-directed erotic narratives, such as erotic romances or slash fic, 'presumably is not masturbation-enhancement'. In the arena of sexually explicit slash fiction, Bauer (2012, p. 74) laments that 'in a blatant neglect of slash fiction's sexual appeal and arousing function, the subgenre of fan fiction is often reduced to its alleged political message of gender equality in academic accounts'. Part of this reluctance to acknowledge the sexually exciting elements of how and why women engage with SEM may well be related to the idea that whereas men consume pornography, women consume erotica—and erotica here is presented as a 'purified realm of sexual freedom and equality, with higher, and more complex, holistic intentions than the singular and mundane one of arousal' (Ross, 1989, p. 185). I will go on to discuss what women feel are the distinctions between pornography, erotica and romance (and how they relate these terms to their own creation and consumption of SEM) in Chaps. 4 and 6. The refusal to acknowledge the centrality of sexual pleasure to why and how women engage with m/m SEM was noted by respondents, with one stating, 'I think it's important not to downplay the masturbation thing. I feel it's part of a narrative that treats all pleasure as suspect, and sexual pleasure, particularly women's sexual pleasure, as Something That Must Never Be Mentioned' (British, 25–34, in a relationship, heterosexual).

m/m SEM Viewers

Seventy-two per cent (72 per cent) of the women who responded watch m/m visual pornography. Three-quarters (75 per cent) of women who watch m/m pornography also watch m/f pornography, and 57 per cent watch f/f pornography. However, 73 per cent of porn viewers express a preference for m/m pornography over other types (see Fig. 1.2). Ninety-

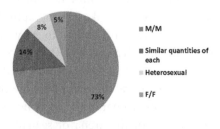

Fig. 1.2 What type of pornography do you tend to consume the most of?

one per cent (91 per cent) of the 365 porn viewers use pornography as a masturbatory aid.

m/m SEM Readers

The majority of respondents are readers as well as viewers. Eighty-four per cent of respondents are involved, to a greater or lesser extent, with slash fandom. Three quarters (75 per cent) also read heterosexual erotica, and 60 per cent also read lesbian erotica. Almost two-thirds (61 per cent) read romance novels, going some way to disprove Symons's assertion that 'the majority of slash fans … infrequently read mainstream romances' (Symons, in Salmon & Symons, 2001, p. 5).

Now we know who these women are, it's time to better explore what it is they enjoy about m/m sexually explicit content, and how this ties in to their feelings about sex, gender, and sexuality more generally. Chapter 2 examines the most common reason given by respondents for enjoying m/m pornography—that they find men, and particularly the spectacle of two men having sex, attractive. Many respondents state they enjoy m/m porn because it is marketed to a target audience they feel they have more in common with (gay men as opposed to heterosexual men), and invites them to adopt a point of view that is more in-keeping with their own sexual preferences and desires where 'men are the objects of sexual attraction, instead of the women' (American, 25–34, single, heterosexual). To this extent, several of the themes that emerged from the analysis as to why female respondents enjoy watching m/m pornography can be situated within some of the wider literature concerning the notions of the 'gaze' (see, e.g., Mulvey, 1989) and the existence (or not) of a 'female gaze'.

Chapter 3 examines in more detail what the 84 per cent of respondents who participate in slash fandoms enjoy about sexually explicit slash fiction. It looks at the sense of community and security provided by these spaces, and the opportunity they provide women to explore issues around gender and sexuality. Chapter 4 builds on previous work that has examined women's engagement with pornography, and how it relates to their engagement with romance and erotica as media genres (see, e.g., Juffer,

1998; Radway, 1984; Smith, 2007). It explores what this sample of women who consume or produce m/m erotic content see as the primary differences between pornography and erotica. It also looks at the extent to which many of the women I spoke to identify as male, either when reading, writing, watching, or fantasising about m/m sexually explicit content.

Chapter 5 examines the difficulties presented to women in this sample by heterosexual (and, to some extent, lesbian) pornography, in terms of both the lack of agency afforded to female actors because of the wider political and economic situation of women, and the lack of evidence, or rather, 'authentic' evidence of female desire. It looks at why the women I spoke with might therefore see m/m pornography as a viable alternative, answering Angela Carter's (1979) call for 'a moral pornography'. This chapter also examines what women describe as the 'eroticising equality' (Dyer, 2004; Pugh, 2005) of gay sex, and explores the experiences of a subsection of the sample who spoke about how issues with their own bodies, and in some cases a history of previous sexual abuse (committed by men), mean that m/m porn offers a comfortable space to explore their own sexuality and sexual identity which heterosexual pornography does not.

Chapter 6 explores the role of romance and love in participants' use of m/m erotica and pornography. A large section of the sample discussed how important the relationship (or perceived relationship) between the characters is when they are reading or watching m/m erotic content. This chapter investigates this, and what it might have to offer to the long-standing, though not uncontested, assertion that men like 'porn' and women like 'erotica' (see, e.g., Williams, 2007). Chapter 7 explores the concept of m/m sex as queer sex. Many women spoke of how m/m pornography or erotica offers an opportunity for expression of non-normative sexuality, and that their engagement with it allows them to push boundaries and explore other kinds of kink. Cante and Restivo (2004, pp. 142–143) argue that m/m porn is always 'non-normative, whether one conceives the non-normative as a violation of patriarchal law, or, more experientially, as the excess attached to feeling different and acting like an outsider', adding that 'all-male pornography at some point also becomes the field for the (utopian) reinvention of the world eternally promised by identity politics'. This chapter investigates how m/m porn can be seen as subverting the patriarchal order by challenging masculinist values, providing a protected space for non-conformist, non-reproductive and non-familial sexuality, and encouraging many sex-positive values.

Chapter 8 examines the taboo nature of women watching all-male sex and ties into previous thinking around eroticism and transgression (Bataille, 1957/1986; Heiman, 1977). It also examines issues raised by the prospect of women intruding on the 'sexual territory' of 'The Other' and the fetishisation of gay male sexuality. It examines participants' wider involvement with the gay community and gay activism, and looks at the involvement of gay men in the slash community. The final chapter looks at how the perception of women's involvement in the consumption of SEM is changing in this post *Fifty Shades …* world. It explores how the 525 women surveyed and interviewed see women's consumption of porn as having changed since they first engaged with m/m SEM. It also examines how engagement with m/m porn and erotica has changed the women's own views around gender, sex, and sexuality.

Ultimately this book aims to shine a light on the under-researched area of female desire, something which I believe is fundamentally important. For, as Daniel Bergner observes, 'Eros lies at the heart of who we are as human beings, yet we shun the study of our essential core, shun it perhaps most of all where it is least understood, in women. Where there should be an abundance of exploration, there is, instead, common assumption, unproven theory, political constraint, varieties of blindness' (Bergner, 2013, p. 195). This book starts some of that exploration—and I hope others will follow.

Notes

1. Much of Chivers' research was carried out measuring sexual response in women using vaginal photoplethsymography. A plethsymograph is a two-inch long glassine tube that is inserted into the vagina, beams light against the vaginal walls, and measures the illumination that reflects back. In this way, it measures the blood flow to the vagina. Surges of blood bring about

a process called vaginal transudation, the seeping of moisture through the cells of the canal's lining. So, indirectly, the photoplethysmograph gauges vaginal wetness. A problematic aspect of comparative research carried out using vaginal photoplethysmography is it focuses on measuring vaginal blood flow, dilation, and lubrication, and then compares these data with data from penile photoplethysmography, which measures penile blood flow. This treats the vagina and penis as fundamentally 'the same' in terms of what they can tell us about sexual arousal. However, as Alice Dreger (2014) points out, 'the vagina is not the homologue to the penis… The penis's homologue is the clitoris'. She goes on to explain that this is why it is the clitoris which becomes erect when a woman is sexually excited, and why many women need clitoral stimulation to achieve orgasm. Dreger uses the analogy of automatic salivary response vs. taste preference with regards to exposure to food to better explain her issue with most sexual arousal studies, pointing out that our mouths may automatically start salivating to both coffee and peanut butter, but this doesn't tell us anything about *tastes*, that is, what we actually enjoy consuming. She states that 'sex researchers have been doing the equivalent of comparing women's salivary responses to various foods to men's gastric responses to those same foods'. Research studies carried out using clitoral measurements instead of vaginal responses have found that clitoral photoplethysmographs (which measure clitoral blood volume) tend to be more sensitive to inhibition of sexual response in contrast to vaginal devices (Gerritsen et al., 2009, p. 1678), leading researchers to conclude that 'VPA [the vaginal response] may be a more automatic, preparatory response rather than a measure of genital arousal *per se*'. However, there has not yet been any systematic attempt to replicate the results of the studies coming out of Chivers' lab to see if the results pertaining to women's flat arousal profiles to heterosexual, lesbian, and m/m pornography can be replicated using clitoral measurements.

2. Although there are many slash stories devoted to f/f relationships—called 'femslash'—the term 'slash' generally refers to m/m relationships. This division is not unproblematic; Webb (2012, p. 18) notes that 'it's a shame that even in a literature dominated by female writers and readers the feminine is segregated—that the masculine is still default and the feminine still requires a prefix'.

3. *Yaoi* is an acronym for the phrase 'yama nashi, ochi nashi, imi nashi' (no climax, no resolution, no meaning) which was coined in the late 1980s to

describe the more explicit forms of BL manga. The term refers to the fact that some of these short stories were not meant to be viewed as fully developed narratives, but were rather just scenes and snippets, *oishii tokoro dake* (only the yummy parts). What constituted a 'yummy part' was usually a scene involving sexual contact between the two male protagonists. As such *yaoi* has much in common with PWP stories (Plot? What plot? or, alternatively, porn without plot) in slash fic.

4. Fanshipping (sometimes just shipping), a term derived from the word 'relationship', is the desire by fans for two or more people, either real-life people or fictional characters, to be in a relationship, romantic or otherwise.

5. The tweets have since been deleted, but you can read a response to them here: http://www.devonhunter.info/archives/tag/spencer-reed/ (accessed 5 December 2017).

6. Acafan: an academic who self-identifies as a fan.

7. Although not always: see Malamuth (1996) and Tolman and Diamond (2001) for a more nuanced overview of SEM, gender differences, and evolutionary psychology.

8. F-lock refers to the process of changing the settings on your Livejournal blog so that only people you have accepted as 'friends' can see it—in effect, it means you can 'lock' everything you have written on your personal page, including previously publicly available posts, so it is only accessible to your 'friends'.

9. AO3 [Archive of Our Own] is a multi-fandom archive designed to host web-based fan fiction as well as fandom nonfiction. The archive contained 2 million fanworks as of 20 December 2015. See http://fanlore.org/wiki/Archive_of_Our_Own (accessed 5 December 2017).

References

Abramson, P. R., & Pinkerton, S. D. (1995). *With pleasure: Thoughts on the nature of human sexuality*. Oxford: Oxford University Press.

Attwood, F. (2005). 'Tits and ass and porn and fighting': Male heterosexuality in magazines for men. *International Journal of Cultural Studies, 8*(1), 83–100.

Bacon-Smith, C. (1992). *'Enterprising women': Television fandom and the creation of popular myth*. Philadelphia: University of Pennsylvania Press.

Bailey, J. M. (2008). What is sexual orientation and do women have one? *Contemporary Perspectives on Lesbian, Gay and Bisexual Identities, 54*, 43–63.

Bataille, G. (1957/1986). *Eroticism: Death and sensuality* (M. Dalwood, Trans.). San Francisco: City of Light Books.

Bauer, C. K. (2012). *Naughty girls and gay male romance/porn: Slash fiction, boys' love manga, and other works by female 'cross-voyeurs' in the US academic discourses*. Hamburg: Anchor Academic Publishing.

Beggan, J. T., & Allison, S. T. (2009). Viva Viva? Women's meanings associated with male nudity in a 1970s 'For Women' magazine. *The Journal of Sex Research, 46*(5), 446–459.

Bellas, A. (2015, November 10). Women's fandoms: Unruly desires, perverse pleasures. *Teensecreenfeminism blog*. Retrieved from https://teenscreenfeminism.wordpress.com/2015/11/10/womens-fandoms-unruly-desires-perverse-pleasures/

Bergner, D. (2013). *What do women want? Adventures in the science of female desire*. London: Canongate.

Blair, M. M. (2010). 'She should just die in a ditch': Fan reactions to female characters in boys' love manga. In A. Levi, M. McHarry, & D. Pagliassotti (Eds.), *Boys' love manga: Essays on the sexual ambiguity and cross-cultural fandom of the genre* (pp. 110–125). Jefferson, NC: McFarland & Company, Inc.

Boyd, K. S. (2001). *'One finger on the mouse scroll bar and the other on my clit': Slash writers views on pornography, censorship, feminism and risk*. PhD dissertation, Simon Fraser University. Retrieved from http://summit.sfu.ca/item/7501

Braun, V., & Clarke, V. (2006). Using thematic analysis in psychology. *Qualitative Research in Psychology, 3*(2), 77–101.

Bruner, J. (2013). *I 'like' slash: The demographics of facebook slash communities*. PhD dissertation, University of Louisville. Retrieved from http://ir.library.louisville.edu/cgi/viewcontent.cgi?article=1169&context=etd

Buruma, I. (1984). *Behind the mask: On sexual demons, sacred mothers, transvestites, gangsters, drifters and other Japanese cultural heroes*. New York: Pantheon.

Bury, R. (2005). *Cyberspaces of their own: Female fandoms online*. New York: Peter Lang.

Busse, K. (2006). My life is a WIP on my LJ: Slashing the slasher and the reality of celebrity internet performances. In K. Hellekson & K. Busse (Eds.), *Fan fiction and fan communities in the age of the internet* (pp. 207–224). London: McFarland.

Busse, K., & Hellekson, K. (Eds.). (2006). *Fan fiction and fan communities in the age of the internet*. London: McFarland.

Butler, H. (2004). What do you call a lesbian with long fingers? The development of lesbian and dyke pornography. In L. Williams (Ed.), *Porn studies* (pp. 167–197). London: Duke University Press.

Cante, R., & Restivo, A. (2004). The cultural-aesthetic specificities of all-male moving-image pornography. In L. Williams (Ed.), *Porn studies* (pp. 142–166). London: Duke University Press.

Carter, A. (1977). A well-hung hang-up. In Nothing sacred: Selected writings (pp. 100–105). London: Virago.

Carter, A. (1979). *The Sadeian woman: An exercise in cultural history*. London: Virago.

Chivers, M. L., & Bailey, J. M. (2005). A sex difference in features that elicit genital response. *Biological Psychology, 70*(2), 115–120.

Chivers, M. L., Rieger, G., Latty, E., & Bailey, J. M. (2004). A sex difference in the specificity of sexual arousal. *Psychological Science, 15*(11), 736–744.

Chivers, M. L., Seto, M. C., Lalumière, M. L., Laan, E., & Grimbos, T. (2010). Agreement of genital and subjective measures of sexual arousal in men and women: A meta-analysis. *Archives of Sexual Behaviour, 39*, 5–56.

Cicioni, M. (1998). Male pair-bonds and female desire in fan slash writing. In C. Harris & A. Alexander (Eds.), *Theorising fandom: Fans, subculture and identity* (pp. 153–177). New Jersey: Hampton Press.

Ciclitira, K. (2004). Pornography, women and feminism: Between pleasure and politics. *Sexualities, 7*(3), 281–301.

Devereux, G. (1967). *From anxiety to method in the behavioural sciences* (Vol. 3). Berlin: Walter de Gruyter GmbH & Co KG.

Diamond, L. M. (2008). *Sexual fluidity: Understanding women's love and desire*. Cambridge, MA: Harvard University Press.

Diamond, S. (1985). Pornography: Image and reality. In V. Burstyn (Ed.), *Women against censorship* (pp. 40–57). Vancouver: Douglas & McIntyre.

Donnerstein, E. I., & Malamuth, N. M. (Eds.). (1984). *Pornography and sexual aggression*. London: Academic Press.

Dreger, A. (2014, August 5). The problem with sexual arousal studies. *Pacific Standard*. Retrieved from https://psmag.com/social-justice/problem-sexual-arousal-studies-87383

Driscoll, C. (2006). One true pairing: The romance of pornography and the pornography of romance. In K. Hellekson & K. Busse (Eds.), *Fan fiction and fan communities in the age of the internet* (pp. 79–96). London: McFarland.

Dwyer, S. C., & Buckle, J. L. (2009). The space between: On being an insider-outsider in qualitative research. *International Journal of Qualitative Methods, 8*(1), 54–63.

Dyer, R. (2004). Idol thoughts: Orgasm and self-reflexivity in gay pornography. In P. Church Gibson (Ed.), *More dirty looks: Gender, pornography and power* (pp. 102–109). London: BFI.

Ellis, B. J., & Symons, D. (1990). Sex differences in sexual fantasy: An evolutionary psychological approach. *Journal of Sex Research, 27*, 527–555.

Evans, A., & Stasi, M. (2014). Desperately seeking methods: New directions in fan studies research. *Participations: Journal of Audience & Reception Studies, 11*(2), 4–23.

Falzone, P. J. (2005). The final frontier is queer: Aberrancy, archetype and audience generated folklore in K/S slashfiction. *Western Folklore, 64*(3/4), 243–261.

Fazekas, A. (2014). *Queer and unusual space: White supremacy in slash fanfiction.* MA dissertation, Queen's University. Canada. Retrieved from https://qspace.library.queensu.ca/bitstream/handle/1974/12609/Fazekas_Angela_M_201411_MA.pdf?sequence=1

Fielding, D. M. (2013). *Normalising the deviance: The creation, politics, and consumption of sexual orientation and gender identities in fan communities.* BA dissertation, Hamline University. Retrieved from http://digitalcommons.hamline.edu/dhp/7/

Fine, M. (2002). *Disruptive voices: The possibilities for feminist research.* Ann Arbor: University of Michigan Press.

Foucault, M. (1980). *The history of sexuality* (Vol. I). New York: Vintage.

Fung, R. (1996). Looking for my penis: The eroticised Asian in gay video porn. In Bad Object-Choices (Ed.), *How do I look? Queer film and video* (pp. 145–168). Seattle, WA: Bay Press.

Furness, H. (2014, August 12). George RR Martin: Women beg me to write more gay sex scenes for *Game of Thrones*. *The Telegraph*. Retrieved from http://www.telegraph.co.uk/culture/tvandradio/game-of-thrones/11027457/George-RR-Martin-women-beg-me-to-write-more-sex-scenes-for-Game-of-Thrones.html

Gerritsen, J., van der Made, F., Bloemers, J., van Ham, D., Kleiverda, G., Everaerd, W., et al. (2009). The clitoral photoplethysmograph: A new way of assessing genital arousal in women. *Journal of Sexual Medicine, 6*(6), 1678–1687.

Green, S., Jenkins, C., & Jenkins, H. (1998). 'Normal female interest in men bonking': Selections from the Terra Nostra Underground and Strange Bedfellows. In C. Harris & A. Alexander (Eds.), *Theorising fandom: Fans, subculture and identity* (pp. 9–38). New Jersey: Hampton Press.

Gunn, R. (1993). On/Scenities: Porn for women? *Body Politic, 4,* 33–36.

Gunter, B. (2002). *Media sex: What are the issues?* Mahwah, NJ: Lawrence Erlbaum Associates.

Hayes, S., & Ball, M. (2009). Queering cyberspace: Fan fiction communities as spaces for expressing and exploring sexuality. In B. Scherer (Ed.), *Queering paradigms* (pp. 219–239). Oxford: Peter Lang.

Heiman, J. R. (1977). A psychophysiological exploration of sexual arousal patterns in females and males. *Psychophysiology, 14,* 266–274.

Herbenick, D., Reece, M., Schick, V., Sanders, S. A., Dodge, B., & Fortenberry, J. D. (2010). Sexual behaviour in the United States: Results from a national probability sample of men and women ages 14–94. *The Journal of Sexual Medicine, 7*(5), 255–265.

Hicklin, A. (2014, October 14). The gospel according to Benedict. *Out Magazine.* Retrieved from https://www.out.com/out-exclusives/2014/10/14/poised-make-alan-turing-his-own-sherlock-star-benedict-cumberbatch-no-stranger-sexual-politics-and-bullying

Hinton, L. (2006). *Women and slash fiction.* BA dissertation, James Madison University. Retrieved from http://www.jmu.edu/mwa/docs/2006/Hinton.pdf

Ingulsrud, J. E., & Allen, K. (2009). *Reading Japan cool: Patterns of manga literacy and discourse.* New York: Lexington Books.

Jamison, A. (2013). *Fic: Why fanfiction is taking over the world.* Dallas, TX: Smart Pop.

Jenkins, H. (1992). *Textual poachers: Television fans and participatory culture.* New York: Routledge.

Jonquil. (2009, September 2). *Highway to the meta zone.* Dreamwidth blog. Retrieved from http://jonquil.dreamwidth.org/867288.html?format=light

Juffer, J. (1998). *At home with pornography: Women, sex & everyday life.* New York: New York University Press.

Kanuha, V. K. (2000). 'Being' native versus 'going native': Conducting social work research as an insider. *Social Work, 45*(5), 439–447.

Laumann, E. O., Gagnon, J. H., Michael, R. T., & Michaels, S. (1994). *The social organization of sexuality: Sexual practices in the United States.* Chicago: University of Chicago Press.

Levi, A. (2009). North American reactions to Yaoi. In M. I. West (Ed.), *The Japanification of children's popular culture: From Godzilla to Miyazaki* (pp. 147–173). London: Scarecrow Press.

Lothian, A., Busse, K., & Reid, R. A. (2007). 'Yearning void and infinite potential': Online slash fandom as queer female space. *English Language Notes, 45*(2), 103–111.

Lulu. (2013). *AO3 census data analysis.* Retrieved from http://centrumlumina.tumblr.com/post/63373124511/mm-fans-sexuality-and-gender

Mackinnon, K. (1997). *Uneasy pleasures: The male as erotic object.* London: Cygnus Arts.

Madill, A., Jordan, A., & Shirley, C. (2000). Objectivity and reliability in qualitative analysis: Realist, contextualist, and radical constructionist epistemologies. *British Journal of Psychology, 91*(1), 1–20.

Malamuth, N. (1996). Sexually explicit media, gender differences and evolutionary theory. *Journal of Communication, 46*, 8–31.

Martin, F. (2012). Girls who love boys' love: Japanese homoerotic manga as trans-national Taiwan culture. *Inter-Asia Cultural Studies, 13*(3), 365–383.

Matsui, M. (1993). Little boys were little girls: Displaced femininity in the representation of homosexuality in Japanese girls' comics. In S. Gunew & A. Yeatman (Eds.), *Feminism and the politics of difference* (pp. 177–196). New South Wales: Allen & Unwin.

McCutcheon, J. M., & Bishop, C. J. (2015). An erotic alternative? Women's perception of gay male pornography. *Psychology & Sexuality, 6*(1–2), 75–92.

McGregor, R. (1996). *Japan swings: Politics, culture and sex in the New Japan.* St Leonards: Allen & Unwin.

McKee, A., Albury, K., & Lumby, C. (2008). *The porn report.* Melbourne: Melbourne University Press.

McLelland, M. (2000). Male homosexuality and popular culture in modern Japan. *Intersections: Gender, History, and Culture in the Asian Context, 1*(3). Retrieved from http://espace.library.uq.edu.au/view/UQ:141361

McLelland, M. (2001). Why are Japanese girls' comics full of boys bonking? *Intensities: A Journal of Cult Media, 1*(1), 1–9.

McNair, B. (2013). *Porno? Chic!* London: Routledge.

Meyer, U. (2010). Hidden in straight sight: Trans*gressing gender and sexuality via BL. In A. Levi, M. McHarry, & D. Pagliasotti (Eds.), *Boys' love manga* (pp. 232–257). Jefferson: McFarland and Company.

Minkel, E. (2014, October 17). Why it doesn't matter what Benedict Cumberbatch thinks of Sherlock fan fiction. *New Statesman.* Retrieved from http://www.newstatesman.com/culture/2014/10/why-it-doesn-t-matter-what-benedict-cumberbatch-thinks-sherlock-fan-fiction

Mizoguchi, A. (2003). Male-Male romance by and for women in Japan: A history of the subgenres of Yaoi fictions. *U.S.-Japan Women's Journal, 25*, 49–75.

Mizoguchi, A. (2011). Theorizing comics/manga genre as a productive form: Yaoi and beyond. In J. Berndt (Ed.), *Comics worlds and the worlds of comics: Towards Scholarship on a Global Scale* (pp. 143–168). Kyoto: International Manga Research Centre, Kyoto Seika University.

Moran, C. (2016, March 9). 12 things about being a woman that women won't tell you. *Esquire*. Retrieved from http://www.esquire.co.uk/culture/advice/a9641/things-men-dont-know-about-women-caitlin-moran/

Morley, D. (1989). Changing paradigms in audience studies. In E. Seiter, H. Borchers, G. Kreutzner, & E. M. Warth (Eds.), *Remote control: Television, audiences, and cultural power* (pp. 16–43). New York: Routledge.

Morrison, T. G., Ellis, S. R., Morrison, M. A., Bearden, A., & Harriman, R. L. (2006). Exposure to sexually explicit material and variations in body esteem, genital attitudes, and sexual esteem among a sample of Canadian men. *The Journal of Men's Studies, 14*, 209–222.

Morrissey, K. (2008). *Fanning the flames of romance: An exploration of fan fiction and the romance novel.* MA dissertation, Georgetown University. Retrieved from https://repository.library.georgetown.edu/bitstream/handle/10822/551540/17_etd_kem82.pdf

Mowlabocus, S., & Wood, R. (2015). Introduction: Audiences and consumers of porn. *Porn Studies, 2*(2–3), 118–122.

Mulvey, L. (1989). *Visual and other pleasures.* London: Macmillan.

Nagaike, K. (2003). Perverse sexualities, perverse desires: Representations of female fantasises and Yaoi Manga as pornography directed at women. *U.S.-Japan Women's Journal, 25*, 76–103.

Nayar, S. J. (2011). A good man is impossible to find: Brokeback Mountain as heteronormative tragedy. *Sexualities, 14*(2), 235–255.

Neville, L. (2015). Male gays in the female gaze: Women who watch m/m pornography. *Porn Studies, 2*(2–3), 192–207.

Nicholas, L. J. (2004). The association between religiosity, sexual fantasy, participation in sexual acts, sexual enjoyment, exposure, and reaction to sexual materials among black South Africans. *Journal of Sex & Marital Therapy, 30*(1), 37–42.

Noble, B. (2007). Queer as box: Boi spectators and boy cultures on Showtime's *Queer As Folk*. In M. L. Johnson (Ed.), *Third wave feminism and television: Jane puts it in a box* (pp. 147–165). New York: IB Tauris.

Paasonen, S. (2010). Good amateurs: Erotica writing and notions of quality. In F. Attwood (Ed.), *Porn.com* (pp. 138–154). New York: Peter Lang.

Pagliassotti, D. (2010). Better than romance? Japanese BL manga and the sub-genre of male/male *romantic* fiction. In A. Levi, M. McHarry, & D. Pagliassotti (Eds.), *Boys' love manga: Essays on the sexual ambiguity and cross-cultural fandom of the genre* (pp. 59–83). Jefferson, NC: McFarland & Company Inc.

Penley, C. (1991). Brownian motion: Women, tactics, and technology. In C. Penley & A. Ross (Eds.), *Technoculture* (pp. 135–161). Minneapolis: University of Minnesota Press.

PornHub. (2014). *What women want.* Retrieved from http://www.pornhub.com/insights/what-women-want/

PornHub. (2015). *More of what women want.* Retrieved from https://www.pornhub.com/insights/women-gender-demographics-searches

Pugh, S. (2005). *The democratic genre: Fan fiction in a literary context.* Bridgend, Wales: Seren.

Radway, J. (1984). *Reading the romance: Women, patriarchy, and popular literature.* Chapel Hill: University of North Carolina Press.

Ramsay, G. (2017). Straight women seeing gay porn: 'He's too good looking!'. *Porn Studies, 4*(2), 157–175.

Reid, R. A. (2009). Thrusts in the dark: Slashers' Queer practices. *Extrapolation, 50*(3), 463–483.

Reinhard, C. D. (2009). *If one is sexy, two is even sexier: Dialogue with slashers on identity and the internet.* Roskilde: Roskilde University Publications. Retrieved from http://dspace.ruc.dk/bitstream/1800/4062/1/Reinhard_2009_slash_identity.pdf

Rich, A. (1980). Compulsory heterosexuality and lesbian existence. *Signs, 5*(4), 631–660.

Ross, A. (1989). *No respect: Intellectuals and popular culture.* London: Routledge.

Rubin, G. (1992). Thinking sex: Notes for a radical theory of the politics of sexuality. In C. Vance (Ed.), *Pleasure and danger: Exploring female sexuality* (2nd ed., pp. 267–319). London: Pandora Press.

Russ, J. (1985). *Magic mommas, trembling sisters, puritans and perverts: Feminist essays.* Trumansburg, NY: Crossing.

Salmon, C., & Symons, D. (2001). *Warrior lovers: Erotic fiction, evolution, and female sexuality.* London: Weidenfeld & Nicolson.

Schauer, T. (2005). Women's porno: The heterosexual female gaze in porn sites 'for women'. *Sexuality & Culture, 9*(2), 42–64.

Schulman, S. (1994). *My American history: Lesbian and gay life during the Reagan and Bush years.* London: Cassell.

Shaw, S. M. (1999). Men's leisure and women's lives: The impact of pornography on women. *Leisure Studies, 18*(3), 197–212.

Smith, C. (2007). *One for the girls!: The pleasures and practices of reading women's porn*. Bristol: Intellect Books.

Sutherland, J. (2006, February 14). Slashing through the undercult. *The Telegraph*. Retrieved from http://www.telegraph.co.uk/culture/books/3650072/Slashing-through-the-undercult.html

Suzuki, K. (1998). Pornography or therapy: Japanese girls creating the Yaoi phenomenon. In S. A. Inness (Ed.), *Millenium girls: Today's girls around the world* (pp. 243–267). Maryland: Rowman & Littlefield Publishers.

Tablesaw. (2009, September 2). *The pervy survey*. Dreamwidth blog. Retrieved from http://tablesaw.dreamwidth.org/421853.html

Taylor, J. (2011). The intimate insider: Negotiating the ethics of friendship when doing insider research. *Qualitative Research, 11*(1), 3–22.

The Metro. (2008, October 14). Women who like to watch gay porn. *The Metro*. Retrieved from http://metro.co.uk/2008/10/14/women-who-like-to-watch-gay-porn-30888/

Thorn, M. (2004). Girls and women getting out of hand: The pleasures and politics of Japan's auteur comics community. In W. W. Kelly (Ed.), *Fanning the flames: Fans and consumer culture in contemporary Japan* (pp. 169–186). New York: State University of New York Press.

Tibbals, C. (2015). *Exposure: A sociologist explores sex, society, and adult entertainment*. Austin, TX: Greenleaf Book Group Press.

Tindall, C. (1994). Issues of evaluation. In P. Banister, E. Burman, I. Parker, M. Taylor, & C. Tindall (Eds.), *Qualitative methods in psychology: A research guide* (pp. 142–159). Buckingham: Open University Press.

Tolman, D. L., & Diamond, L. M. (2001). Desegregating sexuality research: Combining cultural and biological perspectives on gender and desire. *Annual Review of Sex Research, 12*, 33–74.

Van Dam, F. S. A. M., Honnebier, W. J., van Zelinge, E. A., & Barendregt, J. T. (1976). Sexual arousal measured by photoplethysmography. *Behavioural Engineering, 3*, 97–101.

Wanzo, R. (2015). African American acafandom and other strangers: New genealogies of fan studies. *Transformative Works and Cultures, 20*. Retrieved from http://journal.transformativeworks.org/index.php/twc/article/view/699/538

Webb, E. (2012). *Slash as genre*. MA dissertation: American University, Washington, DC. Retrieved from http://aladinrc.wrlc.org/bitstream/handle/1961/11138/Webb_american_0008N_10043display.pdf?sequence=1

Wicke, J. (1993). Through a gaze darkly: Pornography's academic market. In P. Church Gibson & R. Gibson (Eds.), *Dirty looks: Women, pornography, power* (pp. 62–80). London: BFI.

Williams, L. (1990). *Hard core: Power, pleasure and the 'frenzy of the visible'*. Los Angeles: University of California Press.

Williams, L. (1992). Pornography on/scene of diff'rent strokes for diff'rent folks. In L. Segal & M. McIntosh (Eds.), *Sex exposed: Sexuality and pornography debate* (pp. 233–262). London: Virago.

Williams, L. (2005). *The erotic thriller in contemporary cinema*. Bloomington: Indiana University Press.

Williams, L. (2014). Pornography, porno, porn: Thoughts on a weedy field. *Porn Studies, 1*(1–2), 24–40.

Williams, Z. (2007, July 25). The market beyond porn. *The Guardian*. Retrieved from   http://www.theguardian.com/commentisfree/2007/jul/25/comment. television

Wischhover, C. (2016, May 16). Why straight young women are obsessed with these gay porn stars. *Esquire*. Retrieved from http://www.esquire.com/entertainment/a44928/straight-women-who-love-cockyboys-gay-porn/

2

Boys on Film

Women like looking. The persistent notion than women's sexuality is less innately visual than men's does not necessarily hold in more recent data. For example, Rupp and Wallen (2009) found that women are likely to spend just as long as men looking at pornographic photos, and seem just as interested—giving similar subjective ratings of engagement. Outside of the lab, women have consistently told researchers that they want to see 'attractive male actors' in heterosexual porn (Janssen, Carpenter, & Graham, 2003; Ramsay, 2017; Reed Hughes and Anderson, 2007), and the market is finally starting to listen. Discussing what women want in porn—and what she therefore tries to create—the award-winning director Petra Joy highlights the importance of porn that 'features male sex objects' (in Catalina, 2011). Women's desire to look at, and to imagine looking at, naked men is not limited to porn films—the most popular reason for reading Boys' Love manga given in Pagliassotti's (2010, *n* = 478) survey was 'I think it's sexy to see same-sex couples making love' (81 per cent), followed by 'I like looking at pictures of pretty boys' (79 per cent), and as far back as the 1980s the radical feminist and critic Joanna Russ (1985, p. 90) was positively joyous about the opportunities that slash fiction provides to 'create images of male bodies as objects of desire', exalting in the fact that it allows women to 'describe male beauty—

© The Author(s) 2018
L. Neville, *Girls Who Like Boys Who Like Boys*,
https://doi.org/10.1007/978-3-319-69134-3_2

not "masculinity", mind you, but the passive, acted-upon glories of male flesh'. As one participant notes: 'Men are so pretty! We deserve more eye candy of that kind' (American, 55–64, married, heterosexual). Another discusses what she enjoys about m/m porn: 'Well, cocks! [laughs] I'm straight so I enjoy looking at the male anatomy in general' (German, 25–34, single, heterosexual).

It is perhaps not surprising, then, that the most common reason given by women for why they watch m/m pornography is the seemingly unradical notion that many women find men attractive, and therefore like looking at them, particularly without their clothes on. This is not limited to pornography: reading about—and therefore imagining—attractive men and the naked male body is also a key draw to women who read erotic literature (both m/m and m/f), and 62 per cent of the women surveyed feel there should be more male nudity in films and television (only 7 per cent feel there should not be, with 31 per cent being unsure or ambivalent).

However, looking, for women, has never been as straightforward as some of these responses might indicate. Part of this is because we don't know how to look—not properly—and part of this is because we aren't given anything to look *at*. While our art, our mass media, our pornography, our fiction, is saturated with images and descriptions of women's bodies, and representations of women's sexuality, 'men's bodies seem to have quietly absented themselves' (Coward, 1984, p. 227; see also Davis, 1991; Saunders, 1989). As one woman comments, 'there's always been *plenty* of female nudity in just about everything. From TV ads, to cosmetic commercials, to your prime-time television... Just not much of men' (American, 18–24, married, bisexual). This is particularly the case when we consider what should be one of the most erotic parts of the male body: the cock. Susan Bordo (1993, p. 698) argues that women's bodies have 'become increasingly common cultural property... By contrast, outside of homoerotic representations ... the penis has grown more, not less, culturally cloaked over time'. While the male nude enjoyed a fair amount of exposure in classical and renaissance (public) art, contemporary penises are strictly a 'no go' area outside of subscription cable channels ('Thank you HBO!' exclaimed one of my participants) and post-watershed TV. As one participant observes, male nudity in the media is 'interesting, [because we] don't get to see much of it in everyday life' (American, 65–74, married, mostly heterosexual). Feona Attwood (2005, p. 87) notes that these 'cultural blind spots' might prevent many women from seeing men erotically—'instead, a dominant discourse of heterosexual hedonism has relied on the female body to represent male sexual pleasure while the male body has remained largely invisible', especially in soft porn texts 'where the male body is quite literally absent from view'.

Scholars have argued that this is a consequence of living in a male-dominated society where men have a vested interest in keeping the erotic spectacle of the nude male body out of sight. As one participant notes, 'the entertainment industry is run predominantly by men, [and] they have little interest in showing [or] producing male nudity. Men don't want males exposed that way: men don't want to be compared to 'movie star' bodies, nor do men want to see 'it all hanging out' on screen' (American, 55–64, married, heterosexual). Lehman (1988, p. 105) believes that traditional patriarchal constructions of masculinity 'benefit enormously by keeping the male body in the dark, out of the critical spotlight. Indeed, the mystique of the phallus is, in part, dependent on it'. As Ms. Naughty (2013, p. 72) observes 'the penis [is] … the last bastion of secrecy, a final preserve of male power'. Men cannot allow themselves to be perceived as vulnerable, or as possessing corporeal sensuality. To do so is to show weakness. By refusing to see the male body as desirable, men affirm that *they* are the ones who desire, who judge, who control. Many women in my study are acutely aware of this phenomenon, with one commenting,

It's OK for a woman to show her breasts [or] butt [or] bush for an R rating, but the second a penis comes into view, it's suddenly NC-17? What in the world is so sacred and inviolable about the male organ that isn't about the female? Breasts by themselves are *way* sexier than an un-erect penis, but for some reason. … No, actually, not *some* reason: *men* have decided that it's OK to show one and not the other. Fucking male patriarchal society [sigh]. Now I'm getting all riled up. Women have given up so much power to men in the realm of sex and what's good [or] right [or] appropriate that it's disgusting (American, 35–44, married, bisexual).

The absence of naked male bodies to look upon has meant that women often don't know *how* to look, even when the opportunity does present itself. Previous studies have shown that both men and women are more comfortable viewing female rather than male nudity, largely due to the greater exposure they have had to female nudes (Eck, 2003). Familiarity not only breeds acceptance, it also creates a pervasive sense that the female body *should* be looked at—it is artistic, it is beautiful, it is soft, it is attractive—whereas the male body is ugly, ridiculous, offensive, or utilitarian. As one participant observes, 'a guy's body is like a jeep. It's utilitarian. For gettin' around. A female body is much more artistic, in my opinion. More worthy of *really* looking at' (American, 35–44, single, bisexual). Parvez (2006) notes that while some women report enjoying looking at men's bodies, other (heterosexual) women claim that women's bodies are more aesthetically pleasing—these are the bodies they like to look at, because these are the bodies they know *how* to look at. Eck (2003, pp. 692, 706) observes that while cultural scripts for female nudity are part of the 'cultural toolkit' (see Swidler, 1986), scripts for male nudity are 'less readily available' and 'incomplete and fragmented'. As such, Eck (2003, p. 692) postulates that neither men nor women 'are culturally adept at the interpretation and use of male nude images'. As one woman comments, 'people always find a dick on TV so shocking, which of course it *is*, because one never sees it' (Brazilian, 25–34, single, heterosexual), with another adding 'a penis is just this scary thing that sends people running from the cinema' (American, 18–24, single, bisexual). In particular, Eck believes that both sexes have particular difficulty in commenting on the male in the soft porn pose—such images require more 'work' by individual viewers because cultural scripts are less readily available. Women are just not used to seeing men frankly portrayed as sex objects. It is difficult to see a thing as beautiful when it is something we are not used to seeing. It is even more difficult to call something beautiful when we are worried we will be judged or laughed at for doing so.

It is clear that the viewing experience for women is more complicated than it is for men. As Betterton (1987, p. 3) has suggested, women have an ambiguous relationship to the nude visual image not just because they are represented so frequently, but also because their role as makers and viewers of images is rarely acknowledged. While men's lifestyle magazines frequently feature scantily clad women on the front cover, you are extremely unlikely to see a topless man on the front of *Cosmo*. *Black Lace* books—and other erotica aimed at women—often have a suggestively posed woman on the front, and it is this female image which guides the female reader into scenes of heterosexual fantasy. Sonnet (1999) asks why it is that material *explicitly* designed for heterosexual arousal has no pictures of men? It appears that women are so unused to seeing the male body as sexy, as something they are allowed to look at, that when it *is* offered to them it can provoke feelings of embarrassment, revulsion, or amusement instead of appreciation or lust. Women's bodies are safer. We *know* they are sexy. We *know* we're supposed to look at them.

Eck (2003, p. 706) thinks this has led to a situation where women have been taught by wider society to portray themselves as hesitant, shy, and disinterested in the eroticised naked male body. As such they tend to 'stumble through their responses [to it] with laughter, embarrassment and even disinterest'—women have been socialised to find the naked male body unattractive. This might explain why the women in Shaw's (1999, *n* = 32) study responded more negatively to a pornographic image of an m/m couple than an f/f couple. Some of the women explained the reasons behind their response, stating that they 'saw no logical reason for reacting more negatively to the men, but that seeing men exposed seemed less "normal" and therefore more objectionable' (Shaw, 1999, p. 205). Similarly, in Eck's (2003) study women spoke about the offensiveness of male genitalia, and the comparative comfort they felt looking at nude female images. Eck (2003, p. 705) notes that 'as a woman it is OK to look at nude women because "everywhere we turn" they are there', but the same cannot be said for naked men: 'by omitting or de-emphasising images of nude men, high culture and popular culture inform women … who is the appropriate object'. As such, Disch and Kane (1996) have pointed out that there might be socially undesirable implications for women who look excessively at naked men. To look critically at men goes against the feminine role and disrupts the established power relationship. Good girls don't look. They particularly don't look at *men*. Instead they get looked *at*. Women looking—*choosing* to look—at male nudity is a transgressive act that challenges socially constructed femininity (Beggan & Allison, 2009). This is perhaps the primary reason why I get funny looks when I talk about women and m/m sexually explicit media at dinner parties, and why most women *don't* look at m/m porn, even though, as I will argue here, it is a type of media that could offer them a way of engaging with erotic content that sidesteps some of the issues raised when watching or reading heterosexual SEM. By looking at the women who do look, we can better understand how these women engage with and process the naked male form.

'What's Funnier than Looking at a Soft Male Penis?': Male Nudity as Comic

Before I move on to discuss the ways in which many women in my sample talk about the beauty of the male body and the pleasure they take in looking at it, it is necessary to explore the limitations placed on this pleasure. While—unsurprisingly—women who engage with m/m SEM don't struggle unduly with feelings of embarrassment or horror when regarding the naked male body, they are acutely aware that much media positions male nudity as either comedic or utilitarian, and note that it is difficult to then regard this type of nudity as sensual.

Partly this is because the male body is supposed to rehearse narratives of hegemonic masculinity. Many writers have examined how the male body *is* erotically available in film, but most suggest that the body must be specularised and submitted to a male gaze, and that the male look at men does not necessarily consist of an explicitly homoerotic look. Neale (1983) highlights the importance of disavowal as a strategy by which the male body can be presented as erotic spectacle without *direct* recognition of the erotic nature of the spectacle. Entire genres of film—the war movie, the sports biopic, the western—are rife with images of men in various states of undress. We are frequently presented with scenes of men stripping down to fight, or to work, or of shirts being removed to apply bandages to wounds—but in this context the (often aggressive) activity engaged in is culturally accepted as masculine behaviour, and the male body on display here is a reflection of that, not an invitation to view it as erotic *per se*. Men are 'active, stripped, sweating, embracing other men' (Neale, 1983, p. 128), but all under the pretext of furthering the plot: 'in order to remind us that while they are on display they also remain in control, still agents of movement' (Neale, 1983, p. 127). We rarely get to see 'images of a soft, disarmed male body' (Neale, 1983, p. 127)—even more rarely do we get to see the 'throwaway' male nude. A body shown to us purely for our visual delight, superfluous to the plot, intended only to titillate and thrill. It is difficult for us to countenance a male figure who is both subject and object, who functions both as a carrier of the plot *and* an object of desire. As one woman argues, 'if a show—let's say like the currently airing *Game of Thrones*—is going to continually parade naked females around in sexualised situations, then I want the same treatment of male nudity in the show. And not just a bare chest on a Southern soldier doing soldier stuff; I mean male bodies just as gratuitously displayed for the viewers' sexual titillation as all the female nudity' (Canadian, 35–44, single, heterosexual). Even in pornography, this workman-like approach to male nudity persists—the male body is not for enjoyment, it is a tool. When it is on display, it is generally mechanised as a piece of equipment (Moye, 1985). Although dominant in much m/f pornography, the man often 'expresses no pleasure or joy in the "act", he is silent as he concentrates on the *job*' (Moye, 1985, pp. 57–58, emphasis added). Instead, sexual pleasure is captured in and expressed through the female body: while men have a job to do (a job that just so happens to require them to remove some or all of their clothes), women 'keep the secret of bodily pleasure' (Moye, 1985, p. 64).

On the occasions when male nudity is not disavowed via action, it is often disavowed via humour. 'Most of the times when men are nude in film, it's meant to be comedic' one participant says, 'Nude woman equals sexy. Nude man equals funny' (American, 35–44, in a relationship, heterosexual). Writing about a recent episode of *Game of Thrones*, Catherine Gee (2016) comments on how viewers were *finally* given a glimpse of male genitals amid 'near-weekly' female nudity. However, the scene involved a minor character complaining that he was suffering from genital warts (funny, huh?), in sharp contrast to the overtly sensual scenes featuring full frontal nudity from award-nominated female actresses in the show. The scene served no narrative purpose, and was apparently deliberately shot from an unflattering angle; '[it] essentially seemed like the director was just throwing in a "see, we will show you male nudity, and did you really want to see that?"' (Hooton, 2016). Noting how the actress Emilia Clarke, who features prominently on the show, has called for a greater equality of nudity—'Free the penis!'—the feminist porn director Ms. Naughty (2016) complains on her blog that 'a brief close-up of a flaccid cock on an unknown actor accompanied by talk of genital warts is not "freeing the penis"'. Gee (2016) concludes that 'there appears to be a golden rule when it comes to genitals on television. Women's are sexy; men's are funny. To see a penis in a sexual—or even just sexy—context on television is a rare thing indeed.' A participant wryly notes, 'after all, what's funnier looking than a man's soft penis and low-swinging balls? Ha ha. I think part of that attitude lies in our nation's uneasiness with homoeroticism, but also the inherent vulnerability of seeing a man at his "weakest"—because apparently a man isn't a man unless his dick is— seven inches or bigger—erect' (American, 25–34, in a polyamorous relationship, bisexual).

Participants feel that it is partly this framing of male nudity that has led many women to publicly express the idea that men look 'silly' or 'funny' without their clothes on. This is a view that has been espoused even from within women's erotica. In their study of the now defunct *Viva*—marketed as a women's magazine geared towards sexually liberated women—Beggan and Allison (2009, p. 455) quote the magazine's editor, Kathy Keeton, as saying, 'my personal feeling, affirmed by many women I have spoken with, is that, with certain exceptions of course, men look silly—vulnerable and self-conscious—posing [naked]'. In this way, women are continuously told that the male form should be regarded as humorous in some way, even by those who are trying to market female-orientated erotica. It is perhaps not surprising, then, that Mackinnon (1997, p. 150) notes a tendency for women to be embarrassed by viewing men as sex objects, commenting on the amount of 'giggling' that accompanies the watching of male strip shows. Even the handful of films which actively celebrate the naked male body (and female desire for it)—such as Channing Tatum's semi-autobiographic *Magic Mike*—often struggle with how to frame such desire as a serious, sensual pursuit. Mercer (2013, p. 88) believes that for the male sex symbol, 'his sexual desirability is an enigma, a puzzle that has to be worked out or made sense of in some way,' and notes that this 'working out' can manifest itself in various ways. In *Magic Mike* he argues that elements of humour are used to 'work out', and in effect legitimate, the act of looking at the sexualised bodies of Tatum, McConaughey, Manganiello et al.

However, there are some indications that this is changing. In their study of female patrons of a male strip club, Montemurro, Bloom, and Madell (2003, pp. 349–350) conclude that 'contrary to stereotypes about women's sexuality, most of the women observed participated in the show to a large extent by unabashed gazing at the scantily clad men, or frantically waving dollar bills to call the dancers to their area'. Others engaged in more 'extreme' (and arguably problematic) behaviour, by grabbing at the dancers and groping their bodies. Montemurro et al. (2003, p. 350) affirm that women patronise strip clubs because they enjoy the voyeuristic elements of the show and they want to 'observ[e] men's bodies in a sexualised manner'—much the same as male patrons at a female strip club (see, e.g., Erikson & Tewksbury, 2000). Rarely did they see the giggling or awkwardness that Mackinnon (1997) found so prevalent. Interestingly, Eck (2003) found that the embarrassment and/or amusement exhibited by her participants in response to male nudity and m/m pornographic images was more pronounced in the older generation. It is perhaps the case that women *are* gradually learning how to look at men, and that cultural scripts are (slowly) changing. As one of my participants says, 'I think we're getting to the place where we are less repressed and can totally admit we are watching a film (*Thor, Captain America*) to see the hot half-naked hot man scene' (French, 18–24, single, bisexual).

Participants are keen to stress that both the normalisation and the sensualisation of male nudity could have positive overall effects for wider society (not just give women something to look at). As one participant comments, 'I've known a lot of guys hurt by the whole "the penis is the best thing you have AND SHAMEFUL" pile of crap here in America. Or "the penis is ugly". No, it's not. It's perfectly alright. It seems absurd anyone would think otherwise but a sense of normalcy can only be resolved by, well, penises in the public sphere' (American, 25–34, single, lesbian). Another tells a story about how her complete ignorance about male genitalia has had a negative impact on her life:

When I was about 13 years old, I was walking home from school alone, when a car pulled alongside me. I stopped and clutched my schoolbooks to my chest while the driver rolled down the passenger's side window. He leaned across the front seat of the car. I thought for sure he was going to ask for directions. I knew not to stand too close to the car, lest I be kidnapped. The man asked me if I knew where Hancock Street was. I had never heard of Hancock Street, so I replied that I didn't know. 'Have you ever seen one of these?' the man asked. I leaned forward to see what the man was talking about. He was gripping some sort of pink tube in his left hand. He held it in his grasp between the front of his pants and the steering wheel. I shook my head no, and the man laughed before driving away. Until I got married, at 31 years old, it had never crossed my mind that the man had shown me his penis. From what I had learned at a Girl Scout meeting where a nurse explained menstruation to girls in my troop who were all about 12 years old, penises were very long so they could deposit the semen into the vagina. A penis was also covered completely in hair. That's the way I imagined it when the nurse explained that hair grows on boys' genitals when they undergo puberty. It infuriates me to this day that I was so ill-equipped to handle anything to do with sexuality. If I had seen a male nude in a film, it may have spared me the horror of thinking there was something disgustingly wrong with my husband when I saw his penis for the first time, or it may have made me recognize that I had been flashed by the stranger looking for Hancock Street. (American, 45–54, single, asexual)

'Women Want Eye Candy Too': The Male as Erotic Object

Clearly the women I spoke with during the course of writing this book *do* look at men. Not only do they look at them, they are often comfortable looking at them, happy to be frank and open in their desire. This is not to say that feelings of shame or embarrassment do not persist, but—perhaps unsurprisingly—the majority of women who responded to a call asking for women who engage with m/m SEM are pretty effusive in the delight they take from the naked male form. It would seem that this is an attitude which is not unique, however, to these women, but is gaining traction in wider society. Waskul and Radeloff (2010) note that men are increasingly being portrayed as both subjects and objects of the erotic gaze of others. Despite their comparative scarcity, you are nevertheless much more likely to see a naked man on your TV screen or on an advertising billboard today than you were twenty years ago. As Bordo (2000, p. 168) notes, 'beauty has (re)disovered the male body'. In contemporary media culture, the sexualised representation of male bodies (particularly male celebrity bodies) is becoming more and more common (Coad, 2008; Gill, 2007; Mercer, 2013; Smith, 2007; Stratton, 2000). Worton (2002, p. 9) argues that the fact that in recent years the male nude body has been made 'publicly – and often provocatively – visible' is indicative of a radical shift in attitudes towards masculinity and is facilitating the establishment of new multiple concepts of male identity.

Examining the changing nature of masculinity and the male sex symbol, Mercer (2013) discusses the scene in *Casino Royale* where Daniel Craig's Bond emerges from the sea in a tight, blue swimsuit that leaves little to the imagination. This image of Craig, dripping and glistening and inviting us to look at him, positions him more in the tradition of 'Bond girls' than Bond himself—it is difficult to watch this scene without recalling Ursula Andress in *Dr No* or Halle Berry in *Die Another Day*. Mercer (2013, p. 81) observes how Craig 'is a vision of male beauty offered to us through a mise en scene that unambiguously foregrounds his sex appeal', and goes on to note how this scene brought about 'fevered discussion' (op cit., p. 81) and 'hysterical excitement' (op cit., p. 83), particularly among female viewers. Mercer (2013, p. 88) feels that Daniel Craig's sex symbol status can be understood within the context of a wider sexualisation of the signs of masculinity that has been taking place over the last 25 years, and can be read alongside other figures whose 'signification is at points equally ambiguous and uncertain' such as David Beckham—the footballer who dared to wear a sarong, and who frequently poses moodily in nothing but his (extremely skimpy) underwear. Beckham therefore is presented as 'an object of sexual desire for an audience that cannot be regarded as either exclusively female or gay' (Mercer, 2013, p. 88). Many of my participants welcome this recent shift in how celebrity male bodies are being presented for a female audience:

T: What is *Magic Mike* except for us to look at? What is that
       moment in *Thor* where Chris Hemsworth walks across
       the screen with his shirt off? That was a money shot for

women. And that never used to happen. And it was barely
commented on [in the press]!
W: It was commented on on our sofa!
T: Exactly, it was like: [noise of joyous exclamation].
W: Sorry, Chris Hemsworth: wow!
T: [appreciative noise] And he's lovely

Suzanne Moore (1988, p. 56) feels that this tendency to dephallicise
many new images of men gives a place for the female spectator, the men
being presented not 'as all-powerful, but as objects of pleasure and desire'.
The concept of men as 'eye candy' has also gained traction within feminist circles, Germaine Greer's (2003) book *The Beautiful Boy* is an attempt
to 'reclaim the pleasures of the youthful male body for a female gaze'
(McLelland, 2005, p. 71). However, m/f pornography has, on the whole,
been slow to respond to this desire to position men as attractive, as having
appealing bodies which viewers want to look at. The feminist porn director Ms. Naughty (2013, p. 71) observes how porn tends to 'cut men out
of the frame, concentrating only on the woman's body. The guys [are]
often unattractive and seem creepy or obnoxious… The camera never
show[s] the man's face during orgasm, which—to me—[is] a travesty.
Men's faces are beautiful at that moment'. In despair at the lack of heterosexual content on offer, when she started her first 'for women' website,
she often browsed through photo sets of naked men that were intended
for a gay audience, choosing the ones she liked the look of and reappropriating them for her female audience. For it is gay sites which tend to
emphasise the beauty of the male body, and the male body *in its entirety.*
While the penis is certainly part of what respondents find attractive in
naked men, it is not the be all and end all, or even the focal point.
Likewise, in written erotica, participants enjoy sensual descriptions of
various parts of men's bodies. In *Ladies Own Erotica*, Sabina Sedgwick
writes a piece called 'Address to a Penis Owner', where she professes, 'we
are not trying to diminish your appendage, but we want to enlarge upon
those parts of you that have been unjustly ignored. These are parts that
are essential to our pleasure: your hair, your eyes, your lips, your tongue,
your chest, your thighs, your voice, and—most importantly—your

hands. It is no accident that our stories have celebrated these greater assets' (in Thurston, 1987, p. 150).

In part, then, attraction to m/m SEM comes from the desire for eye candy, and eye candy is rarely found in heterosexual media. While the movie industry may be starting to switch on to the idea that many female viewers might appreciate a glimpse of Channing Tatum's butt, pornography still tends to elevate female stars over male ones. In her collection of essays on the porn industry, Chauntelle Tibbals (2015, p. 113) notes that 'no one pays attention to the guys in porn' and that the vast majority of household name porn stars are women. She adds that the only arena where this isn't the case is in the m/m genre: 'gay porn has produced a hefty handful of stars over the decades'. This may well go some way to explaining why women are interested in it—if we accept that women are interested in the male as sex object, the male as celebrity, the male as pin-up, then why wouldn't they look to m/m porn to find this? For in much heterosexual porn, as the porn actor James Deen has pointed out, men are 'the assist, not the star' (Deen in Buchanan, 2013).

Peeping Tomboys: Women as Voyeurs

The term 'male gaze' was introduced by the feminist scholar Laura Mulvey in 1975. Building on the ideas of Foucault (1963)—who had discussed the use of a 'controlling' gaze being used at all times in the panopticon as a tool of surveillance, thus creating a relationship between observation, power, and knowledge, and Lacan (1961)—who had introduced the idea of the 'gaze' as a way of analysing visual culture and understanding how a spectator views the people or objects they are presented with, Mulvey argued that, in classical narrative cinema, this 'gaze' is essentially male (Neville, 2015). Mulvey maintained that in narrative cinema men control the gaze; that they do all the looking, and that women are merely passive recipients, being viewed. It is certainly the case that the vast majority of what we watch (and read, for that matter) is from the male perspective—authored, directed, and filmed by men, and mostly straight cis-gendered white men at that. Maureen Ryan (2014) hypothesises that this lack of female writers, directors, and camera crew in Hollywood may have contributed to the overwhelming norm of the male gaze. If those behind the camera are mostly male, then, as Ryan explains, 'what they don't want to see usually doesn't get shot'. The same is arguably true for much pornography.

In our sexually imbalanced world, viewed through the lens of this male gaze, Mulvey (1975, p. 11) posits that 'pleasure in looking has been split between active/male and passive/female'. The man's scopophilic pleasure ('a ravenous desire to look') arises from 'using a person as an object of sexual stimulation through sight' (Greven, 2009, p. 19). And this 'person' is generally a woman. Indeed, the woman in film is coded for strong visual and erotic impact so that she may connote *to-be-looked-at-ness*. As John Berger (1973, p. 47) once wrote, 'men look at women. Women watch themselves being looked at'. Women in narrative cinema are therefore objectified, voyeuristically, for both the straight male director and the straight male spectator. From this it is posited that men are socialised to stare at women as objects in order to control them and prevent them from 'looking' back—that is, from having any power of their own (Neville, 2015). Endemic here is the notion that the gaze objectifies its target and empowers its owner; in other words, that looking is better than being looked at—something I will come back to later in this chapter. Several women I spoke to are very aware of this inequality in gazing, with one explaining, 'nudity in films is accompanied by a covert discourse of power, in that it spectacularises the body and makes it available for erotic consumption, and, while I don't have a problem with that *per se*, I *do* have a problem with the inequality with which that power discourse is applied to male and female bodies. Breasts on screen are commonplace; full-frontal female nudity is less common, of course, but still overwhelmingly outweighs male full-frontal nudity, and the erect penis is taboo in everything that's not actual porn. This implicitly sets up the naked female body as to-be-consumed, while implying that there's something inherently wrong with consuming the naked male body on screen' (British, 25–34, single, heterosexual).

There has been criticism of the way Mulvey's theory has been over-stretched to apply to a range of cultural products it was not originally intended for, and Mulvey herself has stated that she wrote it as a 'polemic' and that a more 'nuanced perspective' might be helpful (in Sassatelli,

2011, p. 128). A number of writers have specifically questioned the use-fulness of the concept of the gaze when applied to pornography, arguing that the pornographic gaze is different to that which exists within narrative cinema because the intended effect(s) of the respective films differ. Schroeder (2000, p. 7) points out that the 'transformation of the porn film into a private viewing experience has altered its relation to the viewer(s), encouraging viewer engagement in masturbation or sexual intercourse and aimed at maximising pleasure through the creation of changing, inconstant, viewing positions and identificatory relations with characters'. However, despite these critiques, certain facets of the idea of the male gaze have—understandably—been adopted to understand the dynamics involved in viewing heterosexual pornography (e.g. Ellis, O'Dair, & Tallmer, 1990; Williams, 2004). After all, much like narrative cinema, 'the publicly available content of sexual fantasy is almost totally defined by men's needs, as is the content of pornography' (Simon & Gagon, 2005, p. 213).

It is perhaps not surprising then that many of the women I spoke with state they enjoy m/m porn because it is marketed to a target audience they feel they have more in common with (gay men as opposed to heterosexual men), and invites them to adopt a point of view that is more in-keeping with their own sexual preferences and desires, where 'men are the object of sexual attraction, instead of the women' (American, 25–34, single, heterosexual). Many dislike the way that most heterosexual porn invites them to view the sex acts occurring from a 'male' perspective—noting the way that the camera tends to linger on female anatomy and that men are 'ugly and out of focus at best, and just a disembodied cock at worst' (Australian, 18–24, single, bisexual). However, they are also acutely aware that this is porn that *still* isn't made for them, that they are still, to some extent, voyeurs: '[While] I like that it's porn made for an audience other than straight men, [it's] still men, admittedly. But it's a start' (American, 18–24, in a relationship, heterosexual).

The all-pervasive nature of the male gaze has led some scholars to argue that the only possible mode of a woman looking at a male body comes through masquerade—a woman looking through a man's eyes (Doane, 1987). To this extent, Marks (1996, p. 127) believes that 'to look sexually at men I must masquerade as a gay man, i.e. provisionally borrow a male gaze'. Marks (1996, p. 130) argues that theories of imaging the male body still assume a masculine viewing subject (be it gay or heterosexual), and as such the female viewer still faces the problem of how to look: 'the male body remains like Teflon, off which female looks glance with nary a scratch'. It is certainly true that throughout history the erotic male nudes that have been created were not made for women to look at—they were made by men for each other. For this reason, Sarah Kent (1985, p. 77) argues that 'women are used to living vicariously—viewing their culture voyeuristically and translating its material, as best they can, to serve their own needs'. According to Eck (2003, p. 694) women are 'just learning to be voyeurs. Although [they] may be more accustomed to seeing male bodies, they are not as accustomed to having those bodies 'offered' to them'. In other words, women cannot possess a gaze of their own, the nearest they can come to achieving scopophilic pleasure is to snatch looks at men intended for other men. Some of the women in my study are very aware of the way they are positioned as voyeurs, with one noting 'I more often react to a hot boy by thinking it would be hot to see him being fucked than to think of being fucked by him. I guess my appreciation of the male body, such as it is, is mostly voyeuristic and empathetic, rather than hands-on' (British, 35–44, single, demisexual).

As such, Kent (1985, pp. 85–87) argues that it is logical that images created for the (homosexual) male gaze, such as Robert Mapplethorpe's photographs, have much more potential to excite and titillate than images created for the (purported) female gaze, such as pin-ups, or 'playmales' as she refers to them. She observes that it is:

> clear that the museums, galleries, and art history books are filled with male nudes to which women can respond with erotic pleasure and through which they can explore sexual options, even though the images were intended for masculine eyes and express homoerotic desires. This has certain advantages for the female viewer who is eavesdropping on a man-to-man communication. Her presence is neither expected nor taken into consideration—it is irrelevant to the construction of the image and the message it contains. She can, therefore, indulge in her voyeurism unselfconsciously like a fly on the wall, while her sexual interest is con-

firmed though identification with the author of the image. (Kent, 1985, p. 87)

The problem with 'playmales', Kent believes, is that there is a conflict between the power relations between the sexes and between the viewer and the viewed. Men are used to being in control. Men are used to being the ones who gaze. So while the playmale may appear to put himself at the disposal of the female viewer, he is also trying to simultaneously maintain a position of sexual dominance. Kent argues that while the female pin-up and the homoerotic male nude tend to be acquiescent or submissive, playmales 'try to assert their independence and control the observer's responses', through their positioning, gaze, body language and so on (Kent, 1985, p. 87). Bordo (1993) agrees, noting that while male strippers for women are touted as a 'what's good for the goose is good for the gander' development, they rarely exhibit themselves fully naked to women the way female strippers do to men. Instead, Bordo (1993, p. 700, emphasis added) argues, that 'what is eroticised in the male stripper routines is not the strip, not the exposure of nakedness, but the teasing display of phallic *power*, concentrated on the hard, pumped-up armour of muscle and covered frontal bulge, straining against its confinements. Their penises they keep to themselves.'

The 'borrowed' male gaze is not the same as an active, powerful female gaze though. Kaja Silverman (1992) argues that voyeurism, far from being a dominant viewing position, presents a situation in which one is *least* in control. To adopt a voyeuristic position is to deprive any viewer of a powerful viewing position. Women in my sample note this and often express a desire to be more empowered as viewers and consumers. Many of them do feel that a female gaze exists, and moreover that it empowers and excites them. They feel there has been a rise in mainstream films that reject or flip the male gaze, with one noting that while 'you didn't start to see the camera "make love" to action heroes until Brandon Lee and later Keanu Reeves, now we've got Daniel Craig [and loads of others]' (American, 45–54, in a polyamorous relationship, bisexual). In terms of erotica, they particularly link the female gaze to amateur or community-based SEM—from home-made pornography (heterosexual and homosexual), to slash fiction, to Tumblr pages focusing on the male nude and m/m sex. These types of media are seen as both female-created and female-controlled—and therefore empowering. Noting the link between the female gaze and women-produced SEM within slash fandom, Coppa (2008) observes that it is interesting that the first *Star Trek* slideshow (as an early form of vidding[1]) emerged in the same year as Mulvey wrote *Visual Pleasure and Narrative Cinema* (1975). Second-wave feminism had 'popularised ideas of female independence and sexual subjectivity, priming women to take control of the camera' and many vids reverse, or at least complicate, traditional scopophilia of the kind Mulvey describes, 'casting men as objects of visual desire and addressing sexist problems in visual texts' (Coppa, 2008, p. 2.1). To this extent, Nagaike (2003) argues that women engaging with m/m SEM is consistent with a more radical interpretation of the female gaze, wherein women looking at the sexual interactions of male lovers can be seen as an ideological challenge to the gendered power structure of men as gazing subjects and women as visual objects.

This is not to say that women are *never* voyeurs in the sense that Kent describes. Indeed, for some of the women I spoke with, the voyeuristic nature of viewing both the homoerotic male nude and m/m pornography is part of the thrill, what Mackinnon (1997, p. 162) refers to as 'the naughtiness of illicit viewing' (see Chap. 8 for further discussion on this). However, some women are adamant they do possess a gaze their own, and that it is through looking at the naked male body that they are best able to exercise their look. Whether or not this gaze is 'female', however, is a subject of further discussion.

A Gaze of One's Own?: Male Bodies and the Genderless Gaze

A number of respondents, particularly those who are alive to the queer possibilities of women watching m/m SEM, reject the concept of a 'gendered' gaze entirely. It should be noted that within a lot of the discourse around visual culture, the concept of the male gaze has become seen as something almost ubiquitous, a cliché, a lazy metaphor for the patriarchy.

Many object to the fixity of the alignment of passivity with femininity and activity with masculinity, as well as the failure to account for the female spectator (de Lauretis, 1984; Kaplan, 1983; Silverman, 1980; Stacey, 1991). Dhaenens, Vam Bauwel, and Biltereyst (2008, p. 337) point out that this is likely because feminist film theorists such as Mulvey have tended to overlook 'real' women, focusing instead on theoretical frameworks. Similarly, Halberstam (1995, p. 166) critiques Mulvey's 'excessively neat formula for the increasingly messy business of erotic identification', noting that 'the most relevant reformulations of spectator-ship take note of the multiple gendered positions afforded by the gaze and provide a more historically specific analysis of spectatorship'. Halberstam (1995, p. 166) suggests that a 'less psychoanalytically inflected theory of spectatorship is far less sure of the gender of the gaze. Indeed, recent discussions of gay and lesbian cinema assume that the gaze is queer or multidimensional.'

Evans and Gamman (1995, p. 13) state that they want to shift the course of the debate by engaging with what Constantine Giannaris (cited in Evans & Gamman, 1995, p. 13) refers to as 'genderfuck'—claiming this helps to acknowledge that there are in fact 'many perverse but enjoy-able relations of looking'. 'Genderfuck' here is a term used to describe confusions in gender recognition, with the observation that the imagined 'self' has the freedom to mutate into alternative manifestations. The idea of a 'genderfucked' gaze is not a new one (Neville, 2015). Building on the early Lacanian concept of the 'gaze' from within the area of art history, Randolph (2002) states that Michelangelo's David defies homogenous constructions of binary homoerotic and heteronormative gazes, instead permitting an androgynous gaze constantly shifting in time and space. A number of respondents discuss exactly such a shifting gaze, one where they can watch m/m pornography from a number of perspectives, depending on their mood: 'I watch het porn and I can't stand most of it, because the ladies are fake, their reactions, and everything just bugs me. I can view gay porn from an outsider perspective and not see myself in the girl, but rather just enjoy it separately and maybe identify with the top or the bottom, however I am feeling that day' (American, 25–34, single, heterosexual).

This is not just a straightforward 'flipping' of the pornographic gaze to a gazing female and a gazed-upon male. There are similarities here with the work of critics such as Butler, de Lauretis, and Califa, who have raised issues about the position of female (especially lesbian) readers of porn. Both de Lauretis (1994) and Butler (1990) believe in the value and validity of porn as sexual 'fantasy', and Califa (1994) also argues that lesbian sadomasochistic porn functions as a creative fantasy, and therefore possesses subversive possibilities that escape complicity with patriarchal schema. Butler (1990, p. 114) has also argued against the concept of a gendered gaze when viewing pornography, claiming that 'if pornography is to be understood as fantasy, as anti-pornography activists almost invariably insist, then the effect of pornography is not to force women to identify with a subordinate or debased position, but to provide the opportunity to identify with the entire scene of debasement, agents and recipients alike, when those "positions" are clearly discernible in the actions and landscape of masturbatory scenes of triumph and humiliation'.

For Butler, representation in porn is interesting because of how positions 'can perpetually be redrawn' (Butler, 1990, p. 114). In fact, she calls porn 'crucial to read' because of the 'way in which it *fails* to correspond to social positions' (Butler, 1990, p. 114, emphasis added).

'What's Good for the Goose...': Equality and the Pleasures of Being Gazed at

It is clear that in response to a history of female objectification and sexualisation an audience has formed which derives a great deal of pleasure from looking back. The popularity of films such as *Magic Mike* and the steady rise in women attending male strip clubs and revue bars (Montemurro et al., 2003) and live sex shows (Sanders-McDonagh, 2015) suggests that there is a growing desire for women to look at the sexualised male body, or at least, a growing acceptability of the expression of such a desire. To this extent, some of the rhetoric that (rightfully) arose with regards to female objectification now rests on shifting sands. As Zoe Williams (2007) points out in *The Guardian*, 'the rhetoric of objectification relies on the idea that it's one-way traffic, that only men objectify, and only women are objectified. Before you even consider where that leaves homosexuality, you can only accept this model if you take as a starting point that women have no physical imperative'. However, even if we accept that women *do* have a physical imperative, Kenneth Mackinnon (1997, p. 119) asks whether the 'alleged objectificatory harm of pornography [is] lessened or intensified since this sort of erotic experience reinforces object–subject/male–female axes, even if it switches the usual gender relations?' Participants are acutely aware that objectifying men (and the male body) raises these sorts of issues (although they don't always care—as one comments, 'I would absolutely watch exploitative thrillers where the camera pans over guys in a gross fashion and the killer/audience spies on them in the shower. Hell, I watch that kind of stuff with women. I have zero shame about trashy entertainment' (American, 25–34, single, bisexual)).

To explore this accusation, it is necessary to spend some time considering whether objectification *is* always wholly negative—particularly, perhaps, when it is men who are being objectified. Talking about online sites where other users can rate erotic selfies, Waskul and Radeloff (2010, p. 213) postulate that for men, to be seen and appreciated in these ways might be experienced 'not only as novel, but as exciting'. The anthropologist Wim Lunsing (2006, p. 31) agrees, recounting a time that he was dancing in a club in Japan when a woman came up to him and started 'grinding her crotch against [his] buttocks, like gay men may do when dancing in clubs'. Lunsing (2006, p. 31) notes that at the time he had long hair and was wearing cut-off jeans and a crop top, and the fact that the woman was mimicking the 'active male part' in the sexual role division implied that she was 'feminising him'. However, Lunsing (2006, p. 31) asserts that he 'does not know in general what is problematic about being objectified or feminised. Being objectified entails an extent of interest in oneself and if one does not have a sexist view regarding sex differences, being feminised is not something negative'. By all accounts, as a white man, he found the experience of being objectified by a Japanese woman refreshing. While I am not suggesting it should ever be socially acceptable to sexually assault a stranger in a nightclub, it is important nonetheless to interrogate differences in how these behaviours are perceived and responded to. Objectification is not always unwelcome, and it does not always follow rigid gender binaries.

McNair (2013) notes that the term 'objectification' has generally been used in a negative sense, as it is customarily used as reference to the process by which a human subject is reduced to a sexual object, thereby losing a key element of their humanity. Or rather, *her* humanity, since it is usually a her in this paradigm. However, everything can be and often is objectified simply by being perceived by another, and it is not clear that there is something inherently bad about this. As McNair points out, there are, in fact, many circumstances when we want to be viewed, observed, and objectified—at parties, on dates, on social media platforms. While objectification can be experienced as distressing and disempowering, there are occasions when *not* being noticed is extremely disappointing. McNair (2013, p. 12) notes that objectification, in this sense, 'is not a patriarchal imposition on women, but an aspect of human sexuality which encompasses all genders and sexual identities'. While objectification's association with sexism and the patriarchy reflects power relations which have traditionally favoured men, women and men both have the capacity to objectify one another, and while 'unwanted looking is rightly condemned, sexual objectification itself is often invited and welcomed by those to whom it is directed' (McNair, 2013, p. 12). Gill (2009) notes that women have recently begun to participate enthusiastically, as active sexual subjects, in forms of self-representation that earlier generations of feminists regarded as connected to subordination. Likewise, women have begun to lay claim to their ability to objectify men. McNair (2013, p. 100) observes that 'the significant gaze in the act of looking at the body reduced to a sex object is no longer that of the powerful man alone. Now the female also has a gaze, which she will exercise in relation to herself, to other women, and also to men'. He notes how this has gone hand-in-hand with a growing tendency among men to objectify themselves, and a growing emphasis on male grooming and the styling of the male body. Men are now expected to work out and to watch what they eat, as women are. McNair feels that gay culture has led the charge here, and that the spilling over of aspects of gay life into the mainstream means that 'many straight men [are now] embracing self-objectification as a normal, natural part of their public image'. Again, this may help to answer part of the question as to why women engage with m/m SEM—if gay men objectify themselves, would this not be a natural place for women to look?

McNair's (2013) discussion also raises important questions about objectification and power. Writing about the role of the female gaze in the construction of masculinity, Goddard (2000, p. 25) points out that the 'subject' who submits him or herself to the gaze of the other is able to use that submission as a form of power in and of itself, concluding 'the submission is also not entirely as a 'lesser' submitting to a 'superior'— there is a sense of *pride* in the body being displayed. The vulnerability of nakedness is offset by the power of the body's beauty'. Bordo (2000, p. 190) additionally notes that 'passive' does not always describe what is going on when one is the object of the gaze: 'inviting, receiving, responding … are active behaviours'. Furthermore, she argues that attention to appearance involves a lot of work—particularly for men, with male sensuality often placing an emphasis on physical strength and fitness—and is about more than 'sexual allure'—it also indicates one is disciplined and has 'the right stuff' (Bordo, 2000, p. 221).

In a broad sense, then, the formal and thematic validity of visual theory stems from two major questions: Is there a 'gaze' that is firmly gendered? (No). Is the single gaze strongly power-related in such a way? (Perhaps not). Lacan has analysed the issue differently from Mulvey, arguing that the gazing subject can, in turn, be objectified as the gazed-upon object—which calls into question the fixed nature of the power relationships within the gaze. While we typically associate the gaze with an active process, Lacan suggests that the gaze itself is an object, something that serves to trigger our desire visually. The gaze, then, 'is not the look of the subject at the object, but the *gap* within the subject's seemingly omnipotent look. The gap within our look marks the point at which our desire manifests itself in what we see' (McGowan, 2008, p. 6, emphasis added). Greven (2009, p. 23) argues that this interpretation emphasises the idea of the gaze as 'symptomatic of the blinding gap within the very heart of the visual … the rampant, unsatisfiable desire to see and experience pleasure through seeing … scopophilia'. In this sense, concepts of masculinity and femininity are subservient to the gaze, which itself 'is a symptom of engulfing desire' (Greven, 2009, p. 23). Gender imaging is not unidirectional, but works in both directions—the gazer themself is as much influenced by the gaze as is the subject of the gaze. Lacan's scenario of the potential mutuality of the gaze thus calls into question some of Mulvey's contentions, and, more pertinently, several of Dworkin's (1992) assertions about the nature of the gaze in pornography.

We should also consider that gazing is not always about power at all. As the writer Katie Ward (2016) so eloquently writes, 'the human gaze is an act of intimacy. It's why we love it in art'. Building on this idea of intimacy, Bordo (1993, p. 732) conceives of a look where 'the erotics of the gaze no longer revolve around the dynamics of "looking at" or "being looked at" (of penetrating or being penetrated by, of activity or passivity), but around the mutuality of truly *seeing* and being *seen*, a meeting of subjectivities in which what is experienced is the recognition of knowing and being known by another. "Their eyes met and held each other's": a romantic cliché, but how frequently do we really experience the erotic charge of such meetings and "holdings"?'

She asks us to imagine a different sort of sexual paradigm: one in which the subjectivity of the other is experienced neither as threatening nor as essential to the validation of the self, but as offering opportunities for *knowledge* of the other, and thus the possibility of real intimacy with him or her. Many participants allude to this sort of gazing in their discussions, with one commenting that 'we need to … treat everyone's nudity differently … the solution to objectification is subjectification' (American, 25–34, in a polyamorous relationship, bisexual), and another concluding, 'although it's idealistic of me, I like to think that eventually we could get to a point where we can appreciate all kinds of bodies without reducing the people who have those bodies to attractive pieces of meat' (American, 25–34, single, heterosexual).

Opening the Toy Box

While a desire to look at (or imagine) attractive men is one of the primary reasons given by women for why they both watch and read m/m SEM, there is clearly a bit more going on here than straightforward eroticising of men and the male body. After all, these women are not just eroticising men, they are—for the large part—eroticising *gay* men. Much of the literature on slash fiction and BL manga (there is precious little on women and m/m video pornography) has placed female fans of m/m in a category of 'assumed straightness'. Here their interest in men is 'only natural', and can be understood in the same way as male interest in f/f SEM. There are several problems with this assumption. Firstly, as the statistics discussed in Chap. 1 indicate, these women are not *that* straight—55 per cent of my sample identified as something other than heterosexual, and this is broadly in-keeping with other recent survey data from within slash fandom (Fielding, 2013; LuLu, 2013; Morrissey, 2008). Secondly, even when m/m fans are women who are interested in men, it is not apparent that we can necessarily read them as *straight*. They are reading the world with queer eyes, and engaging in a perverse form of interpretation. I will discuss this further in Chap. 7.

In addition, Mulvey's work on the gaze was within the context of male-produced mainstream cinema. Genres like slash and BL differ from conventional texts in several ways. Firstly, they are often (although not exclusively) female-authored and consciously addressed to a mostly female audience. Secondly, the level of audience participation in the fandoms that produce these types of works mean that much content is produced outside of the control of 'patriarchal' publishers. There is therefore no structural need for female consumers of slash or BL to take a male point of view dictated by male artists (Meyer, 2010). Indeed, as Stanley (2010, p. 107) writes, slash and BL have opened up a 'whole new toy box' for women where they are given the chance to 'play with boys and the male body in ways that male authors/artists have traditionally assumed to be their right to manipulate and play with the female body'. In the world of slash fiction 'it is the male body which is on display … and here it has been rendered poseable, penetrable, and subject to disruptions that serve to queer the dominant narratives in playful and irreverent ways'. It is to this 'toy box' that I now want to turn.

Notes

1. Vidding refers to the practice in media fandom of creating videos (very often set to music) from the footage of one or more visual media sources, thereby exploring the source itself in a new way—within slash fandoms vidding often retools scenes or images from the original media source(s) to focus on the romantic and/or sexual tension between two (or more) male characters.

References

Attwood, F. (2005). Tits and ass and porn and fighting': Male heterosexuality in magazines for men. *International Journal of Cultural Studies, 8*(1), 83–100.

Beggan, J. T., & Allison, S. T. (2009). Viva Viva? Women's meanings associated with male nudity in a 1970s 'For Women' magazine. *The Journal of Sex Research, 46*(5), 446–459.

Berger, J. (1973). *Ways of seeing*. New York: Viking Press.

Betterton, R. (1987). *Looking on: Images of femininity in the visual arts and media*. London: Pandora.

Bordo, S. (1993). Reading the male body. *Michigan Quarterly Review, 32*(4), 696–737.

Bordo, S. (2000). *The male body: A new look at men in public and private*. New York: Farrar, Straus & Giroux.

Buchanan, K. (2013, August 1). James Deen on *The Canyons*, social anxiety, and Sasha Grey. *Vulture*. Retrieved from http://www.vulture.com/2013/08/james-deen-the-canyons-fifty-shades-sasha-grey.html

Butler, J. (1990). The force of fantasy: Feminism, Mapplethorpe, and discursive excess. *Differences, 2*(2), 105–125.

Califa, P. (1994). *Public sex: The culture of radical sex*. Pittsburgh: Cleis Press.

Catalina, M. (2011, March 22). Porn, made for women by women. *The Guardian*. Retrieved from http://www.theguardian.com/lifeandstyle/2011/mar/22/porn-women

Coad, D. (2008). *The metrosexual: Gender, sexuality, and sport*. Albany: State University of New York Press.

Coppa, F. (2008). Women, *Star Trek*, and the early development of fannish vidding. *Transformative Works and Culture, 1*. Retrieved from http://journal.transformativeworks.org/index.php/twc/article/view/44/64?__hstc=65709233.99e

d162120c7e894e9a96b328d8ca5e0.1436918400093.1436918400094.
1436918400095.1&__hssc=65709233.1.1436918400096&__
hsfp=1314462730

Coward, R. (1984). *Female desire*. London: Paladin.

Davis, M. D. (1991). *The male nude in contemporary photography*. Philadelphia: Temple University Press.

de Lauretis, T. (1984). *Alice doesn't: Feminism, semiotics, cinema*. Bloomington: Indiana University Press.

de Lauretis, T. (1994). *The practice of love: Lesbian sexuality and perverse desire*. Bloomington: Indiana University Press.

Dhaenens, F., Vam Bauwel, S., & Biltereyst, D. (2008). Slashing the fiction of Queer Theory: Slash fiction, Queer reading, and transgressing the boundaries of screen studies, representations, and audiences. *Journal of Communication Inquiry, 32*(4), 335–347.

Disch, L., & Kane, M. J. (1996). When the looker really is a bitch: Lisa Olson, sport, and the heterosexual matrix. *Signs: Journal of Women in Culture and Society, 21*, 278–308.

Doane, M. A. (1987). *The desire to desire: The woman's film of the 1940s*. Bloomington: Indiana University Press.

Dworkin, A. (1992). Against the male flood: Censorship, pornography, and equality. In C. Itzin (Ed.), *Pornography: Women, violence, and civil liberties* (pp. 515–535). Oxford: Oxford University Press.

Eck, B. A. (2003). Men are much harder: Gendered viewing of nude images. *Gender & Society, 17*(5), 691–710.

Ellis, K., O'Dair, B., & Tallmer, A. (1990). Feminism and pornography. *Feminist Review, 36*, 15–18.

Erikson, D. J., & Tewksbury, R. (2000). The 'gentlemen' in the club: A typology of strip club patrons. *Deviant Behaviour, 21*(3), 271–293.

Evans, C., & Gamman, L. (1995). The gaze revisited, or reviewing Queer viewing. In P. Burston & C. Richardsonm (Eds.), *Queer romance: Lesbians, gay men, and popular culture* (pp. 13–56). London and New York: Routledge.

Fielding, D. M. (2013). *Normalising the deviance: The creation, politics, and consumption of sexual orientation and gender identities in fan communities*. BA Thesis submitted to Hamline University. Retrieved from http://digitalcommons.hamline.edu/dhp/7/

Foucault, M. (1963/2003). *The birth of the clinic* (A. M. Sheridan, Trans.). New York and London: Routledge.

Gee, C. (2016, May 23). Game of Thrones finally showed a penis—But it was a cop out. *The Telegraph*. Retrieved from http://www.telegraph.co.uk/tv/2016/05/23/game-of-thrones-finally-showed-a-penis--but-it-was-a-cop-out/

Gill, R. (2007). *Gender and the media*. Cambridge: Polity Press.

Gill, R. (2009). Supersexualise me! Advertising and the 'midriffs'. In F. Attwood (Ed.), *Mainstreaming sex: The sexualisation of Western culture* (pp. 93–109). London: IB Tauris.

Goddard, K. (2000). 'Looks maketh the man': The female gaze and the construction of masculinity. *The Journal of Men's Studies, 9*(1), 23–39.

Greer, G. (2003). *The beautiful boy*. London: Thames & Hudson.

Greven, D. (2009). *Gender and sexuality in Star Trek: Allegories of desire in the television series and films*. Jefferson, NC: McFarland.

Halberstam, J. (1995). *Skin shows: Gothic horror and the technology of monsters*. Durham, NC: Duke University Press.

Hooton, C. (2016, May 24). *Game of Thrones* finally took Emilia Clarke's advice and 'freed the penis'. *The Independent*. Retrieved from http://www.independent.co.uk/arts-entertainment/tv/news/game-of-thrones-nude-scene-freed-the-penis-in-season-6-episode-5-s6e5-nsfw-a7042826.html

Janssen, E., Carpenter, D., & Graham, C. A. (2003). Selecting films for sex research: Gender differences in erotic film preference. *Archives of Sexual Behaviour, 32*, 243–251.

Kaplan, E. A. (1983). *Women and film: Both sides of the camera*. New York: Methuen.

Kent, S. (1985). The erotic male nude. In S. Kent & J. Morreau (Eds.), *Women's images of men* (pp. 75–105). London: Pandora.

Lacan, J. (1961/2011). *The seminar of Jacques Lacan: Book IX: Identification: 1961–1962*. Retrieved June 20, 2013, from http://esource.dbs.ie/bitstream/handle/10788/159/Book-09-Identification.pdf?sequence=1

Lehman, P. (1988). In the realm of the senses: Desire, power, and the representation of the male body. *Genders, 2*, 91–110.

Lulu. (2013). *AO3 census data analysis*. Retrieved from http://centrumlumina.tumblr.com/post/63373124511/mm-fans-sexuality-and-gender

Lunsing, W. (2006). Yaoi Ronsō: Discussing depictions of male homosexuality in Japanese girls' comics, gay comics and gay pornography. *Intersections: Gender & Sexuality in Asia & the Pacific, 12*, 10.

Mackinnon, K. (1997). *Uneasy pleasures: The male as erotic object*. London: Cygnus Arts.

Marks, L. U. (1996). Straight women, gay porn and the scene of erotic looking. *Jump Cut, 40*, 127–135.

McGowan, T. (2008). *The real gaze: Film theory after lacan*. Albany: State University of New York Press.

McLelland, M. (2005). The world of yaoi: The internet, censorship, and the global 'Boys' Love' fandom. *The Australian Feminist Law Journal, 23*, 61–77.

McNair, B. (2013). *Porno? Chic!* London: Routledge.

Mercer, J. (2013). The enigma of the male sex symbol. *Celebrity Studies, 4*(1), 81–91.

Meyer, U. (2010). Hidden in straight sight: Trans*gressing gender and sexuality via BL. In A. Levi, M. McHarry, & D. Pagliasotti (Eds.), *Boys' love manga* (pp. 232–257). Jefferson: McFarland and Company.

Montemurro, B., Bloom, C., & Madell, K. (2003). Ladies night out: A typology of women patrons of a male strip club. *Deviant Behaviour, 24*(4), 333–352.

Moore, S. (1988). Here's looking at you, kid. In L. Gamman & M. Marshment (Eds.), *The female gaze: Women as viewers of popular culture*. London: The Women's Press.

Morrissey, K. (2008). *Fanning the flames of romance: An exploration of fan fiction and the romance novel*. MA dissertation, Georgetown University. Retrieved from https://repository.library.georgetown.edu/bitstream/handle/10822/551540/17_etd_kem82.pdf

Moye, A. (1985). Pornography. In A. Metcalf & M. Humphries (Eds.), *The sexuality of men* (pp. 44–69). London: Pluto Press.

Mulvey, L. (1975). Visual pleasure and narrative cinema. *Screen, 16*(3), 6–18.

Nagaike, K. (2003). Perverse sexualities, perverse desires: Representations of female fantasises and yaoi manga as pornography directed at women. *U.S.-Japan Women's Journal, 25*, 76–103.

Naughty, Ms. (2013). My decadent decade: Ten years of making and debating porn for women. In T. Taormino, C. Parreñas Shimizu, C. Penley, & M. Miller-Young (Eds.), *The feminist porn book* (pp. 71–78). New York: Feminist Press.

Naughty, Ms. (2016). *Game of thrones*: Three penises is not nudity equality. *Ms Naughty's Porn For Women* Blog. Retrieved from http://msnaughty.com/blog/2016/05/24/game-of-thrones-three-penises-is-not-nudity-equality/

Neale, S. (1983). Masculinity as spectacle: Reflections of men and mainstream cinema. *Screen, 24*(6), 6–18.

Neville, L. (2015). Male gays in the female gaze: Women who watch m/m pornography. *Porn Studies, 2*(2–3), 192–207.

Pagliassotti, D. (2010). Better than romance? Japanese BL manga and the sub-genre of male/male *romantic* fiction. In A. Levi, M. McHarry, & D. Pagliassotti

(Eds.), *Boys' love manga: Essays on the sexual ambiguity and cross-cultural fandom of the genre* (pp. 59–83). Jefferson, NC: McFarland & Company, Inc.

Parvez, Z. F. (2006). The labour of pleasure: How perceptions of emotional labour impact women's enjoyment of pornography. *Gender and Society, 20,* 605–631.

Ramsay, G. (2017). Straight women seeing gay porn: 'He's too good looking!'. *Porn Studies, 4*(2), 157–175.

Randolph, A. W. B. (2002). *Engaging symbols: Gender, politics, and public art in fifteenth-century florence.* New Haven, CT: Yale University Press.

Reed Hughes, K. Y., & Anderson, V. N. (2007). What turns women on? Black and White women's sexual arousal. *International Journal of Sexual Health, 19*(2), 17–31.

Rupp, H. A., & Wallen, K. (2009). Sex-specific content preferences for visual sexual stimuli. *Archives of Sexual Behaviour, 38*(3), 417–426.

Russ, J. (1985). *Magic mommas, trembling sisters, puritans and perverts: Feminist essays.* Trumansburg, NY: Crossing.

Ryan, M. (2014). 'Outlander', the Wedding episode, and TV's sexual revolution. *Huffington Post,* August 29, 2014. http://www.huffingtonpost.com/2014/09/29/outlander-wedding_n_5896284.html

Sanders-McDonagh, E. (2015). Porn by any other name: Women's consumption of public sex performances in Amsterdam. *Porn Studies, 2*(4), 329–341.

Sassatelli, R. (2011). Interview with Laura Mulvey: Gender, gaze and technology in film culture. *Theory, Culture & Society, 28*(5), 123–143.

Saunders, G. (1989). *The nude: A new perspective.* Cambridge, UK: Harper and Row.

Schroeder, K. M. (2000). *The female voyeur and the possibility of a pornography for women: Redefining the gaze of desire.* PhD dissertation, University of South Africa. Retrieved June 20, 2013, from http://uir.unisa.ac.za/bitstream/handle/10500/3079/Schroeder%20K%20M.pdf?sequence=1

Shaw, S. M. (1999). Men's leisure and women's lives: The impact of pornography on women. *Leisure Studies, 18*(3), 197–212.

Silverman, K. (1980). Masochism and subjectivity. *Framework, 12,* 2–9.

Silverman, K. (1992). *Male subjectivity at the margins.* New York: Routledge.

Simon, W., & Gagon, J. H. (2005). *Sexual conduct: The social sources of human sexuality* (2nd ed.). New Brunswick, NJ: Aldine/Transaction.

Smith, C. (2007). *One for the girls!: The pleasures and practices of reading women's porn.* Bristol: Intellect Books.

Sonnet, E. (1999). 'Erotic fiction by women for women': The pleasures of post-feminist heterosexuality. *Sexualities, 2*(2), 167–187.

Stacey, J. (1991). Feminine fascinations: Forms of identification in star-audience relations. In C. Gledhill (Ed.), *Stardom: Industry of desire* (pp. 141–163). New York: Routledge.

Stanley, M. (2010). 101 uses for boys: Communing with the reader in yaoi and slash. In A. Levi, M. McHarry, & D. Pagliassotti (Eds.), *Boys' love manga: Essays on the sexual ambiguity and cross-cultural fandom of the genre* (pp. 99–109). Jefferson, NC: McFarland & Company, Inc.

Stratton, J. (2000). *The desirable body: Cultural fetishism and the erotics of consumption.* Champaign: University of Illinois Press.

Swidler, A. (1986). Culture in action: Symbols and strategies. *American Sociological Review, 51*(3), 273–286.

Thurston, C. (1987). *The romance revolution: Erotic novels for women and the quest for a new sexual identity.* Chicago: University of Illinois Press.

Tibbals, C. (2015). *Exposure: A sociologist explores sex, society, and adult entertainment.* Austin, TX: Greenleaf Book Group Press.

Ward, K. [katiewardwriter]. (2016, Apr 13). The human gaze is an act of intimacy. It's why we love it in art. It's why we feel violated when photos are taken without our permission. [Tweet]. Retrieved from https://twitter.com/katiewardwriter/status/720169023351177216

Waskul, D. D., & Radeloff, C. L. (2010). How do I rate?': Web sites and gendered erotic looking glasses. In F. Attwood (Ed.), *Porn.com* (pp. 202–216). New York: Peter Lang.

Williams, L. (Ed.). (2004). *Porn studies.* London: Duke University Press.

Williams, Z. (2007, July 25). The market beyond porn. *The Guardian.* Retrieved from http://www.theguardian.com/commentisfree/2007/jul/25/comment.television

Worton, M. (2002). *Typical men: Recent photography of the male body by men.* Nottingham: Djanogly Art Gallery.

3

The Joy of Slash

One dimension of female interest in m/m eroticism which *has* been thoroughly explored is the area of explicit slash fiction. Slash fiction is a genre of fan fiction that focuses on interpersonal attraction and sexual relationships between fictional characters of the same sex, believed to have originated in the 1970s when female fans started to compose stories based around *Star Trek* where Kirk and Spock had a romantic—and sometimes sexual—relationship. The slash prefix, as in Roland Barthes' classic post-structuralist text *S/Z* (1970), signals what Sutherland (2006) describes as 'unconventional (i.e. homosexual) relationships, as opposed to the soothingly conventional (heterosexual) ampersand of, say, *Fun With Dick & Jane*'. This 'unconventionality' was a marked aspect of early slash fic: the first few Kirk/Spock [K/S] slash stories in zines[1] were controversial, leading to slash inhabiting a 'marginal and outlaw status for many years' within the Trekker community (Falzone, 2005, p. 244). In his fandom retrospective, Kitson (2009) observes that 'while fans had speculated that there was something in the Kirk/Spock relationship that dare not speak its name, committing the idea to print caused a veritable riot of abuse, and discussion impassioned enough to cause a rift in fan culture'. While many of the disputes addressed the credibility of any erotic tension between the two leads, other Trekkers were explicitly homophobic in their objections to K/S. However, as early as 1988, Henry Jenkins noted that K/S stories had emerged from the margins of fandom toward numerical dominance within *Star Trek* fan fiction. These days, as Cumberland (1999) observes, 'slash is no longer a curious subset of the fan fiction phenomenon, but has become one of the mainstream forms of internet erotica'.

While slash has been regarded with horror by some in the film and television industries (most notoriously, George Lucas[2]), such an attitude is far from ubiquitous, and, as Allington (2007) points out, it is hard to avoid the suspicion that some media industry creatives have begun to draw on slash for inspiration (e.g. Russell T. Davies and *Torchwood*). Producers now often give tacit approval even to sexually explicit fan-works, as they serve as promotional material for the original show—so while there is still an element of transgression in appropriating intellectual property in such a manner, slash fiction itself is often 'both visible and approved' (Booth, 2014, p. 403). This visibility is even more pronounced now that slash stories have largely shifted from being circulated in laboriously handcrafted zines to well-supported global websites. The internet's 'cultural cachet', as well as its properties of wide circulation, have contributed to the expansion of slash fic participation well 'beyond a show's die-hard fanatics' (Levin Russo, 2002, p. 27), and it attracts a broad and diverse readership on sites such as AO3, Livejournal, and Tumblr. Indeed, on dedicated fan fiction sites, such as AO3, slash is extremely common: in Lulu's (2013) analysis of AO3 census data, out of the 10,005 readers and creators of fanfic who responded, 8978 (89 per cent) were involved in m/m fandoms. For women who are interested in m/m SEM, slash sites are also a 'go to' source for consuming male/male eroticism: 84 per cent of my respondents are involved in slash fandom in some way, either as readers, writers, or artists.

Of all the genres of m/m SEM engaged with by the women I spoke to, slash fan fiction emerges as the one they are able to enjoy the most freely and unproblematically. In fact, themes of joy and pure, unadulterated pleasure are incredibly common when respondents speak about both reading and writing slash fic (as well as creating and looking at both fan art and vids). As one woman explains, 'there is this wonderful visceral gut-wrench I get—sort of like the reader's orgasm, I suppose—when I read a story that hits all my buttons at once' (American, 35–44, separated, heterosexual), with another adding 'I love it because it's fun and a turn on' (Canadian, 35–44, married, heterosexual). It's important not to lose sight of this. In both recent academic work and within fandom communities there has been resistance to attempts by scholars to overtheorise slash fandom. Women write and read slash because it's *fun*. They do it because they like it, and because it brings them pleasure. We would rarely ask: why do women go to the cinema? Or: why do women read novels? So what is so special about *this* kind of reading, *this* kind of writing, that it requires complex, often psychoanalytic, theories in order to understand it? In addition, it is highly unlikely that any one theoretical perspective can encompass the incredibly diverse and nuanced reasons women give for their enjoyment of slash fiction (above and beyond the fact that they just *do*). Lackner, Lucas, and Reid (2006, p. 194) have noted how deeply problematic it is to attempt to fit slash consumption and production into 'one theoretical box' instead of acknowledging that a number of explanations might be needed. It is to some of the key explanations provided by the women I spoke with that I will now turn.

'Dead Girlfriend of the Week': The Absence of Strong Female Characters in Mainstream Media

Many respondents discuss difficulties relating to women portrayed in the media, particularly sexually explicit media. From actresses in porn films to heroines in romance novels, the participants I spoke with often find it hard to identify with the women they see on screen or read about in books. This dissociation—which I will discuss further in Chap. 5—acts as a barrier to their enjoyment of many types of media, as well as their arousal in response to SEM featuring women. For women who read or write slash fic, their issues with female representation are even more fundamental—they point out that women are sometimes *quite literally absent* from many of the TV shows and films they consume, and therefore the fandoms they are part of. One participant describes 'an absolute canyon of absence in so much media for female characters that are awesome' (American, 35–44, separated, heterosexual). While there might be token female characters, and even token female (heterosexual) love interests provided for male protagonists, a lot of these texts are unlikely to pass the Bechdel test. As one woman explains 'there are few female characters that are interesting, and even less that actually interact with each other' (French, 35–44, married, lesbian). Strong female characters are a particular rarity in genres not regarded as being traditionally 'female-orientated' (such as action, adventure, sci fi etc.). As one woman complains, 'there are quite simply way more male characters out there than female characters (yay sexism!), so many of the characters I care most about are male. Additionally even where there *are* kickass female characters they are often isolated, (yay tokenization!)' (American, 25–34, single, queer). Male–male duos, however, are a ubiquitous feature of many genres of film and television—the buddy-cop show, the war movie, the fantasy adventure series (Fiske, 1987; Haskell, 1974). It is hard to watch these types of media without coming across two men doing some pretty intensive 'male bonding'. One woman expands, 'I think the problem I have is that most female characters are very flat, there to serve the purpose of being the love interest or the sex object. They don't have the depth I'm looking for, and so it's much easier to turn to the male characters to fill that gap' (American, 25–34, in a relationship, bisexual).

It is perhaps unsurprising, then, that it was hard to write compelling fan fiction m/f romances in the 1970s because of the lack of well-rounded, interesting female characters in most 1970s fandoms. Female characters required so much additional fleshing out that any writing would have had to stray substantially from canon. Against this backdrop, it was easier for potential fan writers to concentrate on the more developed male characters, and the emotional and sexual relationships between them. Why would you want to write about a female character who appeared in a handful of episodes at most, when you had whole series' worth of material exploring the relationships between Kirk and Spock, Bodie and Doyle, Starsky and Hutch, Blake and Avon? One participant notes that she is 'irritated by the industry's tendency to create a romance between two lead characters, decide that both characters must be male, give one of them a one-dimensional female love interest as a cheap 'no homo' device, and call it a friendship. I like when fanfic ignores the beard and puts the romantic element back in the main relationship' (American, 18–24, single, pansexual). As she observes, while some of the male characters I mention here *were* given female love interests at various points in their story arcs, such women were often quickly killed off or otherwise written out of the show. This 'dead girlfriend of the week' scenario did little to provide fans with emotional satisfaction—even more so in cases where the girlfriend in question didn't even die, but was simply discarded between episodes with no explanation. Fans want to see their central characters experience romantic relationships, and such brief and shallow entanglements undermine the idea of romance itself, especially when viewed alongside the depth of the relationships created between the male protagonists. One woman explains,

> let's face it, TV shows take great pains to show us how close the men are as partners, and it's been that way since Kirk and Spock, through Starsky and Hutch, right up to Steve and Danny. When fandom puts the men together as romantic partners, we're just expanding the envelope a very tiny bit. Conversely, the TV shows barely give a nod to possible heterosexual connections. Even when the guy has a girlfriend, it's given about three minutes every fourth episode—if that much! So it's pretty hard to develop a fanfic storyline around an almost non-existent connection (American, 55–64, single, heterosexual).

In addition, a substantial majority of readers of explicit m/m slash read it because they like reading about graphic sex between characters *they already care about*. As I will discuss in the next few chapters, slash fiction is not 'just' porn for most readers, it is porn built on a sturdy bedrock of character and relationship development. As one respondent says 'even in slash that's PWP [porn without plot] there's a shortcut inherent in it—I already know the characters and their relationship to each other, and I already care… I don't think [it would work so well] with "strangers"' (American, 44–55, single, bisexual). These fans are simply not interested in reading about sex between a beloved character and some random woman. They want the emotions, the psychology, the rich insight into a character's inner life, to go with the sex. They want the whole package.

However, while the absence of strong female characters in source texts might hold considerable weight when looking at early 70s and 80s slash fandoms, it is perhaps less relevant an explanation in today's media landscape. Many films and TV series *do* now feature female protagonists every bit as well-developed and nuanced as their male counterparts, characters who are provided with plenty of romantic and emotional plotlines in the source material (Saxey, 2002). Yet the popularity of slash persists, suggesting an ongoing desire for non-traditional, non-heterosexual connections that goes beyond simply not having canon characters to work with. For this reason Scodari (2003, p. 125) claims that while slash writing might have been 'rebellious' in light of texts that did not provide well-crafted female protagonists, viewed alongside shows which feature strong female leads, this point of view becomes more problematic. As Jenkins (1992, p. 190) warns, slash 'runs the risk of celebrating gay male experience (and more traditional forms of male bonding) at the expense of developing [or exploring] … feminine identities'.

While this critique is certainly valid in theory, I would question how grounded it is in real life practices. Three quarters (75 per cent) of my sample also read m/f erotica, including m/f fan fiction, and 60 per cent also read f/f erotica, including femslash. Of the writers I surveyed, 60 per cent write m/f or f/f erotic fiction (with 57 per cent writing from a female character's POV). The majority of participants emphasise that they are happy to both consume and create sexually explicit stories featuring female characters, as long as said characters are strong and well-developed. As one participant expands,

as a woman who bristles at being thought of … [merely] as anyone's wife, who has borne arms in the military, who remains an aggressive tomboy, I find expressions of desire and descriptions of romantic relationships unsatisfying and shallow without … [well-developed female characters]. There are, however, many m/f stories which satisfy this requirement for me. For example, [stories featuring] Hermione Granger almost always do; she is very 'masculine' in her way and a well-written story about her and a man requires acknowledgement of this (American, 25–34, married, bisexual).

This is in-keeping with previous academic work in the area. Meg-John Barker (2002) notes there are more f/f stories in *Buffy*verse than other contemporaneous shows, and postulates that this may well be because there actually *are* lots of strong, likeable female leads in *Buffy The Vampire Slayer*, meaning that fan writers don't need to create or flesh-out poorly developed female characters. As one participant explains, 'Buffy is never expressed as a variation on femininity—she's just a person—so the themes tend to revolve around her interactions and connections with others, as opposed to 'female compulsions to X' (barf)' (Canadian, 18–24, married heterosexual). It is interesting that many of the women I spoke to mention *Buffy* as an example of best practice, even though the show last aired almost 15 years ago:

> Let's break this down: if you look at *Buffy* fandom, whose main characters—credit to Joss Whedon—are actually 50-50 female-male or even 60-40, the most popular pairings are probably actually: Buffy/Angel, Buffy/Spike, Buffy/Faith, Angel/Spike, etc. Everything is basically represented in there! I have never once, for instance, needed to read any *Sex And The City* [slash] fiction because the world is (1) full of strong women getting it on with the men, and (2) sex is on the surface in that world and explored. On the other hand, there is a lot of slash in *West Wing* or in *Supernatural* because there are far fewer compelling women to put in the picture. (American, 25–34, married, heterosexual)

Rose Tyler and the Doctor from *Doctor Who* are another common example of heterosexual pairings enjoyed by participants because the female character involved is interesting, nuanced, and not *de facto* the weaker partner in the couple: 'I wrote an explosion of het between Rose Tyler and the Doctor. I found their power dynamic incredibly interesting—she's a 19 year old shop girl, he's a 900 year old alien with a time machine—but she's also compassionate and wise, and he's wounded, lost, and angry. It's ideal for turning every kind of gendered trope on its ear— he can be the virgin and she can be all worldly—you can play with the pairing on so many levels' (American, 35–44, married, heterosexual).

Likewise, Somogyi (2002, p. 399) points to the popularity of Janeway/ Chakotay fic, concluding that this m/f pairing is 'probably the most popular, in terms of story production, of all the *Star Trek* couples'. While this is a fairly grand conclusion to draw, the existence of such a prolific m/f ship does suggest that—if provided with strong female leads who occupy a position of power and authority such as Janeway—female fans of a show are happy to produce and consume heterosexual erotic fiction.

The enduring popularity of slash, even in an age of more fully-actualised female protagonists, may also be down to the fact that, once they put characters in a heterosexual relationship, producers often seem to run out of ideas for what to do with them. Gwenllian Jones (2002) feels that the popularity of slash might lie in the fact that it offers a less mundane alternative to canon m/f pairings. She notes that *The New Adventures of Superman* went downhill after Lois and Clark got together, as the will they/ won't they excitement of the earlier plot was overtaken by boring, prosaic activities like buying a house, or arguing over who was the best cook. Cult television shows (fertile breeding grounds for slash) rely on a certain distance from everyday reality, as they instead create a fantastic alternative universe. To this extent, always potentiated but never fully realised homoeroticism can 'function as an alternative, less damaging, possibility of the cult fiction's exotic substance' (Gwenllian Jones, 2002, p. 89). Instead of settling down to the humdrum activities that characterise modern live-in relationships, cult shows can create storylines that 'invite and tolerate diverse speculation about characters' "hidden" thoughts or feelings' (Gwenllian Jones, 2002, p. 89).

'Everyone Loves a Good Bromance': Privileged Male Friendship and Homosocial Desire

I have a confession to make: I spent a good part of July 2017, when I should have been finishing this book, watching *Love Island*, a reality show that focuses on heterosexual romance: a number of young men and women are put in a villa and encouraged to 'hook up' with each other—the couple that the audience judges to be the most 'real', the most authentic in their romantic feelings for each other, has the opportunity to win £50,000. What particularly interested me was the couple that generated the most interest, both in the Twittersphere and the mainstream media, weren't even officially a 'couple' at all, but two of the male contestants,

Chris and Kem. Writing in *The Telegraph*, Richard Jones (2017) described them as 'the true star couple of *Love Island*', calling their friendship 'beautiful' and lamenting that Chris could not be the one 'holding Kem's hand' when the latter scooped the prize money. While a lot of the m/f relationships on the show were dismissed as either fake or destined to be short-lived, enthusiasm for the Chris/Kem pairing was almost universal. Numerous viewers entreated the show to allow them to 'couple up', and were delighted when their 'bromance' continued after the show ended (the pair regularly use social media to declare how much they miss each other, and how excited they are to see each other again; they have also been granted their own spin-off show). The answer as to why this 'couple' was so popular with the (largely female) audience of the show can also throw light on why some women are drawn to slash fiction. For while the vernacular may be new, the concept of the 'bromance' is well established in Western culture, as is society's privileging of it.

In comparison to heterosexual romance, which did not emerge until the Age of Chivalry, the homosocial partnership (a 'bromance' by another name) has been a staple of Western romance tradition for at least 2000 years. It is no surprise, then, that the homosocial adventure tale remains so pervasive in Western literature, and therefore in the public imaginary (Fiedler, 1960). The concept of two men forsaking all others in the name of whatever goal they mutually seek is central to our literary consciousness. Often this connection is portrayed as so strong, and so intense, that these two men would give their lives for each other. A romantic, heterosexual entanglement could never hope to compete with such a bond. As one participant comments, 'sexist or wrongheaded or a product of patriarchy though it might be, I totally get off on idealized male friendship. It is extremely unusual for any depiction of women to have that same vibe because our culture just doesn't see female friendship the same way. Even when it is valued, it's treated more realistically and less as some over-the-top Greek myth about swearing eternal brotherhood' (American, 25–34, single, bisexual). Writing in *On Friendship* (1580/2005, p. 138), the renaissance philosopher Michel de Montaigne outlined such an 'ideal' relationship between two men, explicitly linking the homosocial with the overtly homosexual: 'If such a relationship, free and voluntary, could be built up, in which not only would the souls have complete enjoyment, but the bodies would also share in the alliance, so that the entire man would be engaged, it is certain that the resulting friendship would be fuller and more complete'. Some of the women I spoke to agree, with one commenting 'two men can just relate to each other on so many levels of love: romantic, erotic, platonic' (American, 18–24, single, heterosexual). As Joanna Russ (1985, p. 84) has argued in her essay on slash, 'if you ask, "why two males?" I think the answer is that of eighteenth-century grammarians to questions about the masculine-preferred pronoun: "because it is more noble"… No one … can imagine a man and a woman having the same multiplex, worthy, androgynous relationship, or the same completely intimate commitment'. One woman expands, 'there is a particular *strongness*—sorry if that's not the correct word, I'm French—in the love between two men. Not that heterosexual love isn't strong, it's just not the same. It's hard to explain…. It's just *stronger*' (French, 25–34, in a relationship, asexual). Others talked about the 'ferocity' of the love between two men, and the 'more primal' nature of the passion between them.

Eve Kosofsky Sedgwick has written extensively on the relationship between homosociality and homosexuality, which she sees as existing on a continuum. She comments on the physical intimacy and play we see between men in sport, in fraternities, at the climactic moments of war novels, noting that 'with only a slight shift of the optic' these moments can appear 'quite startlingly "homosexual" … for a man to be a man's man is separated only by an invisible, carefully blurred, always-already-crossed line from being "interested in men"' (Sedgwick, 1985, p. 89). Physical and emotional intimacy between men, while not actively discouraged in 'appropriate' arenas such as sport, must generally be interpreted as entirely platonic in order to be socially acceptable. To return to my earlier example, *Love Island's* Chris and Kem regularly told each other they loved each other, they frequently touched and kissed each other, shared a bed, painted each other's nails, exchanged 'eternity' bracelets, and at once point even shaved each other's initials into their pubic hair—intensely physically and emotionally intimate behaviours. However, the assurance of their sexual relationships with two of the women in the show, Liv and Amber, meant their heterosexuality was never in doubt. Chris and Kem are seen as straight, and therefore intimacies between them are also interpreted as 'straight', despite their manifestly queer nature. Chris and Kem's televised bromance is not unique; much popular media depicts relationships between men that could be interpreted as sexual but for the presumption of heterosexuality (Rosenberg, 2007).

All that slash fans do, then, is observe the homosociality they see all around them, and choose to frame it as homosexual. Unlike others, they do not *presume* heterosexuality. They take intimacy between men at face value. Within BL manga fandom this practice has a name: yaoi *me* (literally, the 'yaoi-eye') or yaoi *megane* ('yaoi glasses'). The 'yaoi glasses' that the BL or slash fan uses to read straight or homosocial content as homosexual is 'comparable to other ironic and destabilising reading practices of sexual and gender minorities, as exemplified in practices of drag culture, camp, or "perverse reading"' (Meyer, 2010, p. 232). This way of looking can mean that the avid fan can start to see homosexual dynamics everywhere: between actors, rock stars, sportsmen and even politicians (the Trudeau/Obama 'bromance' led to the emergence of people shipping 'Trubama' on the internet). This does not mean that fans genuinely believe everyone is gay—for the large part, they are aware what they are doing is projection. However, as Meyer (2010, p. 234) argues, what this does do is consciously draw boys and men into the orbit of the fan's desire, 'turning them into objects of voyeuristic pleasure. The female voyeur subversively submits the male objects of her gaze to a "forced homosexualisation"'. Perhaps female voyeurs are not as powerless as we have been led to believe.

Similarly, Henry Jenkins has shown that Sedgwick's work on the homosocial/homosexual continuum can easily be adopted to understand slash, and what draws women to it. Jenkins (1992) argues that the technique of slashing is about bridging the disruption in the spectrum between homosocial and homosexual, and discusses the subtle (and not-so-subtle) hints in canon that suggest romantic potential exists between male characters:

> When I try to explain slash to non-fans, I often reference the moment in *Star Trek: The Wrath of Khan* where Spock is dying and Kirk stands there, a wall of glass separating the two long-time buddies. Both of them are reaching out towards each other, their hands pressed hard against the glass, trying

to establish physical contact... Slash is what happens when you take away the glass... The glass represents those aspects of traditional masculinity which prevent emotional expressiveness or physical intimacy. (Jenkins, 2006, p. 72)

Jenkins is not alone in his belief that it is this emphasis on 'traditional masculinity' that prevents some homosocial texts from becoming openly homosexual. Sean Astin, who played Sam in *The Lord of The Rings* trilogy, noted the sniggering of young men in movie theatres during the emotionally charged scenes between Frodo and Sam in *The Return of The King* (in Smol, 2004, p. 969). They simply could not handle the idea that there might be a deeper, more intimate connection between the two characters than a 'conventional' masculine friendship would permit. Turning to the source material, Smol (2004) speculates that it may well have been Tolkien's belief in the inherent sinfulness of sexuality that prevented the homosocial relationships he portrays between his male characters as being expressed sexually. Woledge (2005a, p. 55) observes that while slash can import the characters' 'masculine' traits from its media source, original mainstream fiction must set up situations to showcase the heroes' masculinity in order to achieve the same juxtaposition, hypothesising that this might be why 'so many mainstream texts exploring intimacy between men choose to use battle themes as a backdrop to their often tender depictions of intimacy'. The fact that slash allows men to express emotions not normally seen in mainstream media is an aspect which fans are particularly drawn to, with one explaining, 'hot guys getting it on with each other and being angsty, having FEELINGS. What's not to like? Hot men with feelings is not a phenomenon I've come across much in my real life' (British, 25–34, single, heterosexual). There is, however, a perception that source texts are beginning to allow male characters to express more emotionality, and that this is also compelling to female viewers.

I think that's one of the reasons why I love Dean Winchester—yes, it's become something of a joke, his OPT (one perfect tear), but it's not often on American TV [or] fiction where you have the quintessential macho male sharing enough of himself to allow his guard to fall and emote. It seems in recent years, we've begun to see men cry more and more in our media, which is great for the generations of boys who will be born and hopefully won't be lashed under the 'real men don't cry' rule. (American, 25–34, in a polyamorous relationship, bisexual)

Salmon and Symons (2001, p. 84) have argued that it is this focus on homosociality—the 'nobility' of the enduring passion that can exist between two men—that means that slash is actually 'less porno' than other forms of erotic fiction, despite its often graphic depictions of sex. In many heterosexual romances and erotic novels, sexual attraction is depicted as the driving force pushing the protagonists together, and sex is often used as a way of establishing a deeper and more concrete bond between the hero and the heroine. In this way, sex leads to love. In slash however, the bond of friendship (or, in some cases, rivalry—more on that later) is firmly in place long before the protagonists get down to it: here love, or (sometimes grudging) respect, leads to sex. The happy-ever-after [HEA] ending we frequently find in slash fic may therefore be regarded as more credible, based as it is not on the heroine's good looks or the hero's physicality and power—things that may fade over time—but a deep, abiding, and tested friendship: 'slash protagonists put their hands in the fire for each other long before romantic love or sex were on the horizon' (Salmon & Symons, 2001, p. 93). This is at the core of the bromance—slash heroes don't just have adventures together *or* fall in love—they do *both*. The historian Francesca Cancian (1990) identifies a relatively new development in romantic culture, the idea that romance makes you a better person, and can make a meaningful contribution to your self-development. Previously, self-development was a masculine narrative, whereas romantic love was a feminine one—men could develop themselves on their own, while women were defined by their attachment to others. Slash fic in many ways fuses these two ideas—male characters often experience self-development over a story arc, via their romantic attachment to other *male* characters as well as via the situations in which they find themselves. It is perhaps not surprising that women are so drawn to this type of egalitarian relationship model.

However, it should be noted that not all slash is 'buddyslash', in the style of the original Kirk/Spock stories. For example, Harry/Draco slash is extremely popular, even though Harry and Draco are arch-enemies throughout much of the *Harry Potter* series. Tosenberger (2008) believes that the joy of an enemyslash pairing is watching the antagonists over-come their differences, at least long enough to have sex. Dislike is recast as sexual tension, and the sex, when it happens, can be explosive. Of course, this is hardly a new convention, and one that has been well-established within traditional romantic fiction; the heterosexual couple's journey from enemies to lovers is a popular romantic trope (James, 2017; Roach, 2010)—*Pride and Prejudice* being an obvious example. Writing about popular musicals, Wolf (2008) highlights that while the principals may begin as rivals (Sarah Brown and Sky Masterson in *Guys and Dolls*), or as enemies (Eliza Doolittle and Henry Higgins in *My Fair Lady*), or as annoyances to each other (Maria and the Captain in *The Sound of Music*), or, at best, in mutual misunderstanding (Nellie and Emile in *South Pacific*), their differences of background or temperament signal they will eventually form a couple—and their progress towards coupledom is all the more engaging because of the obstacles they must each overcome to get there. Akinsha (2009) argues that an important premise for slash is simply an intense m/m relationship, be it a friendship or a rivalry. Because both protagonists are men, the relationship, whether antagonistic or lov-ing, is one between equals—neither is expected to submit to the other or fundamentally change any aspect of their personality or lifestyle for the sake of the other—at least not without negotiation. As one woman explains, 'there are many occasions [in m/f stories] where the woman begins as independent and strong, and the male lead is contemptuous of it. When they eventually get together, she drops everything to be sup-ported by him and have his babies, [which is] infuriating' (British, 45–54, married, heterosexual). Another expands:

> Whereas most fanfic authors fall into the trope of turning female hetero-sexual characters into weak-willed, dependent, fluttering, insecure damsels-in-distress to get their pairing off the ground, it's pretty rare to see a slash author do the same. The two male characters generally remain relatively in-character and do not need to turn suddenly submissive for the relation-ship to germinate. In fact, I think I more often see the opposite—that emotions are revealed and the relationship established in the midst of a conflict between the characters. (American, 25–34, single, demisexual)

Some participants actually express a strong preference for enemyslash fiction. As Tosenberger (2008, p. 190) points out, when the characters are both men, 'part of the pleasure is seeing their negotiation of expectations of male aggression (rather than friendship) in terms of desire'. This is something we are rarely given in the mainstream texts that act as the source material for much slash fic. Greven (2009) argues that while mainstream cinema and television shows explicitly represent homosexuality, what we see far less often is actual *sex* between members of the same gender. As one woman observes, 'you just can't find this shit in real life. It's barely there in the media, but there is so much canonical—or perhaps head-canonical—sexual tension between male characters on television and in movies, and I just ask myself, "Why can't we make them kiss? They do it on *Torchwood*! Where is my gay sex?!"' (American, 18–24, single, bisexual). Greven believes that this inability to represent something 'is a kind of pressure-cooker, one that eventually explodes like a stew left too long under a lid' (Greven, 2009, p. 162). The repression of sex between men—or, at least, the possibility that it might exist—must find some avenue in representation. Greven (2009, pp. 162, 207) maintains that in Hollywood terms, 'repressed same-gender sex finds vent in onscreen violence between men, violence that is usually stylised and ritualised. In terms of homoeroticism, Hollywood representation inscribes the economy of violence over the economy of sexuality … as if the only way to register male-male desire for physical contact is through the impact of fists on flesh'. We can see a good example of this in *Star Trek* which flipped the buddyslash model of writing that accompanied the original series [TOS] to an enemyslash model of writing following 2009's reboot film, which cast Kirk and Spock as antagonists as opposed to allies. Greven (2009, p. 207) feels the *Trek* reboot is 'very much aware of its homoerotic potential … even if it mounts a considerable campaign against it'. He describes Zachary Quinto's Spock, 'with his gamine eyes and earnest-boy haircut' as 'an idealised exotic male figure' and Chris Pine's Kirk as 'a parodistic fantasy of an all-American jock', concluding that the 'ironic distance and violence' between the two characters 'camouflage[s] the homoerotic secret of the film, one that threatens to explode' (Greven, 2009, p. 208). It is easy to see how this kind of unrealised erotic tension might be just as intriguing to slash fans as the unrealised romantic tension between two firm friends.

It is also important here to note that we should not take the abundance of buddyslash fiction to mean that women are *only* interested in earnest, romantic connections between male leads that result in loving, gentle sex. There also exists a substantial body of enemyslash works that have been termed 'dark fics', which tend to include graphic depictions of sex and violence, and often deviate—or at least are seen to deviate—from the source text. As well as focusing on protagonists who don't like each other, dark fics may include rape, torture, orgies, BDSM, and slave situations (Hansen, 2010). Reid (2009, p. 467, emphasis added) maintains that such stories are controversial because they defy conventions of what 'readers, *especially women readers*, are believed to wish for in texts, or to take pleasure from'. Reid believes that this primarily rests upon the simplistic notion that if a woman writes or reads about X it means she wishes to do X or have X done to her. So while romantic and domestic fiction is fine—love, happiness and security are, after all, 'what women want'— dark fics are considerably more problematic. Keft-Kennedy (2008, p. 54) critiques the focus of scholars on romantic forms of slash typified by monogamy, happy endings and vanilla sexual relations, saying that such a focus 'sidestep[s] the existence of vast amounts of slash fiction which deals with the issues of aggressive sexuality, as well as the pleasures associated with it'. Like Reid, she believes that 'the constructions of these violent, yet often strangely tender, representations of masculine characters by female authors ... suggest[s] a threat to traditional conceptions of female desire' (Keft-Kennedy, 2008, p. 73).

Lady Poachers in the Lord's Manor

Memorably advanced by Henry Jenkins in his seminal *Textual Poachers* (1992), slash fans have also been framed as covertly political, surreptitiously reclaiming texts for their own enjoyment in much the same way as a poacher would help himself to the bounty of the Lord's manor under cover of darkness. Jenkins' framework draws on Michel de Certeau's 'poaching' metaphor, which conceptualises reading not as passive absorption of authorial meaning passed down from positions of dominance, but as an 'ongoing struggle for possession of the text and for control over its meanings' (Jenkins, 1992, p. 24). De Certeau (1984, p. 174) speaks of the reader as a poacher, travelling across the land of the Lord, and 'despoiling the wealth of Egypt' for her own pleasure. Central to this understanding is that fans are poachers, not guerrillas—they are not trying to change or overthrow the system, they are just trying to game it. According to Jenkins (1992, p. 26), 'fans operate from a position of cultural marginality and social weakness… [They] lack direct access to the means of commercial cultural production and have only the most limited resources with which to influence the entertainment industry's decisions'. More recent work has challenged some of Jenkins' assertions—after all, as discussed in the introduction, slash fans have growing commercial clout, and, in addition, they often create exciting and novel stories that deviate substantially from the source text(s).[3] As Falzone (2005, p. 252) asks, 'at what point does the poacher/producer cease to travel the lands of the master (narrative), and strike out into previously unexplored and/or unknown lands?'

For Jenkins, slash fiction is much less about sex than it is about creating a rich emotional inner-life for well known characters. He maintains that because women are forced to read male-centred texts, they eventually learn to appropriate them into feminine paradigms of emotional realism—they fixate on the internal and emotional lives of their favourite male characters, and look for ways to expand upon their understanding. He discusses 'the school girl required to read a boy's book, the teenager dragged to see her date's favourite slasher film, the housewife forced to watch her husband's cop show rather than her soap', and views slash fic as a way to 'remake those narratives, at least imaginatively' (Jenkins, 1992, p. 14). In some sense Jenkins' notion of poaching has much in common with Sarah Kent's (1985) concept of women as voyeurs (or, poachers, if you will) that I discussed in the previous chapter—much as we've always had to gaze at erotic male bodies designed for other men to look at and find a way to make them our own, we have also had to take narratives directed at a male audience and find a way to recraft them to fit our own desires. However, the way that Jenkins describes slashers—the lack of agency, the passive voice—does not fit well with how many of these women perceive themselves. Reid (2009) also notes that it is strange that

Jenkins focuses on horror and cop shows, and 'boy's book[s]'—presumably adventure, fantasy, and sci-fi—considering that women have often enthusiastically and actively engaged with these genres, and continue to write slash fic (and original fiction) from within them. They were not 'dragged' into reading or watching these books or shows, but 'were active and willing participants in the consumption and production of [for example] science fiction from the start' (Reid, 2009, p. 472). As one of my participants wryly observes, 'let's not forget that the genre exists because a teenaged girl was stuck at a house party and decided that inventing science fiction sounded more appealing than yet another tiresome threesome with Lord Byron' (British, 35–44, married, heterosexual).

The poaching metaphor also requires us to take a deeper look at the source texts themselves. After all, in order for there to be a poacher, there has to be something worth poaching: you don't sneak out at midnight with your shotgun if there's nothing in the Lord's estate you want to get your hands on. Fans aren't making up the fact that the two characters they're slashing are doing suggestive things on screen. As Saxey (2002, p. 191) points out, slashers 'do not randomly impose psychologically implausible sex on characters'. One woman explains, 'If I don't feel that two male characters are "gay" or would be good in a relationship, I won't read slash erotica about them no matter how well-written it is' (British, 45–54, single, heterosexual). Another adds, 'I distinguish between things that are me reading a text [or] media "with slash goggles on" as it were, and things that I think are kind of essentially what's *really* going underneath the surface of the whole thing. Kirk/Spock is the latter for me' (American, 25–34, married, heterosexual).

The extent to which fans are projecting sexual desire between the male characters of a source text has been an area of some debate within the academy. Looking at Kirk/Spock as an example, Sara Gwellian Jones (2002, p. 82) feels slash may be 'an actualisation of latent textual elements', and Lynne Segal (1994, p. 236, emphasis added) similarly focuses on slashers' powers of interpretation when she writes of 'the sexual and romantic bonds they *construct* between Captain Kirk and Mr Spock'. Woledge (2005b) agrees; she believes that there clearly *is* something there, but since these elements are not an overt part of the show they must be explained as 'subtextual' and 'latent'. Miller (1991, p. 131) has suggested that 'the most salient index to male homosexuality, socially speaking, consists precisely in how a man looks at other men'. Woledge (2005b) notes that eye contact between characters in *TOS* is usually brief, but that this is not the case with Kirk and Spock. She provides numerous examples of long, lingering gazes between the pair, and notes how the direction mimics the stylised presentation of heterosexual attraction in mainstream cinema: focusing on a series of looks cutting from the hero looking at something off-screen, to the heroine (the object of his gaze) looking down and away or glancing briefly in his direction, before cutting back to the hero. Richard Dyer (1995, p. 119) summarises this as 'men stare at women, women submit to being looked at, or at the most steal a glance'. In *Star Trek*, as Stanis and Butler (1995, p. 8, emphasis added) note, 'it's unbelievable the way they *look* at each other. Especially how the Captain looks at Spock, and how Spock just stands there being looked at'.

Allington (2007, p. 48), however, argues that this analysis is far too simple—by applying an encoding/decoding model to K/S Woledge is simply 'translating fan terms into academic ones'. He asks us to consider how this understanding represents the text: homoerotic possibilities are to be recognised in *it*; and how it represents slashers: as *beginning* with what is in the text. Thus, Allington argues, Woledge's reconstruction of the K/S decoding process legitimates slash, presenting *Star Trek*, and not slashers, as the source of the idea that Kirk and Spock have sexual feelings for each other. Within this model, endorsement from the creators of the source material would be the strongest legitimisation that slash consumption could receive: 'the notion that the director of a film or series *planned* for it to be consumed as an erotic representation of homosexual love would thus acquire tremendous appeal: under the ideology of the auteur, it amounts to the implication that the non-slashing majority have actually misread the text' (Allington, 2007, p. 49).

Within this analysis, instead of simply expanding on elements present in the text, slashing becomes a form of queer reading. The practice of queer reading is about repositioning texts outside the boundaries of heteronormativity (Hayward, 2000). Doty (2000) argues that queer reading should not be interpreted as *making* texts queer, but rather as trying to understand how texts might be *understood* as queer. Robert Lang's (2002) queer reading of Hollywood films found homosexual subtexts in classic films such as *The Outlaw* (1943) and *Midnight Cowboy* (1969). Dhaenens, Vam Bauwel, and Biltereyst (2008, p. 343) argue that authors of slash fiction approach the textual material in a similar way to how queer readers approach classic Hollywood cinema, 'they deconstruct traditional narratives and reveal the queer from reading between the story lines'. However, this doesn't mean that queer elements aren't also overtly apparent in source texts. Doty (1993, pp. 2–3) allows for what he calls 'queer moments'—times when straight-identifying people realise that 'heterosexist texts can contain queer elements', and argues they should 'be encouraged to examine and express these moments *as* queer'—for example, when Harry Potter describes Sirius Black as 'very good-looking' (Rowling, 2003, p. 642). Matias Viegener (1993, p. 250) has described such moments as a 'nudge and wink' to a queer sensibility.

However, the debate becomes more complex still. Active forms of reading Hollywood films are performed not only by queer audiences, but also by queer people who work in the film industry, so that many subtexts don't have to be *read into* the text—they are already there and need only to be discovered by those who are attuned to them. 'You got very good at projecting subtext without saying a word about what you were doing,' says screen writer Gore Vidal about his work on *Ben Hur* (1959), which contains a consciously gay subtext in the relationship between Ben Hur and Massala (in Meyer, 2010, p. 235). One participant discusses this in relation to slash:

> Sometimes the male characters in question, on some kind of meta-level, actually are doing it, but the writers/creators of the thing can't or won't admit it and/or fictional characters have a life of their own beyond the work anyway, and maybe that's just somehow the way the thing is going, with or without the consent of anyone. For example, in *Star Trek: Deep Space Nine*, the actor who plays Garak, Andrew Robinson, has said unequivocally quite a few times over the years that he was playing Garak as sexually/romantically interested in his years-long friend and sparring partner, Julian Bashir. So Garak/Bashir, in that sense, is not actually looking for anything more than what's already there. Yes, secondarily, it may be hot [to me] ... but perhaps first and foremost it's there at some level in the production itself... I, of course, also believe Kirk/Spock falls along these lines:

Rodenberry famously said that there was 'enough love there' that if, in the future, the 'Greek ideal of love between two men' … was something practiced, there would be enough love there for that. Well, if we're imagining that hopefully the Twenty-third century is a place where two men can get together without anyone blinking an eye—and I believe it's easy to imagine 240 years from now looking like that!—then we're told there's enough love there for Kirk and Spock, and they'd be together. (American, 25–34, married, heterosexual)

It is for this reason that Tosenberger (2008, p. 187) rejects the notion that slash is inherently transgressive of the canon, noting that an insistence on this 'rather troublingly assigns to the canon a heteronormativity it may not necessarily possess'. However, there *is* a general acceptance that slash is, by its nature, playing on the difference between the overt and the covert in texts. When a show such as *Looking* depicts the lives of homosexual men, it is gay; when a show such as *Sherlock* includes ostensible erotic undertones between its two male leads, it is slashy.

Other scholars have suggested that, far from craving endorsement from the show's creators that the characters they ship *are* in fact queer, many slashers enjoy the unrealised sexual chemistry between male characters—after all, isn't *sneaking* into the grounds of the manor part of the thrill of poaching? Staiger (2005, p. 156, citing Ross, 2002) argues that 'some minorities enjoy maintaining subtexts as just that: subtexts'. In his analysis of fan discussions of *Lord Of The Rings* slash Allington (2007, p. 58) suggests there is what he describes as an 'erotics of the barely perceptible', putting forward that 'it is the uncertainty of the ground on which the slash interpretation rests that gives that ground its fascination'. There is a clear division here between slashers who view the unrealised or latent sexual tension between male characters as a form of queerbaiting,[4] and those who enjoy the furtive nature of the characters' (possible) desire—something I will return to in Chaps. 7 and 8.

Whilst unarguably important, Jenkins' concept of slash readers and writers as textual poachers also glosses over one of the primary reasons women give for enjoying explicit slash fiction (as opposed to, say, gen or crack[5] fic)—that they find it sexually arousing and it gives them what one participant describes as 'that pleasant tingly feeling' (American, 25–34, in a polyamorous relationship, bisexual). As one woman comments, 'well, I'd be a liar if I didn't say that the sex was first and foremost for me. I don't read stories that are below NC-17. I'm shallow, I'm in it for the porn. At the same time, I do enjoy a story where it's *more* than just the porn. The best ones are where it's a good solid plot, interesting characters, inventive storylines *and* porn. I tend to think of it like a great movie that doesn't 'fade to black' on the sex scenes and gives them as much attention as the rest of the movie' (American, 35–44, married, bisexual).

Another adds 'I would be remiss in neglecting the utterly sensual aspects of reading slash. As a sexual being, I enjoy these fictions as fuel for my fantasies, and revel in the feelings of arousal they induce' (French, 18–24, in a relationship, bisexual). Eighty three percent of the women involved in slash fandom in my survey use fic as a masturbatory aid. In addition, 64 per cent of slash writers need to feel sexual attraction to at least one of the characters in the pairing that they write, and 42 per cent need to feel sexual attraction to at least one of the actors playing the characters they write in the source text. This is not unsurprising; as Somogyi (2002, p. 403) notes, it is probably very difficult to write erotic material without feeling any sexual interest in it oneself, and it is logical that fans would construct romantic, erotic, and pornographic stories out of bodies that they find attractive. As one fan explains, 'it's quite difficult to think in detail about people in sexual situations if you just don't find them attractive. I think a lot of people think of fanfiction as a way of women who fancy the actors trying to get a kick, but I personally think it's more the fact that you want to write about somebody who you would enjoy thinking about, rather than somebody who makes you think 'Oh yuck!'" (British, 18–24, casually dating, heterosexual).

Another jokes, 'well, you gotta wanna see the genitals in order to write about them; amirite?' (American, 18–24, married, bisexual).

However, attraction may not always involve conventional, physical beauty. Instead, it can be the dynamic between the two characters which then creates appeal for a pairing.

I don't have to feel like: 'Wow, I wanna jump that guy now', or [have a] would-be-speechless [if I met them] level crush like I have on, say, Tom Hardy. Mmmmm, Tom Hardy. But I do have to see how they might be attractive. Or, more importantly, I have to be able to put myself into the mind-set of character A being attracted to character B. My desire isn't the paramount thing—though I don't tend to want to write about a character I'm repulsed by. The paramount thing when I'm considering whether to write about a character, is the strength of desire, the quality of desire, the uniqueness of desire of the POV character for their object of desire… [It] does help if one of the characters is played by Tom Hardy, though [laughs]. (American, 35–44, single, heterosexual)

The chemistry between characters can often then *lead* to writers and readers finding the actors playing the roles physically attractive. As one writer explains, 'When I first started in *The Eagle* fandom, I didn't find Jamie Bell attractive at all. But looking at [his character] Esca through Marcus' [Channing Tatum's character] eyes I see him as very beautiful, and see all kinds of stuff I now feel drawn to. If you get into your character's head and write through them, then that brings *you* along for the ride' (British, 35–44, married, pansexual).

Jenkins (1992, p. 191), however, consistently plays down the sexual element to slash, noting that while 'slash fans concede that erotic pleasure is central to their interest in the genre … slash is not so much a genre about sex as it is a genre about the limitations of traditional masculinity and about reconfiguring male identity'. Levin Russo (2002, p. 13) disputes his interpretation, maintaining that rather than offer something else ('"male identity", no less') to take precedence over and draw attention away from the smut that readers reluctantly 'concede' is important to them, one could instead propose that 'sexual explicitness can, in itself, be a primary, privileged realm of significance'—particularly for women who have long been ignored as sexual consumers by a male-focused market.

Brownian Motion: Slash and the Politics of Resistance

Constance Penley (1991) goes one step beyond Jenkins, and frames slash as *overtly* political. She points to the largely female control over the production, distribution and consumption of slash as a form of both resistance and creative appropriation. One woman expands on this idea:

I hate it that our stories, our *mythology*, is owned by giant corporations that replicate the misogyny, racism, homophobia etcetera of the culture at large, and that render so many of us completely invisible: the non-heterosexual, the non-sexual, men who are not 'manly', and women who are not beautiful objects of desire. I love grabbing the stories out of their hands—what Livia Penn[6] calls 'stealing the archetypes and dressing them up in frilly Barbie clothes'. I hate it that something as primal as sexual desire is commodified and sold back to us, and what I write is a big 'Fuck You' to all that. We're Robin Hood out here. (American, 45–54, married, bisexual)

Another adds:

I like that we can take something, as a community, that may be intended for a different interpretation and re-invent it for a totally different purpose. Like Riot Grrrls and other feminist radicals, it's like we can take the word 'Bitch' and make it a symbol of empowerment. Similarly, I like the idea of taking a story that is maybe unintentionally sexist or homophobic and taking ownership of the story to make it something totally different, but still using the canon. (American, 25–34, married, heterosexual)

Penley also borrows from the work of Michel de Certeau (1984), who uses the term 'Brownian motion'—which describes the random, zig-zagging movements of microscopic particles suspended in a fluid resulting from their continuous bombardment by fast-moving molecules in the surrounding medium—as a metaphor for creativity. De Certeau goes on to describe Brownian motion as 'the tactical manoeuvres of the relatively powerless when they attempt to resist, negotiate, or transform the system and products of the relatively powerful' (Penley, 1991, p. 139). De Certeau differentiates here between *strategies* and *tactics*; strategies are methods by which dominating and often repressive institutions assert control over time and place. Tactics, however, are used by the weak to exploit tiny fissures, to engage with the possibilities of resistance, and to create their own moments in time and space. In Penley's work, these 'tactics' take the form of a kind of creative guerrilla action, whereby fans rewrite and refigure the relationships in the media they consume to create the kinds of works they want to see. Endemic in both de Certeau and Penley's configurations of Brownian motion is the idea that 'the powerful are cumbersome, unimaginative, and over-organised, whereas the weak are creative, nimble, and flexible' (Fiske, 1989, p. 26). However, in de Certeau's conception the actions of the weak achieve very little, much like how the nudges and bumps of microscopic particles change very little at the macro level in our universe—we can see Brownian motion when we look at smoke through a microscope, but not with our naked eyes. It is a process which takes place around us all the time, but is much too small for us to observe. Parrish (2013, pp. 3, 7) believes that this is how de Certeau would have envisioned the connection: 'as a relevant but ultimately unproductive process in which weak agents bump up against a more powerful agent in a way that does not change anything'. Penley (1991, p. 139), however, argues that slash writers 'went one better' than de Certeau's 'ordinary man'—their type of creative guerrilla action *can* affect things at the macro level—the way that (largely) female fans have taken control of the entire creative process of slash fiction—from writing it, to editing it, to circulating it—has had an impact on both wider society and the original media source. To this extent, Penley views slash as a utopian genre. Many of the women I spoke with agree with her, with one explaining 'my stories tend to be almost utopian—I write the sort of world I want to live in. Realistic? Not really. They are my happy place. And that happy place includes descriptions of sex!' (American, 45–54, single, asexual).

I have argued (Neville, 2018) that online slash communities are better conceived of as *hetero*topias, which Foucault (1986, p. 24) describes as 'real places … which are something like counter-sites, a kind of collectively enacted utopia in which the real sites, all the other real sites which can be found within the culture, are simultaneously represented, contested, and inverted'. Rambukkana (2007, p. 73, emphasis added) highlights the importance of heterotopias being actual spaces (unlike utopias which are simply romantic ideals)—it is the realness of heterotopias that means 'they have a substantive place in politics as spaces where *actual* things can happen'. I will return to the idea that online explicit slash communities can affect real world change in Chaps. 7 and 9.

Interestingly, this view of slash as resistance is not unique to women producing and consuming m/m erotic fiction; it has also been applied to women's porn consumption more generally. DeVoss (2002, p. 90) creates a very similar argument for women-created visual porn sites on the web, which she sees as another example of de Certeau's tactics. Such sites are 'cracks … [which] offer … a space from which we can view women's resistances and appropriation, where we can view women rewriting the narrative of the public and private and asserting their identity and agency in virtual spaces'. Women reappropriating and creating their own pornography in this way is viewed as a kind of transgression, and transgression is something Beasley (2011, p. 27) sees as providing a 'bridging terminology between small-scale, everyday, possibly less self-consciously reflective conduct and more explicit, public, and macro moments in relation to social change'. Likewise, Schauer (2005) describes porn sites 'for women' as an example of what Judith Butler terms 'insurrectionary speech'. Butler (1997, p. 163) defines insurrectionary speech as making cultural articulations—visual representations, texts, or actual speech—into 'instrument[s] of resistance in [a] redeployment that destroys the prior territory of [their] operation'. Finally, Hisatake (2011) posits that slash fans are reading with 'the oppositional gaze', a phrase coined by bell hooks (1992, p. 116). The oppositional gaze is the ability to manipulate one's gaze in the face of structures of domination that would contain it, which opens up the possibility of agency.

Viewpoints such as this have led to accusations that scholars are participating in 'an almost uncritical celebration of fans as "resisters"' (Barker, 1993, p. 180), and other work on slash reception has tended to reject the 'resistance' paradigm (Allington, 2007; Gwenllian Jones, 2002). However, the perspective is interesting for what it can tell us about how SEM consumption can (and does) have the potential to change society and bring about real political and social change. This will be discussed further in Chap. 9.

Slash as Ethical, Feminist Pornography

While not discussing complex theoretical interpretations in the style of Penley and DeVoss, for many respondents slash nevertheless functions as a form of feminist, ethical pornography. Participants spoke about how they find it easy to enjoy slash—and use it as a tool to facilitate arousal—because it does not raise a number of ethical problems they encounter with visual pornography. Namely, it does not involve any real people and so its creation does not raise any concerns with regards to whether anyone is being exploited or coerced. As one woman explains, 'I don't like the fact that pornography basically features real people paid (or, at worst, exploited, not paid) to have sex in front of an audience. That scenario seems so fundamentally unsexy to me, I cannot derive pleasure from it' (British, 25–34, in a relationship, heterosexual). This is particularly true for readers and writers who are in to more extreme kinks (noncon [non-consensual sex] and dubcon [sex where consent is dubious], hard-core BDSM, breathplay, bestiality, incest, underage sex etc.), as it also manages to neatly side-step what MacLeod (forthcoming) has termed 'the consensual catch 22'. This refers to the phenomenon whereby consumers want porn to feel authentic (that is, *not* acted) in order to find it maximally arousing, but simultaneously need to be convinced that they are not engaging with material that represents *real life* non-consent, abuse, or danger to any of the parties involved. One woman explains that because slash is 'not porn with real people' she finds it easier to explore her kinks, adding, 'this may seem strange, but I would hate to objectify a real person, especially if it happens commercially. Nevertheless, there's kinky stuff I'd like to explore in terms of fantasy. Fictional characters do not suffer for it. They are not involved in sex trafficking, are not illegals forced into sexual slavery. I know too much of injustice to forget about it' (Dutch, 25–34, single, heterosexual).

Of course, most written pornography or erotica is able to circumvent this problem—what makes slash further stand out is that it is both free, and community-produced. As Berg (2014, p. 77) has noted, porn, like any industry under capitalism, is always intrinsically exploitative: 'I mean 'exploitation' in the Marxist sense, in that all work under capitalism involves the expropriation of surplus labour'. Slash is able to partially avoid this possibility of exploitation by virtue of the fact it is produced and circulated for free within a community of like-minded individuals[7]—as amateur writing it is, in the truest sense, a labour of love. It also exists outside of the control of patriarchal publishers and porn producers. Positioning most porn as essentially patriarchal, Irigaray (1985, p. 197) writes of the economy of masculine desire that is based on the exchange of women between men. She asks what would happen if female commodities refused to go to market and instead carried out 'commerce' between them-selves: 'exchanges without identifiable terms, without accounts, without end… Without standard or yardstick… Use and exchange would be indistinguishable… Pleasure without possession… Utopia? Perhaps.' For many respondents slash is exactly this: utopia.

This is not to say that slash is entirely beyond criticism in terms of the ethics of production or consumption. As well as facing claims that it fetishises gay men and gay sexuality, and promotes many heteronormative ideals (which I will discuss in Chaps. 6, 7, and 8), slash fandom has also come under fire for the preponderance of what is termed RPS [real-person slash]. RPS is a genre of slash fiction that features celebrities or other real people, and imagines them in homosexual relationships. Acafan Straw (2009, p. 3) reveals how she originally thought RPS was 'morally wrong' and so did not read or write it, mainly because she believed it to be an invasion of privacy as well as a 'denigration of the actor's humanity and worth as a person', and notes that RPS usually ignores an actor's real-life romantic relationships, and yet incorporates his family and friends into the plotlines 'sometimes to an almost stalker-ish degree'. A particularly popular RPS pairing has been that of Harry Styles, formerly of One Direction, and his bandmate Louis Tomlinson. Fellow One Direction band member Zayn Malik told *The Fader* that the existence of so many RPS stories about the pair is 'not funny, and it still continues to be quite hard for them. They won't naturally go and put their arm around each other because they're conscious of this thing that's going on, which is not even true' (in Cooper, 2015). Several respondents were aware of these issues, and reflected on how it deterred them from reading or writing RPS: 'If real people are involved, it ruins it—you can do anything to fictional characters, but real people? Ick! Ethics become involved, and actors'—frequently unappealing—personalities become hard to ignore, and that absolutely ruins slash for me' (Scottish, 45–54, single, heterosexual). As Lee (2003, p. 71) has argued, 'it is considered okay to play with characters, but not with real people'. As such RPS has come to be regarded as 'highly controversial and contentious' in fan spaces (Thomas, 2014, p. 171) and 'roundly denounced' as a legal and ethical grey area (McGee, 2005, p. 173): it is banned from the largest fan fiction site Fanfiction.net.

In defence of RPS, Thrupkaew (2003) argues that as so many celebrities and boy-band members are largely manufactured personas designed for the amusement of the general public anyway, 'why not just run with them'? Celebrities often court attention, and encourage some degree of speculation about their private lives. As such, McGee (2005, p. 174) feels that RPS only 'breaks the rules' by virtue of the fact that it refuses to consume celebrity personas in 'the way intended by Paramount, Warner Bros., or Disney', and argues that since the personas themselves are created to be a commodity, it is not unethical to use them as such. Busse (2005) agrees, noting that celebrities have always been objects of identification and sexual fantasy, especially for teenagers and young adults. The boundaries between reality and fiction become blurred as audiences react to, and appropriate, celebrities in their own fantasy lives, imaging being the celebrity, imaging having sex with the celebrity, imaging what the celebrity's life might be like, how they might have sex with their own partner: 'as such, a version of Real Person [Slash] has always existed, if only in the minds of teenage girls and boys' (Busse, 2005, p. 107). In addition, Piper (2015) notes there are comparisons to be made here between RPS and film and TV texts such as biopics, docudramas, and historical dramas that dramatise real people and events. Romano (2012) invites readers who judge RPS as 'weird' to consider TV shows like *The Tudors* and *The Kennedys* which contain off-the-record moments (including intimate and sexual scenes) that filmmakers construct for viewers. However, many of the women I spoke to remain leery of RPS:

> I have serious reservations about so-called 'real person' fanfiction. Sherlock and John Watson can screw like bunnies and I'll love it. But someone writing about Ben and Martin having sex is a breach of their privacy and so far out of bounds that it makes my stomach churn to think of someone writing or reading that. Especially with Martin and Ben because they've both said that they don't like each other like that, and both are in serious het[erosexual] romantic relationships. Zach Quinto and Chris Pine stories are equally problematic as I understand one is gay and the other straight. But either way, I don't think it's right to write stories about real people—it's like making up gossip about them and spreading it around. (Canadian, 35–44, divorced, heterosexual)

Asides from concerns over specific genres of slash fic (such as RPS), many of the women I spoke with identify slash as not only ethical, but as a form of feminist[8] pornography. While the definition of feminist porn is somewhat slippery, Levin Russo (2007, p. 249) argues that porn can be defined as feminist partly because of its connections 'to material social networks and collective experiences'. Alessandra Mondin (2014, p. 190) emphasises how important the concept of community and shared values are in feminist porn, noting that it is vital that 'producers, directors, and performers share the values of the audiences they are marketing to'. Among the women surveyed here who watch visual pornography, there is a marked preference for home-grown amateur-produced porn, including m/f porn that has female producers and involved women throughout the creative process. As one woman explains, 'most hetero porn I look at is amateur stuff because I'd rather see a goofy-looking husband and wife who honestly enjoy each other under some bad lighting, rather than overly idealized women being humiliated and treated like "things"' (American, 25–34, single, bisexual). This suggests that women—at least women who engage with m/m SEM—like sexual content that allows them to practice creativity and control. For these women slash has much in common with DIY visual porn: reworking old tropes, the production of a creative community, the overlap of readers/consumers and writers/producers. Several respondents also made this connection, with one saying, 'I'm also interested in the politics of porn-making, whether and when it is feminist and empowering; there's interesting crossover in those questions between the fannish and pro[fessional] porn worlds' (Canadian, 25–34). To this extent, slash can certainly be regarded as feminist. As Boyd (2001, p. 102) has argued, 'while [many] slash writers do not set out with a 'feminist agenda', their writing works to resist, and reconceptualise, popular notions of sex, sexuality, pornography, and romance'.

The sense of an accepting and friendly community, invested in each other, is incredibly important to slash fans. Asides from the fact that such a community offers writers an invaluable opportunity to receive constructive feedback on their writing, it also serves to help all members explore their own feelings about sex and sexuality in a safe and supportive environment. Again, we can see that this 'community' element is often important to women when engaging with all types of SEM. Bader (2003) notes that men look at visual porn (alone), whereas women tend to focus on written porn and visit chat rooms (relational). As Lindgren (2010, p. 175) has observed, women (and some men) in today's online porn audience are largely not 'isolated masturbating loners' but instead an 'interactive and creative collective of critical audience members'. Likewise, in their study on women attending a male strip club, Montemurro, Bloom, and Madell (2003) found that a large proportion of the women present use the show and the dancers as a way to bond with their friends, resulting in a shared experience that could be reminisced about later. They postulate that there are considerable differences between female and male patrons in the sexualised atmosphere of the strip club, in that while men tend to ignore each other and focus purely on the dancers, 'for women the experience was mostly about friendship and having a shared experience' (Montemurro et al., 2003, p. 344).

It is also important to note that the community within slash fandom is not as closed off to other forms of queer media as previously thought. Bacon-Smith (1992, p. 248) maintained that 'only a very small number of women who wrote homoerotic fiction inside the community had a prior interest in gay male literature, and few have extended their interest beyond the community once exposed to it'. However, the huge amount of crossover in my data suggests this is no longer true. While only 38 per cent of my sample of slashers had a prior interest in gay literature, and only a quarter (25 per cent) had a prior interest in m/m visual pornography, the majority of them went on to develop an interest in several forms of m/m media following their discovery of slash fandom. Of the 307 respondents who did not have a prior interest in m/m visual pornography, 247 (80 per cent) went on to explore visual m/m SEM after becoming involved in slash; of the 260 respondents who did not have a prior interest in gay literature, 69 per cent went on to explore gay literature.

However, while women involved in slash fandom often engage with multiple other forms of SEM, they often stipulate that slash is by far and away their favourite type of erotic media. Given the fact that it remains one of the few types of SEM that is largely controlled by women, this is interesting for what it says about the gendering of porn: 'whatever other political and literary goals it may have, it is a genre which aims to do something in a way that pleases women' (Pugh, 2005, p. 110). The next three chapters will investigate in more detail what it is about porn that does and does not please women, and why m/m SEM can frequently better offer these pleasures than heterosexual pornography.

Notes

1. Zines are small-circulation self-published works of original or appropriated texts and images, usually reproduced via photocopier. They often deal with topics too controversial or niche for mainstream media.
2. Lucasfilms has previously implied that legal action will not be taken against *Star Wars* fan fiction writers and editors, provided fans do not attempt to publish sexually explicit stories—particularly 'gay' sexually explicit stories. Please see the Fanlore wiki page for more information: https://fanlore.org/wiki/Fandom_vs_The_Courts:_Fan_Fiction_and_Fair_Use.
3. Let us not forget that the phenomenally successful *Fifty Shades of Grey* started life as *Twilight* alternative universe [AU] fan fiction.
4. Queerbaiting is a practice whereby producers incorporate queer subtexts into a show in the hope of expanding the audience by attracting LGBTQ+ folk while avoiding alienating viewers who would disapprove of openly queer characters.
5. In its broadest sense, a crackfic is any story whose premise and events would be completely implausible and/or ridiculous in canon, such as casting all characters as My Little Ponies. It may or may not deal with this premise in a serious way. The name stems from the notion that the author must have been ingesting some pretty strong drugs just to think up the idea, let alone write it.
6. Livia Penn is a blogger and long-term member of media fandom. You can read more about her on her Fanlore page: https://fanlore.org/wiki/Liviapenn (accessed 7 December 2017).
7. Obviously, hierarchies are at work here, and having the time, space and ability to access online SEM, including slash, is deeply embedded in global capitalist social relations. Although women from 40 different countries took part in this study, the demographic data suggests that accessing m/m SEM, including slash fiction, is still a prerogative of White Western women. While slash may be 'free' at point of use, it is not truly free within this framework—in any sexualised economy power relations are classed and racialised, and while online slash fandom spaces may be sites of resis-

tance and struggle, they do not exist outside of power (please see Berg, 2015; Fazekas, 2014; Smith, 2015 for more).

8. While slash fandom can certainly be read as feminist, this is not to say it is exclusively *female* space. Men can and do participate in slash fandom, as both writers, readers, and visual artists. It is important not to erase the important contribution men have made to slash fandom, and scholars such as Joseph Brennan (2014) are intensely critical of academics who continue to link slash exclusively with women.

References

Akinsha, M. K. (2009). *A story of man's great love for his fellow man: Slash fan fiction, a literary genre.* MA dissertation, Central European University. Retrieved from http://www.etd.ceu.hu/2009/akinsha_marja-kristina.pdf

Allington, D. (2007). 'How come most people don't see it?': Slashing *The Lord of the Rings. Social Semiotics, 17*(1), 43–62.

Bacon-Smith, C. (1992). *'Enterprising women': Television fandom and the creation of popular myth.* Philadelphia: University of Pennsylvania Press.

Bader, M. J. (2003). *Arousal: The secret logic of sexual fantasies.* London: Macmillan.

Barker, M. (1993). Seeing how far you can see: On being a 'fan' of 2000AD. In D. Buckingham (Ed.), *Reading audiences: Young people and the media* (pp. 159–183). Manchester: Manchester University Press.

Barker, M. (2002, October 19–20). Slashing the Slayer: A thematic analysis of homoerotic Buffy fan fiction. In: *Blood, text and fears.* Norwich: University of East Anglia. Retrieved from http://oro.open.ac.uk/23340/2/Barker%281%29.pdf

Barthes, R. (1970). *S/Z: An essay.* Paris: Seuil.

Beasley, C. (2011). Libidinous politics: Heterosex, 'transgression', and social change. *Australian Feminist Studies, 26*(67), 25–40.

Berg, H. (2014). Labouring porn studies. *Porn Studies, 1*(1–2), 75–79.

Berg, H. (2015). Sex, work, queerly: Identity, authenticity, and laboured performance. In M. Laing, K. Pilcher, & N. Smith (Eds.), *Queer sex work* (pp. 23–31). London: Routledge.

Booth, P. (2014). Slash and porn: Media subversion, hyper-articulation, and parody. *Continuum: Journal of Media & Cultural Studies, 28*(3), 396–409.

Boyd, K. S. (2001). *'One finger on the mouse scroll bar and the other on my clit': Slash writers views on pornography, censorship, feminism and risk.* PhD dissertation, Simon Fraser University. Retrieved from http://summit.sfu.ca/item/7501

Brennan, J. (2014). Not 'from my hot little ovaries': How slash manips pierce reductive assumptions. *Continuum: Journal of Media & Cultural Studies, 28*(2), 247–264.

Busse, K. (2005). 'Digital get down': Postmodern boy band slash and the queer female space. In C. Malcolm & J. Nyman (Eds.), *Eroticism in American culture* (pp. 103–125). Gdansk: Gdansk University Press.

Butler, J. (1997). *Excitable speech*. New York: Routledge.

Cancian, F. M. (1990). *Love in America: Gender and self-development*. Cambridge: Cambridge University Press.

Cooper, D. (2015, November 17). Zayn Malik's next direction. *The Fader*. Retrieved from http://www.thefader.com/2015/11/17/zayn-malik-fader-cover-story-interview-solo-album-one-direction

Cumberland, S. (1999). *Private uses of cyberspace: Women, desire and fan culture*. Paper presented at the Media in Transition Conference, Massachusetts Institute of Technology, Cambridge, October 8. Retrieved from http://web.mit.edu/comm-forum/papers/cumberland.html

de Certeau, M. (1984). *The practice of everyday life* (S. F. Rendall, Trans.). Berkeley: University of California Press.

de Montaigne, M. (1580/2005). *On friendship*. London: Penguin.

DeVoss, D. (2002). Women's porn sites—Spaces of fissure and eruption or 'I'm a little bit of everything'. *Sexuality & Culture, 6*(3), 75–94.

Dhaenens, F., Vam Bauwel, S., & Biltereyst, D. (2008). Slashing the fiction of Queer Theory: Slash fiction, Queer reading, and transgressing the boundaries of screen studies, representations, and audiences. *Journal of Communication Inquiry, 32*(4), 335–347.

Doty, A. (1993). *Making things perfectly queer: Interpreting mass culture*. Minneapolis: University of Minnesota Press.

Doty, A. (2000). *Flaming classics: Queering the film canon*. New York: Routledge.

Dyer, R. (1995). *The matter of images: Essays on representations*. London: Routledge.

Falzone, P. J. (2005). The final frontier is queer: Aberrancy, archetype and audience generated folklore in K/S slashfiction. *Western Folklore, 64*(3/4), 243–261.

Fazekas, A. (2014). *Queer and unusual space: White supremacy in slash fanfiction*. MA Dissertation, Queen's University, Canada. Retrieved from https://qspace.library.queensu.ca/bitstream/handle/1974/12609/Fazekas_Angela_M_201411_MA.pdf?sequence=1

Fiedler, L. A. (1960). *Love and death in the American novel*. New York: Scarborough Books.

Fiske, J. (1987). British cultural studies and television. In R. C. Allen (Ed.), *Channels of discourse: Television and contemporary criticism* (pp. 254–289). London: Methuen.

Fiske, J. (1989). *Understanding popular culture*. Winchester: Unwin Hyman Inc.

Foucault, M. (1986). Of other spaces. *Diacritics, 16*(1), 22–27.

Greven, D. (2009). *Gender and sexuality in Star Trek: Allegories of desire in the television series and films*. Jefferson, NC: McFarland.

Gwenllian Jones, S. (2002). The sex lives of cult television characters. *Screen, 43*, 77–90.

Hansen, B. (2010). The darker side of slash fanfiction on the internet. In Y. Aris & H. I. R. Daniel (Eds.), *New media and the politics of online communities* (pp. 51–58). Oxford: Inter-Disciplinary Press.

Haskell, M. (1974). *From reverence to rape: The treatment of women in the movies*. New York: Holt, Rinehart, & Winston.

Hayward, S. (2000). *Cinema studies: The key concepts*. London: Routledge.

Hisatake, K. (2011). '*Nothing says I despise you like a blowjob': Opening queer moments for queer spaces in Harry Potter slash fan fiction*. MA dissertation: University of Hawaii at Mānoa. Retrieved from http://scholarspace.manoa. hawaii.edu/bitstream/handle/10125/29630/Hisatake_Kara_Nothing%20 says%20I%20Despise%20You.pdf?sequence=1

hooks, b. (1992). *Black looks: Race and representation*. Boston: South End Press.

Irigaray, L. (1985). *This sex which is not one* (Catherine Porter with Carolyn Burke, Trans.). Ithaca: Cornell University Press.

James, J. (2017). The best enemies-to-lovers romances. *Bookish Blog*. Retrieved from https://www.bookish.com/articles/julie-james-enemies-to-lovers-romances/

Jenkins, H. (1992). *Textual poachers: Television fans and participatory culture*. New York: Routledge.

Jenkins, H. (2006). *Fans, bloggers, and gamers: Exploring participatory culture*. New York: New York University Press.

Jones, R. (2017, July 26). Why Chris and Kem were the true star couple of *Love Island 2017*. *The Telegraph*. Retrieved from http://www.telegraph.co.uk/men/ the-filter/duo-will-last-chris-kem-true-star-couple-love-island-2017/

Keft-Kennedy, V. (2008). Fantasising masculinity in Buffyverse slash fiction: Sexuality, violence, and the vampire. *Nordic Journal of English Studies, 7*(1), 49–80.

Kent, S. (1985). The erotic male nude. In S. Kent & J. Morreau (Eds.), *Women's images of men* (pp. 75–105). London: Pandora.

Kitson, N. (2009, March 2). Day six: Slashing the ties that bind. *Burn Index*. Retrieved from http://www.niallkitson.ie/

Lackner, E., Lucas, B. L., & Reid, R. A. (2006). Cunning linguists: The bisexual erotics of words/silence/flesh. In K. Hellekson & K. Busse (Eds.), *Fan fiction and fan communities in the age of the internet* (pp. 189–206). London: McFarland.

Lang, R. (2002). *Masculine interests: Homoerotics in hollywood film*. New York: Columbia University Press.

Lee, K. (2003). Confronting *enterprise* slash fan fiction. *Extrapolation, 44*, 3–17.

Levin Russo, J. (2002). 'NEW VOY 'cyborg sex' J/7 [NC-17]': New methodologies, new fantasies. *The Slash Reader*. August. Retrieved from http://j-l-r.org/asmic/fanfic/print/jlr-cyborgsex.pdf

Levin Russo, J. (2007). 'The real thing': Reframing queer pornography for virtual spaces. In K. Jacobs, M. Hanssen, & M. Pasquinelli (Eds.), *C'lick me: A netporn studies reader* (pp. 239–252). Amsterdam: Institute of Network Cultures.

Lindgren, S. (2010). Widening the glory hole: The discourse of online porn fandom. In F. Attwood (Ed.), *Porn.com* (pp. 171–185). New York: Peter Lang.

Lulu. (2013). *AO3 census data analysis*. Retrieved from http://centrumlumina.tumblr.com/post/63373124511/mm-fans-sexuality-and-gender

Macleod, P. A. (forthcoming). *Dirty diaries: A grounded ethnographic inquiry into experiences of queer feminist porn*. PhD dissertation, Middlesex University, London.

McGee, J. (2005). 'In the end, it's all made up': The ethics of fanfiction and real person fiction. In P. M. Japp, M. Meister, & D. K. Japp (Eds.), *Communication ethics, media & popular culture* (Vol. 9, pp. 161–181). New York: Peter Lang Publishing.

Meyer, U. (2010). Hidden in straight sight: Trans*gressing gender and sexuality via BL. In A. Levi, M. McHarry, & D. Pagliasotti (Eds.), *Boys' love manga* (pp. 232–257). Jefferson: McFarland and Company.

Miller, D. A. (1991). Anal rope. In D. Fuss (Ed.), *Inside/out*. London: Routledge.

Mondin, A. (2014). Fair-trade porn+ niche markets+ feminist audience. *Porn Studies, 1*(1–2), 189–192.

Montemurro, B., Bloom, C., & Madell, K. (2003). Ladies night out: A typology of women patrons of a male strip club. *Deviant Behaviour, 24*(4), 333–352.

Neville, L. (2018). 'The tent's big enough for everyone': Online slash fiction as a site for activism and change. *Gender, Place and Culture*. Online first http://dx.doi.org/10.1080/0966369X.2017.1420633

Parrish, J. J. (2013). Metaphors we read by: People, process, and fan fiction. *Transformative Works and Cultures, 14*. Retrieved from http://journal.transformativeworks.org/index.php/twc/article/view/486/401

Penley, C. (1991). Brownian motion: Women, tactics, and technology. In C. Penley & A. Ross (Eds.), *Technoculture* (pp. 135–161). Minneapolis: University of Minnesota Press.

Piper, M. (2015). Real body, fake person: Recontextualising celebrity bodies in fandom and film. *Transformative Works and Culture, 20*. Retrieved from http://journal.transformativeworks.org/index.php/twc/article/view/664/542

Pugh, S. (2005). *The democratic genre: Fan fiction in a literary context*. Bridgend, Wales: Seren.

Rambukkana, N. (2007). Is slash an alternative medium? 'Queer' heterotopias and the role of autonomous media spaces in radical world building. *Affinities: A Journal of Radical Theory, Culture, and Action, 1*(1), 69–85.

Reid, R. A. (2009). Thrusts in the dark: Slashers' queer practices. *Extrapolation, 50*(3), 463–483.

Roach, C. (2010). Getting a good man to love: Popular romance fiction and the problem of patriarchy. *Journal of Popular Romance Studies, 1*(1). Retrieved from http://jprstudies.org/wp-content/uploads/2010/08/JPRS1.1_Roach_GettingGoodMantoLove.pdf

Romano, A. (2012). The shipping news. *The Backlot*. Retrieved from http://www.newnownext.com/the-shipping-news-october-1-2012/10/2012/

Rosenberg, D. (2007). Confessions of a lesbian feminist slasher. *Off Our Backs: The Feminist Newsjournal, 37*, 51–52.

Ross, S. (2002). *Super(natural) women: Female heroes, their friends, and their fans*. Unpublished PhD dissertation, University of Texas at Austin.

Rowling, J. K. (2003). *Harry Potter and the order of the Phoenix*. New York: Scholastic Press.

Russ, J. (1985). *Magic mommas, trembling sisters, puritans and perverts: Feminist essays*. Trumansburg, NY: Crossing.

Salmon, C., & Symons, D. (2001). *Warrior lovers: Erotic fiction, evolution, and female sexuality*. London: Weidenfeld & Nicolson.

Saxey, E. (2002). Staking a claim: The series and its slash fiction. In R. Kaveney (Ed.), *Reading The Vampire Slayer: An unofficial critical companion to Buffy and Angel* (pp. 187–210). New York: Tauris Parke Paperbacks.

Schauer, T. (2005). Women's porno: The heterosexual female gaze in porn sites 'for women'. *Sexuality & Culture, 9*(2), 42–64.

Scodari, C. (2003). Resistance re-examined: Gender, fan practices, and science fiction television. *Popular Communication, 1*(2), 111–130.

Sedgwick, E. K. (1985). *Between men: English literature and male homosocial desire.* New York: Columbia University Press.

Segal, L. (1994). *Straight sex: The politics of pleasure.* London: Virago Press.

Smith, N. (2015). Queer in/and sexual economies. In M. Laing, K. Pilcher, & N. Smith (Eds.), *Queer sex work* (pp. 13–22). London: Routledge.

Smol, A. (2004). 'Oh … Oh … Frodo !': Readings of male intimacy in 'The Lord of the Rings'. *Modern Fiction Studies, 50*(4), 949–979.

Somogyi, V. (2002). Complexity of desire: Janeway/Chakotay Fan Fiction. *Journal of American and Contemporary Cultures, 25*, 399–404.

Staiger, J. (2005). *Media reception studies.* New York: New York University Press.

Stanis, K., & Butler, S. (1995). Stranger than fiction. *First Time, 43*, 4–33.

Straw, A. (2009). *Squeeing, flailing, and the 'post-Jared-and-Jensen glow': An ethnography of Creation Entertainment's March 2009 'Salute to Supernatural' conventions.* BA dissertation: Penn State University. Retrieved from http://www.personal.psu.edu/als595/blogs/amandalynn125/papers/ethnography.pdf

Sutherland, J. (2006, February 14). Slashing through the undercult. *The Telegraph.* Retrieved from http://www.telegraph.co.uk/culture/books/3650072/Slashing-through-the-undercult.html

Thomas, B. (2014). Fans behaving badly? Real person fic and the blurring of the boundaries between the public and the private. In B. Thomas & J. Round (Eds.), *Real lives, celebrity stories: Narratives of ordinary and extraordinary people across media* (pp. 171–185). New York: Bloomsbury.

Thrupkaew, N. (2003). Fan/tastic voyage: A journey into the wild, wild world of slash fiction. *Bitch Magazine.* Retrieved from http://bitchmagazine.org/article/fan-tastic-voyage

Tosenberger, C. (2008). Homosexuality at the online Hogwarts: Harry Potter slash fanfiction. *Children's Literature, 36*, 185–207.

Viegener, M. (1993). Kinky escapades, bedroom techniques, unbridled passion, and secret sex codes. In D. Bergman (Ed.), *Camp grounds: Style and homosexuality* (pp. 234–256). Amherst: University of Massachusetts Press.

Woledge, E. (2005a). From slash to the mainstream: Female writers and gender blending men. *Extrapolation, 46*(1), 50–65.

Woledge, E. (2005b). Decoding desire: From Kirk and Spock to K/S1. *Social Semiotics, 15*(2), 235–250.

Wolf, S. E. (2008). 'Defying gravity': Queer conventions in the musical wicked. *Theatre Journal, 60*(1), 1–21.

4

'Don't You Know that It's Different for Girls'

'Nice women like erotica,' one of my participants states, 'whereas porn—porn is for sluts' (Scottish, 45–54, single, heterosexual). It is perhaps not surprising that my participants are well aware of the gendered connotations of being a woman who engages with sexually explicit media—particularly SEM that defies the conventional notion of what a woman *should* like (which is certainly not m/m). Willis (1983, p. 464) neatly describes the sort of SEM women are 'allowed' to engage with as 'beautiful, romantic, soft, nice, and devoid of messiness, vulgarity, impulses to power, or indeed aggression of any sort. Above all, emphasis should be on *relationships*, not (yuk) *organs*'. Many of the women I spoke with confirm the view that m/m porn—especially (though not exclusively) visual m/m porn—is not something we are supposed to like. Porn is for men; m/m porn is for gay men. As one woman explains, 'men have always been allowed to talk about porn and about their sexual interests, and I feel somewhat confined when that isn't OK for women. For example, Barney on *How I Met Your Mother* talks about how he likes girl-on-girl, but you'd never hear a woman say anything of the sort, especially not on TV' (American, 18–24, single, heterosexual). While the majority of participants feel that the cultural landscape is starting to change, with women being increasingly recognised as 'sexual in their own right' there is still a

© The Author(s) 2018

L. Neville, *Girls Who Like Boys Who Like Boys*,
https://doi.org/10.1007/978-3-319-69134-3_4

firm belief that 'it shocks people that *nice* women [watch or] read gay male porn' (Scottish, 45–54, single, heterosexual). For some women the restrictions on them engaging with m/m SEM are not merely external (i.e. socially induced), they are also internal, with one talking about 'the vague remnants of shame that having any sort of sexuality as a woman still engenders in me. I don't like the idea of me being associated with the things my filthy mind conjures. It makes me uneasy' (English, 25–34, single, heterosexual).

Instead, romance is seen as the traditional form of SEM (although easy on the 'E') for women. While men can get their kicks from hardcore visual pornography (including 'regular good old-fashioned girl-on-girl action', as Chandler so memorably describes it), women are meant to limit themselves to a few dog-eared pages of 'good bits' in a Harlequin historical romance. This is not to say that women don't enjoy romances—61 per cent of my sample read romance novels, and I will discuss the importance of both romance and 'love' in SEM in Chap. 6— but the majority of women I spoke with have chosen to reject the traditional romance formula. They want authenticity, rawness, passion and adventure (all at the same time, if possible). And they believe they are more likely to find one, or all, of these elements in m/m SEM—from gay porn films to slash fiction—than they are in heterosexual texts.

It is also perhaps not altogether surprising that women may produce their own SEM from a male perspective. Recall Henry Jenkins' (1992) assertion in the previous chapter that women are 'forced' from childhood to read 'boys' books'. Think of Laura Mulvey's (1981) concept of the male gaze which governs most of the visual material that hits our screens. Exposed to male-authored texts, be they visual or written, women learn to see and interpret the world as men do. Mulvey (1981, p. 13) makes a case for what she calls 'visual transvestism', stating that 'for women (from childhood onwards) transsex identification is a habit that very easily becomes second nature'. Doane (1991, p. 25, emphasis added) writes similarly, noting that 'while the male is locked into sexual identity, the female can at least *pretend* she is other—in fact, sexual mobility would seem to be a distinguishing feature of femininity in its social construction'. However, both these explanations are embedded in a long-standing feminist narrative stretching back to Simone de Beauvoir (1949/1973) that male-identification occurs because women have been taught to other *themselves*, that is, to see themselves as men see them. It is also possible, as I discussed in Chaps. 2 and 3 and will return to in Chap. 7, that the women in this study see themselves as fluid in terms of sexual response to arousing stimuli, both in terms of gender identification and sexual orientation. Women might not be 'othering' themselves when they tap into their own 'maleness', but merely acknowledging a potential in all of us for sexual ambiguity. In her work on desire between women in narrative cinema Stacey (1987, p. 61, emphasis added) criticises 'the rigid distinction between either desire *or* identification so characteristic of psychoanalytical film theory' as it 'fails to address the construction of desires which involve a specific interplay of *both* processes'. A large proportion of the women I spoke with often identify as male, if not in a day-to-day sense, certainly in a sexual sense. Talking about their own positionality as a woman watching, reading, or writing about men having sex with men, they discussed how they often feel male-identified when engaging with explicit texts. This does not stretch only to their consumption of m/m SEM, over half (55 per cent) of participants in the sample state that they imagine themselves as a man during the course of their sexual fantasies and when masturbating. Of those respondents, 96 per cent imagine themselves with another man (or multiple men), 57 per cent with another woman (or multiple women), 33 per cent imagine themselves (as a man) masturbating, 36 per cent imagine being with male and female partners at the same time, 7 per cent imagine themselves with gender diverse/trans people, 7 per cent imagine themselves with mythical/magical creatures, and 9 per cent imagine themselves watching others have sex (from a male point of view). As one respondent explains, 'I feel much more comfortable [watching and writing m/m sex] and I click into it much better. Because in a way I've always thought that way—and I'll share a huge piece of personal information here … when I masturbate I think of myself from a male point of view and stuff like that as well, so obviously it's a key part of me and has been for a very long time' (British, 35–44, married, pansexual).

In this chapter I will explore what women who engage with m/m SEM see as the differences (and similarities) between 'porn' (traditionally perceived as being aimed at men) and 'erotica' (traditionally perceived as being aimed at women) and how this relates to their self-perception as female consumers, and, indeed, their self-perception of being male- (or, more pertinently, gay-male-) identified. In addition, I will share their thoughts on preferences for erotica and pornography from a male vs. a female point of view [POV] and whether they prefer a male POV in general literature. For readers and writers of m/m erotic fiction, I will investigate whether they identify with the 'top' (insertive partner during anal sex) or exclusively with the 'bottom'[1] (receptive partner during anal sex), as has been previously alleged (Bacon-Smith, 1992). Is SEM really that different for girls?

Naughty or Nice? Women and the Porn vs. Erotica Debate

Not only has porn been historically perceived as not 'for' women, it has also been explicitly framed as being 'anti' women. During the mid-1970s to 1980s (a period sometimes known as the 'Porn Wars') debates on pornography deeply polarised the feminist movement. Feminist thinkers and activists such as Andrea Dworkin and Catharine MacKinnon positioned porn as violence against women—not as metaphor, not as speech, but as actual violence (Marks & Neville, 2017; see also MacKinnon, 1993). On the basis of this conflation, and with the support of conservatives and religious fundamentalists, Dworkin and MacKinnon drafted, and briefly passed into law, an ordinance that would ban pornography as a civil rights violation in the U.S. (Dworkin & MacKinnon, 1988). Schauer (2005, p. 45) argues that what seems to underlie much of MacKinnon and Dworkin's (Dworkin, 1992; MacKinnon, 1993) indictment of porn is the assumption that there is 'something like a "normal", natural female sexuality, devoid of dominance/submission; a type of sexuality that is "free", non-aggressive, non-phallic, and lightly lesbian'—certainly women who possess this 'normal' and 'natural' female sexuality would not be in to m/m pornography. However, it's not entirely clear what kind of SEM—if any—such women *would* be in to. Kenneth Mackinnon (1997, p. 104) notes that while anti-porn arguments have been 'largely silent on the issue of sex', their implication is that 'women feel no strong sexual desires, certainly no lust'.

While the perception of women as lacking sexual desire is not apparent among my participants (for obvious reasons!), the spectre of the 'Porn Wars' still hangs heavy over many of the women I spoke to, particularly those who identify as feminist. As one respondent explains, 'most of my friends are old feminists like me, and we come from a culture of anti-porn, [seeing porn] as an industry that is solely for straight men and exploits women, [whereas we are] pro-women's rights and lesbian rights. So, it's been quite hard to come out as a writer of porn, and not always seen as a good thing' (English, 45–54, in a relationship, a little bent). For some participants, the term 'erotica' is therefore seen as less loaded, less problematic, less attached to a painful and complex history than the term 'porn'—even if they view the difference between the two as 'purely semantic' (American, 25–34, single, bisexual). For, as Mackinnon (1997, p. 9) points out, unlike pornography 'the erotic has been claimed for women by certain feminists'. Erotica, then, is often simply defined in opposition to porn, so that it is everything that porn is not: erotica does not objectify women or re-enact male/female power relations, and does not use an exploitative style.

Porn by any Other Name: Differences in Semantics

Gayle Rubin (in English, Hollibaugh, & Rubin, 1981, p. 50) has roundly criticised what she sees as the chauvinism of this type of 'erotica' model, calling it 'the missionary position of the women's movement' because of its exclusion of a whole range of sexual variations, from promiscuity to BDSM. Many sex-positive scholars similarly argue that attempts to distinguish erotica from pornography are often rooted in classism, and posit that such rigid distinctions can cause harm by contributing towards the stigma and whorephobia that marginalises people in the sex industry. Writing in *The Establishment*, Tina Horn (2016) argues that 'the implication is that good (educated) people are aroused by erotica, and bad (trashy) people are aroused by porn'. Even Angela Dworkin (1981, pp. 9–10) maintained that such distinctions are largely class-based—

unfounded on any substantial differences—and are instead tied in with masculine habits of reception, commenting 'in the male sexual lexicon, which is the vocabulary of power, erotica is simply high-class pornography; better produced, better conceived, better executed, better packaged, designed for a better class of consumer'. In this sense, erotica is just more of the same; slightly posher porn for the boys. This perspective was roundly rejected by the women in my sample (nearly all of whom regard erotica as something that could please and arouse women); however, many are sensitive to the accusations of classism levelled at the porn/erotica dichotomy. As one asserts, 'I really dislike the term "erotica"…—it's a way of saying "*my* stuff is lovely life-affirming erotica, *yours* is just nasty old porn"' (American, 55–64, in a relationship, bisexual). Some women therefore prefer to call their writing, reading, or viewing material 'porn'—in a sense of reclaiming the word. One woman explains, 'erotica has connotations of lace draped artistically over the naughty bits, of some coyness and delicacy, of sex with socially redeeming qualities—e.g. erotica has romance, too, so it's all right for women to like it, because it gets us all worked up and ready for committing to men. So I've made a point of insisting … that *I* wasn't writing erotica, I was writing *porn*' (Scottish, 45–54, single, heterosexual). Others, however, reject the term, feeling it doesn't sum up the richness or complexity of the types of m/m SEM they engage with: '"porn" is objectifying, cold, and vulgar… [I like] sex with an actual storyline' (Australian, 25–34, single, bisexual).

In terms of slash fiction, there has been controversy over Russ's (1985) use of the term 'pornography' to describe the genre (see, e.g., Bacon-Smith, 1992), but much like Horn (2016) she maintains that the porn/erotica distinction simply boils down to 'call[ing] something by one name when you like it and another when you don't' (Russ, 1985, p. 79). Some male scholars within slash fandom have also been critical of attempts by slashers to reject the 'pornography' label. Brennan (2014a, 2014b) highlights the pornographic elements of slash by pointing to the use of manips in the fanart that often accompanies stories. Short for 'photomanipulation', manips are pictures that are enhanced or altered using photographic software. In slash manips, images of male characters can be layered with gay pornographic material to create sexually charged stills. Brennan (2014a, pp. 256, 261) argues that by 'virtue of their visual and collage quality, slash manips make explicit the importance of pornography in slash … [and] make visible the unique contribution of men and the influence of gay pornography' on the genre. In this sense, women and gay men who enjoy slash fiction have very similar tastes in what turns them on.

Boys Wank, Girls Sigh: Differences in Affective Response

Juffer (1998, p. 104) agrees that attempts to differentiate porn from erotica are often class-based, but feels this is more to do with format than style or content, noting that the difference has historically been tied to an aesthetic privileging 'the literary—broadly defined—as juxtaposed to the threat of the image'. Susanna Paasonen (2010, p. 139) observes that the tendency to understand porn in terms of the visual is common, 'yet this ignores the fact that the history of pornography has largely been one concerning the written word'. She discusses how the proliferation in online written erotica we have witnessed since the mid-1990s has failed to provoke any significant public uproar, and contrasts this with the animated debates that have arisen around online visual pornography. Indeed, as Paasonen points out, much online written erotica has been greeted with enthusiasm for the possibilities it offers for the exploration of sexual experimentation and fantasy in 'safe', anonymous, and textual online spaces—particularly for women, and markedly in the case of slash fiction (Leiblum, 2001; Cumberland, 2003).

However, while Paasonen (2010) acknowledges that the division between pornography and erotica is often artificial, and can have more to do with taste and moral judgement than any substantive differences, she nevertheless feels that the two separate notions can be useful in describing the different interests of texts. Although it may be tempting to see erotica as a mere euphemism for pornography, she argues that there *is* something specific to the genre of porn; namely its 'explicit carnality, its unabashed commitment to the sexual, and its power to move and arouse' (Paasonen, 2010, p. 150). Likewise, she maintains that erotica also has facets which distinguish it from pornography: 'a "good story" … one involving plot and character development, complexity, and non-explicit elements' (Paasonen, 2010, p. 144). Differences between textual modalities such as porn and erotica are therefore matters of degree rather than matters of kind. In other words, they are not 'poles at either end of a scale, but axes between which every story can be plotted' (Driscoll, 2006, p. 91), and which give rise to different kinds of consumer sensations. The affective power of erotica revolves around desire and emotional realism, whereas the affective power of porn depends on the detailed, if overblown, depictions of sexual arousal, sexual acts, and sensations. Porn, then, is highly instrumental, aimed at making the consumer feel and do specific things: get turned on, masturbate or have sex, climax. In this sense pornography is a cultural form 'defined by its content (sex) [and] its intention (to sexually arouse)' (McNair, 2013, p. 18). While people can be turned on by not-porn, this is either accidental, or, in the case of erotica, not the primary objective. For something to be porn, arousal must be its intention, its *raison d'etre*. As one participant describes it, 'porn exists only to titillate. [Whereas] I like to think of erotica as thinky porn' (American, 25–34, single, bisexual). Paasonen (2010) therefore argues that decisions about 'categories' should be based on 'affective movement rather than hierarchical judgement' (Paasonen, 2010, p. 154), and while acknowledging that the boundaries between the two can be 'overlapping and leaky' (Paasonen, 2010, p. 151), she believes that the distinction is still useful.

Juffer (1998, p. 106) used such affective responses to distinguish between porn and erotica, with one consisting of a 'quick masturbatory fix' and the other depictions of 'the complex nature' of desire. Many of the women I interviewed also distinguish between pornography and erotica along these lines, describing texts as porn if they constitute 'wank material' (American, 35–44, single, heterosexual) and erotica if they are not necessarily something they would consider masturbating to. As one woman explains, '[the difference is] almost along a chart of sexual arousal to completion for me. Erotica definitely arouses, and may even get you physically wet, but I don't often masturbate to it. Porn gets you to sexual orgasm/completion' (American, 25–34, married, heterosexual). Another memorably comments, 'porn is mostly for wanking, erotica is more towards inspiring the imagination towards wanking, and romance is more about making your heart feel like it's wanking' (Canadian, 25–34, single, lesbian). Despite the fact that the women I spoke with could be considered as pretty sexually liberated, simply by virtue of their engagement with m/m SEM, there is still a certain amount of discomfort in talking about masturbation. One woman describes talking about masturbation as 'like telling someone about the shit you just took—some things are best left private' (American, 25–34, single, heterosexual). Another adds that masturbation is rarely discussed within slash fandom communities, even though she assumes it is a frequent occurrence: 'there seems to be an unspoken rule in fandom that you don't really bring up masturbation. We can *imply* certain things ('I'll be in my bunk', etc.), but I think because we're all sharing these characters that if we went around talking about how we got off thinking of Character A and Character B fucking last night, the characters would start to feel 'sticky' in our minds' (Canadian, 25–34, single, semi-asexual). As Lauren Rosewarne (2011, p. 70) observes, 'we seem to understand intellectually that the majority of people masturbate, [but] there appears to be distaste with piecing the story together and accepting that *someone* is buying the porn and that masturbation often accompanies viewing [or reading]'. Masturbation remains for many a symbol of moral weakness, if no longer an outright perversion. Even if the taboo has weakened significantly in recent years, it is still a stigmatised act, particularly for females (Hogarth & Ingham, 2009; Kaestle & Allen, 2011). Perhaps this is one of the lasting areas of difference between how women and (gay) men engage with m/m SEM.

However, differentiating porn from erotica along these lines ignores the fact that many texts can serve as both masturbatory material *and* a more complex study of emotions and characters. Particularly with regards to written m/m SEM, many participants speak of reading a long story which provides them with a variety of complex pleasures, and then returning to read the sex scenes in isolation time and time again as an accompaniment to masturbation:

> I'll read a long story, and I'll love it—the plot, the characters, everything. If I really love a story and there's some hot sex in it, I'll bookmark it so I can just go back to those bits the next time I'm feeling horny. All the set-up's already there in my mind, so those bits work really well to get me off.

Come to think of it, I used to do the same with [visual] porn. Before I got in to [m/m] I had all these explicit bits from movies saved on my laptop—I knew the characters already so wanking to those clips was much more satisfying than some random porno (British, 35–44, married, heterosexual).

There are also wider social dangers with relying entirely on affective response to distinguish between porn and erotica. As Russ (1985, pp. 90–91) has argued, material that is presented outright as a sexual turn-on—fantasy intended as masturbation fodder—can be a lot less harmful than material presented 'as if it were a thoughtful and complex depiction of real life'. One of my participants expands:

I don't distinguish between erotica and porn. I just find it a kinda problematic separation, in a classist sort of way. Like, it always seems to be "ooh well artistic elegant high-class people like erotica, but all those trashy skanks down there want their awful, disrespectful, dirty porn". And in a kink-shaming and even sex-negative way, too. It always seems to imply that erotica is "better" than porn. But that's stupid. If it encourages unhealthy ideas, that's potentially a problem, but I've seen romance novel "erotica" that encourages even more shitty, misogynistic, rapey ideas than most porn I've seen [or] read (Australian, 18–24, single, bisexual).

...Is Good for the Gander? Differences in Intended Audience

Other differences between porn and erotica raised by participants focus on perceived audiences. Erotica has certainly traditionally been viewed as 'for women', and to this extent regarded as different from pornography, that is aimed at men. While not necessarily taking a Dworkin/MacKinnon stance that views porn as intrinsically harmful or violent towards women, a lot of women in my study view much m/f porn as being sexist and problematic: 'erotica is usually risqué and more likely to be queer, [whereas] porn is the oversexualised media produced by the porn industry that often perpetuates certain incorrect or harmful ideas about sex and is mostly aimed at men, even if it's called "lesbian porn"' (American,

18–24, single, lesbian). As the feminist porn director Erika Lust notes, 'the problem with porn is not that it's porn… It's not that it's explicit sex, I think that bit is great about it. But the bad part is that most of it has very sexist ideas and a very sexist vision of the world' (Lust, in Thompson, 2015). Porn aimed at women—erotica if you will—is seen as being less sexist—more tender and less explicit. However, as several feminist critics note, this could well be a reflection of social conventions that say female sexuality is different from that of men, and that porn must therefore be 'dressed up' and made 'warm, human, funny … with wholly different parameters to male porn' if women are to engage with it (Moran, 2011, p. 35). As one participant states, 'porn supposedly made for women tends to be boring. What's with all the soft, glowing lighting? Do these people think women only have sex in clouds?' (Filipino, 25–34, single, heterosexual).

However, many lab studies[2] would suggest that this soft, glowly cloud sex *is* the kind of porn that women prefer. Pearson and Pollack (1997) found that female undergraduates reported significantly greater subjective levels of arousal when viewing a porn film produced by (the late, great) Candida Royalle, whose company, Femme Productions, focused on films designed for women, than a male-produced porn film. Similarly, Janssen, Carpenter, and Graham (2003) discovered that male and female respondents reported more arousal to film clips selected by their own, rather than the opposite, gender. It would appear that women know what women want, which may also go some way to explaining the popularity of slash fiction. However, as Jane Ward (2013, p. 135) notes, while a large body of research indicates women do indeed have group preferences for 'erotica' as opposed to 'pornography', even these 'female' (or, in some senses, 'feminist') preferences have been 'marketed to us, and arguably mirror simplistic cultural constructions of femininity, such as the notion that women's sexuality is more mental or emotional than physical'. If women feel erotica (or 'porn for women') is the only kind of pornography they can respectably access, then this may explain its popularity. One woman explains, '"erotica" is a term people use to pretend women aren't horndogs too, and also a marketing term for written porn' (American, 25–34, single, bisexual).

Neither can we say with any certainty that porn produced by and for women *is* necessarily categorically different from male-produced pornography. Hardy (2001) argues that *Black Lace* positions itself as feminist, but draws on conventions of male-orientated porn, and although it allows for female erotic subjectivity, old forms of eroticism remain largely intact. Ciclitira (2004) also notes that the owners and beneficiaries of *Black Lace*, as in most porn, are men. However, Sonnet (1999, p. 169) discusses how, set against 'the historical and cultural domination of pornography "for men by men"' *Black Lace* comes with the promise that it has been written by a female author—it is 'erotic fiction by women for women'. As such, Sonnet argues, it claims to 'provide a *woman*-defined space for the enjoyment of sexually explicit material' (Sonnet, 1999, p. 169). To this extent it has much in common with slash fiction, another genre that has been historically viewed as 'by women, for women'. Many women emphasise the importance of this element to their enjoyment of woman-produced erotic fiction:

> For so long it's been taboo for women to find sex hot … You're supposed to have this "slut in the bedroom/lady in the street" mentality and behaviour if you're a woman in American or British society. And for so long we've been forced into seeing heterosexual sex as the only acceptable form of sex that, really, any acknowledgement that a woman can find sex between two other [same sex] people, or between themselves and someone else, as erotic, pleasurable, healthy and *normal* is almost exciting in itself—which is just damn sad. So I say, go girls go! Tell it, tell all about it and don't leave anything out and be proud of it (American, 35–44, married, bisexual).

Bauer (2012, p. 78), however, cautions against taking this to mean that m/m slash texts are therefore intrinsically 'female' in some way: 'By over-emphasising the "feminine" characteristics of slash fiction as a genre that is romantic rather than pornographic, the absolute difference between "men" and "women" is performatively reinstated in scholarly discourse'.

The Thinking Woman's Porn: Differences in Plot and Characterisation

Hardy (2001, p. 438) argues that erotica is a hybrid genre—rooted in the conventions of romance, but learning lessons from the directness of porn—and as with any hybrid 'some individual examples bear a stronger resemblance to one parent than the other'. Hardy concludes that perhaps what really distinguishes women's erotica from porn is less the content of the scenes, than the attempt to provide a much more elaborate context for them—erotica has plot, erotica has characterisation. Many participants share this view, with one explaining: 'erotica has some characterisation—it requires explicit sex, [but] the sex is generally pretty plausible … [and] it often has plot. [In] porn characterisation is not required, the characters may not act like remotely believable humans, [the] sex acts may actually be ludicrously impossible … [and] any plot is pretty flimsy' (American, 25–34, in a polyamorous relationship, queer). In *The Other Victorians* Stephen Marcus (1966) argues that one of pornography's defining features is the elimination of external realities. It exists in 'no place'—the locale, when named at all, is irrelevant to the plot. Similarly, it exists in 'no time'—the significant time elements of the story are only how long a sex act or a series of sex acts last. It has no characterisation, no plot; instead porn 'characteristically develops by unremitting repetition and minute mechanical variation' (Marcus, 1966, p. 279). Pornography is therefore in many ways, as Marcus argues, a utopian genre. It is 'always summertime in pornotopia, and it is a summertime of emotions as well—no one is ever jealous, possessive, or really angry' (Marcus, 1966, p. 276). If we accept this definition of porn, then sex within the context of slash fiction—one of the most popular genres of m/m SEM among my sample—with its reliance on meticulously well-crafted characters and emotional development, is decidedly non-pornographic on all counts.

However, some psychologists have long argued that women are not *necessarily* more invested in plot and characterisation in their SEM than men are, if we look at the content of their sexual fantasies as opposed to their responses in the artificial environment of the lab. Bader (2003, p. 212) observes from looking at Nancy Friday's extensive collection of sexual fantasies, that 'the differences in the form and content of men's and women's fantasies are often quite minimal'—both enjoy quick advancement to the sex act, little in the way of seduction or emotional complexity, employ the use of 'crude' language, and focus on body parts. This leads him to conclude that women want many of the same things as men, but have difficulty in being what he terms 'sexually ruthless' because their guilt and worry about hurting others make them so attuned to the inner states of their partners that 'they are unable to let go and surrender to the rhythms of their own excitement' (Bader, 2003, p. 226). Not all studies support Bader's hypothesis, however. Kimmel and Plante (2002) analysed 340 fantasies from 249 women and 91 men, and found multiple gender differences—from language to sexual activities—in both content and form. Women's were longer, more detailed, and more romantic; men's were more active, with women using 'a more passive linguistic style' (Kimmel & Plante, 2002, p. 72[3]). However, similarly to Ward (2013), Kimmel and Plante also feel these differences are likely to be rooted in social structures and differential sexual scripting. Cultural norms encourage women to cast themselves as fantasy objects of desire, whereas men are taught to see themselves as sexual actors, filled with sexual agency.

Perhaps what is different about women who engage with m/m SEM, then, is that they *do* see themselves as sexual actors—whether they like more explicit 'porn' or more plotty 'erotica', they know what they like and how they like it. Is this an intrinsically 'masculine' quality? Is it simply that these women are male-identified? Let's not forget Henry Jenkins' (1992) claim that m/m readers have, to a certain extent, been socialised as men due to their exposure to male-authored cultural products, particularly books. It is to these books that I will now turn.

Be Your Own Hero: Reading as a Man

Most women who read are, in some ways, already accustomed to reading 'as a man'. Male protagonists are still the majority in genres such as mysteries, thrillers, fantasy, and sci fi, all of which have large female readerships. As one woman recounts, 'reading from a male point of view is probably a preference acquired through habit rather than being a conscious choice. Most of the mainstream books I read are from a male point of view, and I think this is because I prefer to read adventure stories, old 1920s detective novels, and spy stories from 60 years ago' (British, 45–54, single, heterosexual). Even female authors often write from a male perspective, and, indeed, some also view themselves *as* men when they write. The science fiction author Ursula K. Le Guin (2004, p. 3) writes about how she identifies as a man, insomuch as for her, the writer *is* a man: 'That's who I am. I am the generic he, as in … "a writer knows which side his bread is buttered on". That's me, the writer, him. I am a man'. The interaction between a reader and a fictional character is complex and multifaceted (Cohen, 2001), and assuming that female readers or viewers can't or wouldn't want to identify with male characters requires taking an extremely limited view of the audience's power to imagine and the text's power to evoke. After all, Tennison (in Green, Jenkins, & Jenkins, 1998, p. 19) notes that we frequently read about characters who are completely removed from us: 'Why do we read (with relish) about space pirates, neurotic rock stars, or melancholy Danish princes? Fiction isn't about reasonable wish-fulfilment or simple identity matches'.

Jenkins (1992) describes three groups of women who he sees as reacting differently to commercial texts: (1) those who primarily read women's fiction and enjoy the female voice, (2) those who more fully assimilate masculine reading interests and enjoy fiction on those terms, and (3) women who experience conflict between socialised interests and commercial products and who may therefore 'colonise' masculine media texts by reconceptualising stories to focus on interpersonal relationships (e.g. slash). The vast majority of women in my study utterly reject the idea of being confined to one of these three groups (this is not to say they don't exist, rather, they do not describe the women I spoke with). On the whole they liked all sorts of texts—from chick lit to Hemmingway (the archetype of the 'male' author)—as one explains, 'I like reading from Harry Potter's POV as much as I love reading Elizabeth Bennet's' (Belgian, 25–34, married, heterosexual). However, there is a real distinction in their preferences for erotic fiction, where 41 per cent of my sample prefer reading from the male perspective (6 per cent preferring a female POV and 53 per cent having no preference), and general fiction, where only 10 per cent prefer reading from the male perspective (10 per cent preferring a female POV and 77 per cent having no preference)—so maybe I should not be so quick to dismiss Jenkins' categories, if we take them as applying specifically to *erotic* literature.

In the field of erotic m/f romances it has long been known that women readers have a soft spot for male POVs. However, up until the 1980s Harlequin authors were actually prevented from using the male POV by their publishers, who clearly operated solidly within the idea that the (female) reader always identifies with the heroine (Kinsale, 1992). Burley (2003) notes a distinct shift to the hero's voice in many erotic romance novels from the mid-1990s onwards. In modern texts the POV often shifts between the heroine and the hero, suggesting that many women readers have no problem identifying with the subjective experience of an ostensibly male character. In fact, women actively welcome the male voice. In Thurston's 1985 survey of romance readers, over 70 per cent wanted the hero's POV included in the novel; it was the number one 'most-liked story attribute'. Romance writer Laura Kinsale (1992, p. 39) argues that women enjoy identifying with the hero as much, if not more than, the heroine, noting that 'within the [female] reader there are masculine elements that can and need to be realised'.

In fact, Kinsale (1992, p. 32) asserts that 'in romance it is the hero who carries the book'. She claims that in the dynamics of reading a m/f romance, the female reader *is* the hero, and also is the heroine-as-object-of-the-hero's-interest (the place-holder heroine): 'the reader very seldom *is* the heroine in the sense meant by the term 'reader identification'. There is always an element of analytical distance' (Kinsale, 1992, p. 32). She refutes Radway's (1984) position that the heroine is at the centre of the book, affirming, 'I think she is wrong. One hundred percent dead blind wrong. I flatly believe that *the man carries the book*' (Kinsale, 1992, p. 36). While Carol Thurston (1987) observes that 'readers are no longer satisfied with seeing only how the New Hero responds, they now want to look inside his head', Kinsale goes one step further, stating, 'romance readers have never had any intention of stopping so short as a mere look' (1992, p. 34). As one of participants describes,

> I have a sneaking suspicion [I like erotic fiction from a male POV] because I've always wondered what it would be like to be a man. Even as a child I

wondered what it would be like to be a man when I grew up. It's not that I have any issue with my own gender identity, it was just something that interested me. And whenever I thought about it from a sexual point of view—especially as a horny teenager—it was always men together, possibly because it was men I myself was attracted to (British, 25–34, single, heterosexual).

For Kinsale (1992, p. 37) the desire to experience the male POV may be a result of sexual admiration: 'a simple, erotic, and free-hearted female joy in the existence of desirable maleness. Hey, women *like* men'. However, she feels the preferential hero-identification exhibited by readers of erotic romances—and, indeed, the readers of m/m SEM in this study—needs further examining. What does it mean to a woman to feel—to want to keenly feel—what the male character feels as she reads? Kinsale (1992, p. 37) believes that when a woman reader identifies with a hero, she can 'realise the maleness in herself'. She is then able to 'experience the sensation of living inside a body suffused with masculine power and grace…, [she] can explore anger and ruthlessness and passion and pride and gentleness and vulnerability … In short, she can *be* a man' (Kinsale, 1992, p. 37). Kinsale stresses, however, that this is a *fictional* man, and does not necessarily mean the reader wishes to be a man in real life. Writing on slash fiction, Joanna Russ (1985, p. 89) agrees: it is not so much that the female readers of explicit m/m slash want to *become* male, rather they want the 'sexual intensity, sexual enjoyment, the freedom to choose' which is generally only afforded to men and to male characters. Looking at it this way, it is, as Lynne Segal (1994, p. 238) notes, 'all too easy to see why in fantasy women may choose male figures for erotic identification, as well as for objects of desire.' When reading m/m SEM women not only get to sexually admire a hero, they also get to *be* a hero.

Building on this, Chen (2007) presents a model of reading that has much in common with the 'genderfucked' gaze I discussed in Chap. 2 with regards to viewing pornography. In this model of reading, the imagined 'self' has the freedom to mutate into alternative manifestations. As Chen (2007, p. 38) explains, 'in offering and guiding the reader's fantasy pleasure, the romance reader may take on a variety of positions in multiple identifications with the heroine, hero, or the process of living, and therefore experience pleasure through each position'. Hence, 'pleasure is produced when the old fixed boundaries are eroded and new possibilities are tried on' (Chen, 2007, p. 38). Saxey (2002) feels that a woman reading slash nearly always engages in this mode of reading, seeing the process as necessitating a fluidity, a crossing over, between genders that goes beyond what happens in more traditional forms of writing and reading. By identifying with one or more of the gay characters, readers don't just take on a traditionally male gender role, but also a traditionally male sexual position, which allows them to experience themselves as penetrator (as well as penetrated). Meyer (2010, p. 233) has called this process 'creative transvestism': 'like putting on drag, creative transvestism is a technique that is not just available for transsexuals, but for everyone. The trans-gendered identification of… [BL and slash] fans and authors might last for the short moment of the romantic or sex scene, or for a lifetime' (Meyer, 2010, p. 247). For a number of women in my study, this 'creative transvestism' is not unique to their experience of the reading or watching of explicit m/m texts—it is something that is a key part of how they identify on a sexual level: 55 per cent of participants state that they imagine themselves as a man during the course of their sexual fantasies. It is this group of women—over half the sample—that I now want to discuss.

'I Always Knew I Was Different…': Tomboys and Girlfags

Traditional Western thinking holds that sex (if not gender) and sexual orientations are inborn, unchangeable, and organised in dichotomies such as man/woman, male/female, gay/straight, lesbian/gay-male, transsexual/cissexual etc. While this has been resolutely rejected by many queer scholars and activists,[4] it remains a pervasive idea. However, Meyer (2010, p. 233) points out that discussing both BL and slash fans within this framework is difficult, as they present us with a world where 'the boundaries of sexual orientation and gender are in flux and sometimes non-existent: a world in which straight characters can suddenly turn gay…, swap social gender and even physical sex…, and nothing can be taken for granted where sex and gender is concerned'. The process of identifying across the conventional notion of gendered and sexed dichotomies is something that Shiller (2004) refers to as 'Gender Meltdown' (similar to the concept of genderfuck introduced in Chap. 2). For many queer scholars the world of Gender Meltdown is an exciting world, full of freedom and play. For, as Noble (2007, p. 158) notes, 'there is something thrilling about disconnecting the biological body from the desiring gaze'.

However, this is not to say that Gender Meltdown does not have its downsides, or that women who cross-identify find it easy to express themselves in our society. In *Female Masculinity* (1998), Jack Halberstam encourages us to see masculinity as a quality independent of gender, one that can occur in women as well as men. However, in later work, Halberstam (2002, p. 358) shows that, while seen as admirable in men, masculinity in women has often been seen as highly undesirable—its negativity strengthened by linking it to ugliness and monstrosity. Relatedly, McNair (2013, p. 98) points out that there has always been a link between women who express an interest in explicit sexual representation and a concordant lack of femininity, arguing that 'women, bad girls who did not play by the rules … were branded as "tomboys", as deviants and weirdos, as figures of fun'. Salmon and Symons (2004, p. 99) also posit that female slashers might be 'disproportionately former tomboys', although they make the link more because of the adventure and sci-fi aspects of the genre than because of the cross-identification that occurs. Hogan and Hudson (1998, p. 556) describe tomboyism as a 'temporary visa to male territory', and note that it is considered 'acceptable' in Western culture until age 12 or 13—which is interesting, seeming as it is unlikely that cross-identification simply 'stops' at the point of puberty; instead it is more likely that women become less free to express 'masculine' elements of identification. Additionally, Hogan and Hudson (1998) point out that the tomboy identity can be experienced by women who develop into either straight or queer adults, and that it crosses racial, ethnic, class, and regional lines with only slight variation. One woman I spoke to combines several of these elements, when she explains:

I do worry that [if] people [know I'm into m/m] they won't 'get' it or may be freaked out by the homosexual nature ... or will find it too subversive or 'weird' in general, sadly. Or that they will see the perhaps even more intimate thing about it for me ... which is that it's in some way a 'trans' act, as it were. I am often imagining myself *as* a gay male in these erotic situations. I imagine that may be challenging to some people. That being said, with my most intimate friends, sister, and my fiancé..., I have talked openly over the years about how, while I am actually very happy in my female physicality and body and so don't feel trans or queer in that sense, there had always—even pre-slash-reading days—been part of me that identifies with maleness and with gay maleness in particular... As a very intense tomboy as a child, I often identified with the male protagonist in the piece: Peter Pan, Aladdin, Robin Hood. I think this had as much to do ... with the fact that that they clearly had a lot more fun and got to do a lot more and have a lot more adventures than Wendy, Jasmine, or Maid Marion in said things. Still, it was very easy for me to imagine myself in those male roles, even from an early age. I have thought about this in general a lot with regards to feminism. The accepted wisdom in Hollywood ... is that men come out to see movies about men. The underlying assumption here, of course, is that women will come out to see movies about men or women—being that there are still so few women-cast movies and so many all-men movies— which implies to me that women have always been expected to 'identify', as it were, across gender lines. They have been forced to exercise what I would say is actually a normal [and] very wonderful human function and identify with *humans*, full stop, regardless of gender, much more than men have. (American, 25–34, in a relationship, heterosexual)

There has been increasing acknowledgement in the literature that women[5] might be more prone to this kind of Gender Meltdown than men. Jacobs (2007) discusses the concept of the 'cross-voyeur', applying it to internet porn users who peruse selections beyond the boundaries of their niche sites and communities, and notes that cross-voyeurs are often, although not exclusively, women. This cross-identification is not limited to any particular type of media. According to Nielsen ratings in 2001, 52 per cent of the (US) viewers of *Queer As Folk* were women, which surprised the show's producer, Shelia Hockin (in Shiller, 2004). Shiller (2004) postulates that 'straight women might be the ultimate Queer quotient when it comes to watching *Queer as Folk* by inhabiting that twilight-zone, the marginal, the Other—qualities of the Queer... Women now have fantasy access to back rooms they could never get into before. The straight female fans might be fags in mental drag; they might be Queer as folk.'

Academics have also made links between cross-identification during media consumption and transsexuality more generally. In an interview with Liz Kotz, Judith Butler comments:

> What strikes me as extremely interesting is there's a very *mundane* sense of transsexuality that most people who theorise on gender or sexuality haven't yet taken into account, and it has to do with the possibility of cross-gender identification... I think that what happens in cross-gendered identification is extremely interesting and could be understood on a continuum with transsexuality. (Butler, in Kotz, 1992, p. 88)

Controversial data from the fields of psychology and physiology suggests that women with higher testosterone levels (Udry, 1988) and higher masculinity scores on the Bem Sex-Role Inventory (Daitzman & Zuckerman, 1980) have a stronger interest in sex than other women. Walsh (1999) argues that women who are interested in porn may be closer to men in terms of attitudes and behaviours relating to sexuality than those who do not. It may then be that a number of women who enjoy m/m SEM identify as 'gay men trapped in women's bodies' (Meyer, 2010; Thorn, 2004). While some have rejected such claims as pathologising (Nagaike, 2003), others have embraced it. Sedgwick (1993, p. 209) famously wrote about herself that, although she identified as a woman, her identification as a gay person was firmly a male one: 'identification 'as' a gay man', adding that one of her most formative early influences was 'a viscerally intense, highly speculative (not to say inventive) cross-identification with gay men and gay male cultures' (Sedgwick, 1993, p. 14).[6] Some queer participants felt similarly, with one explaining, 'despite the fact that my significant other is female and we've been together for thirty years, [f/f] is of little interest in my fantasy life. Plus, my significant other and I relate to each other in our shared fantasies as "male"' (American, 45–54, in a relationship). Similarly Jill Nagle (1997,

p. 122) writes about her perception of her sexual and gender identity, stating, 'I didn't want to be boxed and dismissed as "female". I belonged in the space marked "BOY'S ROOM". I wanted in; to the clubhouse and into the hot house and into some juicy boyflesh'. She discusses her own experience of being attracted to a gay man where she thought, 'I want this man… I want this man as only a man wanting another man can want' (Nagle, 1997, p. 123). Nagle (1997, p. 125) struggles with how to define herself: 'A fag hag? Not quite. A bi-dyke with a dildo in tow? Closer, but… I wanted to lovingly wrestle my equal in strength to the ground; I wanted to feel our cocks together. Our real cocks, warm and throbbing…'. Indeed, it is difficult to think of how best to describe this phenomenon, although many have tried.

The terms 'girlfag' and 'transfag' were coined in the late 1990s to describe people who are female-assigned at birth and feel an intense fascination for, and identification with, gay men (Queen & Schimel, 1997). Bagemihl (1997) compares slash fans to 'fag hags' and female-to-gay-male [f-t-g-m] trans folk, noting how similar many of their narratives are when asked to talk about how they came to realise what they found sexually exciting. He takes a statement from a f-t-g-m trans person, and comments on its similarity with statements made by slashers (indeed, we can see the resemblance to some of the participant comments included in Chap. 6): 'My first sexual fantasies were of a man hugging and caressing a boy and of men kissing each other… What made gay men more sexually attractive than straight men? Simply the fact that they were aroused by other *men*' (in Bagemihl, 1997, p. 387, emphasis added). According to Meyer (2010) the difference between a girlfag and a transfag is one of degree rather than quality—she observes that a person might strongly identify with, and as, a gay man, while still also maintaining a female identity. One of the women I spoke to provides an example of what this might look like:

> when I'm actually in my sexual fantasies, it's almost always as if I've transformed or been transformed into a guy… I very, very rarely fantasise about people I actually know—it usually squicks me out—and I think there has only been one person that I've *extensively* fantasised about having sex with—because me plus a person I know *really* squicks me out. He was one

of two male roommates I had that were friends, and I kinda had a crush on him but also kinda 'slashed' him and his friend together in my mind. The fantasy I had about him was basically that I was a shapeshifter and he asked me to shift into Friend since he had a hardcore crush on Friend but Friend was straight. So I did and he fucked me and it was *amazing*. Possibly the best thing my id has ever come up with (American, 18–24, single, queer).

While Bagemihl (1997, p. 397) argues that we need to encourage and cultivate this 'spirit of polymorphous perversity' in order to 'help forge a new vision of society, one that is radically polygendered', other scholars have been more critical. Walters (1996, p. 857) is concerned that this viewpoint leads to a tendency to be 'like, let us make a theory from our own sexual practice', such as, '"I'm a cross-dressing femme who likes to use a dildo while watching gay male porn videos with my fuck buddy who sometimes likes to do it with gay men. Hmm, what kind of theory can I make from that?"… The notion of "the personal is political" [should] … not mean "let us construct a theory from individual personal experiences"'. Rather Walters feels in order to identify as a trans, or queer, there needs to be 'some notion of collective experience, shared experience' (Walters, 1996, p. 857).

It is also possible there might be something about m/m SEM that lends itself to cross-identification. Writing about the importance of gay porn in the gay community, Fejes (2002, p. 98) argues that, for the gay male, 'sexuality and identity is articulated desire, which itself is a fluid construct'. He points out that there is no 'normal' way to be gay that is reinforced through law, medical or physiological knowledge, custom, or socialisation. Instead, for the gay male, there is no extrinsic goal to a gay sexuality other than the fulfilment of its own desire, meaning there is 'the possibility for the creation of many different homosexual identities and sexualities' (Fejes, 2002, p. 99)—including, perhaps, the gay-male identified woman. I will go on to discuss the ethical and social ramifications of women identifying with and as gay men, and of women producing and consuming m/m SEM in Chap. 8. However, the possibility of cross-identification also raises questions about whether or not women *can* feasibility 'pass' as men, gay or otherwise, in terms of the texts they create. Can women write 'authentic' m/m erotica? And is there such a thing as a 'male' authorial voice to begin with? I will address these questions in the following section.

Create Your Own Hero: Writing as a Man

It is not clear that erotic texts are firmly gendered in any meaningful way. Paasonen (2010) points out that written erotica is *not* an exclusively female domain. Reader feedback on the Literotica website suggests that men and women contribute as both writers and readers, 'making the idea that there are characteristically "male" or "female" modes of sexually explicit writing unconvincing' (Paasonen 2010, p. 147). It is, however, a pervasive myth. Hardy (2001) discusses how for many years the identity of the author of *The Story of O* was contested, with some claiming such an explicit text must be written by a man. The confirmation that it was, indeed, written by a woman shows that 'one's biological sex does not determine the nature of one's discourse, nor does one's discourse reveal one's true nature' (Hardy, 2001, p. 448). Likewise, Sharp (1999) expresses her exasperation that many journalists believe *Black Lace* books have secretly been written by men because they feel that women's writing would be softer and more romantic.

Not only does the notion of women's writing as intrinsically more soft or romantic ignore the contribution of men to the romance genre—e.g. the phenomenal success of male authors such as Nicholas Sparks—it also ignores the fact that m/m romantic fiction aimed at a gay male audience often follows the traditionally 'feminine' happily-ever-after convention, such as Vincent Virga's *Gaywick*. In addition, there is a long history of women involved with writing m/m romantic and erotic fiction, including writers such as Marguerite Yourcenar, Mary Renault, Louise Welsh, Diana Gabaldon, Annie Proulx and Anne Rice. Interestingly, though, women writers are sometimes excluded from the 'gay canon'. James Keller, in his study *Anne Rice and Sexual Politics*, argues that the 'authenticity' of the depictions of male homosexuality in Rice's novels is not only undermined by the narrative conclusions, but also by the 'conventionality of her [personal] life [married to a man and family orientated]' (Keller, 2000, p. 1). Winnberg, Fåhraeus and Jonsson (2008, p. 3) note that very little has been done in terms of understanding how 'female writers not only write *about* men, but *write* men (and perhaps even write *as* men)'.

Most of the work that does exist constitutes female writers' own reflections on the process. For example, English scholar turned romance novelist Linda Barlow (1992, p. 50) writes about how her male POV character represents 'the darker side of [her]self, the powerful male figure on whom [she] was projecting all [her] own aggressiveness and rage'. She adds, 'as a male, he could do all the things that had been traditionally forbidden to me. He personified the freer, wilder, more libidinous self. On some deep level, I *was* [my male hero]'. Calvin Thomas (2006, p. 5) is therefore alive to the queer possibilities writing can offer, observing that a key way for heterosexuals to be queer is 'not so much 'in the sheets' (taken as a metonym for fucking) as '*on* the sheets' (taken as a metonym for writing)'. Similarly, Winnberg et al. (2008, p. 4) note that while Halberstam's (1998) study of female masculinity 'deals with masculine women, one can extrapolate from [his] arguments a corollary critical engagement with female writers' textual masculinity' (Winnberg et al., 2008, p. 4).

There may be an explanation for this ability to write across genders provided within the field of psychology—and it may be particularly apt for this group of women, given that so many of them (74 per cent) are involved in *creating* m/m SEM in some way—writing, drawing, collaging, vidding, website designing. Csikszentmihalyi (1996) notes a predisposition he refers to as 'psychological androgyny' apparent in the creative mind-set. He observes that, in nearly all cultures, men are brought up to be 'masculine', and to disregard and repress those aspects of their temperament that the culture regards as 'feminine', whereas women are expected to do the opposite. However, creative individuals 'to a certain extent escape this rigid gender stereotyping' (Csikszentmihalyi, 1996, p. 45). When tests of masculinity/femininity are given to young people, we see that creative and talented women are more dominant and tough than other women, and creative men are more sensitive and less aggressive than their male peers (Norlander, Erixon, & Archer, 2000; Stoltzfus, Nibbelink, Vredenburg, & Hyrum, 2011).

Csikszentmihalyi (1996, p. 45) claims that psychological androgyny refers to a person's ability to be 'at the same time aggressive and nurturing, sensitive and rigid, dominant and submissive' regardless of gender.

This gives them a wider behavioural repertoire and more responses to draw from—hence its link with creativity. Similarly, Jayne Stake's (1997) research on how people integrate traditionally 'masculine' and 'feminine' characteristics suggests that successful 'real life' integrations are associated with well-being and enhanced self-esteem. When called upon to be both expressive *and* instrumental, participants in her study felt better about various work situations they described. Building on Stake's work, Kimmel and Plante (2002, p. 75) ask if sexuality might be another real-life situation where 'the merging of traditionally gender-linked traits could benefit participants', suggesting that a combination of stereotypically masculine and feminine sexual behaviours could lead to both genders reaping the benefits of 'women's increased sexual agency and men's increased intimacy'.

While both Halberstam's notion of female masculinity (and Winnberg, Fahraeus and Jonsson's riff on it with their idea of female textual masculinity) and Csikszentmihalyi's notion of psychological androgyny could explain why so many women feel able to write from a male POV, this does not necessarily show that they are able to do it successfully. Indeed, many scholars (particularly from the field of BL manga) have argued that they cannot.

'Men with Heart Boners': The Perils of Writing Sex Across Genders

On the one hand, slash characters are often 'men in every sense of the word' (Salmon & Symons, 2001, p. 88), not only possessing many traits classically associated with hegemonic masculinity—strength, bravery, leadership—but also occupying traditionally male 'professions'—police officers, space explorers, secret agents, soldiers, superheroes. On the other hand, a criticism that has long been levelled at both slash and BL characters is that they come across as far too 'feminine' to convince as genuine men. McLelland (2000, p. 13) argues that women writers draw upon the mainstream representation of homosexual men as 'somehow feminine', but 'treat this stereotype favourably' creating the figure of the 'beautiful youth', an androgynous being who possesses a 'female' capacity for sensuality and emotional intuition, but yet experiences 'all the advantages of a male body'. Matsui (1993) similarly believes that although the characters in BL comics are boys, female readers experience them in the same way as they do the protagonists of heterosexual manga romances, that is, as the self, not as the other. She maintains that the boys in BL are 'the girls' displaced selves', and that their appeal lies in the fact that they can be portrayed as possessing sexual agency and aggressive desire in a way that female characters cannot: 'they signify … the possession of the phallus as opposed to the feminine "lack"' (Matsui, 1993, p. 178). The fact the characters are nevertheless boys despite their androgynous appearance and feminine attributes means that they provide female readers with the freedom to imagine themselves acting beyond the strict boundaries placed on them in Japanese society (Shamoon, 2004). Fujimoto (1998) argues that this frees girls to imagine an idealised fantasy of love between boys in a sentimental way that does not threaten their own sense of self or world view: 'compared to the pure (that is, imaginary) love in boy-love comics, heterosexual sex seems frightening and dirty' (Shamoon, 2004, p. 97). Russ (1985) makes a similar argument with regards to slash fic, claiming that such stories are not really about male homosexuals, rather they depict a female version of sexuality acted out on and by male bodies. Homosexuality, then, is merely a trope that serves to purify romantic relationships from the 'tarnished male-female framework of heterosexual love' (Fujimoto, 1991, p. 283).

Other scholars disagree with this interpretation. Stanley (2010, p. 100) has strongly critiqued the psychoanalytical reading of male characters as women readers' displaced selves, saying that such a reading 'emphasises negative, compensatory motivations, leaving women, as so often in non-feminist psychoanalytic theory, making up for a lack of something'. She also, pertinently, asks why, if both characters are male, a female reader would 'limit [her] identification merely to the more effeminate one, especially if female readers are seeking to compensate for a feminine "lack"' (Stanley, 2010, p. 100). Wood (2013, pp. 45–46) also roundly rejects this interpretation, arguing that to view homosexual narratives as merely a cover for heterosexual fantasies is 'a reverse form of closeting that rejects surface-level homoeroticism and pushes it back into the realm of connotation while reinforcing prevailing heterocentrist paradigms' which have maintained that 'expressions of queerness are *sub*-textual, *sub*-cultural, *alternative* readings, or pathetic and delusional attempts to see something that isn't there' (Doty, 1993, p. xii). Neither is it an interpretation that finds much support among the women I spoke to. One complains, 'I often have to defend my preferences of writing [and] reading. Men would never excuse themselves over liking two girls together, but as a woman, I get answers like "oh, you just compensate for your non-existing relationship status" or "you just write stories about women trapped in men's bodies because you're a feminist" or some such, or [they] just ridicule it and I have to argue against it' (German, 25–34, single, heterosexual).

Slash readers and writers have also been criticised for a tendency to particularly 'feminise' one partner in the pairing. Driscoll (2006, p. 84) argues that many fanfic communities 'understand slash pairings as having a more or less feminised "bottom" and a more active "top"'. Salmon and Symons (2001, p. 85) agree, claiming that in slash the 'main POV character [tends] to be the smaller of the two, lighter in colouring, physically weaker, more seductive, more in touch with his emotions, and quicker to perceive the existence of mutual love'. They also assert that this more 'feminine' character—the central POV—tends to bottom more frequently. Kinsella (2000, p. 117) believes that female readers will then often identify with the 'slightly more effeminate male of a couple'. However, it is very unclear how or why these scholars reached this conclusion. Due to the prevalence of slash fic from a broad range of fandoms it is extremely difficult to draw any overarching conclusions about who tends to do what to whom, or how central POV characters are portrayed. In my own—naturally limited—experience, I have seen what they describe happen. I have also seen the exact opposite happen. Generally, women in my sample refute this perspective, with one woman complaining, 'I am really, *really* tired of the fandom clichés that assume that in m/m fiction, the bottom equals feminine and the top equals masculine. Really, really tired of it. Make it stop!' (American, 45–54, married, bisexual). The majority (87 per cent) of women in my study have no preference for erotic fiction written from either a 'top' (insertive partner during anal sex) or 'bottom' (receptive partner during anal sex) perspective (with 9 per cent having a preference for 'bottom' perspective stories and 4 per cent having a preference for 'top' perspective stories). In terms of identification, participants *are* more likely to identify with the 'bottom' (26 per cent) than the 'top' (6 per cent) when reading or watching SEM, mainly because being 'female bodied' they can 'relate to the sensations of being penetrated more' (American, 18–24, single, pansexual), or, as one woman notes in dismay, 'Jesus—it's all because I identify with the idea of being penetrated, isn't it?' (American, 18–24, single, bisexual). Again, though, the majority (68 per cent) identify as both, depending on their mood, the nature of the media they are engaging with, or any number of other factors. Many women utterly reject the top/bottom convention in its entirety, with one woman affirming, '[identifying as being a] top [or] a bottom really squicks me out. As a bi female, I've never felt like my real-life relationships have been defined by my sexual positions, because it varies from encounter to encounter' (American, 25–34, in a relationship, bisexual). The majority of women prefer 'top/bottom roles [that] are interchangeable, depending on the participants' mood at the moment' (American, 55–64, married, heterosexual), with one adding 'hell, [I like it when] they switch mid-fuck' (American, 35–44, single, heterosexual). As Morrissey (2008, p. 97) has argued, the idea that one of the pairing must take on a 'female' role 'overlooks the work being done to broaden and alter men's sexual roles, moving away from the binaries of active/passive or top/bottom to something more flexible and open' (Morrissey, 2008, p. 97). One woman elucidates, 'it boggles me when people get so obsessive about topping and bottoming. I mean, power dynamics *are* crucial to how hot I find a thing, but penetration is not the be-all and end-all of power and control in sex' (British, 35–44, single, demisexual). It also overlooks the fact that some women engage with m/m SEM precisely because there *aren't* women involved (not their bodies, not their emotions)—in fact, the primary reason given by some of my respondents for what they enjoy about m/m pornography is the absence of female actresses and characters. It is these women which I will now address.

Notes

1. While the terms 'top' and 'bottom' are rightfully controversial, laden as they are with connotations of power and control (as well as risking conflation with BDSM roles) I use them here and in my survey as they remain the most commonly used terms within m/m SEM fan communities to understand receptive and insertive anal sex partners.

2. Laboratory studies can add to our knowledge of women's sexual responses, and help us to better understand what turns women on. However, as in all areas of psychology, there is a limit to what lab studies can tell us. The artificial environment of the lab is not analogous to the environments in which people would usually engage with SEM, and the rules and regulations that govern behaviour in the lab mean that participants cannot respond in the ways they might in the real world. For example, in many studies measuring response to SEM participants are not allowed to masturbate (as it would affect the results). This is in direct contrast to the world outside the lab, where pornography and masturbation 'go together like a BBQ and a beer... [Where, in fact] the main effect of exposure to pornography *is* masturbation' (McKee, Albury, & Lumby, 2008, p. 79, emphasis added).

3. See also Leitenberg and Henning's (1995) meta-analysis of sexual fantasy literature which found very similar results.

4. For further insight, I recommend this easy-to-follow blog post on the sex/ gender controversy by Will at Skepchick: http://skepchick.org/2013/10/ 44379/. (accessed 7 December 2017).

5. I realise the irony of using this term when writing about gender and sex fluidity—I mean, simply, people who self-identify as women during their day-to-day lives.

6. Sedgwick's claim to '*be* a gay man' has faced a fair amount of backlash from within the queer community, something I will return to in Chap. 8.

References

Bacon-Smith, C. (1992). *'Enterprising women': Television fandom and the creation of popular myth*. Philadelphia: University of Pennsylvania Press.

Bader, M. J. (2003). *Arousal: The secret logic of sexual fantasies*. London: Macmillan.

Bagemihl, B. (1997). Surrogate phonology and transsexual faggotry: A linguistic analogy for uncoupling sexual orientation from gender identity. In A. Livia & K. Hall (Eds.), *Queerly phrased: Language, gender, and sexuality* (pp. 380–401). Oxford: Oxford University Press.

Barlow, L. (1992). The androgynous writer: Another point of view. In J. A. Krentz (Ed.), *Dangerous men and adventurous women: Romance writers on the appeal of the romance* (pp. 45–52). Pennsylvania: University of Pennsylvania Press.

Bauer, C. K. (2012). *Naughty girls and gay male romance/porn: Slash fiction, Boys' Love Manga, and other works by female 'cross-voyeurs' in the US academic discourses.* Hamburg: Anchor Academic Publishing.

Brennan, J. (2014a). Not 'from my hot little ovaries': How slash manips pierce reductive assumptions. *Continuum: Journal of Media & Cultural Studies, 28*(2), 247–264.

Brennan, J. (2014b). 'Fandom is full of pearl clutching old ladies': Nonnies in the online slash closet. *International Journal of Cultural Studies, 17*(4), 363–380.

Burley, S. (2003). What's a nice girl like you doing in a book like this? Homoerotic reading and popular romance. In S. Strehle & M. P. Carden (Eds.), *Doubled plots: Romance and history* (pp. 127–146). Jackson: University Press of Mississippi.

Chen, E. Y. (2007). Forms of pleasure in the reading of popular romance: Psychic and cultural dimensions. In S. Goade (Ed.), *Empowerment versus oppression: Twenty-first century views of popular romance novels* (pp. 30–41). Newcastle: Cambridge Scholars Publishing.

Ciclitira, K. (2004). Pornography, women and feminism: Between pleasure and politics. *Sexualities, 7*(3), 281–301.

Cohen, J. (2001). Defining identification: A theoretical look at the identification of audiences with media characters. *Mass Communication & Society, 4*(3), 245–264.

Csikszentmihalyi, M. (1996). *Creativity: Flow and the psychology of discovery and invention.* New York: Harper Collins.

Cumberland, S. (2003). Private uses of cyberspace: Women, desire and fan culture. In D. Thorburn & H. Jenkins (Eds.), *Rethinking media change: The aesthetics of transition* (pp. 261–279). Cambridge, MA: The MIT Press.

Daitzman, R., & Zuckerman, M. (1980). Disinhibitory sensation-seeking, personality, and gonadal hormones. *Personality and Individual Difference, 1*, 103–110.

de Beauvoir, S. (1949/1973). *The second sex*. New York: Vintage Books.

Doane, M. A. (1991). *Femmes fatals: Feminism, film theory, and psychoanalysis*. London: Routledge.

Doty, A. (1993). *Making things perfectly queer: Interpreting mass culture*. Minneapolis: University of Minnesota Press.

Driscoll, C. (2006). One true pairing: The romance of pornography and the pornography of romance. In K. Hellekson & K. Busse (Eds.), *Fan fiction and fan communities in the age of the internet* (pp. 79–96). London: McFarland.

Dworkin, A. (1981). *Pornography: Men possessing women*. London: The Women's Press.

Dworkin, A. (1992). Against the male flood: Censorship, pornography, and equality. In C. Itzin (Ed.), *Pornography: Women, violence, and civil liberties* (pp. 515–535). Oxford: Oxford University Press.

Dworkin, A., & MacKinnon, C. A. (1988). *Pornography and civil rights: A new day for women's equality*. Organizing Against Pornography. Retrieved from http://www.nostatusquo.com/ACLU/dworkin/other/ordinance/newday/TOC.htm

English, D., Hollibaugh, A., & Rubin, G. (1981). Talking sex: A conversation on sexuality and feminism. *Socialist Review, 58*, 43–62.

Fejes, F. (2002). Bent passions: Heterosexual masculinity, pornography, and gay male identity. *Sexuality & Culture, 6*(3), 95–115.

Fujimoto, Y. (1991). Shojo manga ni okeru 'shonen ai' no imi [The meaning of 'boys' love' in shojo manga]. *Nyu feminizumu rebuy* [*New Feminism Review*], May, 2, pp. 280–284.

Fujimoto, Y. (1998). *Watashi no ibasho wa doko ni aru no? Shojo manga ga utusu kokoro no katachi* [Where do I belong? The shape of the heart as reflected in girls' comics]. Tokyo: Gakuyo Shobo.

Green, S., Jenkins, C., & Jenkins, H. (1998). 'Normal female interest in men bonking': Selections from the Terra Nostra Underground and Strange Bedfellows. In C. Harris & A. Alexander (Eds.), *Theorising fandom: Fans, subculture and identity* (pp. 9–38). New Jersey: Hampton Press.

Halberstam, J. (1998). *Female masculinity*. Durham, NC: Duke University press.

Halberstam, J. (2002). The good, the bad, and the ugly: Men, women, and masculinity. In J. Kegan Gardiner (Ed.), *Masculinity studies* (pp. 344–367). New York: Columbia University Press.

Hardy, S. (2001). More Black Lace: Women, eroticism and subjecthood. *Sexualities, 4*(4), 435–453.

Hogan, S., & Hudson, L. (1998). *Completely queer: The gay and lesbian encyclopaedia*. New York: Henry Holt.

Hogarth, H., & Ingham, R. (2009). Masturbation among young women and associations with sexual health: An exploratory study. *Journal of Sex Research, 46*(6), 558–567.

Horn, T. (2016, March 21). Why the dichotomy between porn and erotica is false and destructive. *The Establishment*. Retrieved from http://www.theestablishment.co/2016/03/21/why-the-dichotomy-between-porn-and-erotica-is-false-and-destructive-steinem/

Jacobs, K. (2007). Academic cult erotica: Fluid beings or a cubicle of our own? *Cinema Journal, 46*(4), 126–129.

Janssen, E., Carpenter, D., & Graham, C. A. (2003). Selecting films for sex research: Gender differences in erotic film preference. *Archives of Sexual Behaviour, 32*, 243–251.

Jenkins, H. (1992). *Textual poachers: Television fans and participatory culture*. New York: Routledge.

Juffer, J. (1998). *At home with pornography: Women, sex & everyday life*. New York: New York University Press.

Kaestle, C., & Allen, K. (2011). The role of masturbation in healthy sexual development: Perceptions of young adults. *Archives of Sexual Behaviour, 40*(5), 983–994.

Keller, J. R. (2000). *Anne rice and sexual politics: The early novels*. Jefferson, NC: McFarland & Company.

Kimmel, M. S., & Plante, R. F. (2002). The gender of desire: The sexual fantasies of women and men. *Gendered Sexualities, 6*, 55–77.

Kinsale, L. (1992). The androgynous reader: Point of view in the romance. In J. A. Krentz (Ed.), *Dangerous men and adventurous women: Romance writers on the appeal of the romance* (pp. 31–44). Pennsylvania: University of Pennsylvania Press.

Kinsella, S. (2000). *Adult manga: Culture and power in contemporary Japanese society*. Richmond: Curzon Press.

Kotz, L. (1992). The body you want: Liz Kotz interviews Judith Butler. *Artforum, 31*(3), 82–89.

Le Guin, U. K. (2004). *The wave in the mind: Talks and essays on the writer, the reader, and the imagination*. Boulder, CO: Shambhala Publications.

Leiblum, S. R. (2001). Review: Women, sex, and the internet. *Sexual and Relationship Therapy, 16*(4), 389–405.

Leitenberg, H., & Henning, K. (1995). Sexual fantasy. *Psychological Bulletin, 117*(3), 469–496.

MacKinnon, C. (1993). *Only words*. Cambridge, MA: Harvard University Press.

Mackinnon, K. (1997). *Uneasy pleasures: The male as erotic object*. London: Cygnus Arts.

Marcus, S. (1966). *The other victorians. A study of sexuality and pornography in mid-nineteenth century England*. London: Weidenfeld and Nicolson.

Marks, L. H., & Neville, L. (2017, May 15). Gilead: An antiporn utopia. *Nursing Clio*. Retrieved from https://nursingclio.org/2017/05/15/gilead-an-antiporn-utopia/

Matsui, M. (1993). Little boys were little girls: Displaced femininity in the representation of homosexuality in Japanese girls' comics. In S. Gunew & A. Yeatman (Eds.), *Feminism and the politics of difference* (pp. 177–196). New South Wales: Allen & Unwin.

McKee, A., Albury, K., & Lumby, C. (2008). *The porn report*. Melbourne: Melbourne University Press.

McLelland, M. (2000). The love between 'beautiful boys' in Japanese women's comics. *Journal of Gender Studies, 9*(1), 13–25.

McNair, B. (2013). *Porno? Chic!* London: Routledge.

Meyer, U. (2010). Hidden in straight sight: Trans*gressing gender and sexuality via BL. In A. Levi, M. McHarry, & D. Pagliasotti (Eds.), *Boys' love manga* (pp. 232–257). Jefferson: McFarland and Company.

Moran, C. (2011). *How to be a woman*. London: Ebury Press.

Morrissey, K. (2008). *Fanning the flames of romance: An exploration of fan fiction and the romance novel*. MA dissertation, Georgetown University. Retrieved from https://repository.library.georgetown.edu/bitstream/handle/10822/551540/17_etd_kem82.pdf

Mulvey, L. (1981). Afterthoughts on 'visual pleasure and narrative cinema'. *Framework, 15/16/17*, 12–15.

Nagaike, K. (2003). Perverse sexualities, perverse desires: Representations of female fantasises and yaoi manga as pornography directed at women. *U.S.-Japan Women's Journal, 25*, 76–103.

Nagle, J. (1997). Stroking my inner fag. In C. Queen & L. Schimel (Eds.), *PoMoSexuals: Challenging assumptions about gender and sexuality* (pp. 122–126). San Francisco: Cleis Press.

Noble, B. (2007). Queer as box: Boi spectators and boy cultures on showtime's *Queer As Folk*. In M. L. Johnson (Ed.), *Third wave feminism and television: Jane puts it in a box* (pp. 147–165). New York: IB Tauris.

Norlander, T., Erixon, A., & Archer, T. (2000). Psychological androgyny and creativity: Dynamics of gender-role and personality trait. *Social Behaviour and Personality: An International Journal, 28*(5), 423–435.

Paasonen, S. (2010). Good amateurs: Erotica writing and notions of quality. In F. Attwood (Ed.), *Porn.com* (pp. 138–154). New York: Peter Lang.

Pearson, S. E., & Pollack, R. H. (1997). Female response to sexually explicit films. *Journal of Psychology & Human Sexuality, 9*(2), 73–88.

Queen, C., & Schimel, L. (Eds.). (1997). In C. Queen & L. Schimel (Eds.), *PoMoSexuals: Challenging assumptions about gender and sexuality.* San Francisco: Cleis Press.

Radway, J. (1984). *Reading the romance: Women, patriarchy, and popular literature.* Chapel Hill: University of North Carolina Press.

Rosewarne, L. (2011). *Part-time perverts: Sex, pop culture, and kink management.* Oxford: Praeger.

Russ, J. (1985). *Magic mommas, trembling sisters, puritans and perverts: Feminist essays.* Trumansburg, NY: Crossing.

Salmon, C., & Symons, D. (2001). *Warrior lovers: Erotic fiction, evolution, and female sexuality.* London: Weidenfeld & Nicolson.

Salmon, C., & Symons, D. (2004). Slash fiction and human mating psychology. *Journal of Sex Research, 41*, 94–100.

Saxey, E. (2002). Staking a claim: The series and its slash fiction. In R. Kaveney (Ed.), *Reading The Vampire Slayer: An unofficial critical companion to Buffy and Angel* (pp. 187–210). New York: Tauris Parke Paperbacks.

Schauer, T. (2005). Women's porno: The heterosexual female gaze in porn sites 'for women'. *Sexuality & Culture, 9*(2), 42–64.

Sedgwick, E. K. (1993). *Tendencies.* Durham, NC: Duke University Press.

Segal, L. (1994). *Straight sex: The politics of pleasure.* London: Virago Press.

Shamoon, D. (2004). Office sluts and rebel flowers: The pleasures of Japanese pornographic comics for women. In L. Williams (Ed.), *Porn studies* (pp. 80–103). London: Duke University Press.

Sharp, K. (Ed.). (1999). *The Black Lace book of women's sexual fantasies.* London: Black Lace.

Shiller, R. (2004). The show has never been written for straight women: So why is *Queer as Folk* making women wet? *Fab Magazine*, p. 260. Retrieved from http://archive.fabmagazine.com/features/womenwet/index.html

Sonnet, E. (1999). 'Erotic fiction by women for women': The pleasures of post-feminist heterosexuality. *Sexualities, 2*(2), 167–187.

Stacey, J. (1987). Desperately seeking difference: Desire between women in narrative cinema. *Screen, 28*(1), 48–61.

Stake, J. (1997). Integrating expressiveness and instrumentality in real-life settings: A new perspective on the benefits of androgyny. *Sex Roles, 37*, 541–564.

Stanley, M. (2010). 101 uses for boys: Communing with the reader in yaoi and slash. In A. Levi, M. McHarry, & D. Pagliassotti (Eds.), *Boys' love manga* (pp. 99–109). Jefferson, NC: McFarland & Company, Inc.

Stoltzfus, G., Nibbelink, B. L., Vredenburg, D., & Hyrum, E. (2011). Gender, gender role, and creativity. *Social Behaviour and Personality: An International Journal, 39*(3), 425–432.

Thomas, C. (2006). Crossing the streets, queering the sheets; or, 'Do you want to save the changes to queer heterosexuality?'. In R. Fantina (Ed.), *Straight writ queer: Non-normative expressions of heterosexual desire in literature* (pp. 1–8). Jefferson: McFarland Press.

Thompson, J. D. (2015). Invisible and everywhere: Heterosexuality in anti-pornography feminism. *Sexualities, 18*(5/6), 750–764.

Thorn, M. (2004). Girls and women getting out of hand: The pleasures and politics of Japan's auteur comics community. In W. W. Kelly (Ed.), *Fanning the flames: Fans and consumer culture in contemporary Japan* (pp. 169–186). New York: State University of New York Press.

Thurston, C. (1987). *The romance revolution: Erotic novels for women and the quest for a new sexual identity.* Chicago: University of Illinois Press.

Udry, J. R. (1988). Biological predispositions and social control in adolescent sexual behaviour. *American Sociological Review, 53*, 709–722.

Walsh, A. (1999). Life history theory and female readers of pornography. *Personality and Individual Differences, 27*(4), 779–787.

Walters, S. D. (1996). From here to queer: Radical feminism, postmodernism and the lesbian menace (or, why can't a woman be more like a fag?). *Signs: Journal of Women in Culture and Society, 21*(4), 830–869.

Ward, J. (2013). Queer feminist pigs: A spectator's manifesto. In T. Taormino, C. Penley, C. Shimizu, & M. Miller-Young (Eds.), *The feminist porn book* (pp. 130–139). New York: The Feminist Press.

Willis, E. (1983). Feminism, moralism and pornography. In A. Snitow, C. Stansell, & S. Thompson (Eds.), *Desire: The politics of sexuality.* London: Virago.

Winnberg, J., Fåhraeus, A., & Jonsson, A. (2008). Introduction: Female masculinity or textual masculinity. *Nordic Journal of English Studies, 7*(1), 1–9.

Wood, A. (2013). Boys' Love anime and queer desires in convergence culture: Transnational fandom, censorship and resistance. *Journal of Graphic Novels & Comics, 4*(1), 44–63.

5

'Sometimes It's Hard to Be a Woman'

It's not easy being a woman who consumes pornography. Despite the amount of joy and pleasure the women in my study testify to when engaging with erotic content, they still spend a lot of time talking about the negative aspects of being both a woman and a porn consumer. These aspects are especially profound in a world which isn't yet geared up to see women *as* porn consumers. Many of the women I spoke with over the course of writing this book tried to articulate to me what they like about m/m pornography by first telling me what they *don't* like about m/f pornography: the way they perceive women as being treated and/or exploited in heterosexual porn, the invisibility of female sexual pleasure, the fact that identifying with the female actress makes them less able to enjoy the eroticism of looking or makes them feel uncomfortable with their own bodies, or how watching or reading about m/f sex can trigger painful memories of past sexual abuse. All these things can act as barriers for women who want to engage with SEM. As Clarissa Smith (2012, p. 167) notes, 'female consumers of pornography are constantly dogged by questions of harm, subordination, objectification, and authenticity, and the need to consider women's well-being before their own pleasures in watching or reading porn'. For the women I spoke to, engaging with m/m SEM

© The Author(s) 2018
L. Neville, *Girls Who Like Boys Who Like Boys*,
https://doi.org/10.1007/978-3-319-69134-3_5

is a way to sidestep some of these questions and start putting their own pleasures first.

Much of this ties in with some of the anti-porn arguments memorably advanced by Dworkin (1989, 1992) and MacKinnon (1993) that I discussed in the previous chapter—that pornography is dangerous because pornographic images of women are responsible for women's subordination in society generally. This is a bold and controversial position, but even if taken to be partially true (which for many women in my sample it is), such a perspective can present a real moral and ethical conundrum for women who engage with SEM. This issue is, of course, not unique to the women in my study—although they have, perhaps, found a more radical way to address it. Karen Ciclitira (2004) notes that many of the women she interviewed about their porn use had difficulty reconciling their enjoyment of heterosexual porn with their identification as feminists, citing Dworkin's anti-porn work as a major contributor to this tension. Similarly, the feminist porn director Ms. Naughty (2013) has eloquently written on how concerns about the treatment of female performers can stop female viewers from enjoying porn, and Lawrence and Herold (1988) report a strong feminist orientation as being associated with unfavourable attitudes towards SEM and infrequent SEM use. One of my participants reflects on her conflicted attachment to, and enjoyment of, m/f porn, demonstrating the fraught nature of female sexuality in a misogynistic society: 'if I'm in the mood to be aroused by degradation, I watch heterosexual porn. Or, if I don't feel very good about myself that day I might watch heterosexual porn. Heterosexual porn makes me feel better physically, but worse mentally and emotionally' (American, 18–24, single, bisexual). Sonnet (1999, p. 174) writes about this as the 'bad conscience of being complicit in the objectification of other women'. As one of my participants explains, 'when I watch women [in m/f porn], I spend the whole time wanting to put bathrobes on them and go feed them chicken soup. Not sexy' (American, 45–54, married, bisexual). For Sonnet, a way to avoid this as a female consumer is to engage with feminist pornography, or women-authored erotica such as *Black Lace*.

However, for the women in my study, engaging with m/m erotic content offers a more definitive solution. In much m/f pornography there is no room for the woman's story. She does not do, she is instead done to.

Feminist m/f pornography has to work very hard to escape this formula, especially given entrenched notions about power and submission with regards to penetration, whereas in m/m SEM men are doing things to or with other men—there is no woman to potentially feel bad for. As one interviewee describes, 'If you're watching … heterosexual pornography and anal is going on, it's usually quite degrading to the woman, it's very much seen as if they're being held down, and [forced] into it… Obviously there's some gay porn where that's [also] the case—but, there's a lot of gay porn where it's just a loving act, or they're just hot, or they're both really in to it… So [in watching m/m] are we putting up a barrier between ourselves and pornography to stop ourselves entering it and feeling degraded or feeling used and stuff? Maybe when there's just two men, we're just not going to enter that space, so it's something we can take from without anything being taken from us, and us being made to feel anything we don't want to feel' (British, 35–44, married, pansexual).

Bader (2003, p. 221) links this discomfort about the treatment of women in porn to the feminisation of poverty, and the idea that women have historically 'trade[d] sex for love' and financial security. A lot of participants are unable to move beyond the idea that m/f pornography offers more of the same historic social and economic suppression of women, giving us actresses who are fucking for money, not because they want to. Obviously in our Western capitalist society most of us do our jobs because we get paid, and sex work is no exception. Work is work: much as I have loved writing this book, there have been times I would have gladly set the whole thing on fire were it not for the threat of unemployment hanging over my head. However, as discussed in Chap. 3, the women in my sample place huge value on authenticity in their porn—authentic desire, authentic pleasure, authentic *love* for the sexual act(s) carried out. While many of them have no issue with sex work *per se* (and support female performers' rights to work free from stigma and discrimination), they have an issue with the kind of sex *they* consume being somebody else's *work*. For these women, the sex they want to consume, the sex of their fantasies, shouldn't be *work*. A key draw of m/m SEM is that the male actors make it look like fun: 'gay men in porn love sex, and it rarely seems forced' (British, 25–34, married, bisexual). Inherent here is the notion that men love sex, and take part in pornography for reasons other than straight financial gain.

For the women in my sample, the motivations of female actors in porn seem less clear. These attitudes reflect the findings of Parvez's (2006) interview study with 30 self-identified heterosexual women who report enjoying heterosexual porn, where the authenticity of the female performer's pleasure was rated the most important feature of any given porn scene. Parvez notes that interviewees' previous experiences helped shape their perception of 'authentic' porn, with uncertainty over the female performer's enjoyment and motivation varying with respect to interviewees' economic backgrounds and experience(s) with sexual violence and coercion. Women with a history of economic struggle and/or sexual abuse were more likely to question authenticity and motivation, presumably, Parvez concludes, because of their own negative experiences of physical and emotional labour and sexual coercion, or lack of choice. Indeed, for many of the women in my study who have experienced sexual abuse, m/f SEM is a 'no go' area. Only m/m SEM can offer them the pleasures of looking at or reading sexually explicit texts without the risk of being triggered or re-traumatised. Other women simply dislike seeing the female body represented in SEM—either because it reminds them uncomfortably of the imperfections of their own bodies or sexual performance, or, in the case of heterosexual women, because they find female sexuality and genitalia actively unpleasant. As one participant explains, 'I don't find female bodies easy to [relate to] in an erotic sense. I can't bring myself to think of anything attached to a uterus—that horrifying vomitter of Mordor, thwarter of romantic plans, and ruiner of silky undies—as [either] erotic [or] beautiful [or] sexy' (Zimbabwean, 25–34, single, asexual/omnisexual). In all of these cases, the male body presents uncomplicated and even de-gendered access to the pleasures of pornography.

Issues with how women are represented in SEM are compounded in my sample by the fact that it is very difficult to 'see' female sexual pleasure. When presented with two men on the screen, respondents are better able to believe that both actors are enjoying the experience, and the sexual desire and pleasure between them therefore feels more authentic. This is not just because of the greater economic and social choices offered to men under capitalism (Penny, 2011), but because of the very visual cues that indicate male sexual desire ('the outward validation of spurting penises' as one participant describes it) and the general attitude women feel is evinced by male porn actors (as opposed to female porn actors), who are regarded as 'enjoying each other more rather than simply playing to the camera' (American, 55–64, married, Kinsey 1[1]). This is often further couched in what women describe as the 'eroticising equality' (Dyer, 2004; Pugh, 2005) of gay sex: the idea that men can enjoy sex (including porn-sex) more than women, not just because of the greater financial and cultural choices open to them, but also because the very nature of the types of sex acts performed in m/m pairings mean that neither one is automatically privileged or in a position of power over the other simply by virtue of penetration. Many respondents feel this gives a different set of power dynamics to m/m porn than to m/f porn, which makes it more exciting, as well as allowing a greater 'range' of behaviours. Several mention how they enjoy the potential for roughness, and even violence, in m/m SEM as 'characters in gay pornography are seemingly more able to be rough without it being distasteful [or] non-consensual' (Zimbabwean, 25–34, single, asexual/omnisexual). In this sense, m/m SEM offers women an opportunity to explore and enjoy their own sexuality and sexual identity in a way that m/f pornography does not—it makes it just that little bit easier to be a woman.

'It's Hard to Miss a Hard-On': The Authenticity of Male Desire

In her essay on SEM produced 'by women for women', Esther Sonnet (1999, p. 184) argues that we need to move to 'a place where women's enjoyment and pleasure are paramount' in our pornography—but for many women in my study this is hard, simply because they are not sure what 'women's pleasure' in SEM might look like. Linda Williams (1990, p. 50) argues that one of the pleasures of watching porn derives from seeing the truth of the body, what she terms 'the frenzy of the visible', noting that 'hardcore desires assurance that it is witnessing not the voluntary performance of female pleasure, but its involuntary confession'. However,

she concedes that it is extremely difficult to objectively measure orgasmic
excitement in the portrayal of female pleasure. While male pleasure (or
what is assumed to be pleasure) in porn can be portrayed by showing the
erect penis and ejaculation, the physiology of the vagina makes the reality
of female sexual pleasure much more difficult to represent. As McKee,
Albury, and Lumby (2008) point out, we can't assume a woman is coming in porn just because she says she is. As one interviewee explains,
'When I'd look at it [het porn], I'd just think: "Oh My God, she's so
thin!" And my brain would just not… I just couldn't get off on it basically, I just couldn't even watch it. A [friend of mine] lent me some "feminist" porn with this guy who was, like, the biggest male porn star … and
he's very attractive … [and she said], "This is good this film, this is a good
one—you'll like this." And she sent it to me, and I just… I just didn't like
it, I didn't think the girl was enjoying it—how did I *know* she was having
an orgasm again? And again. And again… With the men you can *tell*
they're both enjoying it, you can *see* they've had an orgasm' (British-
Italian, 45–54, married, heterosexual). The majority of women I spoke
with agree that 'most simulations of female pleasure [in porn] are unconvincing [and] unsatisfactory' (American, 18–24, single, pansexual).

In m/m porn, however, it is 'more obvious that they're both enjoying
it—what with erections and everything' (British, 45–54, in a relationship, a little bent). Richard Dyer (1985, 2004) argues that the come shot
in m/m porn is important precisely because it relates to the importance
of the visible in male sexuality. He writes that within gay sex, seeing
another's orgasm is 'delightful' because 'it is a sign that the other is excited
by one and is even a sort of gift, a giving of a part of oneself' (Dyer, 2004,
p. 104). He also stresses the realism of the moment. While the actors are
just that—actors—they are also real people having real sex, and their
climaxes are also real. Male come shots are rarely faked—we really are
seeing someone ejaculate. While the sex and climax are happening in the
story, and in the fictional world of the porn film, they are also happening
on a set. It is for this reason that male pleasure feels more 'authentic' to
many of the women in my sample, with one explaining, 'so much—okay,
all—of the enjoyment of sex for women is internal. Men can't *hide* the
fact that they're enjoying their partner rimming them, and I find that hot.
With women, I can't help but think about all the reasons other than the

enjoyment of sex that she might be doing this' (American, 25–34, single, heterosexual). Believing in the authenticity of the pleasure shown on screen makes it easier for women to enjoy guilt-free orgasms of their own while watching pornography. As one woman notes, 'you kind of want to know people are getting off while you're getting off, don't you?' (British, 35–44, married, pansexual). Even in written SEM, the perception that it is easier to realistically portray male sexual pleasure persists: 'the ways men are described as being aroused are much easier to "see" in your imagination and stay "in scene" than the ways women are typically described as being aroused. A woman, for instance, will never grind her erection into someone's hip. Kinda hard to miss that cue' (Canadian, 35–44, divorced, heterosexual).

Additionally, there is a strong sense among some of the women in my sample that same-sex partners are more proficient at pleasuring each other because of their familiarity with their own (male) bodies and preferences, after all 'men totally understand how the other enjoys the sex, what he's physically feeling, what it's like to have a cock…' (British, 45–54, single, bisexual) (see also McCutcheon & Bishop, 2015). While there is an awareness that men featuring in m/m pornography might not necessarily *be* sexually attracted to other men, and that they might be acting in m/m films purely for financial reasons ('gay-for-pay' as it is known), many women try to avoid this by actively seeking out amateur or queer pornography. One explains, 'when I watch [gay] porn it's often bears who are heavily pierced and stuff. Not because I find them attractive, but because you know this is what they like to do…, you know this is the stuff they're into, and this is their everyday sexuality that just happens to be on camera. Whereas I'd have absolutely no interest in watching two straight blokes go at it, because it's unnatural behaviour for them' (British, 35–44, married, pansexual). There is also a (perhaps unfounded) perception that the gay-for-pay phenomena is not particularly widespread, despite the fact that porn scholar Jeffrey Escoffier estimates the number of gay-for-pay performers in gay pornography at around 35–40 per cent (Escoffier, 2003, p. 216). However, writing as a gay performer and producer, Lucas (2006) describes how, in his experience, performers rarely take part in scenes they do not want to, and choose their roles (receptive/insertive) based on their desires.

This is not to say that representations of male sexual pleasure are immune from critique, but they certainly circumnavigate a lot of the difficulties presented to female viewers by porn featuring women. Tucker (1990, p. 270) criticises radical feminist analyses of gay porn which argue that the erection and male ejaculation are symbols of female objectification and subjugation within all forms of porn, and asks what an 'ethical erection or ejaculation' would entail, since such clarification is never provided. Certainly my respondents seem to view these manifestations of male physical pleasure as the closest thing to an 'ethical' orgasm they are likely to see represented in SEM.

Avoiding the Sexual Minefield

Not only does m/m porn offer women more assurances as to the pleasure being experienced by performers, it also side-steps a lot of the political issues endemic in m/f SEM: what one participant referred to as 'the sexual minefield'. Dekker and Everaerd (1989) found that female sexual arousal in response to SEM is facilitated when participants perceive their identification figure as being in control of, or dominating, the sexual interaction. It is telling that a lot of the women I spoke to struggle to find this in m/f SEM, either written or visual. As one participant describes:

> I think I like it [m/m SEM] because they're men... I'm a feminist, I love shagging [laughs], I love heterosexual sex, *having* it. But when I read, when I write, I associate with the women—I can't help that, they're like me... And God, it's a minefield! It's just a minefield. Every movement in the sexual act becomes political... [But] If I've got [two male characters] and one is giving [the other] a blowjob, it doesn't mean anything, it's just hot, or not. It either works or it doesn't. But a woman giving a guy a blowjob, if he puts his fucking hand on her head, suddenly: 'Who does he think he is?' My brain just goes... I can't stand it!' (British-Italian, 45–54, married, heterosexual)

A number of women find that m/f SEM that avoids this same sexual minefield by firmly centring the woman in the sexual acts depicted tends to also be 'vanilla' and 'boring': 'too many floral metaphors and soulful gazes, not enough raunchy stuff' (American, 25–34, single, bisexual). As discussed in previous chapters, women are visual, and women can be extremely kinky. Lots of women *like* hands on the backs of heads during oral sex scenes. The problems arise when the hand is always a man's hand, and the head is always a woman's head. As one woman explains, 'I like two equally strong [men] engaging in hate-sex. This can involve fighting. Now, if some man threw me into a wall, or fought with me prior to sex, I would think he was trying to hurt me, and I would blow a gasket. Two strong men can do such things and it just ends in mind-blowing sex' (British, 45–54, married, heterosexual). In Shaw's (1999; *n* = 32) study, women responded much more negatively to pornographic shots depicting violence, dominance, or coercion if the subject of the photo was a woman rather than a man. Their responses indicated that this was because (1) as women, they related more strongly to violence against women, and (2) violence against men was seen as more 'artificial', 'unrealistic', or even 'ridiculous' because they felt men would not find themselves in such situations unless by choice (Shaw, 1999, p. 203). Many women in my study reinforced this concept: 'It's strange, when I see kinks like bondage or erotic asphyxiation in a het context, my immediate reaction is to assume something negative. Or at least [to be] ambivalent about the consent of the situation. I can't enjoy the images… When I see the same in a gay context… I am somehow assuming by default that consent has been given—which is ridiculous!—but gay porn means freer enjoyment [of that kind of stuff], I guess' (German, 25–34, in a relationship, mainly heterosexual). Partly this perception is because of men's greater economic and social power, and partly it is because men are assumed to be each other's physical match: if they don't like what's happening to them, they can physically stop it. 'I prefer that even if a top has his cock down another man's throat, you know that the bottom probably *has the ability* to shove him away or stop an action he doesn't like,' explains one woman, 'whereas a hundred pound woman is likely powerless against a man in the same situation' (American, 18–24, single, bisexual).

Jung (2004, p. 34) points out that m/m SEM allows for exploring scenes of dominance and submission, and even violence, in a safe environment over equal male bodies, which have 'never been constructed as sites of subordination in the way female bodies have'. Without invoking institutions of gender inequality, the female consumer is free to identify with either the dominant or the submissive or simply remain a voyeur to the exchange. To this extent Jung believes that taking up the tropes of pornography as gender inequality but rewriting them over male bodies is 'more than just female traffic in men' (Jung, 2004, p. 34), although it may at times be a tongue-in-cheek revenge for centuries of male 'traffic in women' (more on that later); and the reversal can be highly disconcerting for dominant masculine culture. In addition, the fact that overt gender politics are removed from the power dynamics between an m/m pairing means that male participants are free to assert their 'masculinity' without it necessarily being an exercise in dominance. 'I like the strength in men's bodies pushing against each other, and the potential for roughness,' one woman explains, '[even if] … it is never achieved… And if it *is*, it's more equal between them' (American, 35–44, married, pansexual). Coward (1984, p. 231) refers to the attractiveness of this 'unchecked masculinity' in the gay male subculture, noting that 'these characteristics are constructed as desirable in this context, presumably as a sort of celebration of power which is safe as a game between people of the same sex, but entirely problematic between men and women'.

It is clear that to talk about the erotics of power in heterosexual relationships raises complex questions about the politics of gender difference. However, in m/m SEM Nagaike (2003, p. 84) argues that female readers and viewers can be 'liberated from feelings of guilt and shame connected with deriving sexual excitement from their identification with (abjected and objectified) female characters who appear in pornography directed at men'. She believes that identifying instead with male characters (and projecting their sexuality on to them), women can obtain the 'ambivalent and balanced status' of both identifying with, and at the same time dissociating from, the protagonists in a scene, therefore achieving what she sees as a safe and comfortable involvement with the pornographic (Nagaike, 2003, p. 85). Rosie Gunn (1993, p. 336) agrees, noting that as there are no women present in m/m porn she doesn't 'feel bound into an ideological discourse about the misrepresentation of my likeness'. She concedes that heterosexual porn offers her 'small moments of pleasure' but goes on to say that these are 'usually followed by feelings of displeasure and disempowerment' (Gunn, 1993, p. 336). While she appreciates the way that feminist porn directors are engaging with the idea of creating porn that is enjoyable for female viewers, she nevertheless maintains that 'gay male porn seems to offer me more possibilities [for pleasure] for the moment' (Gunn, 1993, p. 336).

The avoidance of the sexual minefield gives women a sense of freedom, and affords them the liberty to enjoy SEM as opposed to struggling with what it might mean for them or say about them as women. Within the context of m/m women can be free from the 'violence and harassment' that Buckley (1994, p. 176) sees as 'mechanisms for the containment and management of women's bodies and sexuality'. By attempting to depoliticise porn in this way, some of the 'fun' is put back into it, at least for the women I spoke to. For, as Judith Butler (in an interview with Kotz, 1992, p. 89) notes, there is 'among gay men, a certain focus on pleasure and sexuality that [i]sn't always available in women's communities highly mediated by feminism'. Not only can m/m take the work out of creating porn, it can take the work out of consuming it.

The Eroticising Equality of Sex Between Men

Not only does m/m SEM provide a more 'egalitarian model for gazing' (Isola, 2010, p. 89) as discussed in Chap. 2, it also provides a more egalitarian sexual dynamic, and this dynamic can, in and of itself, be extremely erotic for some women. The feminist pornographer Candida Royalle has discussed how female viewers prefer pornography where sexual partners have equal roles as far as sexual desire, sexual pleasure, and power are concerned (in de Wit, 1987). However, this can be difficult to achieve when much (although obviously not all) m/f SEM rests on a dynamic of men as penetrators and women as penetrated. While it is easy to refute the dominance of the act of penetration at a theoretical level—and I will attempt to do just this later on in this chapter—the fact remains that for many of the women I spoke to, being penetrated implies a surrendering of sorts, and a giving up of power: 'being penetrated is an inherently passive act, something that happens *to* you, not something you *do*' (American, 25–34, single, heterosexual).

Pugh (2005, p. 110) notes that one thing that women particularly like about m/m SEM as opposed to f/m SEM is the 'eroticising equality' of the sex acts represented, noting that 'it is difficult in any sex scene involving penetration to make the two participants completely equal and avoid any hint of dominance'. However, men offer the potential to be 'reversible couples' (Nagaike, 2003, p. 88)—seemingly offering so many more possibilities in terms of the representation of multiple sexual pleasures. For, as Bishop (2015, p. 19) has argued, 'sex sans power is typically portrayed in gay pornography by virtue of the participants maintaining the option of versatility if they desire'. One participant expands, 'I like the direct, presumed mutual pleasure of the sex [in m/m] too. The natural equality of desire in it… It's like because they are both men they are presumed to both like the sex [and be] equally enthusiastic about sex. Sex is not something that is done *to* a man, even if it's being physically done to him' (English, 25–34, single, heterosexual).

Susan Bordo (1993, p. 720) delights in the fact that there is 'something deeply subversive of sexism in homoerotic representations which "neutralise" the dominance of the penetrator and depict a kind of "democracy" of sexual position, in which active/passive roles appear so easily reversible and none is privileged'. The potential for either member of the pairing to take or surrender control at any given moment is what can make m/m SEM incredibly erotic. For, as Marks (1996, p. 132) states, what many SEM consumers want is not 'two free and equal, Habermasian ideal subjects, but two people between whom power relations are continually being negotiated. Eroticism relies on this shifting and promising inequality … upon a tension between the sense of control and submission on each person's part'. The concept of tension, of shifts and unpredictability, is what lends m/m SEM some of its appeal:

> in het [SEM] … it's always the same. The man is the aggressor, the woman the accepter, and the woman is the psychological as well as the physical "bottom". The details change, but we know how it will end right from the beginning. The woman is automatically seen as "lesser", "weaker", "receptive", "done to" instead of "doing" … [In m/m] there's no pre-ordained "script". Everything has to be negotiated. … It's a tossup as to how the men involved will handle sex between them, and there are so many more per-

mutations than between man/woman (American, 55–64, single, heterosexual).

Constance Penley (1991, p. 154) highlights this 'eroticising equality' as one of the key draws of slash fiction, noting that writing about two men 'avoids the built-in inequality of the romance formula in which dominance and submission are invariably the respective role of male and female'. Henry Jenkins (1992, p. 194) agrees, observing that in slash 'both characters can be equally strong and equally vulnerable, equally dominant and equally submissive, without either quality being permanently linked to their sexuality or their gender'. In Hayes and Ball's (2009) experience, the bottom in any given sex scene in slash is not always the submissive or weaker party in any sense, and the interplay of power between the two characters generally shows they both have ways of asserting dominance and showing vulnerability. The power each exercises complements the other, rather than being at odds with it. Pugh (2005) believes that it is rare in slash for one partner to permanently 'top', either physically or emotionally. Either characters will have sex in ways other than penetrative, or alternate roles. Many participants agree, with one noting 'part of what I enjoy about slash … is the fluidity of sexual practices that are possible between two (or more) men compared to het sex, which often seems to require penis-in-vagina sex to be considered complete, and brings with it a lot of cultural baggage about how sex "should be"' (British, 35–44, married, heterosexual).

Waugh (1985, p. 30) therefore argues that m/m porn in particular, and gay sexuality more generally, undermine the widespread assumption in the porn debate that penetration is in and of itself an act of political oppression: 'a sexual act or representation acquires ideological tenor only through its personal, social, narrative, iconographic, or larger political context'. In m/m porn 'gay men fuck and suck and are fucked and sucked, etc., in a wide range of combinations and roles not determined by gender; sometimes roles are determined by sexual practice, body type, age, class, race … but just as often this is not so' (Waugh, 1985, p. 34). Fejes (2002, p. 107) believes that m/m porn films are thus able to 'explore a wide range of positions of the sexual subject without falling into the power dynamics of a gender based structure of domination. The gay males in these films can be both aggressive and passive, both tops and bottoms, both emotionally hard and cold, and soft and vulnerable'.

Not all scholars, however, agree with Waugh's interpretation. Clarissa Smith (2007, p. 150) notes that pornography featuring m/m sex is authenticated through 'the built-in assurance in Dworkin's work' that the free will of men is never in doubt. However, she also points out that this ignores Dworkin's analysis of gay male porn as simply a 'reworking or feminisation of men through the visual stylizations of female submission' (Smith, 2007, p. 151). Dworkin (1989) argues that simply because women are almost never present in m/m porn does not necessarily lessen the overall misogynistic meaning of m/m porn films. Indeed, the lack of women in m/m porn can be seen as increasing its offensiveness, as men who are the recipients, or 'passive' in the sexual act of penetration, are viewed as being submissive and therefore feminised (Dworkin, 1989, p. 23), thus 'adding gender transgression and emasculation to this dystopia of unrestrained masculine sexual aggression and violence' (Fejes, 2002, pp. 96–97). Morrison (2004, p. 169) agrees, stating that the medium's 'determination to be fiercely "masculine", and its eschewal of anything remotely feminine, may explain its misogynistic elements and its disturbing tendency to conflate pleasure and pain'. The gay feminist scholar John Stoltenberg is unequivocal on this: 'the "faggot" is stigmatised because he is perceived to participate in the degraded status of the female' (Stoltenberg in Jeffreys, 2003, p. 89, scare quotes added). According to Jeffreys (2003, p. 89), this 'hatred of the feminine' is a major reason why 'gay men are so attracted to the exaggerated masculinity portrayed in gay male pornography'.

Christopher Kendall's (1993, 1997, 1999, 2011) position builds on this radical feminist perspective on m/m porn, and stresses that the power differential that exists between gay male porn performers should be attributed to a patriarchal social system that subjugates and oppresses women. Basing his work in subject/object (Mulvey, 1975), Kendall feels that the 'top' is coded as larger, both physically and in terms of penis size, and is both more dominant and aggressive than the 'bottom'. As the former more closely approximates hegemonic standards of masculinity, he experiences certain privileges denied his 'submissive' counterpart. As such, Kendall believes much m/m porn depicts 'large, hyper-masculine men … who find sexual arousal through the infliction of pain on socially feminised sexual subordinates (read: gay men)' (Kendall, 2011, p. 54). While Kendall acknowledges versatility, he disagrees that such an occurrence subverts the power differentials at work in society. Much like Stoltenberg, he sees 'position swapping' in m/m porn as problematic rather than positive: 'if a man is shown being assfucked, he will generally be shown assfucking someone else in turn—this is to avoid the connotation that he is at all feminised by being fucked' (Stoltenberg, 1989, p. 132). This perspective is resolutely rejected by other scholars such as Stychin (1992, 1995) and Lucas (2006) who contend that versatility is 'the sine qua non of truly egalitarian sex' (Bishop, 2015, p. 11).

Stychin (1992, p. 892) attacks the radical feminist position, claiming instead that 'the flexibility of positions—of both fucking and being fucked—does not reinforce male power. Instead, it demonstrates the ridiculousness of suggesting that real value is coterminous with sexual position… [It is] absurd … [to] equat[e] human values with the arbitrariness of the sexual choice to be a "top" or a "bottom"'. Anna Marie Smith (1995, p. 203) points out that this entire line of thinking is in itself perpetuating misogyny and homophobia: the idea that 'men being dominated and penetrated by other men are "abused" and "degraded" because they are being "treated like women"' is both profoundly anti-gay and anti-woman. As one participant observes, 'sex doesn't always have a top and a bottom; [and] penetration isn't the be all and end all of every sexual relationship. To assume so is heteronormative and unimaginative' (Canadian, 25–34).

The radical feminist position also appears to assume heterosexuality is the default—and that we therefore need to interpret m/m porn through a heterosexual lens. For Butler, 'gender' is a construct and not an unproblematic expression of one's sex. Butler (2006, p. xiii) argues against seeing heterosexuality as 'the origin and the ground' from which all sexualities are constructed; within the terms of her analysis there is no 'ground' point for sexuality. Moreover, Butler suggests that conceiving of gender roles as being inherently singular ('masculinity', 'femininity') and inherently hierarchical is problematic: 'if gender hierarchy produces and consolidates gender, and if gender hierarchy presupposes an operative notion of gender, then gender is what causes gender, and the formulation culminates in tautology' (Butler, 2006, p. xiii). As Thompson (2015, p. 761) argues, 'to see potentially transgressive and/or queer pornographies as always-already premised on a heteronormative and patriarchal model loads heterosexuality with possibly misplaced assumptions, endowing it with a power, a rigidity, and weight that it might not, in fact, wield'. Fejes (2002, p. 97) argues that a fixation on penetrator/penetrated as being analogous to male/female 'reflects an inability or an unwillingness to move beyond a heterosexist understanding of sex and grant legitimacy and respect to the unique nature of the gay male experience'.

Eroticising Equality: Does It Really Exist?

The concept of 'eroticising equality' as expressed via versatility is core to many of my participants' enjoyment of m/m SEM partly because they believe that it reflects real-life MSM practices: 'as I understand it, few men are exclusively top or bottom, most like to mix it up, and some just don't like anal sex at all—which is kind of what you'd expect really' (British, 45–54, single, heterosexual). There is a prevalent notion that real life m/m sex is 'fairly switchy', so that 'whether they're topping or bottoming is less determined by "the relationship" than "it's Tuesday" or "I'm tired, you do the work"' (American, 55–64, in a relationship, bisexual). Indeed, numerous studies have shown that the majority of gay men self-label as versatile; that is, instead, of seeing themselves as 'tops' or 'bottoms' they practice both insertive and receptive sexual intercourse (Coxon et al., 1993; Hart, Wolitski, Purcell, Gómez, & Halkitis, 2003; Lyons, Pitts, & Grierson, 2013; Wegesin & Meyer-Bahlburg, 2000; Wei & Raymond, 2011; Wilcox, 1981). As far back as 1965, Hooker noted that, 'few individuals prefer and predominantly engage in modes of sexual gratification for which any term defining a typical 'sex-role' can be assigned. Variability, interchangeability, and interpartner accommodations seem to preclude role categorization for the majority' (Hooker, 1965, p. 24). Looking over recent research it appears that the proportion of men who self-label as versatile is increasing (Lyons et al., 2013), and there is also emerging evidence that gay men, particularly young gay men, view versatiles as the ideal partner type (Johns, Pingel, Eisenberg, Santana, & Bauermeister, 2012).

Although the terms 'top' and 'bottom' in this context describe anal sex behaviours, there is evidence to suggest that MSM [men who have sex with men] *may* also associate them with gender roles. Wegesin and Meyer-Bahlburg (2000, p. 56) found that several men in their focus groups acknowledged an association between bottoming and perceived femininity, with one commenting 'if that's the role you are playing (woman's) in a homosexual partnership, then you must be more the bottom and the woman', and another adding 'and women will be less than men and therefore bottoms are less that tops. This may be a reflection of society's general misogynist attitudes.' The associated stigma attached to being a bottom meant that many men who preferred receptive anal sex presented themselves publicly as tops (Wegesin & Meyer-Bahlburg, 2000, p. 58). However, they also noted what they described as a 'pervasive reluctance' among their sample to 'pigeonhole individuals or their identities' (Wegesin & Meyer-Bahlburg, 2000, p. 57).

Both Kippax and Smith (2001) and Hoppe (2011) explored the power dynamics between tops and bottoms, and concluded that power and anal intercourse are more complexly related than previously assumed. Though behaviours might be perceived as dominant or submissive with respect to position and physicality, perceptions of an individual sexual act are equally, if not more, important in assessing and explaining sexual power differences. Some men who prefer being receptive during anal intercourse [RAI] feel empowered because of their ability to offer themselves as receptive and produce pleasure for their partners; and, conversely, other RAI partners report enjoying the position specifically because they feel dominated by the insertive partner. Moskowitz, Rieger, and Roloff (2008, p. 192) comment that 'anal intercourse … [is] more than simply a sexual behaviour enacted between individuals. It seems representational and more indicative of larger relational issues and psychological aspects'. Hoppe (2011, p. 212) concludes that there may not be a '"true" direction in which power or pleasure flow', and narratives such as these should be read as 'strategies men use to make sense of their sexual lives as bottoms in terms of both pleasure and power'.

There are very few systematic studies on the prevalence of exclusive topping/bottoming in the porn industry, but it seems that most male performers are versatile. A 2009 Austrian study on gay pornography has shown that at least 82.4 per cent of all men performing in the male porn industry are versatile at one point or another during their career (Michelides, 2009, cited in Gill, 2010). Michelides (2009, cited in Gill, 2010) considered the performances of 5556 actors, and found that only 10.8 per cent performed exclusively in the top role, and only 6.8 per cent appeared exclusively in the bottom role. Mackinnon (1997) notes that gay stars who have previously exclusively topped tend to get paid more to bottom—as a break from the norm—and this generates excitement in viewers. While this suggests that dominance/submission remain a vital part of the meaning of the pornographic representation of sex in the gay context, gay porn 'fosters a belief in the relative variability and relative unpredictability of dominance/submission partners' (Mackinnon, 1997, p. 160). Nevertheless, Richard Dyer (1985, p. 28) notes that while the pleasure of anal sex is represented in much m/m pornography, the narrative is 'never organised around the desire to be fucked, but around the desire to ejaculate' and hence the 'pleasure of being fucked … takes a backseat'.

Jobs for the Boys: Equality, Labour, and the Radical Re-tooling of the Male Body

The concept of equality that so many women enjoy in m/m SEM goes beyond the erotic—it extends to the romantic and the intimacy of the everyday. After all, who gets to fuck whom doesn't only have political implications, but emotional ones too. Writing about her experience of pegging her male lovers, the writer Susie Bright (1998) says:

> I would like more women … to know the pleasures of ravishing their husbands and boyfriends. … Because it's a deep emotional pleasure to be the one who holds the world in her hands, so to speak—to be on top and going inside. When a man is vulnerable to you in that way, he's not only having physical pleasure from his prostate, he's also giving himself to you in such

a completely open way that it can't help but be intensely—dare I use the word—*romantic*, in an ultimate, far-out, upside-down kinda way.

Within wider narratives, such as slash stories and other types of m/m erotic fiction, it is not just dominance and submission, or physical roughness or violence, that carry different ramifications than they do within the m/f dynamic. Emotional responses, housework, helping or 'rescuing' each other from potential danger, parenting etc. all take on a different timbre when the two people in the pairing are both men: 'when two *men* are equals, they can be *very* equal' (American, 35–44, single, bisexual). So when two male lovers are presented together in a long-term, intimate relationship, they will be expected to share physical and emotional labour. There are no 'boy jobs' and 'girl jobs' here. To this extent the gay man is both 'the recognised peer *and* the lover of a male' (Decarnin, 1981, p. 10), a position many women would like to hold, but can struggle to in our sexist culture. Some fan scholars have argued that such scenarios of ideal utopian partnerships function as 'a safety valve for the stress women experience in their daily lives and in their relationships with men' (Cicioni, 1998, p. 174).

In this way slash fiction is able to work out some of the tensions that exist in traditional m/f romances, something which it can do in quite extreme ways. Mpreg, for example, is a genre of slash that explores the concept of (cisgendered) male pregnancy. Ingram-Waters (2015, p. 1.1) describes mpreg as a 'thought experiment about gender, sexuality, and the male body', highlighting that 'only in the realm of fiction is pregnancy possible for human cisgender men'. While the idea of mpreg may seem pretty 'out there',[2] case studies like Berit Åstrom's (2010, p. 1.2) on mpreg in *Supernatural* slash demonstrate that it can also be remarkably conventional: 'what may at first seem like resistance may in the end reinforce heteronormative structures'. Constance Penley (1997, p. 131) sees mpreg as 'an extreme retooling of the male body'. However, Åstrom's (2010, pp. 5.1, 1.1, 7.1) reading is more cautious; she considers the ways that male pregnancy stories can bring with them 'female-gendered features' and can lead to 'quite heteronormative stories', although they can certainly also produce narratives that 'challenge our notions of gender, identity, [and] sexual and social practices, as well as parenthood'. From a feminist perspective, Hunting (2012, p. 6.9) argues that while placing pregnancy on a male body is subversive, 'inscribing natural (often accidental) reproductivity onto homosexual sex works to assimilate the queer characters and their sex acts into traditional heteronormative goals of sex' and into what Edelman (2004) calls a culture of reproductive futurism.

However, Ingram-Waters (2015) believes that fans often approach mpreg in a nuanced and complex way, sensitive to the fact that it can serve to reinforce heteronormative stereotypes. For example, even if there is an accepted 'local knowledge' that the partner who 'bottoms' should then carry the pregnancy, writers often resist 'gender norms that dictate that the pregnant man should be somewhat feminised' (Ingram-Waters, 2015, p. 4.21), for example, by switching sexual positions (so that the pregnant man tops during pregnancy). The writers she spoke with were very careful not to have pregnancy 'compromise the character's masculinity' (Ingram-Waters, 2015, p. 4.33). Ingram-Waters (2015, p. 5.1) notes that, on the face of it, male pregnancy might seem like a refusal of queerness, but nevertheless for her it is a phenomenon that redefines cisgender masculinity: it 'stretche[s], [breaks], and realign[s]' the boundaries of both pregnancy and masculinity. However, Suzuki (1998, p. 265) warns against us interpreting such stories as being necessarily feminist: 'pregnancy, rather than being a backdrop for the exploration of women's unequal status in society, becomes in these stories a dramatic technique for revealing how [male] partnerships are deepened'.

No Girls Allowed: M/M SEM and the Evacuation of the Female Body

It is easy to see why the perceived equality of m/m SEM might appeal to female consumers, but it is important to note that many porn scholars, such as Thomas Waugh (1985), do not view gay porn as intrinsically feminist. Rather, by failing to offer a 'safe space' for women—and, indeed, by rendering them (largely) invisible—Waugh suggests that gay male porn is complicit in the oppression of women. Several academics have voiced concern over women's interest in a genre of SEM that evacuates the female body, and asked why is it that women are so alienated from their own bodies that they choose to watch, or read, or write erotic fantasies only in relation to a non-female body?

Well, on the whole, they don't, not exclusively: 75 per cent of the women in my sample read m/f erotica, and 69 per cent of those who watch m/m porn also watch m/f porn. Sixty per cent also read f/f erotica, and just over half (53 per cent) of m/m porn watchers also watch f/f porn. We can see from this that the majority of women who consume m/m SEM have broad interests in different types of SEM, including heterosexual and lesbian works that involve the female body. There is, nevertheless, a marked preference for m/m SEM (74 per cent of the sample prefer it over other pairings), and a portion of participants who exclusively focus on m/m content. Many participants have reflected on this preference:

> as a straight-identified woman in a monogamous, years-long relationship with a man, this sometimes freaks me out [and] baffles me, because it makes me wonder: where is my female fantasy in my real life, which is a heterosexual one, getting fulfilled in my erotic fantasy life? At the same time, I know the brain is a bizarre and wondrous organ, and that sexual fantasy and reality are fluid and interesting beasts, and that to worry about these things too much is probably silly (American, 25–34, married, heterosexual).

For some women their preference for m/m SEM is a simple case of not finding women attractive. As one woman expands, 'women aren't sexually arousing to me. The only woman I could watch all day is Kate Upton, but I would prefer she keep some clothes on' (American, 25–34, married, heterosexual). For others, seeing or reading about women in sexual situations makes it too difficult to keep reality out of their fantasy life: 'for example, if someone is performing cunnilingus, I get caught up in wondering when the last time she showered was, and I hope it doesn't smell like mine when it gets whiffy, and then I start getting all self-conscious' (American, 25–34, married, bisexual). For others, it is more complex. Many report feeling a sense of alienation from their own (gendered) bodies, often to such an extent that they cannot enjoy SEM where other female bodies are present. 'I hate my body,' one explains, 'because I have body issues and low self-esteem, it's far too easy to self-insert into the fantasy [if it features women], and that just mucks the whole thing up once I see myself in the 'scene'" (Canadian, 35–44, divorced, heterosexual). Another discusses how 'the ease with which females in erotica tend to experience orgasms contrasts strongly with my sexual experience, which is not as easy. I don't need to resent my inability to orgasm vaginally more than I already do' (American, 25–34, in a polyamorous relationship, bisexual). Penley (1991, p. 154) notes that the bodies that these women feel alienated from are modern female bodies, 'bodies that are a legal, moral, and religious battleground, that are the site of contraceptive failure, that are publicly defined as *the* greatest potential danger to the foetuses they house, that are held to painfully greater standards of physical beauty than those of the other sex'. In this sense, a feeling of alienation is only natural.

Some of the women I spoke to feel threatened by the sexual acts depicted in m/f porn, and others feel concerned that men will only be satisfied by women who have bodies like porn stars. Watching these 'perfect' bodies, belonging to these 'orgasmic' women is therefore very difficult for them: 'I find myself comparing my own body to the female character's, and it just starts a long and nasty spiral of bad body image. I've never found a [story] where a woman like me is having amazing, fantastic sex' (Puerto Rican, 18–24, single, unsure of sexuality). In Shaw's (1999) study, several women also talked about feelings of jealousy, and how they would like to look like the women in porn stills they were shown; others talked about how these images of beautiful women with perfect bodies made them feel inadequate, self-conscious, and dissatisfied with their own bodies.

The absence of women in SEM removes feelings of inadequacy and jealousy—as one participant succinctly puts it, 'two hot guys, no girl to be jealous of' (American, 25–44, married heterosexual), and therefore the 'threat' that can be presented by attractive, sexually assertive women. Scodari (2003, p. 114) equates slash with male-targeted porn featuring 'lesbian' encounters, positing that they may have the same motivation: removal of the competition and the desire to frame both attractive characters of the opposite sex as 'performing for and serving only the individual indulging in the fantasy'. Occasionally, the removal of perceived 'threats'—both to the consumer, and to the idealised m/m pairing—can become problematic, particularly in the realm of slash fiction and BL where it can result in the eradication or demonisation of canon female characters. Blair (2010) notes that female characters in slash and BL may be seen as having the potential to have a negative impact on the relationship between the story's main (m/m) couple, especially if the character is one who has had a romantic or sexual relationship with one of the male characters in canon. Blair (2010, p. 110) believes that it is because of this that comments about female characters in fan spaces are 'frequently very negative and occasionally virulently, even violently, misogynistic'. Blair (2010, p. 112) agrees with Scodari that there is a certain amount of jealousy involved with the rejection of female characters, but frames it slightly differently, claiming that a woman consuming m/m SEM may 'identify the female character as a source of competition, regardless of the fact that the two men … are involved with each other. The men are still the object of desire for the reader. This means characters who threaten the relationship between the men could also be seen as threatening the desire of the reader'.

Davies (2005, p. 199) argues that this is understandable, on the grounds that while the slash fans she has spoken to are 'willing to share' their favourite characters, they will only do so with other men, 'not with half-their-age female co-stars'. This is not simply a question of jealousy, or of threat, but of a desire for realism and authenticity (once again). The hostility of some slash fans towards female characters in the types of cult TV shows that attract a wide slash following has not gone unnoticed within the media industry. Straw (2009, pp. 15–16) describes an interview with the three central male cast members of *Supernatural* (Jared Padalecki, Jensen Ackles, and Misha Collins) regarding Collins' concern about how fans would respond to his character.

Collins: At first I was nervous because I know that some of the other characters who have been introduced to the show haven't gone over well … especially some of the women…
Ackles: Yes
Padalecki: *All* of the women
Collins: All women

Padalecki: Women are not welcomed by the fans
Collins: This is an incredibly sexist group of people
Padalecki: Against their own sex
Collins: But fortunately I am, to date, not a woman … so I have that
             going for me

However, Flegel and Roth (2010, p. 3.7) argue that the case could be made that this misogyny is, in part, a 'by-product of the show's own over-arching misogyny', particularly in Seasons 3 and 4, which feature many female villains and numerous examples of gendered and sexualised insults and violence. As discussed in Chap. 3, the bulk of the problem here could lie in the source texts themselves, not in how fans have interpreted or recreated them. Indeed, when Blair (2010) surveyed BL fans on their opinions of female characters, her participants responded that they primarily disliked the women in BL because they were portrayed as weak, fawning, and overly emotional. Participants stated that they enjoyed strong, likeable female characters, but there were very few of them about—as discussed in Chap. 3.

The absence of women as romantic protagonists also means that slash can offer women a chance for emotional escapism, an opportunity to explore feelings of pain, jealousy, emotional angst, and loss from a safe distance. Many fan scholars have noticed the prevalence of hurt/comfort [H/C] stories with slash fandom. H/C is a term used to describe stories where one character comforts another after they have been physically or emotionally hurt. Parrish (2016) describes these stories as being of the 'we found love in a hopeless place' variety, as they often occur against a background of trauma or danger (war-torn countries, prison camps, dystopic futures). However, she notes that it often 'isn't the place that feels hopeless, but an element of the character's story—a past trauma, struggle, or loss—and the love isn't so much an outgrowth of it, but a salve for it' (Parrish, 2016). While H/C can occur in all types of fan fiction, it seems to be a particularly popular trope within slash fic, where pleasure is generated for many readers by positioning male characters as both the sufferers of pain and the receivers of comfort (Fathallah, 2010). This is perhaps unsurprising; after all, there is plenty of space for emotion and vulnerability—as well as comforting and nurturing—in cultural scripts of femininity, so there is less of an impetus to give such dynamics within m/f or f/f pairings a specific name. Bacon-Smith (1992) maintains the H/C dynamic is the cornerstone of slash fiction, serving as an outlet for denied female pain, and a providing a feminine reworking of the hypermasculinist dominant-culture narrative—in this way slashers are able to 'work out' tragedy or unhappiness in their own lives. While this theory has been received with scepticism by slash fans themselves, some fan scholars such as Fathallah (2010, p. 3.1) have conceded that 'elements of [Bacon-Smith's] theory strike a half-embarrassed chord' with them. Writing about her own experience with H/C slash fiction, Fathallah admits that she desires the characters she identifies with to be made vulnerable, because vulnerability is not something she herself can afford: 'I do not want to be vulnerable and I am not a victim, not in real life. Not 99 percent of the time. Yet perhaps H/C fic is my little pressure valve—when the irrational, embarrassed part of myself that feels unfairly wounded and wants to be comforted lives vicariously through a character for a moment' (Fathallah, 2010, p. 3.1). However, she goes on to stress 'not a female character. That is uncomfortable, and too close to home' (Fathallah, 2010, p. 3.1). When they speak about H/C, women in my study tend to echo Fathallah's sentiments: 'I do not find hurt/comfort with a female character as appealing as with a male character… I imagine it has to do with the fact that in mainstream media, women are usually presented as the victims in these sorts of situations… The power dynamics are also important—in a H/C situation, the person being hurt is usually in a less-dominant role than the person who rescues/comforts. If the character is male, I am not troubled by the patriarchal overtones of such a situation' (American, 25–34, single, queer). When it is a male character who is experiencing pain, or emotional anxiety, or desperate longing, or trauma, women are able to explore and engage with those emotions at a safe distance. Just like in explicit m/m visual pornography—when women aren't in the scene there are no women to potentially feel bad for. Again, the absence of sad or inadequate or rejected women make being a female reader just that little bit easier.

'Up Yours, Boys!' The Notion of Payback in M/M SEM

For a small portion of my sample, it is clear that the objectification of men's bodies acts as a form of payback for women's objectification in patriarchal culture as a whole. As one woman explains, 'men should get to experience the same body issues women ... face. We need Tina Fey and Amy Poehler singing 'I saw your dicks' at a future Oscars to see how male actors feel about it' (American, 35–44, single, bisexual). Another adds, 'we objectify women, and our bodies are sources of entertainment and amusement... I think men [should be made to] feel equally as vulnerable and exposed as we do' (American, 25–34, married, sapiosexual).

McLelland (2005, p. 72) observes that 'it is clear that many women find the manipulation of male characters in a sexual fantasy setting empowering'. One woman agrees, explaining 'I feel that because I'm from an area and family that thinks less of females ... the power fantasy of dominating the male gender that has long oppressed me is gratifying' (American/Alabama Cherokee tribe citizen, 25–34, married, queer). Hisatake (2011, p. 19) believes this sense of empowerment is particularly acute when women are *creating* m/m SEM: by bringing together two male characters and orchestrating their relationship the woman is now 'pulling the strings' rather than occupying the traditional female position of 'an 'object' or mere catalyst of desire within [a] story'. Women and queer people are often denied this kind of agency in traditional media texts (not to mention in real-life), and the flipping and reversing of traditional power dynamics can give an erotic thrill in and of itself.

Tina Anderson (quoted in Isola, 2010, p. 89) explains that BL and slash allow for the enjoyment that comes with 'visual recreation without the self-examination. That's what's so beautiful about it. Women don't have to think about being the ones abused and played with.' Aoyama (1988, p. 196) goes a step further, suggesting that sex between men that takes place in a violent context becomes 'an act of revenge' on the part of women consumers who now 'become a spectator rather than a prey'. As one participant divulges, 'there's a little thrill of revenge when reading about men getting abused just like women. It's nasty, but it makes one feel better about the general situation of women in society to remember that this can happen to men too' (German, 25–34, single, heterosexual). Some women express similar views about visual SEM: 'I like that there's no women [in m/m porn] being slapped around and verbally abused, or doing things that generally hurt or are no fun in reality and pretending to like it… I'm okay with men being slapped around and objectified, because I'm kind of a jerk. They don't have to deal with the kind of shit women do all around that, so it's more like a novelty' (American, 25–34, single, bisexual).

'It Doesn't Trigger Me': M/M Porn and Histories of Abuse

There are a small number of women in my study who identify as rape or abuse survivors,[3] and go on to discuss how this makes consuming SEM featuring women extremely difficult for them. As one explains, 'due to my own negative experiences with sex, I have a hard time reading about and believing in women enjoying sex, or for sex between a man and a woman to be an act of love' (American, 18–24, single, bisexual). Another notes how she 'finds [m/f] triggery', adding that 'a mixture of my history of m/f abuse and my own body, which does not experience very much sexual sensation, makes [SEM] featuring females uncomfortable for me. I cannot read about female characters in sexual roles because of how often they're given Magical Sexyparts of the Unlimited Stimulation and Capacity for Orgasm variety. It makes me feel shitty about my luck of the draw, like I'm missing out on something, which is very triggery for me as a survivor' (American, 18–24, in a relationship, heterosexual). This is particularly the case when engaging with texts that feature elements of BDSM: 'any form of dominance [or] powerplay involving women brings back uncomfortable memories of my experience with rape' (Zimbabwean, 25–34, single, asexual/omnisexual). The emotional distance provided by not having women featuring in viewing or reading materials often means that women who have experienced abuse are able to respond much more intensely to m/m SEM than they would to other types. As one woman explains, nothing in my real life makes me feel so dizzy with want. Nothing in my real life constricts my chest and makes my limbs tingle. It helps me feel a desire that I can't feel in my real life. Part of this may be due to my history of sexual abuse. I am just able to feel way more, both emotionally and physically, through a fictional exploration of [male] characters I love (American, 18–24, in a relationship, heterosexual).

This is not to say that m/m SEM is devoid of themes of sexual, physical, or emotional abuse. In fact, much has been made of the prevalence of non-consensual sex (noncon), rape, and sexual encounters where consent, though possibly given, is dubious (dubcon) in slash fiction and BL manga. In Pagliassotti's (2010) survey, 50 per cent of participants thought rape and physical torture were acceptable plot points in BL stories. Pagliasotti provides many possible reasons for the popularity of violent themes in BL, including Suzuki's (1998, p. 258) suggestion that women write rape scenes into BL manga as a form of resisting the social stigmatisation of rape by portraying 'male protagonists, loved by the very partners who rape them, as imbued with innocence'. In these cases Suzuki (1998) believes that such a plotline may serve to alleviate a BL-reading rape survivor's sense of guilt or shame.

Discussing the prevalence of rape and violence in *yaoi*, Thorn (2004, p. 177) speculates that 'by projecting experiences of abuse onto male characters, [women readers] are able to come to terms in some way with their own experiences of abuse'. Fujimoto (1998, p. 140, cited in Thorn, 2004, p. 179) maintains that through the abuse male characters are subjected to, 'women are freed from the position of being unilaterally violated, and gain the perspective of the violator, of the one who watches'. We can see these dynamics at work in one of my focus groups, where a participant talks about how writing sadomasochistic m/m fiction helped her to work through the trauma of the sexual abuse she had experienced as a teenager:

H: I was never a rape victim, but I was a sexual abuse victim [as a teenager], and I had a lot of anger about those issues… [I liked the fact that when writing slash] I was in control of those two very powerful men. And I made them do things to each other that I don't even want to think about [laughs]. There was a lot of sadomasochism in those stories, and a lot of… It was me acting out via my writing… And because they were doing it to each other, they weren't doing it to *me*… I didn't want men doing it [sadomasochism] to women, I wanted men to suffer for being *men* at that point, that's how that started. As it evolved—because those were *nasty* stories, it was not nice—as it evolved, as I grew up and got better I wrote much less nasty stories. I didn't want men to be hurting each other anymore, but I still found it very sexy. Two men together.

D: So it was quite a cathartic process for you?

H: Oh yeah. Absolutely it was. And I-

D: I mean, do you feel like that was quite a big part of your healing?

H: Oh, absolutely. It was just about the only thing that I had that fixed that.

D: Did you not have any professional help?

H: No. Nothing like that.

Pagliassotti (2010) also believes that non-con scenes might be considered more acceptable in BL manga than heterosexual romance for all women, not just abuse survivors, because the female reader doesn't feel compelled to identify with the victim by virtue of her gender. Fujimoto (2004, p. 87) states 'no matter how much those rape or gang-rape scenes (and there are truly a lot of them!) resemble male-on-female assaults, if it is men depicted then [they] cannot get pregnant, lose their virginity, or become 'unsuited for marriage''.

It is this focus on jealousy, body insecurities, feminist outrage, and previous trauma that led Bacon-Smith (1992) to view slash very much as a literature of alienation; these were women, she believed, who felt intimidated by real life men, and were unable to form meaningful romantic bonds with them. Such a view is uniformly rejected by the majority of the women I spoke to here (including many of those who had experienced abuse), and the data on relationship statuses does not support it either—89 per cent of women in the sample have had romantic/sexual relationships, and of those currently in a romantic relationship, a further 89 per cent are with men (or a mixture of men and women in the case of polyamorous relationships). Webb (2012, p. 21) argues that, far from being a passive, needy form of sexual gratification for women who are either uncomfortable in their own skin or afraid of heterosexual intimacy—a 'medicine for loneliness'—female interest in m/m SEM instead expresses a 'vivacious and tenacious interest in the possibilities of the heart'. Indeed, the heart is very much a focal point in much SEM that appeals to women. While I have stressed the importance of the physical, the visceral, the carnal in the previous few chapters, I would be doing my participants a disservice if I did not discuss the huge emphasis many of them place on the importance of love and intimacy in their SEM. Much as women may enjoy explicit m/m sex, it seems good old-fashioned romance hasn't lost its appeal quite yet.

Notes

1. Defined as: predominantly heterosexual, only incidentally homosexual.
2. Mpreg fan Lyric refers to mpreg as belonging to 'the weird part of the internet… The [parts where] people … are like 'WTF?'" (Lyric, in Shrayber, 2014).
3. This was not a question that I specifically asked respondents, either during interviews, focus groups, or the survey. Some participants, however, spontaneously divulged their experiences with violence and sexual abuse while answering other questions.

References

Aoyama, T. (1988). Male homosexuality as treated by Japanese women writers. In G. McCormack & Y. Sugimoto (Eds.), *The Japanese trajectory: Modernization and beyond* (pp. 186–205). Cambridge: Cambridge University Press.

Åstrom, B. (2010). 'Let's get those Winchesters pregnant': Male pregnancy in *Supernatural* fan fiction *Transformative Works and Cultures, 4*. Retrieved from http://testjournal.transformativeworks.org/index.php/twc/article/view/135/141

Bacon-Smith, C. (1992). *'Enterprising women': Television fandom and the creation of popular myth*. Philadelphia: University of Pennsylvania Press.

Bader, M. J. (2003). *Arousal: The secret logic of sexual fantasies*. London: Macmillan.

Bishop, C. J. (2015). 'Cocked, locked, and ready to fuck?': A synthesis and review of the gay male pornography literature. *Psychology & Sexuality, 6*(1), 5–27.

Blair, M. M. (2010). 'She should just die in a ditch': Fan reactions to female characters in boys' love manga. In A. Levi, M. McHarry, & D. Pagliassotti (Eds.), *Boys' love manga: Essays on the sexual ambiguity and cross-cultural fandom of the genre* (pp. 110–125). Jefferson, NC: McFarland & Company, Inc.

Bordo, S. (1993). Reading the male body. *Michigan Quarterly Review, 32*(4), 696–737.

Bright, S. (1998, May 22). Move over, Ken, it's 'Bend Over Boyfriend'. *Salon*. Retrieved from http://www.salon.com/1998/05/22/nc_22brig/

Buckley, S. (1994). A short history of the feminist movement in Japan. In J. Geld (Ed.), *Women of Japan and Korea: Continuity and change* (pp. 150–186). Philadelphia: Temple University Press.

Butler, J. (2006). *Gender trouble: Feminism and the subversion of identity* (2nd ed.). New York: Routledge.

Cicioni, M. (1998). Male pair-bonds and female desire in fan slash writing. In C. Harris & A. Alexander (Eds.), *Theorising fandom: Fans, subculture and identity* (pp. 153–177). New Jersey: Hampton Press.

Ciclitira, K. (2004). Pornography, women and feminism: Between pleasure and politics. *Sexualities, 7*(3), 281–301.

Coward, R. (1984). *Female desire*. London: Paladin.

Coxon, A. P., Coxon, N. H., Watherburn, P., Hunt, A. J., Hickson, F., Davies, P. M., et al. (1993). Sex role separation in sexual diaries of homosexual men. *AIDS, 7*, 877–882.

Davies, R. (2005). The slash fanfiction connection to bi men. *Journal of Bisexuality, 5*(2–3), 195–202.

de Wit, B. (1987). Candida Royalle. *Playgirl, 1*, 102–105.

Decarnin, C. (1981). Interviews with five faghagging women. *Heresies, 12*, 10–15.

Dekker, J., & Everaerd, W. (1989). Psychological determinants of sexual arousal: A review. *Behavioural Research Therapy, 27*, 353–364.

Dworkin, A. (1989). *Pornography: Men possessing women*. London: The Women's Press.

Dworkin, A. (1992). Against the male flood: censorship, pornography, and equality. In C. Itzin (Ed.), *Pornography: Women, violence, and Civil Liberties* (pp. 515–535). Oxford: Oxford University Press.

Dyer, R. (1985). Male gay porn: Coming to terms. *Jump Cut, 30*, 27–29.

Dyer, R. (2004). Idol thoughts: Orgasm and self-reflexivity in gay pornography. In P. Church Gibson (Ed.), *More dirty looks: Gender, pornography and power* (pp. 102–109). London: BFI.

Edelman, L. (2004). *No future: Queer theory and the death drive.* Durham, NC: Duke University Press.

Escoffier, J. (2003). Gay-for-pay: Straight men and the making of gay pornography. *Qualitative Sociology, 26*(4), 531–555.

Fathallah, J. M. (2010). H/C and me: An autoethnographic account of a troubled love affair *Transformative Works and Cultures, 7.* Retrieved from http://testjournal.transformativeworks.org/index.php/twc/article/view/252/206

Fejes, F. (2002). Bent passions: Heterosexual masculinity, pornography, and gay male identity. *Sexuality & Culture, 6*(3), 95–115.

Flegel, M., & Roth, J. (2010). Annihilating love and heterosexuality without women: Romance, generic difference, and queer politics in *Supernatural* fan fiction *Transformative Works and Cultures, 4.* Retrieved from http://journal.transformativeworks.org/index.php/twc/article/view/133/147

Fujimoto, Y. (1998). *Watashi no ibasho wa doko ni aru no? Shojo manga ga utusu kokoro no katachi [Where Do I Belong? The Shape of the Heart as Reflected in Girls' Comics].* Tokyo: Gakuyo Shobo.

Fujimoto, Y. (2004). Transgender: Female hermaphrodites and male androgynes. *U.S.-Japan Women's Journal, 27*, 76–117.

Gill, A. (Ed.). (2010). *Gay sex files: Tops, bottoms and versatiles.* New York: Brian Phillippe.

Gunn, R. (1993). On/scenities: Porn for women? *Body Politic, 4*, 33–36.

Hart, T. A., Wolitski, R. J., Purcell, D. W., Gómez, C., & Halkitis, P. N. (2003). Sexual behaviour among HIV-positive men who have sex with men: What's in a label? *Journal of Sex Research, 40*(2), 179–188.

Hayes, S., & Ball, M. (2009). Queering cyberspace: Fan fiction communities as spaces for expressing and exploring sexuality. In B. Scherer (Ed.), *Queering paradigms* (pp. 219–239). Oxford: Peter Lang.

Hisatake, K. (2011). *'Nothing says I despise you like a blowjob': Opening queer moments for queer spaces in Harry Potter slash fan fiction.* MA dissertation: University of Hawaii at Mānoa. Retrieved from http://scholarspace.manoa.hawaii.edu/bitstream/handle/10125/29630/Hisatake_Kara_Nothing%20says%20I%20Despise%20You.pdf?sequence=1

Hooker, E. (1965). An empirical study of some relations between sexual patterns and gender identity in male homosexuals. In J. E. Money (Ed.), *Sex research: New developments* (pp. 24–52). New York: Holt, Rinehart & Winston.

Hoppe, T. (2011). Circuits of power, circuits of pleasure: Sexual scripting in gay men's bottom narratives. *Sexualities, 14*(2), 193–217.

Hunting, K. (2012). *Queer as Folk* and the trouble with slash *Transformative Works and Cultures, 11*. Retrieved from http://journal.transformativeworks.org/index.php/twc/article/view/415/315

Ingram-Waters, M. (2015). Writing the pregnant man *Transformative Works and Cultures, 20*. Retrieved from http://journal.transformativeworks.org/index.php/twc/article/view/651/544

Isola, M. J. (2010). Yaoi and slash fiction: Women writing, reading, and getting off? In A. Levi, M. McHarry, & D. Pagliassotti (Eds.), *Boys' love manga: Essays on the sexual ambiguity and cross-cultural fandom of the genre* (pp. 84–98). Jefferson, NC: McFarland & Company, Inc.

Jeffreys, S. (2003). *Unpacking queer politics: A lesbian feminist perspective.* Malden, MA: Polity Press.

Jenkins, H. (1992). *Textual poachers: Television fans and participatory culture.* New York: Routledge.

Johns, M. M., Pingel, E., Eisenberg, A., Santana, M. L., & Bauermeister, J. (2012). Butch tops and femme bottoms? Sexual positioning, sexual decision making, and gender roles among young gay men. *American Journal of Men's Health, 6*(6), 505–518.

Jung, S. (2004). Queering popular culture: Female spectators and the appeal of writing slash fan fiction. *Gender Queeries, 8*. Retrieved from http://www.genderforum.org/fileadmin/archiv/genderforum/queer/jung.html

Kendall, C. N. (1993). 'Real dominant, real fun': Gay male pornography and the pursuit of masculinity. *Saskatchewan Law Review, 57*, 21–58.

Kendall, C. N. (1997). Gay male pornography after Little Sisters Book and Art Emporium: A call for gay male cooperation in the struggle for sex equality. *Wisconsin Women's Law Journal, 12*, 21–82.

Kendall, C. N. (1999). Gay male pornography/gay male community: Power without consent, mimicry without subversion. In J. Kuypers (Ed.), *Men and power* (pp. 157–172). Halifax, NS: Fernwood Press.

Kendall, C. N. (2011). The harms of gay male pornography. In M. Tankard-Reist & A. Bray (Eds.), *Big Porn Inc: Exposing the harms of the global pornography industry* (pp. 53–61). Melbourne: Spinifex press.

Kippax, S., & Smith, G. (2001). Anal intercourse and power in sex between men. *Sexualities, 4*, 413–434.

Kotz, L. (1992). The body you want: Liz Kotz interviews Judith Butler. *Artforum, 31*(3), 82–89.

Lawrence, K., & Herold, E. S. (1988). Women's attitudes toward and experience with sexually explicit materials. *The Journal of Sex Research, 24*, 161–169.

Lucas, M. (2006). On gay porn. *Yale Journal of Law & Feminism, 18*, 299–302.

Lyons, A., Pitts, M., & Grierson, J. (2013). Versatility and HIV vulnerability: Patterns of insertive and receptive anal sex in a national sample of older Australian gay men. *AIDS and Behaviour, 17*(4), 1370–1377.

MacKinnon, C. (1993). *Only words*. Cambridge, MA: Harvard University Press.

Mackinnon, K. (1997). *Uneasy pleasures: The male as erotic object*. London: Cygnus Arts.

Marks, L. U. (1996). Straight women, gay porn and the scene of erotic looking. *Jump Cut, 40*, 127–135.

McCutcheon, J. M., & Bishop, C. J. (2015). An erotic alternative? Women's perception of gay male pornography. *Psychology & Sexuality, 6*(1–2), 75–92.

McKee, A., Albury, K., & Lumby, C. (2008). *The porn report*. Melbourne: Melbourne University Press.

McLelland, M. (2005). The world of yaoi: The internet, censorship, and the global 'Boys' Love' fandom. *The Australian Feminist Law Journal, 23*, 61–77.

Michelides, C. (2009). *Männlichkeitskonstruktionen der Pornografie zur Jahrtausendwende [Constructions of masculinity in pornography at the turn of the millenium]*. Austria: Wien.

Morrison, T. G. (2004). 'He was treating me like trash, and I was loving it…' Perspectives on gay male pornography. *Journal of Homosexuality, 47*(3/4), 167–183.

Moskowitz, D. A., Rieger, G., & Roloff, M. E. (2008). Tops, bottoms and versatiles. *Sexual and Relationship Therapy, 23*(3), 191–202.

Mulvey, L. (1975). Visual pleasure and narrative cinema. *Screen, 16*(3), 6–18.

Nagaike, K. (2003). Perverse sexualities, perverse desires: Representations of female fantasises and yaoi manga as pornography directed at women. *U.S.-Japan Women's Journal, 25*, 76–103.

Naughty, M. (2013). My decadent decade: Ten years of making and debating porn for women. In T. Taormino, C. Parreñas Shimizu, C. Penley, & M. Miller-Young (Eds.), *The feminist porn book* (pp. 71–78). New York: Feminist Press.

Pagliassotti, D. (2010). Better than romance? Japanese BL manga and the sub-genre of male/male *romantic* fiction. In A. Levi, M. McHarry, & D. Pagliassotti (Eds.), *Boys' love manga: Essays on the sexual ambiguity and cross-cultural fandom of the genre* (pp. 59–83). Jefferson, NC: McFarland & Company, Inc.

Parrish, R. (2016, March 2). What is hurt/comfort and why do we love it? *Heroes and Heartbreakers*. Retrieved from https://www.heroesandheartbreakers.com/blogs/2016/03/what-is-hurt-comfort-and-why-do-we-love-it

Parvez, Z. F. (2006). The labour of pleasure: How perceptions of emotional labour impact women's enjoyment of pornography. *Gender and Society, 20,* 605–631.

Penley, C. (1991). Brownian motion: Women, tactics, and technology. In C. Penley & A. Ross (Eds.), *Technoculture* (pp. 135–161). Minneapolis: University of Minnesota Press.

Penley, C. (1997). *NASA/Trek: Popular science and sex in America*. New York: Verso.

Penny, L. (2011). *Meat market: Female flesh under capitalism*. Alresford, UK: John Hunt Publishing.

Pugh, S. (2005). *The democratic genre: Fan fiction in a literary context*. Bridgend, Wales: Seren.

Scodari, C. (2003). Resistance re-examined: Gender, fan practices, and science fiction television. *Popular Communication, 1*(2), 111–130.

Shaw, S. M. (1999). Men's leisure and women's lives: The impact of pornography on women. *Leisure Studies, 18*(3), 197–212.

Shrayber, M. (2014, March 11). What exactly is Mpreg? A male pregnancy enthusiast explains. *Jezebel*. Retrieved from http://jezebel.com/what-exactly-is-mpreg-a-male-pregnancy-enthusiast-expl-1651553874

Smith, A. M. (1995). 'By women, for women and about women' rules OK?: The impossibility of visual soliloquy. In P. Burston & C. Richardson (Eds.), *A queer romance: Lesbians, gay men and popular culture* (pp. 199–215). New York: Routledge.

Smith, C. (2007). *One for the girls!: The pleasures and practices of reading women's porn*. Bristol, UK: Intellect Books.

Smith, C. (2012). 'I guess they got past their fear of porn': Women viewing porn films. In X. Mendik (Ed.), *Peep shows* (pp. 155–167). London: Wallflower Press.

Sonnet, E. (1999). 'Erotic fiction by women for women': The pleasures of post-feminist heterosexuality. *Sexualities, 2*(2), 167–187.

Stoltenberg, J. (1989). *Refusing to be a man: Essays on sex and justice*. Portland, OH: Breitenbush Books.

Straw, A. (2009). *Squeeing, flailing, and the 'post-Jared-and-Jensen glow': An ethnography of Creation Entertainment's March 2009 'Salute to Supernatural' conventions*. Unpublished dissertation: Penn State University. Retrieved from http://www.personal.psu.edu/als595/blogs/amandalynn125/papers/ethnography.pdf

Stychin, C. F. (1992). Exploring the limits: Feminism and the legal regulation of gay male pornography. *Vermont Law Review, 16*, 859–900.

Stychin, C. F. (1995). *Law's desire: Sexuality and the limits of justice*. London: Routledge.

Suzuki, K. (1998). Pornography or therapy: Japanese girls creating the yaoi phenomenon. In S. A. Inness (Ed.), *Millenium girls: Today's girls around the world* (pp. 243–267). Maryland: Rowman & Littlefield Publishers.

Thompson, J. D. (2015). Invisible and everywhere: Heterosexuality in anti-pornography feminism. *Sexualities, 18*(5/6), 750–764.

Thorn, M. (2004). Girls and women getting out of hand: The pleasures and politics of Japan's auteur comics community. In W. W. Kelly (Ed.), *Fanning the flames: Fans and consumer culture in contemporary Japan* (pp. 169–186). New York: State University of New York Press.

Tucker, S. (1990). Radical feminism and gay male porn. In M. Kimmel (Ed.), *Men confront pornography* (pp. 263–276). New York: Crown.

Waugh, T. (1985). Men's pornography: Gay vs. straight. *Jump Cut, 30*, 30–35.

Webb, E. (2012). *Slash as Genre*. MA dissertation: American University, Washington, DC. Retrieved from http://aladinrc.wrlc.org/bitstream/handle/1961/11138/Webb_american_0008N_10043display.pdf?sequence=1

Wegesin, D. J., & Meyer-Bahlburg, H. F. (2000). Top/bottom self-label, anal sex practices, HIV risk and gender role identity in gay men in New York City. *Journal of Psychology & Human Sexuality, 12*(3), 43–62.

Wei, C., & Raymond, H. F. (2011). Preference for and maintenance of anal sex roles among men who have sex with men: Sociodemographic and behavioural correlates. *Archives of Sexual Behaviour, 40*(4), 829–834.

Wilcox, R. R. (1981). Sexual behaviour and sexually transmitted disease patterns in male homosexuals. *British Journal of Venereal Diseases, 57*, 167–169.

Williams, L. (1990). *Hard core: Power, pleasure and the 'frenzy of the visible'*. Los Angeles: University of California Press.

6

'...Always Should Be Someone You Really Love'

Porn kills love, we are told. The pornkillslove.com website reliably informs us that 'pornography is full of ideas and beliefs that are completely opposite of what real relationships are like. Instead of love and affection, pornography is all about domination, disrespect, abuse, and selfishness'. There are no shades of grey offered here. Porn is porn. Love is love ('real life, real love ... real people' the website asserts). However, for many of the women I spoke to, porn and love are not polar opposites. Instead, it is the fusion of these two things that gives them the most pleasure: sexually and emotionally. When discussing what they like about m/m visual pornography, approximately a quarter of respondents make the explicit proviso that they only watch films, clips, or gifs where the actors seem to 'genuinely like each other' (American, 45–54, single, bisexual) and where they are 'obviously enjoying each other—smiling and laughing' (American, 35–44, single, bisexual). Not only do they often therefore express a preference for amateur pornography, but also for pornography where there appears to be an existing romantic relationship between the men featured:

© The Author(s) 2018
L. Neville, *Girls Who Like Boys Who Like Boys*,
https://doi.org/10.1007/978-3-319-69134-3_6

M: I do now, occasionally [watch gay porn]. But I find a lot of it is a bit too 'wham bam thank you man' for me. I want… I mean, the ones I enjoy most is where I see little touches and kisses, and—

J: They're boyfriends!

M: Exactly. And when there's a little bit more there, and I'm like: oh, that's nice, that's cute.

Another woman explains 'I want an emotional, romantic attachment [in my porn]… I know bisexual men who are only interested in having sex with other men, but can't ever see themselves having a romantic relationship with a man: the idea of watching them couple, or whatever, wouldn't do it for me—I want them to feel the love! Along with the shagging' (British, 35–44, married, pansexual). Given the emphasis many of my participants place on authenticity in their SEM, as discussed in previous chapters, this is not that surprising. However, it's not just that many of the women I spoke with want 'authentic' sex in their SEM, they quite often want *romance* too. This returns us to some of the ideas discussed in Chap. 4: that pornography is 'for men', whereas erotica is 'for women'. What is interesting, though, is that just as often it is not erotica which is positioned as porn's antithesis in the popular imaginary, but the romance novel. Indeed, Salmon and Symons (2004, p. 96) note that for some time now 'romance novels have been called, with … justification, women's pornography'.

Again, here, we have the idea that romance—unlike porn—is soft and non-explicit—and that this tells us something important about the nature of female sexuality. As Ann Barr Snitow (2001, p. 317) observes, 'how different is the pornography for women, in which sex is bathed in romance, diffused, always implied rather than enacted at all. This pornography is the Harlequin romance'. However, romance isn't necessarily about softness or euphemism—romance stories can be *extremely* explicit, as NC-17-rated slash fiction demonstrates—it's also about mystery and excitement. It is about chemistry, and watching or reading about interactions between two (or more) people who are as interested in each other's minds as they are in each other's bodies, even in the context of a seemingly 'casual' encounter (Russ, 1985). As one participant explains, '[I like] writing that is centred around romance—[but] that also has a sexual payoff. Romance is a shamed genre in publishing and often the writing is not as sophisticated as I'd like. And even in romance, the sex is often not explicit! Obviously, I read not only for the romantic denouement of passionate understanding, but also for the often unbelievably arousing set pieces of kink and sex… I want both' (American, 25–34, married, bisexual).

We should also remember that while romantic fiction is rarely thought of as a radical space, it *is* a genre—one of the only genres—that is consistently governed by an active, desiring female gaze. This suggests that romance is an important element of female sexual desire. In the 1970s John Cawelti (1976, p. 42) speculated that 'the coming age of women's liberation will invent significantly new formulas for romance, if it does not lead to a total rejection of the moral fantasy of love triumphant'. While I am not arguing that the romance has not changed significantly since the 1970s, it is not apparent that the 'moral fantasy of love triumphant' has been entirely rejected. Popular romance still tends to follow familiar, well-worn paths—although it is 'a far more malleable and flexible form' than it is given credit for (McAlister, 2014, p. 300)—and it is often precisely this formula that many romance readers find both compelling and comforting. This is true for many of the women in my sample who read explicit m/m romances and slash fiction: 'not only is it hot, the kinds of [stories] I tend to read have, if not a happy ending, at least a hopeful one, and I find them emotionally satisfying. I haven't had a lot of that in real life, and I wouldn't necessarily say it's a substitute, but it's a kind of enjoyable escape, knowing that, whatever they go through, the protagonists are going to end up together in the end … [because] they love each other' (American, 25–34, single, heterosexual).

Jodi McAlister (2014) has referred to this inextricable intertwining of sex and love in the romance genre as 'compulsory demisexuality'. People who identify as demisexual *need* to feel a strong emotional connection with someone in order to feel sexual attraction to them: it is part of their sexual orientation.[1] In the romance, the protagonists are often presented as demisexual—meaning that sex is only truly pleasurable for them when they are in love (McAlister, 2014). Often this is the case for the consumer too: *they* need to believe that the partners have an emotional bond (or at least have the potential to have an emotional bond) in order to find the sex between them truly arousing. Women's desire for this type of connection in romance novels can also be found in their preferences for porn more generally. For example, when Shaw (1999) showed women in her study a series of (m/f) pornographic photos, she found that several respondents were unhappy with the lack of affection, or 'warmth', portrayed in the pictures (Shaw, 1999, p. 204). The sexual explicitness wasn't a problem, but, much like some of my participants, they felt that sexuality should be in the context of a loving relationship. It is for this reason that some of the women I spoke to like m/m pornography, which one describes as being 'more sentimental' than m/f porn (American, 18–24, in a relationship, lesbian); and m/m erotic fiction, which another discusses as being something which 'touches [her] heart,' adding, 'yeah, that means that first and foremost it's not about pornography for me; it's about love, love stories' (German, 25–34, single, asexual). It would seem when it comes to m/m SEM, a good many of the women in my sample are vicariously demisexual.

This combination of sex and romance has proved incredibly popular among readers of m/m SEM. In her study of nearly 8000 fanfic fandoms, Morrissey (2008) found that by far and away the most popular stories were *romantic* stories that feature m/m pairings. While most fans said they read similar amounts of the major story types (m/f, m/m and gen), their favourite story was nearly always one which focused on male homosexual romance. In Dru Pagliassotti's (2010) survey of BL readers, a romantic storyline was very important in terms of enjoyment of the text. The largest group in the survey reported that the single most important element of BL manga was 'slowly but consistently developing love between the couple', and in qualitative comments many participants situated BL manga directly within the romance genre. As with my sample, where 63 per cent of women read romance novels, Pagliasotti found very similar crossover appeal between the genres; of her 478 BL manga readers, 72 per cent report reading m/m romances and 55 per cent read m/f romances. Pagliassotti (2010, p. 60) therefore believes that slash is a subgenre of the Western popular romance.

A lot of these women love love. They love it in their porn, they love it in their erotica, and they love it in their novels. Not only that, but a number of women liken the experience of both discovering their interest in m/m sexuality, and discovering slash stories,[2] as being like *falling* in love. For many of the women I spoke to, m/m SEM is not simply about getting off, it is a genre that speaks directly to their hearts.

A Brief History of Love: Slashing the Romance Narrative

Linda Williams (1990, p. 6) has dismissed the porn/erotica distinction discussed in Chap. 4 precisely because of this blurring of the borders between 'mass-market romance fiction for women' and pornography. Indeed, the boundary between romance and pornography is porous. Jagodzinski (1999) discusses how the two genres have always shared a connection, with the novel reaching maturity at the same time as modern pornography became easily accessible in print. Both genres 'had to be read in secret; both were regarded as especially harmful to the sensitive or naïve reader' (Jagodzinski, 1999, p. 134). To this day they are often both seen as being in poor taste, as being 'trashy', lowbrow literature or art, as predictable, and as cultural forms that are regarded as having 'less value for being so predictably *effective*' (Driscoll, 2006, p. 95, emphasis added).

The historian Thomas Laqueur (1992) notes that the rise of the novel in the eighteenth and nineteenth centuries was accompanied by a debate about the dangers of allowing women to indulge in such a fantasy-provoking item. The novel was seen as encouraging women to retreat from social interaction into their own private world, awakening dangerous romantic, and even sexual, passions. A host of erotic images from the same era suggest that reading novels also encouraged women to masturbate (McKee, Albury, & Lumby, 2008). Laqueur (1992, pp. 203–204) feels that the cloud over the romance was the same cloud that now hovers over porn, which 'represented in its purest form the power of literature to arouse the imagination and make itself felt upon the body'. Caught in the fervour of 'reading mania' women were seen as seduced by novels, and, incapable of telling fiction apart from reality, impressed by their 'untruthful, exaggerated, or bizarre depictions' of love and romance (Schindler, 1996, p. 68). Even non-sexually explicit novels, by encouraging women to have fantasies, were thought to be a form of porn in the nineteenth century. The language used by contemporary social commentators with regards to concerns about the romance mirrors a lot of the language used in the 'porn panic' articles we read today about young men becoming addicted to visual pornography (Barnett, 2016). We can see similar distinctions made between highbrow and lowbrow media; texts which are useful and educational versus those which are entertaining at best, and at worst, dangerous; and the gendering of consumers (and therefore those who are most at 'risk') as male and female. Paasonen (2010) notes that these divisions, first constructed around the romance, paved the way for dismissals of many popular genres, particularly ones aiming at affective and sensuous responses, such as pornography and horror.

A similar parallel exists between romance novels and slash fic, in that they have both often been looked down upon by cultural commentators. The romance novel's notorious 'tacky' covers and purple prose, and the fan's intense focus on a media product and eroticisation of celebrities, as well as the shared focus on relationships, has led to a devaluation of both genres (Morrissey, 2008). Salmon and Symons (2001) have criticised fan scholars for underestimating or glossing over the similarities between slash fic and mainstream romances. They argue the two genres have a great deal in common: graphic depictions of sexual activities, shifting POVs, egalitarian love relationships and, generally, a happily-ever-after ending. Salmon and Symons (2001, p. 61, emphasis added) describe the romance novel as 'at once women's erotica *and* women's adventure fiction'. In their opinion slash fic goes one better than traditional m/f romances as, during the course of the 'adventure', female readers are offered the chance to be a 'co-warrior' instead of 'Mrs Warrior' (Salmon & Symons, 2001, p. 89). Hypothesising that slash would therefore hold a great deal of appeal to female romance readers, Salmon and Symons (2001) asked members of a mainstream romance readers' group, none of whom had read m/m before, to read an m/m romance novel and then complete a questionnaire. Seventy-eight per cent[3] of the women who completed the survey said they enjoyed the novel as much as they enjoyed the heterosexual romances they regularly read. This suggests that what is important about both these types of text is the *romance*, the development of an emotional and sexual connection, not the gender of the characters.

Nearly all the women who said they enjoyed the m/m romance said they would have enjoyed it *more* if the sex scenes had been more graphic, suggesting that women generally 'enjoy explicit descriptions of [m/m and f/m] sexual activities when they occur in the context of a loving relationship' (Salmon & Symons, 2001, p. 80). As one of my participants states, 'what I enjoy about [slash] is what I love about any nice love story with characters I like. I love K/S for the same reason I love Elizabeth Bennet and Mr. Darcy together' (American, 18–24, in a relationship, bisexual).

Despite these clear parallels, there has been some controversy over attempts to label slash as 'romance'. Russ (1985, p. 82) describes the resentment caused by descriptions of slash as simply 'Barbara Cartland in drag', and Penley (1997, p. 167) dismisses reading slash stories as romance, claiming this 'slights the pornographic force' of the genre. However, she acknowledges that romance *is* important to slash writers, moving 'imaginatively to what *they* wanted: a better romance formula, and compelling pornography for women' (Penley, 1997, p. 489). To this extent, there is a case to be made that slash is essentially romance, but with more (and arguably better) sex. The sex in slash is merely the icing on the relationship cake—it does not define the genre, and neither is the primary function of slash stories pornographic, insomuch as they are not *explicitly* designed to arouse (although they often do) nor to accompany masturbation (although, again, they often do, as discussed in Chap. 3). One of the slash writers in my study discusses this:

> I have no problem with people referring to my writing as porn, I sometimes call it that myself, but I think I'm being very flippant, because even a thousand-word written just-a-fuck will still have stuff that I've written, intended sub-textually, to show that it's more than just porn... If I'd written something very explicit, I would be disgruntled to find it left everybody cold, but I'd also not expect it to be just for somebody to rub one off to. I wouldn't mind if they did—I've had feedback where people have said 'I tried to keep up with each of the characters' and stuff like that, you know?—which I find quite flattering, but I'm more interested in people *connecting* with the characters, whether it's sexual or emotional. (British, 35–44, married, pansexual)

According to Catherine Driscoll, this perspective sees romance as having the ability to subvert pornography's distance from, and depersonalisation of, sexual relationships, instead recasting sex in terms of love and intimacy, and producing a feminist reworking of porn whilst never becoming it. For, as she notes, 'porn is to romance as male is to female, and slash cannot be porn' (Driscoll, 2006, p. 83). This is not to say that many elements of porn are not present in slash, however. As discussed in Chap. 4, PWP is a very popular category of slash, both in my sample and in other studies. The most popular choice of story in Bruner's (2013; $n = 43$) study was by far and away NC-17 rated (92 per cent) and 60 per cent of her sample reported enjoying PWP. However, Jung (2004) argues that in slash fandom sex nearly always translates into love. Even if it doesn't within any individual story, the metanarrative is still clear—these are two characters who know each other and whose lives are interwoven with each other's. Even if they hate each other, they still share a kind of intimacy that would be anathema to most characters in porn. It may, to paraphrase Lady Gaga, be a bad romance (full of revenge and horror), but it is, nevertheless, still a romance.

Emoporny: Reframing the Romance

To better understand the connections between romance and porn in women's m/m SEM preferences, it is necessary to examine how much of women's investment in romance as an integral part of erotic content is socially constructed, and therefore whether or not this represents a *real* difference in SEM preferences between genders. Morrissey (2008) argues that one of the primary reasons romance novels are not more 'pornographic' is because of the need to conform to society's expectations of women's sexual desires and behaviours. Romances cannot be porn because women cannot be seen to be consumers of porn—so they have to use code words and suggestive details. While many may find the manner in which such texts go out of their way to avoid using words like penis or clitoris ridiculous, these euphemisms 'indicate the many restrictions and limitations placed on women's sexuality within our society. Obscuring these elements has also allowed [erotic romance novels] to remain under the social radar' (Morrissey, 2008, p. 51). Burley (2003, p. 137) posits that readers, editors and publishers are careful not to label 'romance' as 'porn' because they don't want their novels 'consigned to 'adult' bookstores where nice girls rarely venture'. The majority of women in my sample reject the 'delicate' approach romance novels can sometimes take towards sexual description, but that does not mean they reject romance itself:

> [If I pick up a] romance it means that I'm going to get flowery euphemisms for body parts and sex acts. [I prefer something more] like real life, [where] you get the emotion, the attraction, the characterization and the connection, but you also get the payoff using grown-up words: penis, cunt, vagina, ass, etc. You get the messy awesome fucked-out aftermath and the sometimes painful and horrible realization that things don't always work out the way you thought they would (American, 35–44, married, bisexual).

There is much evidence to suggest that romance novels can perform a similar function for women as video porn does. A study by Coles and Shamp (1984; n = 24) found that readers of erotic romances engaged in sex more frequently than non-readers, and were also more likely to use fantasies to enhance the experience of sex. They hypothesise that erotic romances can provide a form of sexual stimulation to their readers—a kind of mental foreplay—and so can be conceived of as a form of 'softcore' pornography that women find socially acceptable and nonthreatening (Coles & Shamp, 1984, p. 208). They feel that the 'vast sales' of erotic romance novels 'suggest that women are interested in meeting their own sexual needs but are still confined by traditional social and sexual stereotypes' (Coles & Shamp, 1984, p. 208). Similarly, Wu (2006; n = 770) found that female readers of erotic romances report higher sex drives and a greater number of orgasms required for sexual satisfaction than female non-readers (although, incidentally, they score lower than men on these attitudinal variables). Interestingly, several of the women I spoke to comment on how their male partners approve of their use of m/m SEM because 'it benefits [their partners] in terms of [their] excitement' (American, 25–34, in a relationship, bisexual). As one woman explains, 'my husband likes that slash makes me physically interested in sex. He clearly considers it my version of porn' (American, 45–54, married, bisexual). Stephanie Burley (2003, p. 135) points out that while there is a 'series of codes explicitly limiting discussion of romance to the realm of the "heart" as opposed to the "body" [that] keeps us from recognising readers as sexual agents', there clearly is a strong connection between reading romances and sexual expression. She notes a similar coyness around masturbation as some of my participants noticed in slash fandom (see Chap. 4), observing that 'even when specific physical effects are described by readers, as in pounding hearts and stomachs full of butterflies, the tendency is to turn a demurring eye away from the narrative of embodied physical pleasure ... masturbation is never mentioned overtly' (Burley, 2003, p. 136). She does, however, draw attention to the success of 'hands free' stands for reading romances 'in bed'.

The reluctance to discuss masturbation and the emphasis on SEM that frontlines love and relationships may well be a facet of women's 'compulsory demisexuality' (McAlister, 2015a). In coining this term McAlister acknowledges that she is borrowing from Adrienne Rich's (1980) concept of 'compulsory heterosexuality'—the idea that women are innately sexually orientated towards men and that to deviate from this 'norm' is a perversion of their natural state. For McAlister, compulsory demisexuality is a discourse that assumes a similar sort of innate orientation. Just as Rich contended that heterosexuality is culturally encoded as compulsory for women, so McAlister contends that demisexuality is now culturally encoded as compulsory for women: 'sexual desire and romantic love are tied together in [the] socially sanctioned image of female sexuality, to the extent where the two are indistinguishable' (McAlister, 2015a, p. 10). This is not to say that romance is not *actually* important to women, or to signify a return to the feminist rhetoric that surrounded romance novels prior to the work of scholars such as Modleski and Radway in the 1980s— that they are 'clear cut patriarchal propaganda' (Wood, 2008, p. 11), containing a 'monolithically pernicious and disabling ideology ... a species of "false consciousness" which could, and should, be resisted' (Stacey & Pearce, 1995, p. 13). However, the social compunction for women to express an interest in romance, love, and intimacy cannot be overlooked.

Lisa Diamond (2008) questions the extent to which women's preference for monogamy and intimacy exists as an innate phenomenon. While her longitudinal study on women and desire found that intimacy *was* important for sexual desire to her participants, they weren't always achieving closeness with the same person: 'relationships were being traded in periodically, and in the realm of sexual fantasy, they were being betrayed all the time' (Diamond, in Bergner, 2013, p. 127). Diamond challenges the presumption that women need more emotional meaning in their SEM, while men are more objectifying: 'the stereotypes of male versus female, that male desire is far more promiscuous, seem more and more open to question' (Diamond, in Bergner, 2013, p. 128). Indeed, when Morrison and Tallack (2005; n = 17) examined lesbian and bisexual women's perception of f/f porn by presenting focus groups with two pornographic films, one targeting heterosexual men and another aimed at a lesbian audience, they did not find the clear-cut results they were expecting. While the lesbian-orientated sequence was generally viewed as having greater intimacy and authenticity, not all participants regarded it as possessing greater erotic value, or being 'better'. In fact, a number criticised it for being too 'mushy' (Morrison & Tallack, 2005, p. 23). Some of the women in my study feel similarly, with one stating that f/f pornography 'doesn't do much' for her as it's 'incredibly "mushy" and over-sentimental' which puts her off as she prefers 'more aggressive erotica' (American, 25–34, married, bisexual). Another adds:

> If somebody could tell me where to find thousands of movies like that famous one Annie Sprinkle made of the hot black UPS delivery woman fucking her, I would be all over that. In practice, by-lesbians-for-lesbians porn isn't something I just stumble across, and its reputation is a little granola crunchy and wholesome for my tastes. I [do] love the f/f and f/transwoman porn samples on Kink.com though. (American, 25–34, single, bisexual)

Similarly, in their study of 30 male and 32 female undergraduate students, Fisher and Byrne (1978) found no major differences in responses on self-reported arousal questionnaires to pornographic content that was prefaced either with a 'love' or a 'lust' scenario (e.g. sex with a partner, a sex worker, or a chance encounter). Both men and women were more aroused by the casual sex theme than sex with a partner, leading Fisher and Byrne (1978) to conclude that romantic or affectional emphasis is not a precondition for female arousal by erotica. Heiman (1977) also found that women were no more responsive (either subjectively or physiologically) to romantic script elements than men were, and that erotic content alone was responsible for arousal in both sexes.

Data from these types of studies are generally taken to mean that women are just as aroused by explicit, pornographic content as men are; not that men also might be invested in intimacy or romance in SEM but feel similarly socially constrained into *not* saying so (a compulsory promiscuity, if you will). Men—including gay men—are often framed as being interested only in graphic and emotionally meaningless sex in their pornography. Mark McLelland (1999, p. 98) points out that gay culture and gay magazines in Japan tend to contain scenes of violent sex and portray men as 'sex maniacs'. Men and the male body are thus presented in much the same way as in media aimed at heterosexual men: 'hypermasculinist' figures whose primary interest is 'in maximising and demonstrating [their] virility through [their] ability to get sex' (McLelland, 1999, p. 98). He argues that the only difference between m/m porn and m/f porn is the object, and that searching for depictions of 'enduring and loving' relationships in m/m porn is as futile as looking for them in heterosexual pornography (McLelland, 1999, p. 99). McLelland's view is not universal, however. In his 'how to' book on writing m/m fiction, the author Josh Lanyon (2008, p. 18) comments that 'the stand-out thing about m/m [e.g. slash] versus [erotic fiction written by gay men for gay men] is that there's a distinct sensibility to m/m fiction. In effect, it's gay men in love and making love versus gay men fucking. It's about sensual and evocative details. It's about the choice of language. It's about emotions rather than mechanics'. So far, so similar. However, he then goes on to suggest that writers of any type of m/m erotic fiction should take a leaf out of the slash writer's book. While he is quick to stipulate that 'no, I'm not saying I write like a girl[4]... or that you need to', Lanyon suggests that taking a 'more feminine approach' to a such writing by creating a 'complex romantic relationship' can increase potential readership for *any* explicit m/m text (Lanyon, 2008, p. 19). In other words: gay men will not be put off by a more 'feminine' style of writing, and women will be more drawn to it:

> While many women readers are likely to be disappointed by the lack of emotional intensity in much of gay genre fiction, there's a great deal to

appeal to gay male readers in m/m fiction. After all, the common complaint about porn (assuming you're a guy who *has* a complaint) is the lack of plot or character development, and what m/m fiction attempts to do … is remedy that. (Lanyon, 2008, pp. 25–26)

Lanyon's observation chimes with a survey I conducted with MSM regarding their views on women who produce and consume m/m SEM (Neville, [MSM's thoughts on women and m/m SEM], unpublished raw data; n = 166). Seventy-nine per cent of MSM answered they would be happy to read a sexually explicit m/m story written by a woman, and 84 per cent would choose to watch an m/m pornographic film aimed primarily at a female audience (i.e. directed by a woman, and marketed at women). Much like the women in my sample, the men who responded to my survey feel that SEM produced by women would have a greater focus on emotions and romance—but this is something that the majority of them are open to. As one man explains, 'women are usually a lot better at making believable romances, and making characters more sexy than just bits of flesh' (Swiss, 18–24, gay). Another adds, 'a lot that I've read written by women is a little less macho locker room sleazy kinda stuff, and that appeals to me' (American, 35–44, gay).

Neither is the preference for porn where the actors show genuine affection for each other and appear to be having fun unique to women. In McKee et al.'s (2008) study of 1023 porn users, 82 per cent of whom were men, many respondents spontaneously mentioned that the best kind of porn is where 'you can see real enjoyment'; 'genuine interest'; '[the performers] like what they're doing'; and 'genuine chemistry' exists between them (McKee et al., 2008, p. 41). Such (general) preferences are not limited to m/f pornography either, gay men also like intimacy in their porn. In his comprehensive review of gay male pornography, Bishop (2015) argues that there was a shift in the late 1980s towards more self-affirming material which began to emphasise an emotional connection between sexual partners. One of my MSM respondents comments on this, observing that 'gay [male] porn is very sensual and very intimate—not quite as overdone [as heterosexual porn], and more genuine and erotic' (American, 18–24, bisexual). Interestingly, it is exactly this sensuality that many women allude to. As one explains,

What I like about m/m porn… The look on a guy's face when he's taking a huge cock, and you can tell it's a little uncomfortable, but he's taking it, and then … it's more than comfortable! The occasional hands free come shot? Oh, and the kissing. Definitely the kissing. I don't know what it is about gay porn, but I find that, on average, the makeout portion feels a lot more sincere and realistic than the: 'ahhhh, let's rub our tongues together' kissing I see in a lot of straight porn. I mean, hardcore stuff is great, but seeing two guys just really lost in making out and groping … so sexy! (American, 35–44, single, heterosexual)

As such, Salmon and Symons (2001, p. 68) reject much of this men–porn/ women–romance dichotomy, when they argue that women are 'sexual as well as romantic beings, fully capable of being aroused by hard-core sex scenes' and men 'are romantic as well as sexual beings who fall in love as regularly as women do'. Richard Dyer (1985) believes that much m/m porn serves both these needs. He writes about how many gay porn narratives create: 'a utopian model of a gay lifestyle that combines a basic romanticism with an easy acceptance of promiscuity. Thus the underly-ing narrative is often romantic, the ultimate goal is to make love with the man; but along the way a free-ranging, easy-going promiscuity is possi-ble. … [Gay porn is therefore] a utopian reconciliation of the desire for romance *and* promiscuity, security *and* freedom, making love *and* having sex' (Dyer, 1985, p. 29, emphasis added). This could present a reason as to why m/m is a popular choice among women who value romance and intimacy in their SEM. As Davies (2005, p. 202) has argued, it has the potential to 'hit people in the heart, the brain, and the genitals'.

Do You Remember the First Time? 'Falling in Love' with m/m

Not only do many of the women in my study emphasise the importance of love and intimacy in the m/m SEM they engage with, the language of romance is often employed at a meta level when they discuss how they first came to the discovery of what turns them on. Many spoke about how 'something just clicked' (American, 25–34, married, bisexual) or they experienced a 'revelation' (British, 25–34, in a relationship, heterosexual), with one describing her first experience of engaging with m/m SEM as 'love at first sight' (British, 35–44, married, heterosexual). 'From that first moment, I was hooked', explains another (American, 45–54, married, heterosexual); 'it blew my mind' says a third (German, 35–44, married, heterosexual). One woman shares, 'what I see happening quickens my breath and makes my heart beat a little faster. From the first moment I read a story with a male/male pairing in it, I have been amazed at my own reaction to it' (American, 35–44, married, pansexual). Another recounts:

> I was raised as a very strict Catholic. There were severe punishments for behaving in a manner that was sinful. Things like masturbation, nudity, sex outside of marriage, were things that would land me in hell. Having little to no sex drive, and an inability to experience sexual attraction, made it easy for me to conform to the teachings of my parents and the church. Until I saw *Brokeback Mountain*, I had never experienced a spark of arousal. But during one of the erotic scenes, a lightbulb went off and I suddenly understood what all the fuss about sex was. I had been missing it for my entire life. I am 51 years old now, I was 47 when I first saw the film. (American, 45–54, single, asexual)

Often women describe stumbling across slash or other m/m explicit content, and suddenly realising it was what they had always been looking for: 'I still remember the very first slash fic I ever read, and something just clicked. It wasn't even hardcore, it was totally PG-13 and nothing really happened, but I don't know how else to explain it… For some reason, the Spike/Angel [pairing] just made sense. I've been slashing boys ever since' (American, 35–44, single, bisexual). Due to the paucity of m/m representations in traditional media, many gay men are introduced to gay sexuality by gay SEM, unlike heterosexuals who are typically introduced to sexuality via sex education, films, TV, advertisements, literature etc. (Bishop, 2015). What is interesting is how similar many of the women in my study sound to gay men when discussing the connection between seeing gay sexuality represented in the mainstream media for the first time and their own nascent awareness of their sexual desires. For example, a participant in Morrison's (2004) focus group study with gay men describes, 'I can remember watching a horrible movie with Christopher Reeve and Michael Caine [Deathtrap]… When they kissed in it… I was about 8 years old sitting in a theatre, and it was like a lightning bolt from the top of my head to my toes; it was like someone slapped me' (in Morrison, 2004, p. 183). This mirrors a lot of accounts given by my participants; one remembers how she was taken to the cinema as a child to see *Star Trek: The Motion Picture* and 'against the poor translations of the film in Spanish, [and] without [having seen] the key episode of *Amok Time*, it suddenly hit me—I saw real love right there' (Chilean, 35–44, married, heterosexual). Another explains, 'I saw *The Avengers* and absolutely loved it. [I was] discussing it with a friend, [and] she showed me some Bruce Banner/Tony Stark fanart and I was like: 'This is what is missing in my life'… I fell in love with it and the rest is history' (American, 18–24, single, bisexual).

While several women describe their connection with m/m sexuality as 'intrinsic' (Scottish, 45–54, single, heterosexual), many also recount how, until they encountered m/m in the public sphere, they thought they were the only women to harbour such desires. One woman notes, 'it was inside me from childhood. I saw great relationships between men I was attracted to on-screen, and made up stories in my head. When I was a teenager, I started scribbling the stories in notebooks. When I got online at age 19, I discovered I was not the only person doing this!' (Australian, 25–34, single, heterosexual). Another recounts, 'I was very much into *Buffy the Vampire Slayer*, and just getting used to the internet—around 2004. My partner found some fanfiction online for me, including slash, and I dived in. This was what I'd been waiting for all my life. I'd always found gay male relationships hot and thought I was the only woman who did' (British, 45–55, in a relationship, bisexual).

Participants often liken this first period of discovery of m/m SEM to the beginning phase of a new romance. 'Some of the first pieces [of m/m] I wrote I got very obsessed with, and would write in the middle of the night when the mood took me. It felt like falling in love—seriously', one explains (English, 45–54, in a relationship, a little bent). Another describes her first foray into writing slash fic upon her discovery of it as 'a burst of creativity that resembled a mild manic episode or falling in love' (American, 45–54, married, bisexual). Following on from this period, many women feel their preference in SEM has permanently 'shifted' to m/m, even if they still engage with m/f and f/f content.

> Honestly, I think [my interest in m/m SEM] all started with being sympathetic—thanks to a gay BFF—to the pro-gay marriage movement in the US in high school over a decade ago. I wish I could say that that led to an interest in positive queer representation in the media, which then spiralled into a fetish, because that would be the noble progression of events, but that's not how it happened. I'm not even sure how it happened. Just all of a sudden when I was, like, 17 years old, I was thinking that Sirius and Lupin in *Harry Potter* would make a damn fine couple and revisiting *The X-Files* for the Mulder/Krycek instead of the Mulder/Scully. And then I was slashing House with Wilson from *House* and Ryan Lochte with Michael Phelps and generally pricking up my ears every time there was a sniff of gay in anything from movies, to TV shows, to real life people. Now I follow the gay around like a groupie and watch—exclusively—gay porn. So, in short, it's just something that's been a part of my personality for literally years now. (American, 25–34, single, heterosexual)

For others, their awareness of their interest in m/m sexuality came from spending time with gay men. 'I got a job as an air stewardess and was working with a lot of gay people,' one woman explains, 'and was probably more-than-I-should-have-been interested in their love lives, I was just fascinated by it. I wasn't a total fag hag, I didn't hang out with them *all* the time, but I was definitely very morbidly interested! So there was definitely *something* going on there' (British, 45–54, single, heterosexual). Carol Queen (1997, p. 78) writes similarly of her own dawning understanding of her bisexual identity (having previously come out as a lesbian), speaking of how she always enjoyed the company of gay men, 'listen[ing] raptly to tales of secret cocksucking forays in the park and bathhouse expeditions to Portland or San Francisco… Continu[ing] at every opportunity to sneak looks at their porn'. Several of the older participants lamented the fact they had not realised this important element of their sexuality earlier in their lives: 'I wish I had discovered slash when I was younger. The spark could have been kindled into a fire that I could have shared with a partner, if the circumstances were right' (American, 45–54, single, asexual).

Everyone Likes Happy Endings:
The Demisexual Pornotopia

For many of the women in my sample, the display of love, affection and intimacy they crave in their SEM is often made manifest in a 'happy ending' (pun intended). In visual SEM, this can mean the portrayal of mutual, (seemingly) satisfying orgasms—what massage parlour workers refer to as a 'happy ending'. In written SEM, the happy ending is the protagonists declaring their mutual satisfaction *with each other*. Traditional romances generally go beyond this, and conclude with a happily-ever-after [HEA] ending, with the central couple ending up in a long-term monogamous relationship, usually marriage. Erotic romances have often been described as following the Happy For Now [HFN] model—while the characters may not end up in a permanent monogamous relationship, some sort of emotional connection is usually established between them by the end of the story (Roach, 2016). Orgasm is important in these texts, but it is rarely the final scene, as it is in much visual pornography. As one of the women in my study says, 'it's the emotions that are the money shot for us' (British-Italian, 45–54, married, heterosexual).

Some scholars have seen this differential emphasis as constituting a categorical difference between the two genres. Marcus (1966) has described porn as having a cyclical structure, relying on repeated climaxes: 'kind of like a repeated one-night stand' (Finnish, 18–24, in a relationship, bisexual) as one of my participants describes it. However, while a porn film may have almost as many orgasms as it does scenes, a romance novel has only one climax: 'the moment when the hero and the heroine declare their mutual love for each other' (Salmon & Symons, 2001, p. 69). Porn's emphasis on repeated sexual climaxes, versus romance's emphasis on a single declaration of love, would appear to make romance and porn antithetical to each other. However, texts such as *Fifty Shades of Grey* have shown this is not necessarily the case. As McAlister (2013) points out, the generic frameworks of romance and pornography can easily be fused, 'the repeated climaxes of pornography [can] take place within the single climax structure of the romance'. Thus these type of texts can offer 'instant *and* delayed gratification, sexual *and* emotional pleasure' (McAlister, 2015b, p. 31, emphasis added). They 'break the hard limits between the romance and pornographic genres, creating a discursive space in which women are permitted to access titillating materials while also enjoying the emotional arc of the romance narrative—a demisexual pornotopia' (McAlister, 2015b, p. 32). This is a device commonly employed in slash. As Driscoll (2006, p. 86) notes, in explicit slash stories developing romance is often achieved via sexualised encounters of building intimacy and explicitness, 'drawing on the pornographic convention of the delayed money shot', and the teen romance conventions of bases and scoring. One woman draws further parallels between the two genres: 'the best description of porn I've ever read was a film maker who said something like, "there's no suspense in porn". If this is true, then romance, with its genre-demand that the couple end up together happily ever after or happily for now is, in effect, emotional porn' (American, 45–54, married, bisexual).

There has been some debate about exactly how 'happy' an ending has to be for female consumers to find it satisfying, and this tension also exists within my sample. As one participant explains, 'I don't like unhappy endings with no hope. But everything pink is unrealistic' (Chilean, 35–44, married, heterosexual). In 1984 Janice Radway found that the most important ingredient in a romance is a happy ending, with the second 'a slowly but consistently developing love between hero and heroine' and 'some detail about the heroine and the hero after they have finally gotten together'. In her survey 'lots of scenes with explicit sexual description' wasn't chosen by any of her respondents. However, in Carol Thurston's (1987, p. 129) survey of romance readers carried out in approximately the same timeframe (between 1982 and 1985), 'detailed sexual description' and love scenes made the top five 'most liked story and character attributes' in romances, suggesting that some discrepancy between women is not uncommon. For Radway, romances are deliberately idealised fantasies, that function as a comforting haven for readers who want to escape the problems of their real lives. As such, she views the genre as one which shuns tragedy and violence. As Ricker-Wilson (1999, p. 58) warns, 'once readers venture out of the formulaic romance genre, fiction is a wild card and identification with female protagonists an emotional risk'. Radway's readers identified rape as the most objectionable element in a romance, with 'a sad ending' as runner up. However, a happy ending was the *least* popular choice among BL readers surveyed by Pagliassotti (2010), considered 'most important' by only 6 per cent of her participants. This suggests that women who consume m/m SEM might be more open than mainstream m/f romance readers to the possibility of romantic fiction that contains 'sadness, tragedy, and violence' (Pagliassotti, 2010, p. 66), and be less fixated on happy endings. A woman I spoke to expands, 'I don't necessarily require a happy-ever-after ending, and I prefer tragedy of the *Romeo and Juliet* variety to the merely mundane… I am rarely particularly interested in established relationships that do not progress in any way. If there is going to be a happy ending I am pleased, but like it to be realistic, even within a fantasy context' (British, 65–74, married, heterosexual).

Morrissey (2008, p. 84) argues that slash fic as a genre tends to present 'less than utopian endings' that show relationships 'a little bit closer to the real world' than those found in many m/f romances. She suggests that women readers are interested in romantic stories, but that their desire for a happy ending does not necessarily require marriage and a lifelong commitment, simply an emotional bond and a level of understanding between two people (the HFN ending favoured by erotic romances)—creating what she refers to as 'a new type of romantic promise' (Morrissey, 2008, p. 84).

Bring Me a Higher Love: The Triumph of Gender-Indifference

Despite its potential for queerness, the emphasis placed on monogamous love and a 'happy ending' is partly what has led to female produced m/m SEM such as slash being viewed as both conventional and heteronormative. Kyra Hunting (2012, p. 1.1) remarks on the tension that was produced within the (US) *Queer as Folk* fandom between an 'emotional desire [from fans] for the series to provide a traditional 'happily ever after' for one of its most popular couples' and 'the queerer, less traditional politics frequently articulated in the programme itself'. She notes that female fans of *Queer as Folk* rarely embrace Brian and Justin's version of non-monogamous commitment that is seen on the show, instead preferring to 'reject the canonical narrative that the characters have chosen and develop their own rules for a relationship that privileges monogamy and traditional romance' (Hunting, 2012, p. 5.2). Women do not seem to want a couple who consciously reject marriage at the end of the story, as Brian and Justin do. They don't want a couple that agrees that while they value what they have, they are nevertheless prepared to go their separate ways. Instead, they want the fairy-tale. So, while it may *seem* radical for women to be so invested in producing and consuming sexually explicit stories about same sex pairings, does dropping an m/m narrative into a Disney story, complete with marriage and home-making and babies, really exemplify anything different from the traditional Harlequin romance?

To a certain extent this question can be framed within wider debates around reform vs. assimilation in the LGBTQ+ community. Eric Anderson (2005, p. 47, emphasis added) argues that there has been 'tension between two working ideologies regarding the relationship between homosexuality and the dominant social structure… Assimilationists desire inclusion into the existing social structure' whereas 'reformists … have sought to *transform* dominant social structures'. The assimilationist model—one that uses the argument 'I'm just like you' to win the support of heterosexual allies in the fight for rights such as gay marriage—has been extremely successful, and is widely adopted. Western society now pitches the concept of achieving equality as being able to be married, join the army, and have corporate sponsorship of LGBTQ+ organisations or events, such as Pride (Duggan, 2003). The issue here is that 'substantial critique of these hegemonic institutions' is displaced as queer people instead seek to become part of them (Collier, 2015, p. 3). This mainstreaming dilutes much of the initial gay politics that called for sexual liberation and the eradication of traditional constructions of gender. In terms of slash fiction, Flegel and Roth (2010, p. 4.4) argue that such substitutions[5] 'literalise the 'I'm just like you' argument, simply replacing heterosexual narratives with a homosexual version, while simultaneously erasing both women and gayness in a seemingly queer text'.

Hunting (2012, p. 6.11) argues that when heteronormativity is 'articulated in liberal, pro-gay spaces and uses queer cultural products, its functioning becomes more complex'. Understanding what slash writers, particularly heterosexual women, do with same-sex media characters and whether they represent them as queer or heteronormal ('just like everyone else') is key to understanding slash fic's representational power. For, while marrying off the macho Starsky and Hutch may very well be an act of resistance, portraying Brian and Justin as a happily married monogamous couple can just as easily be seen as imposing heteronormativity on an originally queer text. Hunting (2012, p. 7.3) believes that the 'extent to which it is heteronormativity, rather than gender norms or compulsory heterosexuality, that is so often preserved allows us to investigate the impact that this ideology has on our culture even in pro-gay, reasonably progressive fan spaces'. The fact that many slash stories do offer up happy endings that conform to the heteronormative futurism 'always and in all ways' (Kaler, 1999, p. 4) indicates 'the hold that heterosexism has on the popular imaginary and popular romance' (Flegel & Roth, 2010, p. 5.1).

However, the view of the romance as heteronormative and inescapably straight is slowly changing. Commenting on the commercial success of Anna Cowan's *Untamed* (2013) which features both a cross-dressing hero and a cross-dressing heroine, Jodi McAlister (2016, p. 2) notes there is now a 'considerable appetite for more fluid portrayals of gender' and that many romance readers are 'prepared to reject rigid archetypes'. This does not, however, mean that the ideals of love and intimacy have been abandoned, and certainly the emphasis the women in my study place on these aspects show how important they are to slash as a genre. As one participant explains, 'I like high romance and the idea of soulmates. There's something very satisfying in being able to read vast quantities of stories where no matter what the circumstances, your OTP [one true pairing] will end up together. Fan fiction feeds my craving for melodrama and angst, but also schmoop[6] when I want it' (American, 25–34, single, heterosexual). Woledge (2006) therefore feels that slash takes place in a fantasy world that she calls intimatopia, because its central and defining feature is the exploration of intimacy. Although intimatopic texts can share features of romance and porn, these two genres (in different ways), 'seek to separate sex and intimacy. Intimatopic texts, on the other hand, work to connect these two elements' (Woledge, 2006, p. 99). Intimacy is established before sexual interaction and is maintained after it, in contrast to romantopia, where it is established by sexual interaction and is frequently transitory. In intimatopic texts, then, it is 'intimacy, not sex, that drives human interaction', and this assumption is 'completely normalised within … texts… In today's highly sexualised culture, the *intimacy* of intimatopic slash fiction is [its] most remarkable [feature]' (Woledge, 2006, p. 111). Indeed, Falzone (2005, p. 251) argues that slash is essentially queer *not* because it is about homosexuality, or because it is aberrant, 'genderfucked', or transgressive, but 'because it is transcendent, gender indifferent, and ascribes to a traditional narrative norm in a manner that is lived instead of theorised—that love is the highest ideal'. It is to this debate over whether or not women producing and consuming m/m SEM can be viewed as queer that I now wish to turn.

Notes

1. Demisexuality is also referred to as 'semi sexuality' or 'gray sexuality', and demisexual people might refer to themselves as 'gray-asexuals' or 'gray-aces' for short.
2. For the 84 per cent who were involved in slash fandom.
3. The authors do not provide a sample size.
4. <eye roll>.
5. They are referring here to situations where an m/f couple in the original text are often literally 'swapped out' for an m/m couple—so, for example, stories which follow existing narrative arcs (e.g. *Beauty and the Beast*, or the teen movie *She's All That*) but with both protagonists recast as men.
6. Schmoop describes a fan fiction, or part of a fan fiction, which is sweetly romantic or cute, usually to a degree considered maudlin.

References

Anderson, E. (2005). *Get in the game: Gay athletes and the cult of masculinity.* New York: State University of New York Press.

Barnett, J. (2016). *Porn panic! Sex and censorship in the UK.* London: Zero Books.

Bergner, D. (2013). *What do women want? Adventures in the science of female desire*. London: Canongate.

Bishop, C. J. (2015). 'Cocked, locked, and ready to fuck?': A synthesis and review of the gay male pornography literature. *Psychology & Sexuality, 6*(1), 5–27.

Bruner, J. (2013). *I 'like' slash: The demographics of facebook slash communities*. Thesis submitted to The University of Louisville. Retrieved from http://ir.library.louisville.edu/cgi/viewcontent.cgi?article=1169&context=etd

Burley, S. (2003). What's a nice girl like you doing in a book like this? Homoerotic reading and popular romance. In S. Strehle & M. P. Carden (Eds.), *Doubled plots: Romance and history* (pp. 127–146). Jackson: University Press of Mississippi.

Cawelti, J. G. (1976). *Adventure, mystery, and romance: Formula stories as art and popular culture*. Chicago: The University of Chicago Press.

Coles, C. D., & Shamp, N. J. (1984). Some sexual, personality, and demographic characteristics of women readers of erotic romances. *Archives of Sexual Behaviour, 13*(3), 187–209.

Collier, C. M. (2015). *The love that refuses to speak its name: Examining queerbaiting and fan-producer interactions in fan cultures*. Thesis submitted to The University of Louisville. Retrieved from http://ir.library.louisville.edu/cgi/viewcontent.cgi?article=3268&context=etd

Cowan, A. (2013). *Untamed*. Melbourne: Penguin eBooks.

Davies, R. (2005). The slash fanfiction connection to bi men. *Journal of Bisexuality, 5*(2–3), 195–202.

Diamond, L. M. (2008). *Sexual fluidity: Understanding women's love and desire*. Cambridge, MA: Harvard University Press.

Driscoll, C. (2006). One true pairing: The romance of pornography and the pornography of romance. In K. Hellekson & K. Busse (Eds.), *Fan fiction and fan communities in the age of the internet* (pp. 79–96). London: McFarland.

Duggan, L. (2003). *The twilight of equality? Neoliberalism, cultural politics, and the attack on democracy*. Boston: Beacon Press.

Dyer, R. (1985). Male gay porn: Coming to terms. *Jump Cut, 30*, 27–29.

Falzone, P. J. (2005). The final frontier is queer: Aberrancy, archetype and audience generated folklore in K/S slashfiction. *Western Folklore, 64*(3/4), 243–261.

Fisher, W. A., & Byrne, D. (1978). Sex differences in response to erotica? Love versus lust. *Journal of Personality and Social Psychology, 36*(2), 117–125.

Flegel, M., & Roth, J. (2010). Annihilating love and heterosexuality without women: Romance, generic difference, and queer politics in *Supernatural* fan fiction *Transformative Works and Cultures, 4.* Retrieved from http://journal.transformativeworks.org/index.php/twc/article/view/133/147

Heiman, J. R. (1977). A psychophysiological exploration of sexual arousal patterns in females and males. *Psychophysiology, 14,* 266–274.

Hunting, K. (2012). *Queer as Folk* and the trouble with slash. *Transformative Works and Cultures, 11.* Retrieved from http://journal.transformativeworks.org/index.php/twc/article/view/415/315

Jagodzinski, C. M. (1999). *Privacy and print: Reading and writing in seventeenth century England.* Charlottesville: University Press of Virginia.

Jung, S. (2004). Queering popular culture: Female spectators and the appeal of writing slash fan fiction. *Gender Queeries, 8.* Retrieved from http://www.genderforum.org/fileadmin/archiv/genderforum/queer/jung.html

Kaler, A. (1999). Introduction: Conventions of the romance genre. In A. Kaler & R. E. Johnson-Kurek (Eds.), *Romantic conventions* (pp. 1–9). Bowling Green, OH: Bowling Green State University Popular Press.

Lanyon, J. (2008). *Man, oh man! Writing M/M fiction for cash and kinks.* Palmdale, CA: JustJoshin Publishing Inc.

Laqueur, T. W. (1992). *Making sex: Body and gender from the Greeks to Freud.* Boston: Harvard University Press.

Marcus, S. (1966). *The other victorians. A study of sexuality and pornography in mid-nineteenth century England.* London: Weidenfeld and Nicolson.

McAlister, J. (2013). *Breaking the hard limits: Romance, pornography, and genre in the fifty shades trilogy.* Paper given at The Eighth Global Conference on The Erotic, September 17–19, Mansfield College, Oxford University.

McAlister, J. (2014). 'That complete fusion of spirit as well as body': Heroines, heroes, desire and compulsory demisexuality in the Harlequin Mills & Boon romance novel. *Australasian Journal of Popular Culture, 3*(3), 299–310.

McAlister, J. (2015a). *Romancing the virgin: Female virginity loss and love in popular literatures in the West.* PhD dissertation, Macquarie University. Retrieved from https://www.researchonline.mq.edu.au/vital/access/services/Download/mq:44291/SOURCE1

McAlister, J. (2015b). Breaking the hard limits: Romance, pornography, and genre in the fifty shades trilogy. *Analyses/Rereadings/Theories Journal, 3*(2), 23–33.

McAlister, J. (2016). 'You and I are humans, and there is something complicated between us': *Untamed* and queering the heterosexual historical romance. *Journal of Popular Romance Studies, 5*(2). Retrieved from http://jprstudies.org/2016/07/ you-and-i-are-humans-and-there-is-something-complicated-between-us-untamed-and-queering-the-heterosexual-historical-romanceby-jodi-mcalister/#_ftn12

McKee, A., Albury, K., & Lumby, C. (2008). *The porn report*. Melbourne: Melbourne University Press.

McLelland, M. (1999). Gay men as women's ideal partners in Japanese popular culture: Are gay men really a girl's best friends? *Japan Women's Journal (English Supplement), 17*, 77–110.

Morrison, T. G. (2004). 'He was treating me like trash, and I was loving it...' Perspectives on gay male pornography. *Journal of Homosexuality, 47*(3/4), 167–183.

Morrison, T. G., & Tallack, D. (2005). Lesbian and bisexual women's interpretations of lesbian and ersatz lesbian pornography. *Sexuality & Culture, 9*, 3–30.

Morrissey, K. (2008). *Fanning the flames of romance: An exploration of fan fiction and the romance novel*. MA dissertation, Georgetown University. Retrieved from https://repository.library.georgetown.edu/bitstream/handle/10822/551540/17_etd_kem82.pdf

Neville, L. MSM's thoughts on women and m/m SEM. Unpublished raw data.

Paasonen, S. (2010). Good amateurs: Erotica writing and notions of quality. In F. Attwood (Ed.), *Porn.com* (pp. 138–154). New York: Peter Lang.

Pagliassotti, D. (2010). Better than romance? Japanese BL manga and the subgenre of male/male *romantic* fiction. In A. Levi, M. McHarry, & D. Pagliassotti (Eds.), *Boys' love manga: Essays on the sexual ambiguity and cross-cultural fandom of the genre* (pp. 59–83). Jefferson, NC: McFarland & Company, Inc.

Penley, C. (1997). *NASA/Trek: Popular science and sex in America*. New York: Verso.

Queen, C. (1997). Beyond the valley of the fag hags. In C. Queen & L. Schimel (Eds.), *PoMoSexuals: Challenging assumptions about gender and sexuality* (pp. 76–84). San Francisco: Cleis Press.

Radway, J. (1984). *Reading the romance: Women, patriarchy, and popular literature*. Chapel Hill: University of North Carolina Press.

Rich, A. (1980). Compulsory heterosexuality and lesbian existence. *Signs, 5*(4), 631–660.

Ricker-Wilson, C. (1999). Busting textual bodices: Gender, reading, and the popular romance. *The English Journal, 88*(3), 57–64.

Roach, C. M. (2016). *Happily ever after: The romance story in popular culture.* Bloomington: Indiana University Press.

Russ, J. (1985). *Magic mommas, trembling sisters, puritans and perverts: Feminist essays.* Trumansburg, NY: Crossing.

Salmon, C., & Symons, D. (2001). *Warrior lovers: Erotic fiction, evolution, and female sexuality.* London: Weidenfeld & Nicolson.

Salmon, C., & Symons, D. (2004). Slash fiction and human mating psychology. *Journal of Sex Research, 41,* 94–100.

Schindler, S. K. (1996). The critic as pornographer: Male fantasies of female reading in eighteenth-century Germany. *Eighteenth Century Life, 20*(3), 66–80.

Shaw, S. M. (1999). Men's leisure and women's lives: The impact of pornography on women. *Leisure Studies, 18*(3), 197–212.

Snitow, A. (2001). Mass market romance: Pornography for women is different. In A. B. Snitow, C. Stamsell, & S. Thompson S. (Eds.), *Power of desire: The politics of sexuality* (pp. 245–263). New York: Monthly Review Press.

Stacey, J., & Pearce, L. (1995). The heart of the matter: Feminists revisit romance. In L. Pearce & J. Stacey (Eds.), *Romance revisited* (pp. 11–45). New York: NYU Press.

Thurston, C. (1987). *The romance revolution: Erotic novels for women and the quest for a new sexual identity.* Chicago: University of Illinois Press.

Williams, L. (1990). *Hard core: Power, pleasure and the 'frenzy of the visible'.* Los Angeles: University of California Press.

Woledge, E. (2006). Intimatopia: Genre intersections between slash and the mainstream. In K. Hellekson & K. Busse (Eds.), *Fan fiction and fan communities in the age of the internet* (pp. 97–114). London: McFarland.

Wood, A. (2008). *Radicalizing romance: Subculture, sex, and media at the margins.* Doctoral dissertation, University of Florida. Retrieved from http://etd.fcla.edu/UF/UFE0023561/wood_a.pdf

Wu, H. (2006). Gender, romance novels, and plastic sexuality in the United States: A focus on female college students. *Journal of International Women's Studies, 8*(1), 125–134.

7

'It's a Mixed Up, Muddled Up, Shook Up World'

'I like [m/m] because it's queer,' one of my participants explains, 'I'm totally over heterosexuality' (American, 25–34, single, queer). She is not alone in finding heterosexual SEM tedious, many women in this study agree with her. They speak of how m/m SEM offers an opportunity for the expression of non-normative sexuality, and that their engagement with it allows them to push boundaries and explore other kinds of kink. For example, one woman laments how difficult it is to 'find examples of cross-dressing explored in a respectful and erotic way' in m/f SEM (American, 25–34, single, queer). Another explains that 'you find *mountains* more kink in [m/m], and acceptance of kink is pretty standard … I was actually looking for heterosexual D/s [dominance/submission] … when I first found m/m. It was so beautifully done, I had to see if there was more like it' (Australian, 25–34, single, bisexual). There is a perception that queer visual porn is better than heterosexual porn because the producers 'more often take stylistic risks … than mainstream pornographers—because they often have less to lose' (American, 25–34, single, bisexual). As one woman explains, 'lately there is a lot of really wonderful video porn being filmed, and I find the gay porn companies are being quite creative and daring' (American, 45–54, in a polyamorous relationship, bisexual).

© The Author(s) 2018
L. Neville, *Girls Who Like Boys Who Like Boys*,
https://doi.org/10.1007/978-3-319-69134-3_7

However, while it may be the 'queerness' of m/m sex that appeals to some women, there is a question as to how queer the practice of women using m/m SEM really is. While there is widespread agreement that women producing or consuming m/m SEM can be categorised as 'queer', insomuch as it is 'a practice that problematizes clear straight/gay dichotomies' (Busse, 2005, p. 122), many commentators have noted a tension between creators and consumers of m/m erotic content who are attempting to see a reflection of their own lived queer identities, and those who only 'play at queerness' whist otherwise living a heterosexual (if not heteronormative) life (Lothian, Busse, & Reid, 2007, p. 107). While it is straightforward to view women who engage with m/m as being tolerant and/or liberal in their outlook, it is perhaps less so to view them as undeniably queer. Is there really any 'queerness' going on when women engage with m/m SEM beyond the fact that the actors or characters are presented as having homosexual sex?

As touched on in the previous chapter, this has been a particular area of debate within the arena of slash fiction (Neville, 2018). The sexual orientation of slash writers and readers has been a source of some uncertainty within the literature, but nevertheless, slash fandoms contain a number of women who identify as heterosexual—as do 43 per cent of the women in my sample. Given this, can slash production and consumption really be viewed as queer? Busse (2006, p. 209) comments that while statements about sexual identity are hard to substantiate, 'many women [in slash] acknowledge that their queerness is often restricted to the virtual realm as they live their 'real' heteronormative lives'. She quotes a fan who describes slash fandom as 'the queer minstrel show' (Busse, 2006, p. 209), and goes on to warn that online forums can 'permit a masquerade of queer discourse and thereby trivialise queer identities and experiences' (Busse, 2006, p. 211).

Judith Butler (1993, p. 230) notes that while the term 'queer' has been politically productive as a 'discursive rallying point' for various sexual minorities, as well as for heterosexuals for whom the term expresses an affiliation with anti-homophobic, inclusive politics, too broad a use of the term can create a tension between the critical performance of sexual identities and the material realities of sexual minorities. There is a perception here that, for LGBTQ+ folk, a heterosexual person identifying as queer can feel like an attempt to appropriate the 'good bits' of gay culture—namely the cultural and political cachet—without having to experience the discrimination and stigma that effect non-heteronormative people in their day to day lives (Neville, 2018). Indeed, Beasley, Holmes, and Brook (2015, p. 684) warn of attempts by heterosexuality to 'invite itself along to the fashionably cool queer party without having had to pay the dues of marginalisation'. In her study on slashers and identity, CarrieLynn Reinhard (2009, p. 23) describes how these, sometimes rigid, boundaries that separate insider/outsider status along the lines of real world sexual orientation can cause unhappiness and stress to women participating in online communities around m/m erotic content, and claims that failing to meet the requirements necessary to be part of such a community can 'result in feelings of ostracism and incomplete identity construction'.

On the other hand, if we take 'queer' here as a word for all forms of sexuality that do not conform to the conventional heterosexual model of penetrative sex between an active cisman and a passive ciswoman—or, as Vassi (1997, p. 71) puts it, anything that isn't 'one man and one woman who are fucking to make a baby'—then, yes, women engaging with m/m sex is queer. While this definition of queerness is certainly a broad one, David Halperin (2003, p. 339) warns us that 'even to [try to] define queer … is to limit its potential, its magical power to usher in a new age of sexual radicalism and fluid gender possibilities'—so broad definitions may be on safer ground. Queer theory, which focuses on 'mismatches between sex, gender, and desire' (Jagose, 1996, p. 3), can offer us a useful framework for further exploring the nature of women's engagement with m/m SEM. Queer theory is about reacting against normalised hierarchies (of, e.g., gay vs. straight) and identity politics, and looking outside the boundaries of heterosexual and homosexual communities. The concept of resistance is at the core of queer theory. It is a conscious refusal of labels that define what it is against, and it emphasises a retreat from binary thinking (McIntosh, 1997). To a certain extent, we can see this retreat from the binary exemplified in slash fiction; as Lamb and Veith (1986, p. 253) note, the slash writer 'does not cry "why can't a man be more like a woman?" She instead asks, "why can't we all just be human?"'! According to Hayward (2000), queer theory embraces all 'non-straight' identities. A large proportion of women in this study who identify as heterosexual in terms of their relationship and sexual history discuss how their affinity with non-conventional (and often non-vanilla) SEM makes them feel they aren't 'straight' in the traditional sense. As one woman describes it, 'I'm heterosexual, sure, but I'm certainly a little bent' (British, 45–54, mainly heterosexual, in a relationship).

To this extent, many queer theorists would certainly agree with these women's perceptions of themselves as 'not-straight'. Thomas (2006, p. 2) argues that queer theory's 'great invention' has been to 'denaturalise and disrupt the common-sense assumption' that 'one *must* have a coherent sexual identity of some sort, that eroticism of any kind and all kinds *must* be routed through *some* regulatory political fiction of personhood that can (and must) be affixed with a clearly legible label'. Indeed, Mock (2003, p. 34) believes that the straight/queer binary is something designed by the straight mind anyway; by being essentially opposed to categorical distinctions, queer theory is a theory that 'ultimately strives for its own redundance'. When the oppressions justified by such binary oppositions no longer exist, there will be no need to align oneself politically against their construction. Doty (1993, p. xv) uses the term queer to question the cultural demarcations between the queer and the straight 'by pointing out the queerness of and in straights and straight cultures'; arguably heterosexual women who watch or read m/m SEM qualify as queer in this sense. For while they may be heterosexual in terms of who they have sex with, they are not necessarily heteronormative in terms of their worldview.

In and of itself, heterosexuality is a politically neutral term. Heteronormativity, on the other hand, is far from neutral. It refers to the cultural and institutional systems that make heterosexuality 'seem not only coherent—that is, organised as a sexuality—but also privileged' (Warner, 1999, p. 548). It is heteronormativity which leads most people to assume that a person they have just met is heterosexual unless otherwise informed. Heteronormativity goes beyond just the issue of sexual practices, 'it also refers to the set of values, privileges, and life stages associated with heterosexuality, such as monogamy, marriage, and child-rearing with biological parents' (Hunting, 2012, p. 3.3). Berlant and Warner (1998, pp. 554–555) explain that 'heteronormativity is more than ideology, or prejudice or phobia against gays and lesbians; it is produced in almost every aspect of the forms and arrangements of social life: nationality, the state, and the law; commerce; medicine; and education; as well as in the conventions and effects of narrativity, romance, and other protected spaces of culture'. Heteronormativity is essentially what Jane Ward (2015, p. 35) has described as 'a fetishization of the normal'. Or, as one of my participants simply put it, heteronormativity is 'yawn' (American, 45–54, single, heterosexual).

It is our heteronormative culture that means heterosexual sex is 'in most romance novels, many Hollywood blockbusters, most shows on cable, and everywhere else [we] look' (American, 25–34, single, bisexual), whereas 'alternative sexualities go unrecognised in the majority of mainstream media' (American, 25–34, single, lesbian). For some participants, the wall-to-wall portrayal of heterosexual desire 'can be exhausting on a bad day and boring on a good day' (American, 25–34, single, bisexual). Cante and Restivo (2004, pp. 142–143) argue that m/m porn, on the other hand, is always 'non-normative, whether one conceives the non-normative as a violation of patriarchal law, or, more experientially, as the excess attached to feeling different and acting like an outsider', adding that 'all-male pornography at some point also becomes the field for the (utopian) reinvention of the world eternally promised by identity politics'. To this extent, women engaging with m/m SEM can be seen as subverting the patriarchal order by challenging masculinist values, creating a protected space for non-conformist, non-reproductive and non-familial sexuality, and developing many sex-positive values. This chapter will further explore the queerness of women's desire for m/m sexuality.

Going with the Flow: Women's Sexual Fluidity and m/m SEM

One explanation for female interest in m/m SEM could be women's sexual fluidity: essentially, the idea that women are more open to queer sex (in all its forms) than men. For some time now in feminist scholarship there has been an acknowledgement of the queer nature of women's sexual desire. Since Rich (1980, p. 238) rejected 'the assumption that most women are innately heterosexual', female desire has often been viewed as bisexual in nature. Noting that there are plenty of 'lesbian' shots on 'for women' porn sites, Schauer (2005, p. 59) observes that 'a greater possibility of fluidity ... is accorded to female desire. Nowhere do the sites insist that only "lesbians" or "bisexual" women would find the women-to-women photos attractive. Female sexuality, they seem to suggest, is at least partly bisexual'.

While this is generally taken to mean that female sexual desire is fluid in terms of who (or what) arouses them, it is also possible women are more 'fluid' in terms of how they view arousal more generally. The majority of participants in Hayes and Ball's (2009, p. 220; $n = 16$) study of slash fan communities view sexuality as fluid rather than static, and feel that eroticism has 'more to do with relationships and personal interaction than with sexual activity *per se*'. We can see this echoed in Lisa Diamond's (2008) study of women in the general population, which suggests that women tend to possess what she describes as an 'open gender schema', meaning that they disconnect gender from sexual desire. Diamond (2008, p. 231) urges us not to view love or desire as gender-orientated, pointing out that the complex neurobiological circuitry that enables us to form emotional bonds is 'fundamentally flexible when it comes to the target of bond formation, and is ready to adjust to whatever the environment affords'. To this extent, she advocates 'shifting away from sexual determinism toward a more flexible understanding of sexuality' (Diamond, 2008, p. 236). Using this lens to look at women who engage with m/m SEM it could be argued that not only are these women more open to non-gender-orientated sexual attraction and relationships themselves, but they are also more open to them in others. If these women accept their sexuality as fluid, and believe that their primary mode of attraction is towards the person, not the gender, then it is logical that they would apply this thought process to others. If a relationship between two (or more) people is compelling, then they will find sexual activity between these individuals arousing regardless of the gender combinations involved (m/m, f/f, f/m). As one woman explains, 'to me, it's all about identifying with the character, rather than what their gender is. I don't see gender as very important to be honest, and definitely not a binary' (British, 25–34, in a relationship, pansexual). Another adds, 'the whole slashing thing pretty much reinforces my pansexual world view, in which two people get together on the basis of chemistry and mutual attraction, and not on the basis of penis and vagina' (American, 25–34, single, heterosexual). Not only would this explain the high percentage of non-heterosexual women in the sample (55 per cent), but also the diversity of their interests in SEM, with most women consuming f/m SEM (75 per cent in written format, 60 per cent in visual format) and/or f/f SEM (60 per cent in written format, 46 per cent in visual format) alongside their m/m consumption.

There are various explanations in the literature for why it is that women might present as more sexually fluid than men. We've discussed in earlier chapters how women seem less tied in to their bodies when it comes to experiencing sexual arousal (see, e.g., Laan & Janssen, 2007; Laan, Everaerd, van Bellen, & Hanewald, 1994). Lab studies comparing men's and women's physiological and subjective responses to different types of porn suggest that men's sexual feelings appear to be much more strongly determined by what happens in their body than women's sexual feelings. For men, essentially, whatever the penis says goes. This does *not* mean that women's bodies do not play an important role in women's sexual lives, but that 'more conditions need to be met before women experience bodily sensations as pleasurable and exciting' (Laan & Janssen, 2007, p. 287). As Clarissa Smith (2007) has argued, physiological arousal is only possible in women if other interests, pleasures and activities have been acknowledged and addressed.

Within the field of psychology, reasons for these sex differences in response to SEM tend to fall into three categories: anatomy and sensitivity, learning and attention, and social desirability. In terms of anatomy, it is possible that men might have more cues to detect genital response than women: visual feedback in the form of an erection, coupled with tactile feedback when it presses against clothes and so on. This gives them a more concrete sense of embodied arousal—they are much more tuned in to their bodies' physiological indicators of sexual interest, and much more likely to interpret these indicators at face value. For men, then, physical symptoms of arousal might precede conscious recognition of desire; for women the inverse is perhaps equally as likely.

It is also possible that women undergo quite different learning processes in understanding their bodies' signals. Girls are often encouraged to turn away from their bodies' physiological cues (particularly with regards to menstruation; see Steiner-Adair, 1990), be less interested in learning about their genitalia (Gartrell & Mosbacher, 1984), and masturbate less (Catania, Gibson, Chitwood, & Coates, 1990). Indeed, women who masturbate more often have a higher correlation between physical and subjective measures of sexual arousal than women who either don't masturbate at all or rarely masturbate (Laan, Everaerd, van Aanhold, & Rebel, 1993; Morokoff, 1985). These attentional differences are compounded by wider social and cultural messages about female sexuality, as translated through institutions, media and everyday talk: that women do not have the same sexual desires as men, that their sexual urges are not as strong, that they do not require as much sex to feel happy and fulfilled. Women are, in effect, *trained* to discount their own bodily experiences of sexual desire, not only by being taught not to pay attention to them (or experiment with them via touch), but also because they lack the cultural basis to acknowledge and meaningfully interpret such feelings and experiences. Baumeister (2000, 2004) refers to this as 'differential plastic theory', and posits that women's sexual responses are shaped by cultural, social, and situational factors to a greater extent than men's (see also Youn, 2006).

It is also perhaps the case that women *do* interpret their level of physiological arousal in the exact same way as men do, but that the desire to be socially accepted encourages them to lie about how turned on they are in lab-based pornography studies. Catania et al. (1990) find this third explanation very unlikely, pointing out that the kind of women who volunteer to watch pornography in a psychology lab while a relative stranger measures the wetness and dilation of their vagina, are likely to be fairly liberal in their sexual outlook, and not prone to feeling large amounts of guilt or shame about their sexual needs and desires (see also Malamuth, 1996; Saunders, Fisher, Hewitt, & Clayton, 1985). Laan, Everaerd, and Evers (1995) discuss the frankness of female participants in these sorts of studies—for example, their openness to discussing the arousal they feel in scenes they subjectively report as upsetting or anger-inducing, such as those depicting rape. As such, Laan and Janssen (2007) believe that the reasons for these differences in reported arousal are more likely to be to do with anatomy, sensitivity or attentional focus than social desirability.

In addition, Zurbriggen and Yost (2004) note that, for heterosexual women, (physical) pleasure and desire comprise of two distinct constructs. When men are asked to describe their favourite, or most frequent, sexual fantasies, desire and pleasure tend to be strongly correlated—when they write about desire (of themselves or of their partners), they also write about pleasure. This is not so for women, and Zurbriggen and Yost (2004) speculate that this might spring from differences in lived experiences of heterosexual intercourse. If we take orgasm as an indicator of sexual pleasure, for men we often see a pattern of: experiencing desire, engaging in a sexual encounter, and achieving orgasm. For women, heterosexual intercourse is much less likely to result in orgasm (Haavio-Mannila & Kontula, 1997; Morokoff, 2000), so women are perhaps more used to feeling desire without also experiencing the pleasure of orgasm—meaning that female desire is often more grounded in the mind than in the body.

It could be that this very real detachment from their own physical bodies in terms of arousal—as well as the psychoanalytic aspects already touched on in Chaps. 2, 3, 4, 5, and 6—make it easier for women to imagine other bodies, other physical responses, other synergies between physical reactions and emotional responses than the ones they themselves have or experience. If women's attentional focus, when turned on, is how they *feel* intellectually and emotionally, not what their body is doing, this can perhaps give them a greater sense of fluidity and flexibility in terms of both identification and arousal. We discussed in Chaps. 2 and 4 how a significant proportion of women in my sample fantasise about being men, particularly in sexual scenarios, and in Chap. 2 we explored the idea that women may possess a genderless or genderfucked gaze. Foster (2015, p. 519) notes that 'this singular freedom to range over multiple objects of desire, without necessarily privileging the couple relationship as one's motivation, is also a defining characteristic of bisexuality, popularly understood as an "unpredictable fluidity" between male and female object-choices', and one that disrupts the binarism of hetero/homosexuality. Foster (2015, p. 519) maintains the identity category 'bisexual', as well as this mode of desire, can also be used to understand a woman who

calls a bisexual (or gay) man 'into being through her idiosyncratic practice of reading and/or writing *as if* she were a man'. In short, the practice
of women engaging with m/m SEM is *always* queer, because it always
involves some kind of fluidity. It does not sit neatly in the heterosexual
box.

As John Stoltenberg has argued:

> To be 'orientated' toward a particular sex as the object of one's sexual
> expressivity means in effect having a sexuality that is like target practice—
> keeping it aimed at bodies who display a particular sexual definition above
> all else, picking out which one to want, which one to get, which one to
> have. Self-consciousness about one's 'sexual orientation' keeps the issue of
> gender central at exactly the moment in human experience when gender
> really needs to become profoundly peripheral. Insistence on having sexual
> orientation in sex is about defending the status quo, maintain sex differ-
> ences, and the sexual hierarchy; whereas resistance to sexual orientation
> regimentation is more about where we need to be going. (Stoltenberg,
> 1989, p. 106)

This resistance to sexual orientation regimentation can therefore be
regarded as both queer, and, arguably, positive—it opens up new and
exciting possibilities. As one woman describes, 'I am very interested in
how sexuality can be—in the right circumstances—fluid and situational.
In part, because I was so uncertain of my own sexuality for a long time. I
am asexual, and did not hear about asexuality until I was in my twen-
ties—ironically, by reading *Sherlock* slash. And partly because I have a
friend who is heterosexual, but is in a homosexual relationship simply
because she loves her girlfriend so much' (Australian, 18–24, married,
asexual). Several slash scholars have tied this resistance to rigid sexual
orientation to the process of women writing or reading erotic fiction.
Jenkins (1992) links such resistance to women and slash fiction, and
Somogyi (2002) links it to women's fluidity with regards to sexually
explicit fan fiction more generally. Noting the shifting POVs in Janeway/
Chakotay explicit fics she argues that much m/f fan fiction gives readers
the opportunity to *be* a woman and make love to a woman, to *be* a man
and make love to a man. She feels the interest of women in these types of

stories with their shifting viewpoints—be they m/m, m/f, or f/f—reflects a 'uniquely female sexuality, a sexuality in which having and being are not dichotomous but part of the same thing, where identification and desire merge' (Somogyi, 2002, p. 403). Women's engagement with m/m SEM therefore rejects the notion 'that gender roles are fixed and predetermined and embrace[s] the idea that sexuality can be fluid and filled with various erotic possibilities' (Katyal, 2006, p. 485). To this extent, it is certainly queer.

Girls Just Wanna Have Fun: m/m as a Site of Play

Women engaging with m/m SEM can also be viewed as queer, insomuch as it is an inherently disruptive practice, and one that situates pleasure and playfulness before social norms or rules. This is not the kind of porn women *should* be engaging with, according to social practice, and yet they are—and, as discussed in Chap. 3, one of the primary reasons they do it is because it's *fun*. It brings them joy. It makes them feel good. As one woman complains, 'I often think in these studies [of women and m/m SEM] the simple fact that it's *fun* gets left out' (English, 55–64, single, heterosexual). Foster (2015, p. 521) notes that as children we are often allowed greater latitude in expressing ourselves as gendered, and, to a lesser extent, sexual beings, whereas when we grow old that latitude seems to be gradually reined in until it disappears: there is 'no room [any-more] … for "play"'. Slowly but surely, a lot of the fun, the joy, the sheer staggering *potential*, is sucked out of how we perform both gender and sexuality. To this extent, McLelland (2000, p. 23) argues that BL and slash represent gender not as it is, but how it *should* be 'negotiable, mal-leable, a site of play'.

We can therefore conceive of women watching or reading m/m porn as engaging in a celebration of queer desire. Shave (2004) has used Bakhtin's (1984) work to establish the concept of slash fandom on the internet as a contemporary site of carnival. For Bakhtin (1984), the car-nival is a liminal space, where rules that govern normative behaviour are lifted, and people are able to pursue taboo desires in this unique place outside of time.

Shave (2004) believes the convergence of slash and the internet has created 'a new, imagined, carnival space', and that the concept of carnival helps to provide a more complex understanding of the 'subversive pleasures' created by the intersections between slash fandom and the internet. There are no rules in place at the carnival, and no gatekeepers. A participant points out that slash is 'more interesting than what gets published as it doesn't go through editors. It can be completely off the wall. And it can deal with queer issues that no published literature would ever deal with. You get 'magical-queer-acceptance-land' fantasy fics, for example' (British, 25–34, in a relationship, bisexual). Conceiving of slash as carnivalesque allows us to see how women in these online spaces are experiencing both desire for difference (m/m) and desire for the Other (men) (Sanders-McDonagh, 2016). Bakhtin (1984, p. 255) maintains that in the carnival space the individual body is no longer distinct; it is possible to 'exchange bodies, to be renewed' through a change of costume or mask. Shave notes that the use of pseudonyms in slash fandom can allow for play and movement by providing metaphorical masks for participants. For many women, engaging with m/m SEM also offers the radical opportunity to imaginatively 'exchange' bodies with male actors or characters—to, in effect, *become* different, *become* the Other. Thorn (2004, p. 176) discusses cosplay within fandom and the entailing crossdressing seen at slash cons, likening it to the erotic play seen at carnivals and in other liminal settings (festivals, holidays)—the identification of women as men does not extend only to the realm of the imagination. This can lead slash (and indeed gay porn) to become a site of what Chatterjee and Lee (2017) refer to as *rapture/rupture* for the women involved. Pleasure is paramount here, and conventionality is abandoned, broken, ignored and rejected.

In addition, Booth (2014) notes that the carnival relishes the grotesque, the excessive, the extremes of the human body. He posits that slash fic 'represents this grotesqueness specifically through both its erotic spectacle of the male body[1] and the extension and subversion of the typically heteronormative structure of the original text' (Booth, 2014, p. 402). He observes that the carnival is also a time of hierarchy reversal, creating a specific, ritualised opposition to the *status quo*. Slash fic similarly enacts such hierarchy reversal through the change in gender roles, 'males become passive, sexuality takes precedence over repression, and emotional reactions are placed at the forefront of the narrative instead of backgrounded, as in heteronormative mainstream media texts' (Booth, 2014, p. 402). In much slash, characters who are traditionally presented as heterosexual in the source texts are instead presented as either gay or bisexual, or, at least, as being open to the possibility of homosexual romance or sex. Some slash stories spend much time exploring precisely how and why these 'straight' characters came to experience homosexual desire and/or engage in homosexual sex, often placing them in extreme or unusual situations (prison camps, wars, fuck-or-die, sex pollen, aliens made them do it[2]). One woman remarks that what she 'love[s] most is seeing how other writers get their characters into a sexual relationship when they wouldn't ordinarily go there' (American, 55–64, married, heterosexual). This practice is not unproblematic, something I will return to in the next chapter. However, it is interesting in what it says about the nature of female producers' concepts of queer desire. Ward (2013, p. 137) explains that one of the things she likes about homosexual encounters between adult heterosexuals is that they 'constitute a unique erotic domain characterised by many of the features of childhood sexuality', insomuch as they 'occupy a liminal space within sexual relations, one that sits outside of the heterosexual/homosexual binary and is sometimes barely perceptible as sex. Like childhood sex, it goes by many other names: experimentation, accident, friendship, jokes, playing around, and so on'. She notes that in trying to avoid being mistaken as 'sincere' homosexuals, heterosexuals must get really 'creative' (Ward, 2013, p. 137). This is fun, and, as Ward argues, queer.

Stanley (2010, p. 99) argues that BL and slash are therefore transgressive 'precisely because they are joyous and playful and refuse to take themselves, or the many iconic narratives they subvert, seriously'. They are also transgressive in that they subvert much of the mainstream discourse around heterosexuality (that it is a desirable state of affairs, that to 'come out' as gay or bisexual is inherently traumatic and/or likely to lead to unhappiness and isolation). As one woman complains, 'queer stories in the media … are [often] tragic. *Black Swan* wasn't happy, never mind the fact that it was all inside the main character's head, and *The Kids Are*

Alright wasn't a model relationship either' (American, 35–44, in a relationship, lesbian). Many of my participants note that explicit slash fiction provides a space where readers can engage with gay and bisexual characters who are fulfilled and happy. One participant observes, 'have you ever noticed how gay guys are not allowed to live happily ever after in books or film? One or both always ends up dead' (American, 45–54, heterosexual, single)—slash is seen as providing a counter to this portrayal. In turn, this allows some women consumers to better understand that LGBTQ+ people will not necessarily 'live miserable lives' (American, 18–24, single, pansexual), by offering up texts where non-heteronormativity is celebrated and seen as a site of joy and play.

For female producers of m/m SEM, then, creating this kind of media allows them to 'play' with gender and sexuality, and open themselves up to experimentation, even if they present as heterosexual in day to day life. As one woman explains, engaging with m/m SEM made her 'more open about accepting and understanding people who are not sitting neatly in one labelled box' (Australian, 35–44, queer/dyke, single). She goes on to discuss how her 'gaze is queer, and I am sometimes surprised … [when someone I read as queer] doesn't identify or practice that way. I like it when people are comfortable enough with their gender and sexuality to play with it. For example, for straight men to behave camp or a butch guy to femme up, or a hetero guy to have queer sex … [m/m] lets me enjoy playing with gender and sexuality, and exploring the different ways in which these can be performed.' Another speaks about how the labels attached to sexuality are 'confining' and that she views the 'slash fiction world [as] "queer"' insomuch as she feels it creates a world where 'all of these identities and categories are quite secondary to humanness' (American, 25–34, heterosexual, married). In turn, she believes that 'though only engaging in heterosexual sex with a male-identified partner' she identifies as 'queer, and by queer I mean what I have just talked about: humanness'. There is a clear rejection of community 'policing' in my sample—online slash fiction is very much positioned as a carnivalesque space, a place where 'rules don't apply'. Most of the women I spoke to reject the creation of rules about who is and isn't allowed to engage in fandom, or write m/m sex, and acknowledge that yes, fandom provides a safe space for queer women, but this safe space should be extended to everyone—gay or straight, man or woman, cisgendered or trans (Neville, 2018).

Here we return to the important idea I first highlighted in Chap. 3—that women like m/m SEM because it is fun, and because it brings them both joy and pleasure. O'Brien (2004, p. 125) also argues that porn should be fun, and that the 'representative playfulness' of porn indicates that 'that most fraught of categories, 'sexual identity' need not be dictated by either genitalia or gendered behaviour'. Without wanting to argue myself out of writing this book(!), this remains *the* paramount reason for women engaging with m/m SEM. For as McNair (2013, p. 124) observes, 'fucking is fun, and its representation is a pathway to pleasure ... for its own sake, unadorned and requiring no apology'.

'I'll Be in My Bunk': The Homoerotics of Slash Fandom

Several fan scholars point to the ways in which slash fandom can be conceived of as queer space because it involves elements of homosocial desire between and within the participants themselves. Arguments about women's evacuation from slash stories, such as those discussed in Chaps. 3 and 5, overlook the key point that women *are* and always have been present in slash: the writers and readers *are* the women (Lackner, Lucas, & Reid, 2006). As one participant tells it,

> I now think that it's striking that my entrée into [writing m/m] was together with my best female friend, that it started out as a "social" project for us, which strikes me as similar to the production and consumption of slash erotica online today. Yes, slash fiction is certainly erotica in its truest, perhaps essential sense—something to titillate, arouse, play out sexual fantasy—and I love that about it, but it is also something that comes out of female social interaction, even if only digitally—and I love that too (American, 25–34, married, heterosexual).

Even if the producers and/or consumers of any particular explicit text identify as heterosexual, the process of heterosexual women producing smut for other women is something that can arguably be seen as queer. Social ties are created which undoubtedly have erotic elements. As Busse

(2006, p. 208) argues, the fact that slash communities involve women writing sexual fantasies with and for one another projected through and by same-sex desire suggests that fandom may be a queer female space, 'if not at the level of the text and the writers, then at least at the level of their interaction'. Busse (2005, p. 121) inverts Sedgwick's argument and describes this phenomenon as 'a homosocial—even homoerotic—bond 'between women' where the reader and author are making love over the naked bodies of attractive men'. As one woman recounts, 'in the ten years I've been an active member of fandom …, I've seen a large number of writers become involved romantically and sexually with each other, including some who previously identified as heterosexual. I think there's something to be said for slash and erotica allowing women to voice their own fantasies and desires, and, in sharing that experience with others, to form romantic and sexual connections of their own. The slash community provides a level of intimacy, a safe place, that gives women the freedom to explore themselves and their responses to each other' (American, 25–34, single, lesbian). The romantic/erotic way that slashers talk to each other (e.g. *pets*, *smooches* as ways of expressing thanks for popular stories) can certainly be conceived of as queer—in the absence of real physicality, the virtual one is exaggerated and often sexualised (Lackner et al., 2006). Busse (2006, p. 208) observes that 'emotional intimacy frequently gets translated into images of physical intimacy, so that close fannish ties become verbalised in sexual language'. Elizabeth Guzik (in Busse, 2006, p. 219) calls this the 'erotics of talk' and notes 'no matter what identity or behaviours many women readers and writers of slash claim, there is an unmistakable erotics between and among them'. This is not a concept unique to slash; writing about homoerotic readings of popular romance, Burley (2003, p. 130) argues that 'when we … love our favourite authors, and experience close personal relationships to our fellow readers of erotic literature, we are in fact engaged in homosocial practice'. One participant discusses how she wrote m/f erotica long before she wrote any m/m, explaining, 'round age 14, I had a painfully acute crush on one of my best friends, a female, and we took turns writing erotic scenes between Legolas and our Mary-Sue[3] OFCs [original female characters] to entertain each other. In retrospect, I was sublimating my same-sex interest in her into a safer form of expression' (American, 25–34, in a polyamorous relationship, bisexual).

Sometimes these homosocial ties between women are central to slash's appeal. Cumberland (1999, p. 1) maintains that a 'displacement of affection' follows the initial impulse to seek out websites where m/m erotic texts can be consumed and produced. The original motivation may be a sexual longing that is projected on to a fantasy figure, but this becomes of secondary importance once the online community is discovered. In essence, 'the hero becomes the vehicle rather than the object of affection' and the ultimate function of the 'cultic figure' is to 'provide a site upon which a web of real life friendships can be formed' (Cumberland, 1999, p. 1). For others, the community was always the central draw of slash. One participant observes 'girls love [m/m], which is why I started writing it … Burgeoning lesbian that I was, that was really exciting. It wasn't a perverse thing on my part; it was just that being part of a community of women who were all so enthusiastic was huge for me—especially since in the real world my friend group was slowly turning to all guys, gay and straight' (American, 25–34, in a relationship, lesbian).

Boys Who Do Boys Like Their Girls: The Privileging of Male Bisexuality

Women's interest in m/m SEM can also be viewed as queer insomuch as it often privileges male bisexuality. Not only do the women themselves express a desire that could be categorised as bisexual (Foster, 2015), many of the men who feature in much of the m/m SEM produced and consumed by women (especially within slash) are presented as bisexual.

Numerous scholars have commented on the prevalence of biphobia in both heterosexual (Eliason, 1997) and homosexual communities (Welzer-Lang, 2008). There remains a persistent belief that bisexuality is not a 'real' sexual orientation, and that bisexuals themselves are promiscuous or dishonest (Klesse, 2011). Bisexuality is often regarded as a 'phase', something that a person will grow out of, returning to their 'true' sexuality, be that heterosexual or homosexual. Gender differences are often apparent here; as Ward (2015, p. 20) astutely observes 'when ... women have sex with women, the broader culture waits in anticipation for them to return to what is likely their natural, heterosexual state; when ... men have sex with men, the culture waits in anticipation for them to admit that they are gay'. The fluidity exhibited by bisexuals 'provokes fear, unease, and confusion in monosexuals' which in turn creates an oppressive discourse towards bisexuality, where 'structural oppression stemming from hetero-normativity is aided by the inherently one-sided narrative of homosexuality' (Bucholski, 2014, p. 1). As Angelides notes:

> In order for something to be only one or the other, it is therefore necessary to prohibit a term being both one *and* the other. Anything that is both one and the other contradicts the logic of either/or and must be repressed, disavowed, or excluded. As we have seen, in the hetero/homosexual structure the position of both/and is occupied by bisexuality; hence its contradictory presence must be erased. (Angelides, 2001, p. 188)

Not only do bisexuals experience the same types of homophobic abuse and aggression as homosexuals within heteronormative cultures, they are also often viewed within the gay community as potential traitors to the cause, forcing many to supress their bisexuality when they engage in gay and lesbian activism (McLean, 2008). The feminist sexologist Carol Queen (1997, p. 81) discusses a 'chaste' romance that she conducted with a gay male friend, recounting the time they kissed in a nightclub: 'We made jokes about what bad queers we were, but joking covered our deep fear: we both loved (and needed) our community, its structure, its support. We were misbehaving. What would become of us?' The denial or rejection of bisexuality often leads to bisexual erasure in the mainstream media (as well an absence of male bisexuality in most SEM). As one of my participants complains, '[I want to] mention [the importance of] bisexuality in slash fiction! Things aren't just Gay and Heterosexual. [The fact you haven't asked me about this] feels a real shame, but isn't surprising. I am bisexual and am used to being totally ignored and erased. It is part of the reason why I started writing professionally; to see myself reflected in erotic and romantic fiction' (British, 35–44, in a polyamorous relationship, bisexual).

It is notable, therefore, that male (and female) bisexuality is so prevalent within slash fiction (Coker, 2015). Not only are male characters
often presented as unapologetically bisexual (or, in some sense, post-
sexual), but OT3[4] partnerships are not uncommon. In her analysis of 19
slash fic texts, Dianna Fielding concluded that fics tended to privilege
homosexuality over heterosexuality, and bisexuality over both, noting
'bisexuality, which is usually viewed as deviant, is privileged' (Fielding,
2013, p. 30). As one participant explains, 'I read a lot of *Star Trek* fic, and
one of the things that struck me the most upon entering the fandom was
the attitude that everyone was so accepting of all kinds of relationships.
There's rarely any 'but I don't even like guys' angst, or the hand-wavey
'I've always been bi' exposition. It just *is*' (American, 45–54, single, bisexual). The 'not really gay' idea is often used to bash characters in slash
(with writers accused of 'wimping out' of making a canonically heterosexual character homosexual—something I will return to in the next
chapter), but there's no reason it couldn't be that women find bisexuality
attractive in and of itself. Certainly men seem to find female bisexuality
attractive, given how prominently it features in pornography aimed at
heterosexual men. The reverse, however, is rarely true, even though this
study suggests there would be a receptive market for it. Härmä and Stolpe
(2010, p. 118) note that one of the staples of mainstream porn is the 'oft-
professed bisexuality of female porn stars', but that male actors are presented quite differently: 'men are never asked [in behind the scenes
material] whether they "like to fuck men"'. It would appear that the 'heteroflexibility' (Diamond, 2005) with which apparently straight women
experiment with same-sex activity extends only to female performers in
on-set discourse. While female bisexuality is often trivialised, it is nevertheless visible. In addition, Moorman (2010) notes that on many porn
sites, types of 'lesbian' and 'bisexual' porn, typically focused on the display of women's bodies, are grouped with heterosexual porn, while gay
male porn and bisexual porn that includes guy-on-guy action is generally
not included at all, or is segregated from other categories via a link to a
separate page. Moorman (2010, p. 156) observes that videos featuring
two women and no men might be listed as 'girl-on-girl' or categorised in
relation to particular sex acts, such as 'oral', but m/m porn is 'always
"gay"'. Framed this way, 'lesbian' sex is incorporated as 'girl-on-girl' action

for a straight audience, whereas m/m sex is 'presented as marginal and "Other"' (Moorman, 2010, p. 156). However, this is perhaps underestimating female attraction to male bisexuality. As one participant affirms, 'I actually prefer bisexual/threesomes when watching porn. And there I like both f/m/m and f/f/m' (German, 25–34, single, bisexual).

Likewise, Rooke and Moreno Figueroa (2010) note that while female heteroflexibility is relatively common in swinging circles, male bisexuality is not. When it is touched on, it is done so 'in rather evasive terms, such as "not being worried about close contact"' (Rooke & Moreno Figueroa, 2010, p. 230). Although there were men on the Swingers Date Club website that Rooke & Moreno Figueroa analysed who defined themselves as 'straight but open minded' or 'bisexual', sex between men, unlike f/f sex, was not visible. Rooke and Moreno Figueroa (2010, p. 230) maintain that its absence points to the way that it 'disturbs the dominant heteroflexible visual discourse at work. Heteroflexibility works to titillate other couples and encourage the participation of single bisexual and bicurious women while discouraging potential male homosexual or bisexual swingers'. However, they do quote an interesting post from the Swingers Date Club website that implies this is not necessarily because female swingers would be uninterested in m/m sexual contact: 'John isn't uncomfortable in the presence of other guys and isn't against fumbling with Mary present (*as this would excite her*) but the right situation has never occurred' (in Rooke & Moreno Figueroa, 2010, p. 232, emphasis added). The journalist Mark Simpson recounts a similar tale:

> A separated 'bi-curious' fireman in rural England I met a few times before he went back to his wife recently contacted me to tell me something rather alarming. 'She found out about you,' he said. 'She hacked into my Hotmail account.' 'Oh, shit,' I said. 'What did she do? Throw you out?' 'No,' he said. 'She got turned on! She wants to watch.' The poor guy had to tell her that this really was a kinky bridge too far for him. That he was too much a traditionalist to go down that path … (Simpson, 2006)

However, to date there has been very little research examining women's interest in bisexual, heteroflexible, or sexually fluid men. Rupp and Taylor (2010, p. 29) believe that men do not experience the same kind of sexual fluidity as women, 'although they may identify as straight *and* have sex with other men, they certainly don't make out at parties for the pleasure of women'—unlike the phenomena of 'straight girls kissing', which Rupp & Taylor believe to be relatively widespread. Ward (2015) argues that this common perception that women are sexually flexible and men are sexually rigid has rendered men's sexual fluidity largely invisible. She thinks it does exist, and that women *are* interested in it—'straight men *do* make out at parties for the pleasure of women and engage in virtually the same teasing/kissing/sex-for-show behaviours that straight young women do'—it just receives very little academic or popular attention (Ward, 2015, p. 13). She draws attention to Eric Anderson's (2008) work on young men and sports, where they discuss 'jacking each other off' during threesomes with women and teammates, and other sexually performative behaviour for the benefit of the female gaze. One football player interviewed by Anderson says, 'I'm not attracted to them [men]. It's just that there has to be something worth it. Like, this one girl said she'd fuck us if we both made out. So the ends justified the means. We call it "a good cause". There has to be a good cause' (in Anderson, 2008, p. 109). Another explained, 'there has got to be a reward. If I have to kiss another guy in order to fuck a chick, then, yeah, it's worth it … Well, for the most part it would be about getting it on with her, but, like, we might do some stuff together too. It depends on what she wants' (in Anderson, 2008, p. 109). Not only does this work suggest that men are more than capable of sexual fluidity, it also shows that some women find fluidity and/or bisexuality a desirable trait in their male lovers. As one woman in my study states, 'maybe I'm deviant, but I fantasize about a threesome with two guys and would love the guys—in real life—to want each other too. I'm bisexual myself, so it's easy for me to assume/fantasize that they are bisexual as well' (Dutch, 25–34, in a relationship, bisexual).

While there is evidence to suggest that women *are* more fluid with regards to sexuality than men (Diamond, 2008), recent research supports Ward's view of men as more heteroflexible than previously thought. Robards (2017) has analysed the 'Totally Straight' (r/TotallyStraight) 'subreddit' on social media site reddit—a forum dedicated to sharing gay pornography amongst men who identify as straight. As well as posting recommendations etc., the men who frequent this site also use it to share personal narratives related to contested 'mostly straight' sexual identities. Robards (2017, p. 16) argues that this phenomenon could be representative of 'broader socio-cultural shifts towards less rigidly defined categories and acceptance when it comes to sexual identity'. Anderson and McCormack (2016) found that younger generations of bisexual men report easier coming out experiences, greater disclosure and recognition in relationships, and less attachment to their sexual identities. McCormack and Wignall (2017) posit that porn has played a role in this; many 'mostly' straight men in their study discuss how porn has helped them to understand their sexual desires in a monosexist culture. Over a fifth (20.7 per cent) of the 134 heterosexual men in Downing, Schrimshaw, Scheinmann, Antebi-Gruszka, and Hirshfield's (2016; n = 821) study on SEM use reported viewing porn containing m/m sex.

The move towards flexible, or 'unlabelled' sexual identities is arguably queer, and the fact that many women who engage with m/m SEM are interested in men who experience attraction to *people* regardless of gender is also queer. As discussed in the previous chapter, while women's 'compulsory demisexuality' can be extremely confining, it also has the potential to destabilise heteronormative concepts of desire that focus on monosexism.

Fucking Gender: Women, m/m SEM, and Genderfuck

In Chap. 2 I discussed the possibility of a 'genderfucked' gaze—the idea that the imagined 'self' has the freedom to mutate into alternative manifestations when viewing or reading pornographic material. However, the concept of genderfuck goes beyond the gaze; some queer theorists have suggested it as a political strategy for disrupting the heteronormative narrative. According to Whittle (2005, p. 117) queer theory is almost entirely 'concern[ed with] "genderfuck"', which is a full-frontal theoretical and practical attack on the dimorphism of gender- and sex-roles'. As many queer theorists have argued, sexuality and gender are interrelated but distinctive cultural constructions, and sexuality is not reducible to gender.

However, June Reich (1992, p. 113) acknowledges that there are contradictions inherent in the difference between, say, herself in the shower (as a woman—gendered) and herself in bed (as a femme—sexualised) that need to be articulated, and that the best way to do this is through a theory of genderfuck, which 'deconstructs the psychoanalytic concept of difference without subscribing to any heterosexist or anatomical truths about the relations of sex to gender'. Genderfuck utterly rejects such binarisms as male = masculine, female = feminine, male = aggressive, female = passive etc. Instead, genderfuck 'structures meaning in a symbol–performance matrix that crosses through sex and gender, and destabilises the boundaries of our recognition of sex, gender, and sexual practice' (Reich, 1992, p. 113). When asked about whether they engaged with m/f SEM, a number of women I spoke to state a preference for non-conventional male/female relations. For example, in the arena of slash fiction, a lot of women only like m/f if it is 'genderbending, where an originally male character is turned into a female'—this is seen as preserving both the queerness, and the 'equality … that was inherent in the original characters' relationship, but also gives you the chance to read hot het sex' (American, 25–34, single, queer).

Smith (1997) quotes a section from a letter from his friend, Johnathan Meyer, further explaining genderfuck:

> [Genderfuck] has at least two meanings for me—the first, more obvious, is fucking with gender—distorting, twisting, inverting, playing with, challenging—but still (potentially) retaining and honouring the beauty of any expression of gender/sexuality etc… But the other is fucking gender: making love to gender … it is as much a source of inspiration, joy, anguish, beauty, and entrapment as any other aspect of human existence and human culture. (Meyer, personal correspondence, in Smith, 1997)

Smith (1997) believes that 'the concept of genderfuck opens queer further to playful possibilities of destabilising rigidly gendered boundaries'. Genderfuck then is not limited to sex, but also includes drag, crossdressing, and other forms of gender bending. According to Ward (2013, p. 135), the beauty of queer or genderfucked desire is 'precisely that it is unpredictable, potentially unhinged from biological sex or even gender, and as such, difficult to commodify. A given viewer may have a vagina, but while watching porn, who knows what kinds of subjectivities emerge (male? alien? wolf?)' This chimes with the work of Leo Bersani (1995, p. 103) who considers 'who are you when you masturbate?' to be an insightful question. As Donald E. Hall (2003, p. 109) notes, 'one of those hopelessly complicated and therefore highly intriguing sites is the relationship between solitary or masturbatory sexuality and the question of identity'. Hall is alluding to the fact that the masturbator is essentially having sex with themselves, and therefore masturbation becomes a homosexual-identified activity, but it could equally be argued that who I imagine myself to *be* while masturbating is a site of potential queerness (and genderfuckery). If I imagine myself to be a man having sex with another man while I'm getting off, what am I? A straight woman (after all, I'm imagining having sex with a man)? A gay man (because I'm also a man in this scenario)? A heterosexual woman engaged in a homosexual act (because I'm engaged in an act of self-love)? Trans-identified (because I'm a woman imagining I'm a man)? Queer (because this is an act that is hard to explain through conventional sexual scripts)?

To this extent, the women in my sample who imagine themselves, sexually, *as men who have sex with men,* while watching m/m pornography, reading m/m erotica, or masturbating to their own sexual fantasies (as explored in Chap. 4), are carrying out a queer act. They are embodying the concept of genderfuck. According to Halberstam (1992, p. 51) 'gender is always posthuman, always a sewing job which stitches identity into a body bag'—the emphasis that many of the women in my study place on both the fluidity of gender and sexual identity in the realms of fantasy, and the importance of *humanness* as opposed to gender when thinking about both sex and love, might explain both their preference for nonconventional SEM and the affinity many of them feel for queerness and queer culture. The queerness of being a woman who watches or reads about m/m sex—the queerness of being a woman who imagines herself as a man—may also explain why a number of lesbians enjoy m/m SEM. As one woman summarises, 'I love love *love* [f/f]—for possibly obvious reasons—but there is so little of it. I'll take queer males if I can't get queer girls' (New Zealander, 35–44, single, lesbian). Another adds, 'for me the queer is more important than the form of queer' (American,

25–34, single, queer), with a third acknowledging that 'as a bisexual woman, sometimes I'm attracted to men but I find it helpful not to leave the "queer sphere" mentally' (American, 25–34, married, bisexual). As discussed in the previous chapter, the concept of queer for these women is as much about love as it is about fucking. Reich steals a phrase from Roland Barthes (1975, p. 65) when she refers to a genderfucked body as a '*drag* anchor', adding, 'drag: a performance that interrupts the circulation of the phallus in its attempt to fix, that is, anchor, signification. A drag anchor, far from centring a soul, casts a body loose in a queer sea of love' (Reich, 1992, p. 126).

The Rise of the Queer Heterosexual

For the women in my study who identify as other-than-heterosexual, an interest in other-than-heterosexual SEM simply 'because it is queer' might seem both logical and uncontroversial. However, the interest of heterosexual women in other-than-heterosexual SEM 'because it is queer' raises the possibility that they, too, might be considered as queer. To some extent, this idea can be seen as resonating with the idea of the 'queer heterosexual' (Powers, 1993; Smith, 1997), which Powers (1993, p. 24) describes as the 'testy lovechild of identity politics and shifting sexual norms'. In contrast to some of the objections raised to the appropriation of queer identities by heterosexuals discussed at the beginning of this chapter, Smith (1997) writes about how he claims the identity of queer heterosexual in order to 'further [his] own desires for a world of multiple possibilities rather than as a means of benefitting from queer chic'. Embracing this perspective, the queer activist and director Tristan Taormino (2003) 'welcomes queer heterosexuals into the fold', adding 'being queer to me has always been about my community, my culture, and my way of looking at the world, not just who I love and who I fuck'. For her, it is not surprising that 'all this gender fucking has … rubbed off on heteros, who are ditching the script in favour of writing their own' (Taormino, 2003). Calvin Thomas (2000, p. 15) therefore speaks of the possibility of 'including straights in the queer mesh'. While being aware that 'it is important that queerness isn't appropriated—through either self-serving trendiness or totalising liberation—to support another version of dominant heteronormative order', Roberta Mock (2003, p. 24) nevertheless thinks that the 'erotic potential' of the queer heterosexual should not be ignored.

Others are resistant to the idea of the queer heterosexual. Walters (1996, p. 839) voices concerns that queer has come to stand for 'a sort of meaningless pluralism motivated only by a vague sense of dissent'. She is worried that the deconstruction of identity politics can become a convenient way to avoid questions of privilege, and asks whether we would tolerate this kind of 'passing' in another context. After all, the notion of 'passing' has connotations for LGBTQ+ folk—and people of colour—that hardly suggest liberation. As Walters (1996, pp. 841–842) asks, 'if it is clearly co-optive and colonising for the white person to claim blackness if she or he "feels" black (or even feels aligned politically with the struggles against racism), then why is it so strangely legitimate for a heterosexual to claim queerness because he or she feels a disaffection from traditional definitions of heterosexuality?' Powers (1993, p. 24) herself notes that members of the LGBTQ+ community often show suspicion and anger at heterosexuals who infiltrate their space, and maintains that 'this hostility is completely justified'. Assimilation by heterosexuals can diffuse the focus of queer culture and politics. As a gay friend of Powers' remarked to her, 'you know what happens to a gay club when straights start coming? It becomes a straight club' (in Powers, 1993, p. 24).

However, such a viewpoint positions heterosexuality as defiantly 'not queer'. Beasley and others have critiqued this perception of heterosexuality as 'nasty, boring, and normative' within sexuality scholarship (Beasley et al., 2015, p. 682), and are critical of the tendency to focus on heterosexuality's more negative and disturbing aspects while, at the same time, casting it as uninteresting. Beasley (2011) questions why the concept of transgression is often linked to queerness while heterosexuality is equated with normativity/heteronormativity. She concedes that any discussion of transgression in relation to heterosexuality certainly has to happen in the context of its privileged status, but feels the conflation of heterosexuality and heteronormativity 'presents dominant practices as all of a piece and unchanging' (Beasley, 2011, p. 26). Heterosexuality 'remains a monolith opposite a rainbow of "queer" subjectivities, practices, and lifestyles'

(Schlichter, 2004, p. 549), left in its 'dark, dull corner, its positive potential for joy and social change [is] virtually unacknowledged and unexplored' (Beasley et al., 2015, p. 683). Beasley (2011, p. 26) believes that considering the idea that subversion might be intrinsic within some dominant practices like heterosexuality—rather than necessarily always external to them—'opens up hopeful possibilities'. The current status quo not only assumes that heterosexuality is not politically labile, it also assumes that queer sexualities are *always* politically labile—neither of which are necessarily true. Interestingly, Beasley, Holmes, and Brook (2015, p. 693) include 'gender-ambiguous sexual fantasies' in their list of activities that might be considered 'transgressive' (p. 688) or 'more confronting heterosexual activities' (p. 693). Kath Albury (2002, p. xix) hints at the transgressive potential for women who engage with m/m SEM when she writes that 'a heterosexual woman who actively asserts and exercises sexual agency' might be 'the most perverse of all perverts'. In the area of slash and BL, Meyer (2010, p. 252) notes that 'the queerness of … fans pops out of what is only a shell of conventional straight femaleness' (Meyer, 2010, p. 252).

We can see from the way they talk about the porn they like, the erotica they read, and the content of their fantasies, that most of the women in my study possess a certain amount of sexual fluidity—something which might seem out-of-step with their sexual orientation (43 per cent heterosexual) and relationship choices (87 per cent of the 244 women in a relationship were with a man). However, it could well be that these women are the epitome of Powers' (1993) queer heterosexual. Beasley (2011, p. 30) notes that while there is a growing consensus that identities are not biomedically determined, fixed, or even coherent, this fluidity appears almost exclusively to apply to queer sexualities, 'it drops away sharply in relation to heterosexuality' meaning that 'queered' heterosexuality is seen as an oxymoron. However, Taormino (2003) believes that the queer heterosexual is both real and authentic, viewing them as someone with non-traditional gender expression, someone who is politically and culturally aligned with the queer community even if they 'happen to love and lust after people of a different gender', and often someone who embraces alternative modes of sexuality and relationships, such as polyamory, cross-dressing, and BDSM. Taormino states that while these people might be 'straight-looking and [/or] straight-acting … you can't in good conscience call them straight'. Likewise, Thomas (2006, p. 3) notes that a person who 'is drawn, however tremblingly, to what disrupts identity' may regard themselves as queer, as one of the people who 'vibrate to the chord of queer [even] without having much same-sex eroticism' (Sedgwick, online, quoted in Thomas, 2006, p. 3).

Thomas (2006, p. 5) argues that if 'queer does mark the other side of 'the street' … then that other side … can be a 'site of becoming' to which some heterosexuals desire to cross over'—politically speaking. After all, 'the word queer itself means *across*' (Sedgwick, 1993, p. xii), from the German word *quer*: transverse. Chatterjee and Lee (2017, p. 47) observe that for the German speaker, this meaning still holds primary importance, and resonates with the phrase 'quer denken'—to think outside the box. This concept certainly resonates with my participants, with one asserting that 'to enjoy this kind of thing [m/m] you tend to be the sort of person who thinks outside the box' (Scottish, 25–34, single, bisexual). Another adds that she likes queer porn, and for her the *aesthetic* is what makes porn queer, not the genders or sexualities of the actors involved: 'the bodies involved might be any combination of cis/trans/other, but the aesthetic and attitudes are notably different from mainstream porn. There's less boxing into categories, a wider range of body types, and a sense of collegiality and sex-positivity that makes me enjoy the participants as characters, not just bodies' (Canadian, 25–34). Heterosexuals giving voice to their queer desires can also have positive effects on wider society, something I will return to in Chap. 9. For, as Halley (1993, p. 83) has argued, heterosexual silence on these matters, however unwittingly, joins in a pervasive representation of heterosexuals as 'coherent, stable, exclusively loyal to heterosexual eroticism, and pure of any sodomitical desires or conduct'. By engaging with m/m SEM—and, more importantly, by *talking* about engaging with m/m SEM, by creating spaces, such as online slash fandom, for the discussion of sexuality as well as the sharing of m/m erotica—the heterosexual women in my study are defiantly bucking this convention.

While I would be hesitant to make a definitive case for the existence of the queer heterosexual, a determination to create a welcoming, open, and liberal environment within online spaces dedicated to slash fandom is overwhelmingly apparent in my data. Much of what participants say about their fandom space is echoed in the works of writers such as Leo Bersani (1995, p. 9), who argues that we should be looking to create a kind of community 'that can never be settled, whose membership is always shifting … a community in which many straights should be able to find a place'. As Carol Queen (1997, p. 84) so movingly writes about her desire to go beyond both straight/gay and male/female, '[I want to create] an army of lovers, for an army of lovers cannot fail. I do not want this community to be an alliance; alliances can be broken. I want it to be a deep, dizzying, expectation-defying love affair'. It would certainly seem, as Donna Haraway (1991) has previously suggested, that the politics of affinity have strong potentials to move us beyond some of the limitations of identity politics.

Notes

1. Particularly when we consider the concept of mpreg, as discussed in Chap. 5.
2. For a further discussion and explanation of these tropes, see Chap. 8.
3. A Mary Sue (if female) or Gary Stu (if male) is an idealized and annoyingly perfect fictional character. Often, this character is recognized as an author insert or wish fulfilment.
4. A derivative of OTP [one true pairing], OT3 means one true threesome, and involves three characters instead of two. OTPs may constitute three same sex characters, but often they involve m/m/f or m/f/f partnerships, for example Harry/Ron/Hermione in *Harry Potter* or Jack/Will/Elizabeth in *Pirates of the Caribbean*.

References

Albury, K. (2002). *Yes means yes: Getting explicit about heterosex*. St Leonards: Allen and Unwin.

Anderson, E. (2008). 'Being masculine is not about who you sleep with…:' Heterosexual athletes contesting masculinity and the one-time rule of homosexuality. *Sex Roles, 58*(1–2), 104–115.

Anderson, E., & McCormack, M. (2016). *The changing dynamics of bisexual men's lives: Social research perspectives*. London: Springer.

Angelides, S. (2001). *A history of bisexuality*. Chicago, IL: University of Chicago Press.

Bakhtin, M. (1984). *Rabelais and his world* (H. Iswolsky, Trans.). Bloomington: Indiana University Press.

Barthes, R. (1975). *The pleasure of the text* (R. Miller, Trans.). New York: Noonday.

Baumeister, R. (2000). Gender differences in erotic plasticity: The female sex drive as socially flexible and responsive. *Psychological Bulletin, 126*, 347–374.

Baumeister, R. (2004). Gender and erotic plasticity: Sociocultural influences on sex drive. *Sexual and Relationship Therapy, 19*, 133–139.

Beasley, C. (2011). Libidinous politics: Heterosex, 'transgression', and social change. *Australian Feminist Studies, 26*(67), 25–40.

Beasley, C., Holmes, M., & Brook, H. (2015). Heterodoxy: Challenging orthodoxies about heterosexuality. *Sexualities, 18*(5–6), 681–697.

Berlant, L., & Warner, M. (1998). Sex in public. *Critical Inquiry, 24*(2), 547–466.

Bersani, L. (1995). *Homos*. Cambridge, MA: Harvard University Press.

Booth, P. (2014). Slash and porn: Media subversion, hyper-articulation, and parody. *Continuum: Journal of Media & Cultural Studies, 28*(3), 396–409.

Bucholski, M. (2014). *Intersectionally Bi: The how and why of Bi-negativity*. Unpublished research paper. Retrieved from https://www.researchgate.net/publication/285894995_Intersectionally_Bi_The_how_and_why_of_Bi-negativity

Burley, S. (2003). What's a nice girl like you doing in a book like this? Homoerotic reading and popular romance. In S. Strehle & M. P. Carden (Eds.), *Doubled plots: Romance and history* (pp. 127–146). Jackson, MI: University Press of Mississippi.

Busse, K. (2005). 'Digital get down': Postmodern boy band slash and the queer female space. In C. Malcolm & J. Nyman (Eds.), *Eroticism in American culture* (pp. 103–125). Gdansk: Gdansk University Press.

Busse, K. (2006). My life is a WIP on my LJ: Slashing the slasher and the reality of celebrity internet performances. In K. Hellekson & K. Busse (Eds.), *Fan fiction and fan communities in the age of the internet* (pp. 207–224). London: McFarland.

Butler, J. (1993). *Bodies that matter: On the discursive limits of sex*. London: Routledge.

Cante, R., & Restivo, A. (2004). The cultural-aesthetic specificities of all-male moving-image pornography. In L. Williams (Ed.), *Porn studies* (pp. 142–166). London: Duke University Press.

Catania, J. A., Gibson, D. R., Chitwood, D. D., & Coates, T. J. (1990). Methodological problems in AIDs behavioural research: Influences on measurement error and participant bias in studies of sexual behaviour. *Psychological Bulletin, 108*, 339–362.

Chatterjee, S., & Lee, C. L. (2017). 'Our love was not enough': Queering gender, cultural belonging, and desire in contemporary *Abhinaya*. In C. Croft (Ed.), *Queer dance: Meanings and makings* (pp. 45–66). Oxford: OUP.

Coker, C. (2015). Everybody's bi in the future: Constructing sexuality in the *Star Trek* Reboot fandom. *The Journal of Fandom Studies, 3*(2), 195–210.

Cumberland, S. (1999). *Private uses of cyberspace: Women, desire and fan culture.* Paper presented at the Media in Transition Conference, October 8, Massachusetts Institute of Technology, Cambridge. Retrieved from http://web.mit.edu/comm-forum/papers/cumberland.html

Diamond, L. M. (2005). 'I'm straight but I kissed a girl': The trouble with American media representation of female-female sexuality. *Feminism & Psychology, 15*(1), 104–110.

Diamond, L. M. (2008). *Sexual fluidity: Understanding women's love and desire.* Cambridge, MA: Harvard University Press.

Doty, A. (1993). *Making things perfectly queer: Interpreting mass culture.* Minneapolis, MN: University of Minnesota Press.

Downing, M. J., Schrimshaw, E. W., Scheinmann, R., Antebi-Gruszka, N., & Hirshfield, S. (2016). Sexually explicit media use by sexual identity: A comparative analysis of gay, bisexual, and heterosexual men in the United States. *Archives of Sexual Behaviour.* Retrieved from https://link.springer.com/article/10.1007/s10508-016-0837-9

Eliason, M. J. (1997). The prevalence and nature of biphobia in heterosexual undergraduate students. *Archives of Sexual Behaviour, 26*(3), 317–326.

Fielding, D. M. (2013). *Normalising the deviance: The creation, politics, and consumption of sexual orientation and gender identities in fan communities.* BA Thesis submitted to Hamline University. Retrieved from http://digitalcommons.hamline.edu/dhp/7/

Foster, G. M. (2015). What to do if your inner tomboy is a homo: Straight women, bisexuality, and pleasure in m/m gay romance fictions. *Journal of Bisexuality, 15*, 509–531.

Gartrell, N., & Mosbacher, D. (1984). Sex differences in the naming of children's genitalia. *Sex Roles, 10*, 867–876.

Haavio-Mannila, E., & Kontula, O. (1997). Correlates of increased sexual satisfaction. *Archives of Sexual Behaviour, 26*, 399–419.

Halberstam, J. (1992). Skinflick: Posthuman gender in Jonathan Demme's 'The Silence of the Lambs. *Camera Obscura, 27*, 35–52.

Hall, D. E. (2003). *Queer theories*. London, UK: Palgrave Macmillan.

Halley, J. (1993). The construction of heterosexuality. In M. Warner (Ed.), *Fear of a queer planet: Queer politics and social theory* (pp. 82–102). Minneapolis: University of Minnesota Press.

Halperin, D. M. (2003). The normalisation of queer theory. *Journal of Homosexuality, 45*(2/3/4), 339–343.

Haraway, D. (1991). *Simians, cyborgs, and women: The reinvention of nature.* New York: Routledge.

Härmä, S., & Stolpe, J. (2010). Behind the scenes of straight pleasure. In F. Attwood (Ed.), *Porn.com* (pp. 107–122). New York: Peter Lang.

Hayes, S., & Ball, M. (2009). Queering cyberspace: Fan fiction communities as spaces for expressing and exploring sexuality. In B. Scherer (Ed.), *Queering paradigms* (pp. 219–239). Oxford: Peter Lang.

Hayward, S. (2000). *Cinema studies: The key concepts*. London: Routledge.

Hunting, K. (2012). *Queer as Folk* and the trouble with slash. *Transformative Works and Cultures, 11*. Retrieved from http://journal.transformativeworks.org/index.php/twc/article/view/415/315

Jagose, A. (1996). *Queer theory: An introduction*. New York: New York University Press.

Jenkins, H. (1992). *Textual poachers: Television fans and participatory culture.* New York: Routledge.

Katyal, S. K. (2006). Performance, property, and the slashing of gender in fan fiction. *Journal of Gender, Social Policy and the Law, 14*(3), 461–518.

Klesse, C. (2011). Shady characters, untrustworthy partners, and promiscuous sluts: Creating bisexual intimacies in the face of heteronormativity and biphobia. *Journal of Bisexuality, 11*(2–3), 227–244.

Laan, E., Everaerd, W., & Evers, A. (1995). Assessment of female sexual arousal: Response specificity and construct validity. *Psychophysiology, 32*, 476–485.

Laan, E., Everaerd, W., van Aanhold, M., & Rebel, M. (1993). Performance demand and sexual arousal in women. *Behaviour Research and Therapy, 31*, 25–35.

Laan, E., Everaerd, W., van Bellen, G., & Hanewald, G. (1994). Women's sexual and emotional responses to male- and female-produced erotica. *Archives of Sexual Behaviour, 23*(2), 153–169.

Laan, E., & Janssen, E. (2007). How do men and women feel? Determinants of subjective experience of sexual arousal. In E. Janssen (Ed.), *The psychophysiology of sex* (pp. 278–290). Bloomington: Indiana University Press.

Lackner, E., Lucas, B. L., & Reid, R. A. (2006). Cunning linguists: The bisexual erotics of words/silence/flesh. In K. Hellekson & K. Busse (Eds.), *Fan fiction and fan communities in the age of the internet* (pp. 189–206). London: McFarland.

Lamb, P. F., & Veith, D. (1986). Romantic myth, transcendence and *Star Trek* zines. In D. Palumbo (Ed.), *Erotic universe: Sexuality and fantastic literature* (pp. 236–255). Westport, CT: Greenwood Press.

Lothian, A., Busse, K., & Reid, R. A. (2007). 'Yearning void and infinite potential': Online slash fandom as queer female space. *English Language Notes, 45*(2), 103–111.

Malamuth, N. (1996). Sexually explicit media, gender differences and evolutionary theory. *Journal of Communication, 46*, 8–31.

McCormack, M., & Wignall, L. (2017). Enjoyment, exploration and education: Understanding the consumption of pornography among young men with non-exclusive sexual orientations. *Sociology, 51*(5), 975–991.

McIntosh, I. (1997). *Classical sociological theory*. Edinburgh: Edinburgh University Press.

McLean, K. (2008). Inside, outside, nowhere: Bisexual men and women in the gay and lesbian community. *Journal of Bisexuality, 8*(1–2), 63–80.

McLelland, M. (2000). The love between 'beautiful boys' in Japanese women's comics. *Journal of Gender Studies, 9*(1), 13–25.

McNair, B. (2013). *Porno? Chic!* London: Routledge.

Meyer, U. (2010). Hidden in straight sight: Trans*gressing gender and sexuality via BL. In A. Levi, M. McHarry, & D. Pagliasotti (Eds.), *Boys' love manga* (pp. 232–257). Jefferson: McFarland and Company.

Mock, R. (2003). Heteroqueer ladies: Some performative transactions between gay men and heterosexual women. *Feminist Review, 75*(1), 20–37.

Moorman, J. (2010). Gay for pay, gay for(e)play: The politics of taxonomy and authenticity in LGBTQ online porn. In F. Attwood (Ed.), *Porn.com* (pp. 155–167). New York: Peter Lang.

Morokoff, P. J. (1985). Effects of sex guilt, repression, sexual 'arousability', and sexual experience on female sexual arousal during erotica and fantasy. *Journal of Personality and Social Psychology, 49*(1), 177–187.

Morokoff, P. J. (2000). A cultural context for sexual assertiveness in women. In C. B. Travis & J. W. White (Eds.), *Sexuality, society, and feminism* (pp. 299–319). Washington, DC: American Psychological Association.

Neville, L. (2018). 'The tent's big enough for everyone': Online slash fiction as a site for activism and change. *Gender, Place and Culture*. Online first http://dx.doi.org/10.1080/0966369X.2017.1420633

O'Brien, W. (2004). Qu(e)erying pornography: Contesting identity politics in feminism. In S. Gillis, G. Howie, & R. Munford (Eds.), *Third wave feminism: A critical exploration* (pp. 123–134). New York: Palgrave Macmillan.

Powers, A. (1993). Queer in the streets, straight in the sheets: Notes on passing. *The Village Voice, 29/06/93*, 24–31.

Queen, C. (1997). Beyond the valley of the fag hags. In C. Queen & L. Schimel (Eds.), *PoMoSexuals: Challenging assumptions about gender and sexuality* (pp. 76–84). San Francisco: Cleis Press.

Reich, J. L. (1992). Genderfuck: The law of the dildo. *Discourse, 15*(1), 112–127.

Reinhard, C. D. (2009). *If one is sexy, two is even sexier: Dialogue with slashers on identity and the internet*. Roskilde: Roskilde University Publications. Retrieved from http://dspace.ruc.dk/bitstream/1800/4062/1/Reinhard_2009_slash_identity.pdf

Rich, A. (1980). Compulsory heterosexuality and lesbian existence. *Signs, 5*(4), 631–660. (also 1993 same article, 227–254).

Robards, B. (2017). 'Totally straight': Contested sexual identities on social media site reddit. *Sexualities*. Retrieved from http://journals.sagepub.com/doi/abs/10.1177/1363460716678563

Rooke, A., & Moreno Figueroa, M. G. (2010). Beyond 'key parties' and 'wife swapping': The visual culture of online swinging. In F. Attwood (Ed.), *Porn. com* (pp. 217–235). New York: Peter Lang.

Rupp, L. J., & Taylor, V. (2010). Straight girls kissing. *Contexts, 9*(3), 28–32.

Sanders-McDonagh, E. (2016). *Women and sex tourism landscapes* (Vol. 63). London: Taylor & Francis.

Saunders, D. M., Fisher, W. A., Hewitt, E. C., & Clayton, J. P. (1985). A method for empirically assessing volunteer selection effects: Recruitment procedures and responses to erotica. *Journal of Personality and Social Psychology, 49*, 1703–1712.

Schauer, T. (2005). Women's porno: The heterosexual female gaze in porn sites 'for women'. *Sexuality & Culture, 9*(2), 42–64.

Schlichter, A. (2004). Queer at last? Straight intellectuals and the desire for transgression. *GLQ: A Journal of Lesbian and Gay Studies, 10*(4), 543–564.

Sedgwick, E. K. (1993). *Tendencies*. Durham, NC: Duke University Press.

Shave, R. (2004). Slash fandom on the internet, or, is the carnival over? *Refractory, 6*. Retrieved from http://refractory.unimelb.edu.au/2004/06/17/slash-fandom-on-the-internet-or-is-the-carnival-over-rachel-shave/

Simpson, M. (2006). *Curiouser and curiouser: The strange 'disappearance' of male bisexuality*. Blog post at marksimpson.com. Retrieved from http://www.marksimpson.com/blog/2006/04/26/curiouser-and-curiouser-the-strange-disappearance-of-male-bisexuality/

Smith, C. (1997). *How I became a queer heterosexual*. Paper presented at 'Beyond Boundaries': An International Conference on Sexuality, July 29–August 1, University of Amsterdam. Retrieved from http://culturalresearch.org/qhet/

Smith, C. (2007). *One for the girls!: The pleasures and practices of reading women's porn*. Bristol, UK: Intellect Books.

Somogyi, V. (2002). Complexity of desire: Janeway/Chakotay Fan Fiction. *Journal of American and Contemporary Cultures, 25*, 399–404.

Stanley, M. (2010). 101 uses for boys: Communing with the reader in yaoi and slash. In A. Levi, M. McHarry, & D. Pagliassotti (Eds.), *Boys' love manga: Essays on the sexual ambiguity and cross-cultural fandom of the genre* (pp. 99–109). Jefferson, NC: McFarland & Company, Inc.

Steiner-Adair, C. (1990). The body politics: Normal female adolescent development and the development of eating disorders. In C. Gilligan, N. P. Lyons, & T. I. Hammer (Eds.), *Making connections: The relational worlds of adolescent girls at Emma Willard School* (pp. 162–182). Cambridge: Harvard University Press.

Stoltenberg, J. (1989). *Refusing to be a man: Essays on sex and justice*. Portland, OH: Breitenbush Books.

Taormino, T. (2003, May 6). The queer heterosexual. *The Village Voice*. Retrieved from http://www.villagevoice.com/news/the-queer-heterosexual-6410490

Thomas, C. (2000). *Straight with a twist: Queer theory and the subject of homosexuality*. Illinois: University of Illinois Press.

Thomas, C. (2006). Crossing the streets, queering the sheets; or, 'Do you want to save the changes to queer heterosexuality?'. In R. Fantina (Ed.), *Straight writ queer: Non-normative expressions of heterosexual desire in literature* (pp. 1–8). Jefferson: McFarland Press.

Thorn, M. (2004). Girls and women getting out of hand: The pleasures and politics of Japan's auteur comics community. In W. W. Kelly (Ed.), *Fanning the flames: Fans and consumer culture in contemporary Japan* (pp. 169–186). New York: State University of New York Press.

Vassi, M. (1997). Beyond bisexuality. In *PoMoSexuals: Challenging assumptions about gender and sexuality* (pp. 70–75). San Francisco: Cleis Press.

Walters, S. D. (1996). From here to queer: Radical feminism, postmodernism and the lesbian menace (or, why can't a woman be more like a fag?). *Signs: Journal of Women in Culture and Society, 21*(4), 830–869.

Ward, J. (2013). Queer feminist pigs: A spectator's manifesto. In T. Taormino, C. Penley, C. Shimizu, & M. Miller-Young (Eds.), *The feminist porn book* (pp. 130–139). New York: The Feminist Press.

Ward, J. (2015). *Not gay: Sex between straight white men.* New York: University of New York Press.

Warner, M. (1999). *The trouble with normal: Sex, politics, and the ethics of queer life.* Cambridge, MA: Harvard University Press.

Welzer-Lang, D. (2008). Speaking out loud about bisexuality: Biphobia in the gay and lesbian community. *Journal of Bisexuality, 8*(1–2), 81–95.

Whittle, S. (2005). Gender fucking or fucking gender? In I. Morland (Ed.), *Queer theory* (pp. 115–129). Basingstoke: Palgrave Macmillan.

Youn, G. (2006). Subjective sexual arousal in response to erotica: Effects of gender, guided fantasy, erotic stimulus, and duration of exposure. *Archives of Sexual Behaviour, 35*(1), 87–97.

Zurbriggen, E. J., & Yost, M. R. (2004). Power, desire, and pleasure in sexual fantasies. *Journal of Sex Research, 41*, 288–300.

8

'You Give Me the Sweetest Taboo'

Eroticism has often been rooted in the transgression of social conventions about what is forbidden and what should be hidden from view. Not only has male homosexuality frequently been 'forbidden' (both legally and morally), male homosexual and homosocial worlds have historically been kept hidden from women. Not in the sense that women didn't know about them, but hidden in that they were often supported by male-only institutions and spaces to which women did not have access: boarding schools, universities, the workplace, the military. While this may, slowly, be changing, m/m *sex* is something which remains categorically hidden from the female gaze. The gay sauna is the ultimate boys' club: however far we push the concept of gender equality it is one all-male institution that will never open its doors to female patrons. Given the paucity of m/m sex scenes in much mainstream media, as discussed in previous chapters, and the predominance of m/f sex in erotic romances marketed at women, sex between men holds a great deal of mystique for some women. It is the sex we don't get to see. It is the sex we *never* get to have. Georges Bataille (1957/1986) argues that eroticism is wedded to this idea of transgression, claiming that what we find erotic is inherently disruptive and disorderly, and this is what brings about the feeling of excitement. We like to look at the things we are not meant to see. We like to have—or at least try to have—the sex we must not—*cannot*—have. For, as Meana (2010, p. 119) proclaims, eroticism is the 'wild child of desire … [it] just will not be told what to do'.

It is unsurprising, then, that much pornography hinges on this notion of transgression. As Knudsen, Lofgren-Martenson, and Mansson (2007, p. 39) observe, 'it is in pornography that we find information about the hidden, the forbidden, and the taboo'. Indeed, Laura Kipnis (1996, p. 163) argues that pornography's 'greatest pleasure is to locate each and every one of society's taboos, prohibitions, and proprieties, and systematically transgress them, one by one'. Male SEM consumers have often been positioned as the transgressors of these taboos, but as McNair (2013, p. xi) argues, women are not so very different in their sexualities from men, and often share with them 'an interest in the transgressive' dimensions of the erotic. In fact, it is arguably easier for women to commit 'transgressions' in the realm of SEM than it is for men—after all, so many things are off limits to us. Both consuming porn and looking at the naked male body—staples of the erotic—are things that women are not traditionally expected to do. From the very first time women dip their toes into the waters of eroticism, they are transgressing the boundary of 'appropriate' female behaviour—and this naughtiness can be extremely exciting. As one woman explains, 'watching m/m makes me a little high, because I always feel like I'm doing something forbidden' (French, 25–34, married, lesbian).

In their analysis of female patrons at a male strip club, Montemurro, Bloom, and Madell (2003) note that most of the women present were 'first timers'. They therefore speculate that women attend these shows because it is a 'somewhat mischievous' and 'deviant' activity and that they enjoy the fact that their presence in such a space makes them feel 'bad' or 'naughty' (Montemurro et al., 2003, p. 342). As Lofland (1969, p. 106) has argued, we sometimes engage in deviant behaviour for the sheer fun or 'pleasant fearfulness' that comes from participating in it. Heiman (1977, p. 272) then wonders if perhaps SEM for women 'must be socially unacceptable or norm-breaking in order to be maximally arousing', noting the preference of the women in her study for sexual scenarios that went against contemporary scripts. Women watching m/m porn not only goes against contemporary scripts, it snatches up these scripts with both hands and tears them to pieces. Not only do such women get to enjoy the 'taboo' nature of watching sex they wouldn't normally get to see—what Mackinnon (1997, p. 162) refers to as 'the naughtiness of illicit viewing'—they also get to witness men enjoying something that heterosex has often taught them men don't (shouldn't?) enjoy: penetration. M/M porn gives women sex that they themselves will 'never get to experience' and probably 'shouldn't be watching', and adds to it the sight of 'a man getting enjoyment out of something that is not supposed to be pleasurable, i.e. anal penetration' (American, 25–34, single, bisexual). Jenkins (1992, p. 201) similarly describes slash fiction's subversive qualities as an internalised feature of its subculture, declaring that the 'forbidden' aspects are an important part of its allure.

The French philosopher Bernard Henri Levy (2007) argues that when there is no distance, there is no border, and that the border is required for eroticism precisely because it is the transgression of such a border that stirs desire. For some of the women I spoke to it is this border, this distance between themselves and the men they are watching or reading about, that adds to the thrill of consuming m/m SEM. As Isola (2010, p. 86) explains, male bodies are exciting for women because 'in existential reality, this is not a body to which female artists, authors, or readers have psychological or physiological access'. One of my participants notes that m/m sex is 'very physical, there's still the hint of the taboo about it even now, and there are times when I really wish I could swap bodies so I could experience it for myself. I guess it also has the lure of being something that, unless technology advances hugely in my lifetime, I will never be able to experience—it's literally the unknowable' (British, 35–44, married, bisexual).

Of course, it is not just that women are 'forbidden' from engaging with m/m sex, it is that m/m desire *itself* still carries an element of the taboo. Dyer (1988, p. 57) notes that while there is nothing inherently gay or lesbian about the ideas of privacy, voyeurism and exhibitionism, the fact that homosexual desire is 'forbidden' means 'it may well find expression, as a matter of necessity rather than exquisite choice, in privacy and voyeurism … Furtive looking may be the most one dare to do.' Or, in contrast, 'exhibitionism may take on a special voluptuousness, emerging from the privacy of the closet in the most extravagant act of going public'

(Dyer, 1988, p. 58). As discussed in Chap. 2, women are used to indulging in voyeuristic pleasures. The furtive look is often the only kind we are allowed. It is perhaps natural then, that we might choose to look at the types of SEM that aim to elicit just such furtive glances. As one woman explains, 'heterosexual porn lacks that illicit thrill that I get from m/m, from the subverting of society's norms, which contributes to me not enjoying it as much' (British, 35–44, single, bisexual).

However, transgression inevitably also includes elements of intrusion, encroachment on to the sexual territory of 'the Other'. Women producing and consuming m/m SEM have been accused of what I have termed 'gaypropriation'—exploiting m/m sexual culture in order to achieve sexual satisfaction (Neville, 2018). This chapter will also explore whether this gaypropriation is a transgression too far, or whether it is a positive step that serves to unite women and MSM in terms of common goals: freedom from patriarchal oppression and an end to heteronormativity.

Bad Girls and Badder Boys: The Thrill of Liking Something You Shouldn't

Jenkins (1992) argues that women are less intrigued by f/f pairings than m/m pairings because relations among women have historically been more fluid and less restrictive. After all, lesbianism has never been illegal in the UK, and hence 'the stigma attached to the [historically] quasi-legal status of male homosexuality is absent with respect to lesbianism' (Burke, 1994, p. 195). One of the women in my study discusses how 'male homosexual relationships were part of my 'taboo relationships' fascination when I was younger. I liked the idea of forbidden love in a repressed society' (American, 18–24, single, heterosexual). Taboos with regards to f/f sex are also arguably less entrenched because, unlike m/m sex, they sidestep the thorny issue of male penetration. While the female body is seen as inviting, even welcoming, penetration in the heteronormative imaginary, the male body is understood as 'phallic and impenetrable…, a war-body, simultaneously armed and armoured, equipped for victory' (Waldby, 1995, p. 268). As such, there remains an injunction against what Sartre (1952/2012, p. 615) calls 'men's secret femininity': receptive anal eroticism. Catherine Waldby explains:

> When a man puts his penis in a woman's vagina he is saying, 'look, it is she who is the permeable one, the one whose body accommodates, takes in and lets out, *not* I'. But the possibilities of anal erotics for the masculine body amount to an abandonment of this phallic claim. The ass is soft and sensitive, and associated with pollution and shame, like the vagina. It is non-specific with regard to genital difference in that everybody has one. It allows access into the body, when after all only women are supposed to have a vulnerable interior space. All this makes anal eroticism a suasive point for the displacement or erasure of purely phallic boundaries … But the negative injunction of the phallus against such pleasure is, like all laws, also an invitation to transgression, and it seems likely that this phallic taboo might intensify, rather than disperse, the erotic potential of the anus. (Waldby, 1995, p. 272)

In most m/f SEM, particularly soft-core narratives, the male body remains unpenetrated. Boundaries are not crossed, literally or figuratively. Phallic taboos are not broken. For the most part, anything goes, yet still 'the real remaining taboo … on male penetration' persists, 'while women are routinely penetrated in every orifice, male bodies remain intact' (Attwood, 2005, p. 87). It is perhaps not surprising, then, that the thrill of witnessing the penetration of the male body might carry such an erotic charge for some women. As one of my participants explains:

> two men is automatically going to be hotter than anything else, and I've thought about why … Is it because it's the only sort of sex I'm never going to experience? …. Is it because it's two testosterone-fuelled men having moments of tenderness and stuff? … [Is it] because we're taking two men who we expect to be very traditionally masculine and they're doing something which in our culture is considered *not* to be traditionally masculine—anal sex—so are we getting off on the taboos there …? (British, 35–44, married, pansexual).

It is clear that the relationship between pleasure and shame with regards to (male) anal eroticism is an uneasy one. Writing about her own experience of pegging, the author Susie Bright (1998) says, 'the first time

I ever asked a man if I could fuck him he said absolutely not. After that, I met a few men who definitely liked it… But after they came and cried out and loved every minute of it, I noticed a decided lack of conversation. They were embarrassed that I'd found some secret part of them. I sensed that if I insisted on talking about it, the taboo would get worse.' While Nancy Friday (1981) argues that 'in fantasy, men want exactly what women want: to be done to', this is not something that is frequently acknowledged in our heteronormative culture. Bader (2003, p. 211) explains that men with 'submissive' sexual fantasies are not unusual in his clinical experience, but adds that because such fantasies violate social norms surrounding masculinity, 'they may well be experienced as more forbidden and shameful in men than they are in women, [however] their prevalence is indisputable'.

However, taboos surrounding anal eroticism are frequently violated in m/m pornography. As Bishop (2015, p. 19) explains, 'the unapologetic explicitness of gay sexuality inherent to gay pornography transgresses hegemonic masculinity because it showcase[s] men having sex with one another, something considered to be a … severe violation of masculinity'. Thomas (1999) argues that, even more than drag, being forced to confront these images has shown society that men can have sex with men and still remain 'men'. It is the simultaneous breaking of these taboos around anal eroticism, and the subversion of shame into joy and/or pleasure, that many women find compelling about m/m SEM. The pleasure men can take from receiving anal penetration is paramount here. As one woman elucidates, 'I *love* hot guys getting so much pleasure from doing stuff that men aren't supposed to do… I am sick of the homophobic nonsense that too many supposedly intelligent people spout. This is my way of saying "up yours!"' (American, 45–54, single, heterosexual). The women in my study are not alone in appreciating this aspect of receptive anal intercourse. Tibbals (2015, p. 97) discusses the popularity of films featuring male penetration such as *Beggin' for a Peggin'*, noting how 'the dudes appear to be super happy … it's uplifting'; and in her work on women's porn, Clarissa Smith (2007) discusses the interest shown by some of her participants in a story involving pegging, where a female character uses a strap-on to have anal sex with her boyfriend:

Julie: I really liked that one… It was so different… I mean, he's so macho … so normal but she's … showing him it could be different… Some men are SO uptight!… It was just great!

Alison: She keeps telling him 'don't be macho'… He tries something he would never … he wouldn't know that he wanted … and he has a great time! That's what's great! (in Smith, 2007, pp. 215–216)

Similarly, for the women in my study who discuss taboo, it is the taboo nature of men getting off on anal intercourse that is exciting for most of them, as opposed to the taboo nature of homosexuality *per se*. Thorn (2004, p. 180) believes that the homosexuality displayed in slash and BL is largely abstract, as 'direct familiarity with homosexuality as practice may inevitably dilute the thrill of slash, which draws on a sense of taboo violation'. To this extent he feels m/m SEM may have less appeal for women raised in more progressive social environments, 'with more developed feminist consciousness' for whom homosexuality has little sense of taboo (Thorn, 2004, p. 180). While some women touched on this, the data from my study suggests that the vast majority of women who produce or consume m/m SEM are familiar and comfortable with homosexuality (in fact, many are active in promoting LTGBQ+ rights, as I will go on to discuss). Certainly there is an element of taboo violation, but this mainly stems from how women perceive *men* feel about penetration—it is exciting for them to see men embrace this so-often denied aspect of their sexuality. In addition, part of the taboo-breaking thrill for women engaging with written m/m SEM such as slash, is not just the physical vulnerability of men opening up their bodies to other men, but the emotional vulnerability of men (figuratively) opening up their hearts to other men. As one of my participants explains, 'homosexual erotic fiction appeals to me more than heterosexual erotic fiction because of the fact that homosexual love is still more 'taboo' than heterosexual love, which makes it seem more courageous to approach someone of the same sex romantically or sexually than to approach someone of the opposite sex. Male homosexuals, in particular, have to act against gender norms by showing affection for another male, which in my mind translates to them putting themselves in a vulnerable position, and which makes the emotions seem a bit more real and tangible to me. I am more attracted to the male/male dynamic than female/female, and more attracted to female/female than female/male' (Norwegian, 25–34, single, pansexual). Akinsha (2009) notes how interested a lot of slashers are in this emotional (taboo) relationship. This chimes with Foucault's (1997) assertion that it is the *emotional* side of male homosexuality, rather than the sex, that society finds so hard to accept. He argues that the portrayal of homosexuality 'as a kind of immediate pleasure … cancels everything that can be troubling in affection, tenderness, friendship, fidelity, camaraderie, and companionship' between men, and posits that 'what makes homosexuality "disturbing" [is] the homosexual mode of life, much more than the sexual act itself' (Foucault, 1997, p. 136). Part of what excites women about m/m SEM is male vulnerability, male honesty, male emotionality—as much as male penetration.

All About the p: Penetration and Realism in m/m SEM by Women

It is exactly this focus on penetration in m/m SEM produced by women (particularly slash) which has been criticised by some scholars. After all, there is nothing particularly revolutionary (or queer) about continuing to regard penetrative sex as 'real' sex, and neither does this focus on anal sex necessarily reflect lived MSM experience. On his blog 'Violated', gay male author Jamie Fessenden (2014) writes 'the fact of the matter is, MM romance [written by women] might be *about* gay men, but it isn't really *ours*'. Often such books don't appear to him to be authentic depictions of the real romantic or sexual lives of gay men, with their emphasis on monogamy and anal sex. To this extent, slash fiction has faced criticism for presenting potentially queer narratives in a depressingly heteronormative fashion—relationships between male leads can be seen as typified by an emphasis on monogamy and marriage (as a happy, fairy tale ending), and the manner in which m/m sex acts are written and described often conforms to Gayle Rubin's (1992) hierarchical valuation of sex acts, with (anal) penetration being portrayed as the ultimate, and ultimately most satisfying, type of sex (Hunting, 2012). Several participants comment on the fact that there exist subsets of slash fiction that are 'persistently heterosexual in perspective', in so much as they present a world where 'sex between two men is okay as long as one is feminised and it's all about penetration' (Canadian, 18–24, married, heterosexual). Bury (2005, p. 87), however, rejects the idea that anal sex is always portrayed as the ultimate act of trust/surrender in a mimicry of heterosexual encounters, arguing that the progression from, say, hand jobs, to blowjobs, to anal sex could also be viewed as 'two novices in homosex gaining confidence and skill'. However, this neatly avoids the problematic focus that many slash stories have on 'homosex novices', something I will return to in the following section.

In terms of its portrayal of penetrative sex, slash has also been criticised for its lack of attention to issues such as the threat of STIs (particularly HIV/AIDs) and ignorance of safe sex practices (Cicioni, 1998). While the infamous magically self-lubricating anuses of the early years of slash zines may have disappeared, much slash fiction still skirts around the issues of safe sex practices—after all, as slash writer Morgan (n.d.) argues, there's 'more to avoiding [HIV/]AIDs than slipping on a condom just in time for the main event. If it *is* the main event'. However, this would not appear to be an issue unique to female produced m/m erotica; we need only look to the popularity of barebacking in m/m porn produced for gay men (Dean, 2009, 2015; Mowlabocus, Harbottle, & Witzel, 2013; Scott, 2015) to understand that, for many SEM consumers (regardless of gender), safe sex just ... well, isn't that sexy when portrayed on screen or in writing. The theoretical and empirical work done within gay porn studies can provide reasons for the popularity of bareback sex (despite an awareness of risk) for both male and female viewers. Dean argues that barebacking remains a common occurrence in m/m SEM because of both its perceived intimacy (Dean, 2009) and its perceived 'rawness' (Dean, 2015, p. 224), what he describes as 'raw, unmediated contact with another body'. After all, as Daniel Bergner (2013, p. 26) argues, 'the erotic might run best on something raw'. Part of the appeal of bareback sex in gay male fantasy may well be because it is precisely the kind of sex they *wouldn't* have in real life (Mowlabocus et al., 2013)—and arguably the same argument could be forwarded with regards to female consumers.

One of the draws of m/m sex is that it offers women freedom from all the baggage that comes with heterosex, including pregnancy. If gay sex is partly exciting because it carries less risk (e.g. pregnancy), to substitute one kind of risk for another (e.g. HIV/AIDs) would detract from the fantasy. As Morgan (n.d.) points out, 'there are very few … who would find gay sex with all its potential hazards erotic. There's the cleanliness issue, for one thing. Then there's the very real risk of disease… There's [the potential for] blood and pain and allergies to spermicides used in condoms. There are certain health issues that tend to affect men in later life. There's the embarrassment of natural bodily functions at inappropriate moments. And the list goes on. That level of reality [just] isn't erotic'. While some slash writers have been accused of naïvité for the way in which they approach m/m sex, many writers do have experience of the sex acts they are describing, and are thus perfectly capable of realism if they so choose. For while women cannot *literally* have m/m sex, they can approximate it. As one woman explains:

> Once, at a Pride festival, I had a gay man who was flabbergasted to find that women were writing gay romance. He said, 'Is there sex in your books?' I said yes. He actually said to me, 'But you're a woman. What do you know about giving blow jobs?' I looked right at him and said, 'Honey, I'm straight. I'm not a nun.' At which point he actually blushed and said, 'Wow. I'm sorry. That was a really stupid question, wasn't it?' But the fact of the matter is, this attitude seems to be fairly common among middle-aged gay men—not men in their twenties and thirties so much, but definitely in their forties and fifties. They seem to think that straight women have zero knowledge of sex or of male orgasms. I actually had a male author—who is in his fifties or sixties, I think—say to me, 'I can always tell when a sex scene is written by a woman because no woman will ever know what it's like to have anal sex.' I said, 'Oh really? Because I've had anal sex, and most of the female authors I know have had it too.' He just sat there stuttering. He honestly had never considered the possibility that women have assholes too, and we're perfectly capable of making use of them. (American, 35–44, married, heterosexual)

I'm Only Gay for You: 'Straight' Men in m/m SEM

Many commentators have noted the popularity of 'first time' stories in slash fandom, where one or both characters are portrayed as 'anal virgins' (Salmon & Symons, 2001, p. 87). These often bear a striking narrative resemblance to the popular romance trope of the heroine giving her virginity to the hero (McAlister, 2015). Such 'anal virginity' often exists because the character(s) in question have previously viewed themselves as exclusively heterosexual. In these stories the sex itself is often accompanied by angsting as the hero is forced to rethink his concept of his sexuality and his relationships. Akatsuka (2010) is highly critical of this co-presence of homoeroticism within heteronormativity, especially in stories which feature protagonists' heated denials of actually *being gay*; what Jenkins (1992, p. 220) refers to as the 'I'm not gay, I just fell in love with X' plotline.

Foster (2015) argues that this happens because the heterosexuality of one or both partners represents a significant conflict for the protagonists to have to surmount if they are to have a lasting relationship, and in this way it is simply a novel approach to the classic romance formula. As one woman in my study explains,

> when you have a hetero romance, you know there is nothing standing between the main characters but the plot, while in m/m romance written in our universe, there is a whole cultural barrier than can keep our guys apart. There is so much opportunity for conflict. Maybe they're not out, maybe one of them isn't while the other is, maybe one of them thinks he's straight. They could be married, want children, they could have a whole lifetime of self-loathing behind them because society [or] religion [or] family has always impressed on them how wrong it is. For me, the greater the obstacles two lovers have to overcome to be together, the more wonderful the payoff (Belgian, 25–34, married, heterosexual).

Nevertheless, the 'only gay for X' theme has been viewed as distinctly homophobic by some scholars (e.g. Green, Jenkins, & Jenkins, 1998; Scodari, 2003), and it certainly presents some problems. However, the idea of changing someone's sexual orientation with either the sheer effervescence of your personality or your 'mad bedroom skillz' is erotic in and of itself, particularly when viewed in the context of women's 'compulsory demisexuality' and more open gender schema. It doesn't matter if you weren't 'gay' before, love conquers all. It doesn't matter if you didn't think you would enjoy sex with another man, now you've had it it's the only kind of sex you're ever going to want. Heteronormative, maybe. But, also, romantic. Also, erotic.

Importantly, this trope is by no means unique to female produced m/m SEM. Ogas and Gaddam (2011, p. 131) point out that the 'straight boy turns gay' concept is very popular in gay porn (see also Bozelka, 2013; Mercer, 2011, 2017). In fact, the way this is handled in male-produced m/m SEM is arguably often even more problematic; Moorman (2010, p. 163) notes the popularity within gay culture of porn 'celebrat[ing] "conning" straight men into having gay sex'. The porn site *Haze Him* (marketed at gay men) exclusively focuses on 'straight' college fraternity guys getting hazed into m/m sex. In discussing this site, and its authenticity, Ward (2015, p. 179) notes how 'the gay male scholar who first introduced [her] to the site assured [her] the videos are 'REAL!', which he communicated with more than a glimmer of excitement in his eyes'. As Ward observes (2015, p. 183), it's the fact that 'the seemingly innocent … straight boy is subjected to the most naughty of gay sex acts … that makes the films hot'. After all, taboos are made to be broken. It is this naughtiness that can make m/m porn so exciting.

The popularity of this type of scenario should not be underestimated. PornHub (in Duffy, 2016) data shows that 'straight guys' is the most viewed 'gay' category on their site, with two of the top search terms being 'straight first time' and 'straight friend' (PornHub Insight Research Team, in Duffy, 2016). The Insight Team go on to note that 'gay videos featuring "college roommates" are popular, along with … searches like… "locker room"'. If we accept that men and women have a similar interest in the transgressive nature of the erotic (McNair, 2013), then it is not surprising that women would also enjoy the same kind of m/m SEM as gay men. Jane Ward (2013, p. 135) describes her own experience of watching a series of porn films called *College Invasion* where female porn stars arrive at college fraternity parties in the US and refuse to have sex until the frat boys have engaged in a series of 'feminising and sexually intimate humiliation rituals with one another', such as stripping naked, putting on pink bras and panties, 'bobbing for tampons', and touching each other sexually. Ward notes that she finds these movies 'hot', particularly 'the performative and ritualistic way that straight men touch one another's bodies or order others to do so' (Ward, 2013, p. 136).

Ward (2015, p. 7) also notes that previous research on sex between 'straight' men suggests that this sex often results from 'desperate circumstances', such as situations of heterosexual deprivation that occur in prisons and the military. This way of framing the issue assumes that men only 'engage in homosexual behaviour when [they have] no opportunity for heterosexual intercourse' (DeCecco & Parker, 1995, pp. 12–13). Interestingly Jeffrey Escoffier (2003) has 'resuscitated' this concept of 'situational homosexuality' in his work on gay-for-pay porn stars (here the situational constraints are economic instead of physical), a genre of m/m that many of the women in my study actively avoid. However, this is not to say that situational homosexuality is absent from female produced m/m SEM. In fact, Ward (2015, p. 102) explicitly links what she calls 'the performance of necessary homosexuality' with the 'fuck or die' trope found in slash fiction. 'Fuck or die' happens when the author places two or more characters in a situation that forces sexual intimacy between them,[1] thus creating a plausible motivation for two 'heterosexual' characters to engage in homosexual sex. Although 'fuck or die' has been used as a plot device in many fandoms, it originated from *Star Trek* canon and refers to *pon farr*, part of the seven-year mating cycle of Vulcans. During this period Vulcans undergo a blood fever, become violent, and finally die from the resulting chemical imbalance unless they mate with someone with whom they are emotionally bonded. Many slash writers have used the concept to produce scenarios in which Spock—often stranded or trapped somewhere with only Kirk, or McCoy, or some other male character—enters *pon farr* unexpectedly and is forced to have homosexual sex to avoid death. As Ward (2015, p. 102) observes, 'fuck or die' is 'premised on the idea that all people are capable of acting out of accordance with their core sexual orientation should a desperate situation demand it of them'. Although death is clearly an extreme consequence unlikely to happen in real life, 'fuck or die' remains a useful metaphor for situations in which homosexual urgency is manufactured by heterosexual men and becomes an alibi for homosexual conduct. This is not unique to slash—as

Ward (2015) points out it happens in m/m porn (particularly 'cuckold' films and the frat-boy based *College Invasion* series) and in 'real life' (Ward gives the example of Republican Representative Bob Allen who, when arrested for offering a blowjob to a Black undercover officer, explained that he did so because he feared Black men: 'This [undercover officer] is a pretty stocky black guy, and there's other black guys around in the park that—you know!' (in Ward, 2015, p. 103)). One participant in my study explains that she 'enjoy[s] reading first times, or straight men who under normal circumstances would not engage in sex with other men. I enjoy the taboo aspects of gay porn. I like reading about men who have known other guys for a while, and then something small happens to them where they both just *know*' (Russian, 18–24, in a relationship, heterosexual).

However, the difference here is that slash fiction places an emphasis on both the (often permanent) emotional consequences of situational homosexuality, and the emotional basis for it. After all, in the classic *Star Trek* 'fuck or die' premise, Spock cannot have sex with just anyone in order to survive *pon farr*. He has to have sex with someone who he is emotionally bonded to, who he shares a deep intellectual and/or passionate connection with. Following on from homosexual sex, there is generally a move to acknowledging (and privileging) male bisexuality, as discussed in the previous chapter, and an emphasis on love and compatibility as a stimulant for sexual desire, as opposed to fixed gender-orientation, as discussed in Chap. 6. In this sense there are aspects of the 'gay for X' trope that conform to heteronormative expectations, but equally there are aspects which trouble them.

While the privileging of male bisexuality in women-produced m/m may be positive in some respects, the popularity of straight-acting or bisexual characters or actors in the types of m/m SEM that women engage with has also been viewed as homophobic to the extent that it reinforces some of the binaries it allegedly sets out to challenge (e.g. that 'being masculine' is an inherent or necessary aspect of being a man). McCutcheon and Bishop (2015) observe what they call 'homonegativity' and 'feminegativity' in their sample of women who enjoy m/m porn. Participants in their focus groups often made 'sweeping generalisations' about gay men, such as 'gay men don't use condoms' or 'gay men are fit and take care of themselves' (McCutcheon & Bishop, 2015, p. 84). While

McCutcheon & Bishop note that not all these stereotypes are negative, they nevertheless paint a certain kind of picture of MSM which ignores the diversity of the homosexual experience. Femi-negativity refers to the classification of an individual's gender performance as normal or abnormal (Bishop, Kiss, Morrison, Rushe, & Specht, 2014) and can take the form of prejudicial attitudes towards overtly 'feminine' or camp gay men because they are perceived as violating male gender roles. Women in McCutcheon and Bishop's study expressed a preference for more 'masculine' looking performers, with several participants indicating that they were 'relieved that only 'masculine' gay men were depicted' in the films the researchers showed to the them in the focus groups 'because of their aversion to more feminine gay men' (McCutcheon & Bishop, 2015, p. 87). A minority of the women in my sample also discussed this, with one explaining, 'If I think about a really, *really* campy effeminate guy in [a porn scene] it doesn't seem as hot as if I think about two quite manly masculine men being attracted to each other, and feeling, like, this tempestuous urge and just going at it. That… I don't know why that is, but there is something about the two men being very masculine and yet so attracted to each other that I find hot' (Canadian, 25–34, in a relationship, heterosexual).

However, once again these issues are not unique to women's m/m SEM preferences. There are similar issues with m/m porn produced by and for gay men, with several scholars noting that many gay viewers have a preference for actors who are overtly masculine in their build and behaviour, and reject what they see as feminine or flamboyant men (Harris, 1997). Gay male porn sites typically feature performers who are conventionally attractive and masculine, rather than gender-ambiguous or androgynous in appearance (Moorman, 2010). Moorman (2010, p. 166) notes that gay porn on major porn sites such as YouPorn or PornHub does little to challenge gender norms, in that performers tend to be just as 'conventional … and … masculine' as their heterosexual counterparts. Mowlabocus (2007, p. 61) observes that gay porn is therefore often guilty of the exact same types of gender and body normativity found in heterosexual porn, with its 'toned, often hairless, well-endowed actors', 'hammy narrative', and the promotion of an 'all-American ideology of hegemonic masculinity'. Sites are overwhelmingly white, and men of colour are often pigeonholed (Bernardi, 2006; Fung, 1991). Asian men, for example, are almost exclusively relegated to the role of the 'submissive' and 'feminised' bottom with the sole purpose of pleasing white men (Fung, 1991). Relatedly, Arab, Latino, and Black men are typically depicted as dominant and hypermasculine (Mahawatte, 2004; Ortiz, 1994); often portrayed as heterosexual, they are seen as dominating white partners, and are meant to show an insatiable sexual appetite (Bishop, 2015). I raise these issues *not* to let female-produced m/m SEM off the hook, as it were, but simply to highlight that issues with how gender and race are portrayed in SEM are by no means unique to the types of m/m that women engage with. Much pornography continues to portray both gender and race in deeply problematic ways, something *all* producers need to be more aware of.

Gaypropriation: Women's Fetishisation of m/m Sex

Women consuming and producing m/m SEM has also been accused of what I have termed 'gaypropriation'—exploiting m/m sexual culture in order to achieve sexual satisfaction (Neville, 2018). To this extent, many of the criticisms directed at 'girl-on-girl' pornography created for the heterosexual male consumer can be directed at m/m SEM created for women, such as slash—that it is produced for the voyeuristic 'Other' gaze to the detriment of real homosexuals (Rich, 1980). As one of my participants explains, 'I've seen gay men … saying, you know: "regardless of whether we like the writing, there is a part of us that feels that you're using our sexuality to get off on and we're uncomfortable with that", and you do sort of have to be: are we being intrusive…?' (British, 35–44, married, pansexual). Bee Kee (2010, p. 144) notes that 'some gay men are offended at the idea of becoming "sex objects" for female pleasure', and the gay activist and drag queen Sato Masaki warns, 'when you're spying on gay sex, girls, take a look at yourself in the mirror. Just look at the expressions on your faces! You look just like those dirty old men salivating over images of lesbian sex' (in McHarry, 2010, p. 186). This has led some critics to express concern that homosexual men within slash fiction and BL are simply being presented as an aesthetic to be consumed, and that the queer lives on show are entirely fictionalised accounts, with no reference to social reality. According to Weinstein (2006, p. 615) slash is therefore more 'fascination with' rather than 'representation of' gay relationships. Busse (2006, p. 211) notes that many LGBTQ+ writers and/or readers perceive homophobia within slash writing and its surrounding discourses because of the 'fetishisation of gay sex' and 'the lack of a clear sociocultural and historicopolitcal context'. Akatsuka (2010, p. 172, emphasis added) stresses that while readers and writers of slash may well not deny, or denigrate, the existence of queer individuals in real life, what 'trouble[s]' him is 'not that writers or readers are homophobic, but that they could easily consume [m/m's] queerness without necessarily being *anti*-homophobic'. Some scholars have gone further; Keith Vincent (in McHarry, 2007, p. 186) maintains that slash and BL readers are 'violently co-opting the reality of gay men and transferring it into their own masturbatory fantasy'.

Tanigawa Tamae (in Lunsing, 2006, p. 18) counters the assertion that women watching or reading m/m SEM are like 'dirty old men' watching 'lesbian' porn, by redirecting the consideration of oppression to the female consumer. Tamae argues that gay men themselves are often agents of oppression via their position as men, and it is not at all obvious that women in society are *de facto* more advantaged than gay men. Lunsing (2006, p. 33) argues that 'the implication that gay sex is objectified for the purpose of the sexual liberation of women surely is a queer use of male homosexuality *par excellence*'.

Lunsing (2006, p. 33) feels that some gay men object to women consuming 'their' SEM simply because they want 'depictions of homosexuality to remain in a closet, viewed only by an inner circle of gay men'. Likewise, some of the women I spoke to feel it is important not to dismiss women's engagement with m/m SEM on these grounds, because any expression of female sexuality has value and should be encouraged. One participant stresses that

> 'defending women's right to want to read about two guys getting it on as a sexual preference and aspect of their sexuality versus "appropriation" of the lives and culture of gay men is something I get a bit heated on. If [a]

woman [involved with m/m SEM] also becomes more interested in the civil rights of homosexuals or something, great, but there is enough shaming of women's sexual fantasies and interests in the world and every little bit is awful' (American, 25–34, in a relationship, lesbian).

Others actively resent attempts made by gay men to commandeer women's m/m SEM production, with one asserting that watching m/m is 'part of *my* sexuality, so when someone tells me to get off their territory I'm like: my sexuality is not 'your territory'!' (British, 45–54, married, heterosexual). There are occasions when this results in conflict:

T: It does become a game of one-upmanship… I remember a list on Tumblr of dos and don'ts in gay sex from a gay man telling women what they should definitely *not* write in their sex in slash, because he knows better. And I'm like: I'm sorry, you haven't been involved in every episode of gay sex that's ever happened. Who's to say that my scene of gay sex is not more authentic than yours?

W: Who's to say he's a good lover? Or had good experience? You know…

T: Exactly. Quite. So who's to say that my experience has been more similar to what I'm writing than his, because gay sexuality is a big rainbow, and there's all kinds of different sex acts in there. So, I feel… I've said that it's one-upmanship, and 'I'm speaking from a position of authority and I'm going to educate you on this', and I'm like, well, you need to examine why you think you're more of an authority than I am… I'm willing to engage in a dialogue on this, but not from the point of who's right and wrong—maybe we can learn from each other—[but] that's something that fandom is not very good at.

However, more often women are acutely aware that they are at risk of being appropriative, often more so than gay men they had discussed their m/m use with. As one participant explains, 'generally the gay men I've spoken to are much less discomfited by the idea [that I write m/m] than I am, I feel like I dance on the edge of fetishisation' (British, 18–24, single, bisexual). There is also awareness that some of the concerns around gaypropriation stem from the key role that m/m porn has played in gay life. While heteroporn is generally marginal to the overall construction of heterosexual identity (Trostle, 1993), for the gay male m/m porn 'often serves as an important source for the definition of desire and identity' (Fejes, 2002, p. 95). Gay porn thus occupies a central position in the structure of gay male desire, identity, and community (Bishop, 2015; Clark, 1990; McKee, 1999; Mercer, 2017; Morrison, Morrison, & Bradley, 2007; Sherman, 1995; Tucker, 1990; Waugh, 1996). This may explain why its co-opting by people other than MSM can feel so appropriative. Woledge (2006, p. 103) claims that such appropriation is 'not homophobic so much as homoindifferent'. Slash, for example, makes little use of modern homosexual politics, and the sexuality of the protagonists is often not a big deal. Relatedly, many BL stories contain a strong fantasy element, with a fantastic, historic, or futuristic setting (Shamoon, 2004), and much slash comes from within fantastic or future universes (with some of the biggest fandoms being around *Star Trek, Supernatural, Teen Wolf, Harry Potter* etc.). It is not naïve to assume in such settings that gender and sexuality would not matter, or at least would matter less. These types of stories do not trivialise gay life because they are not 'about' gay men, rather they are about men who are in many ways post-sexual (McLelland, 2001). This in and of itself need not be viewed negatively. For, as Bronski (1984, p. 173) argues, 'gay life has always allowed and promoted fantasy because homosexuality itself is such a forbidden fantasy'. As one participant explains:

> I have heard the arguments from some gay men that m/m slash by women is just objectifying men, that it fetishises gay sex and even that, as it's written by women, it can never be an accurate depiction of gay male relationships. I don't think I know what I think about the first two charges on that list, except to say that I don't think that the slash stories that I've read *do* objectify or fetishise. To the last point I would say that it's like saying only straight men can write, with any authenticity, a fictional account of straight male life. Also not all of these slash stories are *aiming* to be an accurate portrayal of gay male life—in the same way that something like *The L Word* could not claim to be the definitive guide to the entirety of lesbian existence. With regards to the depictions of sex, I'm intelligent enough to know that the sex scenes in slash fic are probably nothing like 'real' gay sex and I can separate the two whilst still enjoying the fictional depiction. (British, 35–44, single, bisexual)

This is not to say that *all* female-produced m/m SEM is apolitical. Martin (2012) observes a clash in women-produced m/m SEM between those who seek to actively de-link slash and BL stories from the topic of gayness via a universalising rhetoric on the beauty of *all* love, versus those who find stories which show a greater fidelity to 'real-life' gay experience far more compelling. However, most people use SEM has a means of escapism, and many women do not like overt political messages in their slash (Bury, 2005). As one woman in my study explains, 'I don't read [issue fic] because a lot focuses on 'queer culture' and despite being a queer woman myself, I find it alienating because ... it feels like I'm being spoken for, and plus I don't read erotica to learn lessons' (American, 25–34, single, bisexual). Despite the rejection by many in my sample of 'issue fic', it should be remembered that slash *has* nevertheless been regarded as more consciously political than much of the source material it draws from. Thrupkaew (2003) notes that slash writers show themselves to be 'much more thoughtful about gender issues than the run-of-the-mill TV shows they use as fodder'. This 'thoughtfulness' can occasionally lead to more direct action. Talking about queerbaiting, a practice whereby producers incorporate queer subtexts into a show in the hope of expanding the audience by attracting LGBTQ+ folk while avoiding alienating viewers who would disapprove of openly gay characters, Collier (2015, p. 120) notes that slash fans are among those who have become 'vocal' in their protests and have refused 'to sit idly by as the shows to which they feel connected to mock, erase, or otherwise dismiss marginalised identities'.

Likewise, previous research has often made links between slash production and consumption and real-world political views and social change. The *content* of female-produced m/m SEM may not be political, but that does mean that the *effects* of such production or consumption are not political. The majority of slashers in Bruner's (2013) survey overwhelmingly supported gay rights. Ninety-seven per cent knew lesbian or gay people, with 70 per cent having close LGBTQ+ friends, and 38 per cent having LGBTQ+ family members. One hundred per cent of her sample believed same-sex marriage should be legal, 92 per cent believed homosexuals should be able to serve openly in the military, and 92 per cent believed that gay people should be able to adopt children. Bruner (2013, p. 62) concludes that not only do heteronormative attitudes have no place in slash fiction, but they also have no place in slash fans' real lives. Similarly, only 13 per cent of the women who took part in this research feel that their involvement with m/m SEM has not impacted on their awareness of issues around gender and sexuality (13 per cent aren't sure, and 74 per cent feel it has had an effect). Sixty-eight per cent also feel that their choice of SEM has some sort of political angle (30 per cent don't think so, and 2 per cent are undecided).

Many participants speak about how their involvement with m/m SEM has impacted on their political and social beliefs and practices using the language of journeying—of moving from a position of ignorance or ambivalence to one of awareness and action (Neville, 2018). There is often a recognition that simply engaging with m/m erotic content is not sufficient to claim any kind of allegiance with real life LGBTQ+ communities, but that it can play an important role in not just raising awareness of gay rights issues, but of moving people towards playing a more active role in community activism (Neville, 2018). As one participant puts it,

> writing and reading slash does not make you an ally, but it can expose you to people who are allies, and give you a window of opportunity to become one yourself. You have to do the work, though; simply enjoying m/m work isn't remotely enough. However, you may begin to pick up on some simple issues; how gender roles are culturally established and enforced, how much disparity there is for marginalised people, and how what you may have thought was "normal" was anything but. Like I said, enjoying m/m can give you a window to see more of the issues at hand (American, 25–34, single, bisexual).

There is also a sense from many participants that this potentially transformative quality of slash fandom should not be dismissed, nor made light of, with one participant observing 'it's easy to hate on tumblrinas who are supporting gay marriage just because of John and Sherlock, but at least they're doing something, right? I think it's a stepping stone to thinking about the world and queerness in general' (American, 18–24, single, QUEER AS HELL).

While it may be the taboo element of m/m SEM that initially draws some women to it, what we then see is often a conscious decision to act to *remove* these taboos going forward. When talking about how their involvement with m/m SEM has changed their own behaviours, some women speak about small-scale changes they have made, such as talking openly about non-normative sexuality to show that 'it's nothing to be ashamed of' (Czech, 18–24, single, heterosexual), calling people out on homophobic 'jokes', and entering into discussions with regards to gay marriage rights and gay adoption rights. Participants note that the m/m fiction they have read, and the associated discussions they have had with other women within the context of online communities such as slash fandom, mean they go into these discussions with 'far better-informed arguments than before' (Belgian, 25–34, married, heterosexual). For others, slash has inspired them to take a much more concrete step into activism, such as attending marches and demonstrations, giving financial support to LGBTQ+ rights organisations, and canvassing for referendums on same sex marriages in the countries or states they live in. As one woman explains, 'I like acknowledging that men can love men and that it is perfectly normal. [Slash] actually got me really active during one of the local anti-gay marriage protests. I helped to organise voting the other way. My little protest. My little way to support equality' (American, 25–34, married, heterosexual). Another participant tells her story:

> Because of my involvement with [m/m erotic fiction], I have volunteered at Boston Pride, donated to It Gets Better, and visited the Out West collection at the Autry museum in Los Angeles, where vignettes from our forum's book, *Beyond Brokeback*, were performed as a stage production. I have worked tirelessly as a volunteer supporting the repeal of DADT [Don't Ask, Don't Tell] and the passage of same sex marriage in Maine and Washington State. (American, 45–54, single, asexual)

Particularly within the context of slash fandom, m/m SEM often serves as a way of women educating themselves about LGBTQ+ realities. As one participant notes, 'before, I was aware of the prejudice [lesbian and gay people face], but for instance I wasn't aware of the brutal danger transgendered people live with far too often' (American, 35–44, single). Other participants feel slash has removed some of their own misconceptions and prejudices about homosexuality, meaning they now are *less* likely to fetishise it. One respondent explains, 'I started out with this thought that there were tops and bottoms and they were totally concrete, and [I] pretty much fetishised homosexuality. But as I learned more, and understood the reality of relationships, sexuality, and the issues of gender, that all changed. This community is very open in talking about current issues regarding sexuality and gender, as well as the potential pitfalls with misunderstandings' (American, 25–34, single, heterosexual). As such, slash has enabled a number of participants to better support people in their lives who have subsequently come out as gay. Several participants in the 45+ age groups speak about having being involved in slash fiction writing since the early 1980s, and as a result feeling more 'prepared' (British, 55–64, married, bisexual) and having a better 'understanding' (British, 55–64, married, heterosexual) when their own children came out as gay. Sometimes slash is the *only* exposure participants have had to positive impressions of LGBTQ+ people. As one woman explains:

> K/S actually played a great part in shaping my belief system. Coming from one of the lesser-known South Asian countries with a conservative culture, my initial reaction to the discovery of the existence of slash was disgust, because that was the accepted belief system around me. But the logic and the rightness of that particular pairing won me over, and made me question why exactly I should oppose someone's love or free will. Once I started questioning automatically acquired traditional beliefs, there was no stopping it. Today, I probably hold very different views on morality from the majority of those around me. The rejection of homophobia in a very homophobic society alone makes me belong to quite a small minority here. (Laotian, 18–24, in a relationship, bisexual)

Some can see how increased personal knowledge around aspects of queer lifestyles is likely to have an impact on others through the nature of their work.

> I'm currently in medical school, and it's amazing to me how some of my classmates—and real doctors—approach sexuality. There is a very narrow window of 'normal', and beyond that, if you're a good physician, you can at least not treat your patient as a freak. It's a profession that exposes us to all sorts of human experiences, and so many of us can't even accept homosexuality, much less asexuality or any of the 'deviant' practices. It makes me terrified to think how many people won't be able to talk to their doctor, get treated and educated properly, because they'll be too busy just trying not to

get labelled as a freak—by a medical professional!—for liking BDSM [for example]. I think that slash fiction made me a more open, more respectful person. I can only hope that it'll make me a better doctor. (American, 25–34, single, bisexual)

Overall, slash is seen as a medium which can 'create better allies, encourage cross-identification, and bring about positive personal changes' (Neville, 2018). Steuernagel (1986, p. 125) maintains that homosexual fiction can make a valuable contribution to the gay rights movement, noting that 'art cannot make a revolution, but it can prepare the ground for one'. Social change involves more than just restructured attitudes and feelings, but what people think and how they feel influences what they do and how they act. If m/m SEM can affect how people think about homosexuality and how they feel towards it, it has the potential to directly influence their behaviour: 'this is the stuff of social change' (Steuernagel, 1986, p. 125).

Homophobia or Homophilia? The 'Special Relationship' Between Women and Gay Men

Much of the discussion around whether women's use of m/m SEM is appropriating rests on the broader debate as to the nature of the affiliation between women and gay men in wider society. The literature has often remarked upon a long-standing 'special relationship' between these two groups, both politically and socially. While the term 'fag hag' has mostly been rejected by academia for being 'homophobic and misogynist' (Sedgwick, 1989, p. 749), in gay circles it has oscillated between 'insult and inclusion' since its first appearance (Moon, 1995, p. 487). Usually referring to heterosexual women attracted to, or simply interested in, gay men or gay culture, the term has often been used in a pejorative way, either to describe women who attempt to come on to gay men, assuming that 'the homosexual man is gay only because he has not found the right woman yet' (Fisher, 1972, p. 66), or women who are confused about their own sexual or gender orientation. Penley (1991, pp. 156–157) therefore rejects the 'hateful term' when applied to women who engage with m/m

SEM, maintaining that it obscures the very real appreciation women have of gay men in their efforts to redefine masculinity, and their feelings of solidarity with them insofar as gay men too 'inhabit bodies that are still a legal, moral, and religious battleground'. Malone (1980, p. 6) views feminists and gay men as natural allies, regarded as 'twin threats to the family structure upon which American morality and the American economic system have long been predicated'. McLelland (1999, p. 77) agrees, identifying gay men as women's 'natural partners and best friends in the battle to win increased space for female subjectivity in conservative institutions such as marriage and the family'.

While the original negative connotations of the term 'fag hag' have not disappeared (Bauer, 2012), the term is now often used either jokingly or approvingly to refer to women who share a close connection with gay men. One of the gay male respondents in Moon's (1995, p. 502) study confirms that he uses the term as a gesture of affirmation, describing it as a way of saying 'you may not be gay, but you're a fag hag, so you're cool now'. Another adds that calling a woman a fag hag is 'kind of inviting the woman to share the stigma of being gay in our society' (Moon, 1995, p. 502). Peter Fisher (1972, p. 66) also writes about what he calls 'the special rapport between homosexuals and women'. He maintains the two primary reasons why gay men and heterosexual women get along are that firstly, gay men have no real sexual interest in women and therefore have greater potential for understanding and sympathising with them, and secondly, the male partners of heterosexual women do not feel threatened by this particular type of m/f friendship. While clearly sexist and outmoded, Fisher's work generated interest in this phenomenon, which has been built on more recently by Russell (Russell, Ta, Lewis, Babcock, & Ickes, 2015; Russell, 2016), who proposes that gay men's lack of motives to either 'mate' with heterosexual women or compete with them for 'mates' enhances women's trust in gay men and increases their willingness to befriend them. Russell (2016, p. v) echoes Fisher's language when he calls this evidence of a 'special connection' between straight women and gay men. Queen (1997, p. 79) speculates that while some straight women may well be attracted to gay men's unavailability, and be focused on trying to craft a 'recognisable heterosexual relationship with one', what she wants is 'a queer connection, a reminder that boys and girls don't have to play those tired old games even when they choose to play with each other'.

Many of the women I spoke to have close relationships with gay men in their day-to-day lives, and 32 per cent of the women in my study who produce m/m SEM (generally slash fiction) have discussed their writing with gay male friends and family members. The response they receive has generally been positive; although some were disinterested, cases of gay male friends feeling exploited or fetishised are rare. One woman discusses how when she mentions she writes m/m to MSM they 'ask if they can read it, usually. My best friend is a gay man and my boyfriend is bi and they've both said my writing made them hard' (British, 25–34, in a relationship, pansexual). Some women report MSM as being incredibly enthusiastic, even about slash fiction: 'the gay guy I did talk to about it said, 'OMG IS THERE JOHN/RODNEY FANFIC OUT THERE??? CAN YOU GET ME LINKS???'' (American, 45–54, single, bisexual). Occasionally the discussion of shared sexual interest brought about a sense of comradeship and bonding:

One of [my best] friends is a gay man. Early on, we were always very simpatico in what we were interested in in literature, movies, TV, etc., but had never talked about what I guess I think of as 'my fandom life online'. When we were getting to know one another as friends do, getting coffee, hanging out, talking shit, etc., he looked at me one day, apropos of seemingly nothing, and was like, 'Do you read fan fiction?' And I was like, pause, 'Yes.' And he was like, 'Slash fan fiction?' And I was like, 'Yes.' And he was like, 'What did you first read?' And I was like, 'Harry/Draco.'

And it was the best moment, most unexpected moment because he just looked at me and burst out laughing. And not in a mean-spirited way but in the way, though, that he had seen something deep about me completely and utterly, and I was like, 'Don't laugh! Oh my god, you've just seen into my *soul*.' And he was like, 'That pairing is *so* obvious!' And I was like, 'Why?' And he was like, ''Cause they're nemeses!'

Turns out he honestly doesn't read or write it, but we have since talked about how I genuinely think Kirk and Spock are meta-queer—meaning that they are queer but that it just hasn't been fulfilled exactly in canon—and he totally gets it, and takes my word for it in fact, but doesn't know *Trek* himself. He once asked me about this, which I think is interesting, while we were hanging out with his boyfriend no less, 'So you've read so much Kirk/Spock that you probably watch the canon stuff differently now?' And I was like, 'Yes'. And he was like, 'That's so amazing and crazy!' And we knew what each other meant and talked about how it was in some ways a 'warped'—not in a negative sense—way of seeing a fictional universe, but in this case a powerful one.

But the reason it was of course embarrassing for me the day he guessed about slash fiction is that he 'saw' my erotic life as well, not just the intellectual one, and could see how we, he as a gay man, and me as a straight woman, overlapped but were also different, etc., and I wonder especially— and will have to talk with him about this at some point—how does it strike him that I read 'his people', as silly as it sounds, to get aroused? Interesting stuff politically and personally there, right? (American, 25–34, married, heterosexual)

Decarnin (1981, p. 10) claims that the 'basis for the eroticisation of gay men by women' is not shared values or goals, but 'sexist culture', which denies women 'men's valued position'. Bauer (2012, p. 41) criticises the way in which Decarnin thus reduces the fag hag phenomenon to 'a side-effect of patriarchy', denying the complexity of the longing to 'become' a gay man that is expressed by some of the women that she interviews. However, Bauer (2012, p. 20) acknowledges that the gay pride movement has had consequences for how heterosexual women associated with homosexual men are portrayed, noting that 'now it [is] the women's turn to be scrutinised and defamed as straight infiltrators of gay culture'.

Moon (1995, p. 493) observes that there are instances where gay men's rejection of heterosexual culture can verge on rejecting *women*, perpetuating the dominant culture's sexist attitudes, even when such men 'share women's oppression under conventional heterosexual ideology'. Moon (1995, p. 499) notes that unlike gay men, women 'are not *assumed* to be part of the gay community, but must one at a time prove themselves worthy of membership'. After all, gay men are primarily socialised as *men*, so it is unrealistic to perhaps expect them to be particularly sensitive to women and their problems. To this extent, gay men have more in common with heterosexual men than they do with women.

To this end, some gay men object to women hanging around gay bars and clubs, as they dislike being made to 'feel like a spectacle all the time' (McLelland, 1999, p. 97). McLelland (1999, p. 97) notes that 'gay men do not view the invasion of gay space by heterosexual tourists, male or female, particularly favourably, nor do they seem to feel the empathy for straight women that some straight women feel for them'. Reflecting on the recent 'uptick' in bad behaviour by straight women in gay venues (particularly as part of hen parties), the drag queen Miz Cracker (2015) asks 'whether [straight people] should be [in queer spaces] at all?' After all, they present one of the few spaces where gay men can 'escape from the hetero panopticon', and being gazed at by women in what should be a 'safe' space can be unnerving (Miz Cracker, 2015). Likewise, some MSM do not appreciate women assuming a 'gay male' identity. Pat Califa (1997) discusses how the practice of women writing gay porn under a male pseudonym is not uncommon, but is not always welcomed. For example, Poppy Z. Brite (1998), a gay-male identified author who mostly writes erotica about gay men, discusses how the gay community responded to her coming out, portraying it as a fairly negative experience:

> What's embarrassing is the naïveté with which I believed readers would take my explanations at face value. 'Oh, she's really a gay man! That explains everything!'… I was completely unprepared for the people who thought my sexuality was some kind of promotional gimmick… I thought I was ready to be called a 'faghag' with 'penis envy', but I wasn't… All I'd really wanted was for my readers, particularly my gay readers, to have a better show at understanding why I wrote the things I did. With a few exceptions, though, the gay press ignored me. (Brite, 1998)

Walters is highly critical of women who 'come out' as gay-male identified. Critiquing Sedgwick, who has likewise claimed to be a gay man, Walters (1996, p. 847) comments, 'this does not even have the naïve honesty of the faghag who simply grooves on the panache of gay men. Sedgwick, the postmodern intellectual subject, must not only identify or sympathise or politically ally, she must *be*'. Likewise, Walters (1996, p. 846) is wary of Sue-Ellen Case's (1991, p. 1) assertion that, 'I became queer through my readerly identification with a male homosexual author', arguing that while it is 'perfectly fine to 'identify' with gay men' what Case's statement illustrates is instead, 'a trend toward a giddy merger with gay men that is left relatively unproblematised'.

Queer Eye for the Naughty Girls: MSM's Thoughts on Women and m/m SEM

Comparatively little work has been carried out asking MSM what they think about women who produce or consume m/m SEM. In the media, gay and bisexual men have generally been presented as viewing female use of m/m porn favourably. For example, gay porn actor, stripper, and dancer Chris Harder (2013) has reflected on how he is now 'shocked at how surprised [he] was in learning that a variety of women enjoy—and get off—on gay porn. And why not? There's certainly plenty of gay men who get off on straight porn or idolize female porn stars—Jenna Jameson are you there?' He adds that as a performer he also feels 'lucky to get some extra love from my burlesque gals who I think have probably watched more of my porn than my gay friends! It's all just a simple reminder to me that our sexualities, desires, and turn-ons are so much more fluid and seemingly incongruous than we realize'. Similarly, in an interview with Katie Welsh (2014) in *The Telegraph*, founder and director of *The Cocky Boys* Jake Jaxson describes how he refers to their female fans as 'porn mums… They post comments, come to our events, and connect with us on Twitter. It's great'. Welsh's piece also quotes Andy Medhurst, a Senior Lecturer at the University of Sussex Centre for the Study of Sexual Dissidence, on the idea of women watching m/m sex being exploitative:

> There's a long history of women being fascinated by aspects of gay male sexuality, ranging from speculating about which pop stars might be gay to the curious corners of slash fiction. Some gay men might find this problematic, but for me it's all part of the flexibility and creativity of desire. It's flattering, in a way, that others find gay sexual identities and practices so intriguing. (Medhurst, in Welsh, 2014)

These opinions are mirrored in my survey soliciting the opinions of MSM on women's m/m SEM consumption and production (Neville, [MSM's thoughts on women and m/m SEM], unpublished raw data; $n = 166$). Sixty per cent of my sample have discussed m/m porn use with female friends, and are aware that women are often interested in m/m sexuality. As such, 75 per cent are unsurprised that 'gay male' is the second most popular category for women visiting PornHub. Nearly all the men I spoke with are very open to women using 'their' porn, and do not, on the whole, find it appropriating. 'I think it's understandable', one explains,

> this is a very presumptuous remark to make, but I think women are poorly catered for and poorly represented in straight porn. Gay male porn—while full of sexist and misogynist discourse—at least avoids the glorification of female pain, for example. I always think women in porn are forced to over-act too—can't be that enjoyable for a lot of women. Finally, I think that gay porn offers something of a "forbidden fruit" for women. It is bad enough that two men are having sex—that a woman is getting off on it really runs against heteronormative values—I think that is very appealing for many women (British, 35–44, gay).

Another agrees, stating 'women like watching dudes get it on, so what? Plus there's a much wider selection of guys in the gay porn category: there's rarely much of a focus on men at all in straight porn, and they're often man-scaped Ken dolls. Or so I hear' (American, 25–44, gay). Echoing the opinion of many of the women I spoke with, one observes 'gay porn does a far better job of showing off the male body and the physicality of male sexuality. Of course women are going to watch it!' (American, 18–24, gay). While many MSM are aware of the taboo appeal of m/m sex for women, this does not tend to phase them: 'it seems to be a trend that people desire quite a lot of that which is off bounds. As a gay guy, I know most gay men have a particular sexual interest in straight men as a fetish. I imagine this is similar' (British, 35–44, gay). As one man notes, 'I think it's awesome. Porn should be democratic: made by everyone for everyone's pleasure' (British, 18–24, gay).

The literature generally portrays MSM as indifferent to women's production of written m/m erotica. One of my participants notes that 'most gay men seem to be aware of the existence of slash, and consider it has no association with their lives. They regard it as "porn for women", and since porn use is widely accepted in the gay community, they leave us to our fun and ignore it' (British, 35–44, married, mainly straight). There is a general sense that while MSM might not feel fetishised by women's production of m/m erotica, they have no desire to consume it themselves. Hardy (1998) found that one of the reasons men gave for disliking a pornographic text was the belief that it had been written by a woman. In terms of slash, Bacon-Smith (1992, p. 247) asserts that gay men 'find it passingly curious, but not engaging in the long term'. McLelland (2000, p. 18) claims that this is because 'the highly idealised "homosexual" characters and fanciful plots' in slash and BL 'do little to foster a sense of recognition or identity in gay male readers'. Writing in the introduction to their book on slash fiction, the psychologist Donald Symons describes how when his co-author Catherine Salmon showed slash fic to gay men they 'laughed' at it, and then showed her examples of the kind of erotica they enjoyed, which had 'an absence of character development and plot' (Symons, in Salmon & Symons, 2001, p. 5). Male readers have critiqued slash saying that sex as described by female writers isn't like that for men—gay, straight, or bisexual, they don't talk or emote about it so much—a slashed hero thus has more to do with what the writers *wish* men were like than what they know men are like (Pugh, 2005, p. 102). However, not all scholars agree on this. When discussing gay masculinity Fee (2000, p. 59) describes men's relationships with one another as traditionally being 'instrumental, distant, and activity-centred', while relationships between gay men are more often characterised by 'disclosure, sharing, and emotional connection'. Having attended an LGBT writer's conference, aca-fan Davies (2005, pp. 199–200) states that a lot of gay and bi men *do* read slash, but are 'more discriminating in their choice of stories, and their reactions to the characters, both within the storyline and the sex scenes'. In her introduction to *Boys' Love Manga*, Levi (2010, p. 3) notes that BL has attracted a 'surprising number' of gay male fans, and posits this might be because of the greater fluidity in BL of gender and sex. She maintains that lability is an accepted part of Japanese fictional understandings and, in BL, this often leads to depictions of fictional worlds in which same-sex relationships and gender shifting are presented as givens without explanation or excuse.

In my sample of MSM, 73 per cent are aware of slash, and very few find it problematic or appropriating. While many find it amusing and/or badly written—'chick-flicky and clichéd' (Spanish, 25–34, gay) and 'cheesy' (British, 35–44, gay)—a significant minority of MSM enjoy it, noting that 'women appear to take the time on the characterisation and offer more rounded characters' (British, 35–44, gay). Most also feel that slash can have a positive impact on wider society: 'if it's helping people explore romance and sexuality, and possibly breaking down over-representation of heterosexuality in the media, then it's probably a good thing' (Australian, 35–44, gay). Seventy-nine per cent of MSM would read an erotic story featuring m/m sex written by a woman. Some are, in fact, avid writers and readers; indeed, the presumption that MSM find slash fetishising or appropriating can sometimes create further problems, in that it assumes gay men are not part of the slash community. Joseph Brennan (2014, p. 248) has discussed how he feels a great deal of 'discomfort' at how Symons characterises slash as an emotion driven, romantic, 'by women for women' genre, as it pushes gay men who are involved in slash to the periphery, excluding them from discussions about the nature of the genre, and ignoring their contributions to slash fandom. He also points out that for male slashers, the process of producing or consuming slash '*is* linked with homosexual life, history, and social issues' (Brennan, 2014, p. 251). While he does not dispute that slash and fannish practice is female dominated, he feels the way scholars have neglected gay men's involvement in the genre has only served to limit the field of study. To this extent, while the taboos of m/m sex are something that both women and gay men can enjoy, the negative connotations of such taboos are something that both women and gay men can work to remove.

Notes

1. It can be, and often is, combined with others such as 'Sex Pollen' or 'Aliens made Them Do It'. There's also a lot of excellent meta works that knowingly wink to this convention.

References

Akatsuka, M. K. (2010). Uttering the absurd, revaluing the abject: Femininity and the disavowal of homosexuality in transnational boys' love manga. In A. Levi, M. McHarry, & D. Pagliasotti (Eds.), *Boys' love manga* (pp. 159–176). Jefferson: McFarland and Company.

Akinsha, M. K. (2009). *A story of man's great love for his fellow man: Slash fan fiction, a literary genre.* Unpublished MA dissertation, Central European University. Retrieved from etd.ceu.hu.

Attwood, F. (2005). 'Tits and ass and porn and fighting': Male heterosexuality in magazines for men. *International Journal of Cultural Studies, 8*(1), 83–100.

Bacon-Smith, C. (1992). *'Enterprising women': Television fandom and the creation of popular myth.* Philadelphia: University of Pennsylvania Press.

Bader, M. J. (2003). *Arousal: The secret logic of sexual fantasies.* London: Macmillan.

Bataille, G. (1957/1986). *Eroticism: Death and sensuality* (M. Dalwood, Trans.). San Francisco: City of Light Books.

Bauer, C. K. (2012). *Naughty girls and gay male romance/porn: Slash fiction, boys' love manga, and other works by female 'cross-voyeurs' in the US Academic Discourses.* Hamburg: Anchor Academic Publishing.

Bee Kee, T. (2010). Rewriting gender and sexuality in English-language yaoi fanfiction. In A. Levi, M. McHarry, & D. Pagliassotti (Eds.), *Boys' love manga: Essays on the sexual ambiguity and cross-cultural fandom of the genre* (pp. 126–156). Jefferson, NC: McFarland & Company, Inc.

Bergner, D. (2013). *What do women want? Adventures in the science of female desire.* London: Canongate.

Bernardi, D. (2006). Interracial joysticks: Pornography's web of racist attractions. In P. Lehman (Ed.), *Pornography: Film and culture* (pp. 220–243). New Brunswick, NJ: Rutgers University Press.

Bishop, C. J. (2015). 'Cocked, locked, and ready to fuck?': A synthesis and review of the gay male pornography literature. *Psychology & Sexuality, 6*(1), 5–27.

Bishop, C. J., Kiss, M., Morrison, T. G., Rushe, D. M., & Specht, J. (2014). The association between gay men's stereotypic beliefs about drag queens and their endorsement of hypermasculinity. *Journal of Homosexuality, 61,* 554–567.

Bozelka, K. J. (2013). The gay-for-pay gaze in gay male pornography. *Jump Cut: A Review of Contemporary Media, 55.* Retrieved from http://ejumpcut.org/archive/jc55.2013/BozelkaGayForPay/

Brennan, J. (2014). Not 'from my hot little ovaries': How slash manips pierce reductive assumptions. *Continuum: Journal of Media & Cultural Studies, 28*(2), 247–264.

Bright, S. (1998, May 22). Move over, Ken, it's 'Bend Over Boyfriend'. *Salon*. Retrieved from http://www.salon.com/1998/05/22/nc_22brig/

Brite, P. Z. (1998). *Enough rope*. Retrieved from http://www.poppyzbrite.com/rope.html

Bronski, M. (Ed.). (1984). *Culture clash: The making of gay sensibility*. Boston: South End Press.

Bruner, J. (2013). *I 'like' slash: The demographics of facebook slash communities*. Thesis submitted to The University of Louisville. Retrieved from http://ir.library.louisville.edu/cgi/viewcontent.cgi?article=1169&context=etd

Burke, M. (1994). Homosexuality as deviance: The case of the gay police officer. *The British Journal of Criminology, 34*(2), 192–203.

Bury, R. (2005). *Cyberspaces of their own: Female fandoms online*. New York: Peter Lang.

Busse, K. (2006). My life is a WIP on my LJ: Slashing the slasher and the reality of celebrity internet performances. In K. Hellekson & K. Busse (Eds.), *Fan fiction and fan communities in the age of the internet* (pp. 207–224). London: McFarland.

Califa, P. (1997). *Sex changes: The politics of transgenderism*. San Francisco, CA: Cleis Press.

Case, S. (1991). Tracking the vampire. *Differences, 3*(2), 1–20.

Cicioni, M. (1998). Male pair-bonds and female desire in fan slash writing. In C. Harris & A. Alexander (Eds.), *Theorising fandom: Fans, subculture and identity* (pp. 153–177). New Jersey: Hampton Press.

Clark, C. (1990). Pornography without power? In M. Kimmel (Ed.), *Men confront pornography* (pp. 281–284). New York: Crown.

Collier, C. M. (2015). *The love that refuses to speak its name: Examining queerbaiting and fan-producer interactions in fan cultures*. Thesis submitted to The University of Louisville. Retrieved from http://ir.library.louisville.edu/cgi/viewcontent.cgi?article=3268&context=etd

Davies, R. (2005). The slash fanfiction connection to bi men. *Journal of Bisexuality, 5*(2–3), 195–202.

Dean, T. (2009). *Unlimited intimacy: Reflections on the subculture of barebacking*. Chicago, IL: University of Chicago Press.

Dean, T. (2015). Mediated intimacies: Raw sex, Truvada, and the biopolitics of chemoprophylaxis. *Sexualities, 18*(1–2), 224–246.

Decarnin, C. (1981). Interviews with five faghagging women. *Heresies, 12*, 10–15.

DeCecco, J. P., & Parker, D. A. (1995). *Sex, cells and same sex desire: The biology of sexual preference*. New York: Routledge.

Duffy, N. (2016, October 5). PornHub reveals what gay guys are searching for. *Pink News*. Retrieved from http://www.pinknews.co.uk/2016/10/05/pornhub-reveals-what-gay-guys-are-searching-for/

Dyer, R. (1988). Children of the night: Vampirism as homosexuality and homosexuality as vampirism. In S. Radstone (Ed.), *Sweet dreams: Sexuality, gender, and popular fiction* (pp. 47–72). London: Lawrence.

Escoffier, J. (2003). Gay-for-pay: Straight men and the making of gay pornography. *Qualitative Sociology, 26*(4), 531–555.

Fee, D. (2000). 'One of the guys': Instrumentality and intimacy in gay men's friendships with straight men. In P. Nardi (Ed.), *Gay masculinities* (pp. 44–65). Thousand Oaks, CA: Sage.

Fejes, F. (2002). Bent passions: Heterosexual masculinity, pornography, and gay male identity. *Sexuality & Culture, 6*(3), 95–115.

Fessenden, J. (2014). My take on women writing MM romance. *Jamie Fessenden's Blog*. Retrieved from http://jamiefessenden.com/2014/06/28/my-take-on-women-writing-mm-romance/

Fisher, P. (1972). *The gay mystique: The myth and reality of male homosexuality*. New York: Stein & Day.

Foster, G. M. (2015). What to do if your inner tomboy is a homo: Straight women, bisexuality, and pleasure in m/m gay romance fictions. *Journal of Bisexuality, 15*, 509–531.

Foucault, M. (1997). *Ethics: Subjectivity and truth*. New York: The New Press.

Friday, N. (1981). *Men in love*. New York: Dell.

Fung, R. (1991). Looking for my penis: The eroticised Asian in gay video porn. In Bad Object-Choices (Ed.), *How do I look? Queer film and video* (pp. 145–168). Seattle, WA: Bay Press.

Green, S., Jenkins, C., & Jenkins, H. (1998). 'Normal female interest in men bonking': Selections from the Terra Nostra Underground and Strange Bedfellows. In C. Harris & A. Alexander (Eds.), *Theorising fandom: Fans, subculture and identity* (pp. 9–38). New Jersey: Hampton Press.

Harder, C. (2013, December 11). *The ladies LOVE Cocky Boys: Fan favourite awards…* Blog post. Retrieved from http://chrisharderfilms.com/?p=67

Hardy, S. (1998). *The reader, the author, his woman, and her lover: Softcore pornography and heterosexual men*. London: Cassell.

Harris, D. (1997). *The rise and fall of gay culture*. New York: Hyperion.

Heiman, J. R. (1977). A psychophysiological exploration of sexual arousal patterns in females and males. *Psychophysiology, 14*, 266–274.

Hunting, K. (2012). *Queer as Folk* and the trouble with slash. *Transformative Works and Cultures, 11*. Retrieved from http://journal.transformativeworks.org/index.php/twc/article/view/415/315

Isola, M. J. (2010). Yaoi and slash fiction: Women writing, reading, and getting off? In A. Levi, M. McHarry, & D. Pagliassotti (Eds.), *Boys' love manga: Essays on the sexual ambiguity and cross-cultural fandom of the genre* (pp. 84–98). Jefferson, NC: McFarland & Company, Inc.

Jenkins, H. (1992). *Textual poachers: Television fans and participatory culture*. New York: Routledge.

Kipnis, L. (1996). *Bound and gagged: Pornography and the politics of fantasy in America*. Durham: Duke University Press.

Knudsen, S., Lofgren-Martenson, L., & Mansson, S. (Eds.). (2007). *Generation P? Youth, gender, and pornography*. Aarhus: University of Aarhus Press.

Levi, A. (2010). Introduction. In A. Levi, M. McHarry, & D. Pagliasotti (Eds.), *Boys' love manga* (pp. 1–10). Jefferson: McFarland and Company.

Levy, B. (2007, January 7). French philosopher and writer Bernard Henri Levy. *The Sunday Times*. Retrieved from https://www.thetimes.co.uk/article/french-philosopher-and-writer-bernard-henri-levy-ch72hhdsgjt

Lofland, J. (1969). *Deviance and identity*. New Jersey, NJ: Prentice Hall.

Lunsing, W. (2006). Yaoi Ronsō: Discussing depictions of male homosexuality in Japanese girls' comics, gay comics and gay pornography. *Intersections: Gender & Sexuality in Asia & the Pacific, 12*. Available at: http://intersections.anu.edu.au/issue12/lunsing.html

Mackinnon, K. (1997). *Uneasy pleasures: The male as erotic object*. London: Cygnus Arts.

Mahawatte, R. (2004). Loving the other: Arab-male fetish pornography and the dark continent of masculinity. In P. Church Gibson (Ed.), *More dirty looks: Gender, pornography, and power* (pp. 127–136). London: BFI.

Malone, J. (1980). *Straight women/gay men: A special relationship*. New York: The Dial Press.

Martin, F. (2012). Girls who love boys' love: Japanese homoerotic manga as trans-national Taiwan culture. *Inter-Asia Cultural Studies, 13*(3), 365–383.

McAlister, J. A. (2015). *Romancing the virgin: Female virginity loss and love in popular literatures in the West*. PhD dissertation, Macquarie University. Retrieved from https://www.researchonline.mq.edu.au/vital/access/services/Download/mq:44291/SOURCE1

McCutcheon, J. M., & Bishop, C. J. (2015). An erotic alternative? Women's perception of gay male pornography. *Psychology & Sexuality, 6*(1–2), 75–92.

McHarry, M. (2007). Identity umoored: Yaoi in the West. In T. Peele (Ed.), *Queer popular culture: Literature, media, film, and television* (pp. 183–195). New York: Palgrave Macmillan.

McHarry, M. (2010). Boys in love in Boys' Love: Discourses West/East and the abject on subject formation. In A. Levi, M. McHarry, & D. Pagliasotti (Eds.), *Boys' love manga* (pp. 177–189). Jefferson: McFarland and Company.

McKee, A. (1999). Australian gay porn videos: The national identity of despised cultural objects. *International Journal of Cultural Studies, 2*(2), 178–198.

McLelland, M. (1999). Gay men as women's ideal partners in Japanese popular culture: Are gay men really a girl's best friends? *Japan Women's Journal (English Supplement), 17*, 77–110.

McLelland, M. (2000). The love between 'beautiful boys' in Japanese women's comics. *Journal of Gender Studies, 9*(1), 13–25.

McLelland, M. (2001). Why are Japanese girls' comics full of boys bonking? *Intensities: A Journal of Cult Media, 1*(1), 1–9.

McNair, B. (2013). *Porno? Chic!* London: Routledge.

Meana, M. (2010). Elucidating women's (hetero)Sexual desire: Definitional challenges and content expansion. *Journal of Sex Research, 47*(2), 104–122.

Mercer, J. (2011). Gay for pay: The Internet and the economics of homosexual desire. In K. Ross (Ed.), *The handbook of gender, sex, and media* (pp. 534–551). London: Wiley-Blackwell.

Mercer, J. (2017). *Gay pornography: Representations of sexuality and masculinity.* London: IB Tauris.

Miz Cracker. (2015, August 13). Beware the bachelorette! A report From the straight lady invasion of gay bars. *Slate.* Retrieved from http://www.slate.com/blogs/outward/2015/08/13/should_straight_women_go_to_gay_bars_a_drag_queen_reports_on_the_lady_invasion.html

Montemurro, B., Bloom, C., & Madell, K. (2003). Ladies night out: A typology of women patrons of a male strip club. *Deviant Behaviour, 24*(4), 333–352.

Moon, D. (1995). Insult and inclusion: The term fag hag and gay male 'community'. *Social Forces, 74*(2), 487–510.

Moorman, J. (2010). Gay for pay, gay for(e)play: The politics of taxonomy and authenticity in LGBTQ online porn. In F. Attwood (Ed.), *Porn.com* (pp. 155–167). New York: Peter Lang.

Morgan. (n.d.). *The erotic versus the realistic: Sex in slash fiction.* Blog post. Retrieved from http://trickster.org/symposium/symp132.html#back

Morrison, T. G., Morrison, M. A., & Bradley, B. A. (2007). Correlates of gay men's self-reported exposure to pornography. *International Journal of Sexual health, 19*(2), 33–43.

Mowlabocus, S. (2007). Gay men and the pornification of everyday life. In S. Passonen, K. Nikunen, & L. Saarenmaa (Eds.), *Pornification: Sex and sexuality in media culture* (pp. 61–71). Oxford: Berg.

Mowlabocus, S., Harbottle, J., & Witzel, C. (2013). Porn laid bare: Gay men, pornography and bareback sex. *Sexualities, 16*(5–6), 523–547.

Neville, L. (2018). 'The tent's big enough for everyone': Online slash fiction as a site for activism and change. *Gender, Place and Culture.* Online first http://dx.doi.org/10.1080/0966369X.2017.1420633

Neville, L. [MSM's thoughts on women and m/m SEM]. Unpublished raw data.

Ogas, O., & Gaddam, S. (2011). *A billion wicked thoughts: What the world's largest experiment reveals about human desire.* New York: Dutton.

Ortiz, C. (1994). Hot and spicy: Representation of Chicano/Latino men in gay pornography. *Jump Cut, 39,* 83–90.

Penley, C. (1991). Brownian motion: Women, tactics, and technology. In C. Penley & A. Ross (Eds.), *Technoculture* (pp. 135–161). Minneapolis: University of Minnesota Press.

Pugh, S. (2005). *The democratic genre: Fan fiction in a literary context.* Bridgend, Wales: Seren.

Queen, C. (1997). Beyond the valley of the fag hags. In C. Queen & L. Schimel (Eds.), *PoMoSexuals: Challenging assumptions about gender and sexuality* (pp. 76–84). San Francisco: Cleis Press.

Rich, A. (1980). Compulsory heterosexuality and lesbian existence. *Signs, 5*(4), 631–660. (also 1993 same article, 227–254).

Rubin, G. (1992). Thinking sex: Notes for a radical theory of the politics of sexuality. In C. Vance (Ed.), *Pleasure and danger: Exploring female sexuality* (2nd ed., pp. 267–319). London: Pandora Press. (also 1984).

Russell, E. M. (2016). *How well, and how quick, do they click? Initial dyadic interactions between straight women and gay (vs. straight) men.* MSc Psychology Dissertation, University of Texas. Retrieved from https://uta-ir.tdl.org/uta-ir/bitstream/handle/10106/25594/Russell_uta_2502M_13364.pdf?sequence=1

Russell, E. M., Ta, V. P., Lewis, D. M. G., Babcock, M. J., & Ickes, W. (2015). Why (and when) straight women trust gay men: Ulterior mating motives and female competition. *Archives of Sexual Behaviour,* 1–11.

Salmon, C., & Symons, D. (2001). *Warrior lovers: Erotic fiction, evolution, and female sexuality*. London: Weidenfeld & Nicolson.

Sartre, J. P. (1952/2012). *Saint Genet: Actor and martyr* (B. Frechtman, Trans.). Minneapolis, MN: University of Minnesota Press.

Scodari, C. (2003). Resistance re-examined: Gender, fan practices, and science fiction television. *Popular Communication, 1*(2), 111–130.

Scott, S. (2015). The condomlessness of bareback sex: Responses to the unrepresentability of HIV in Treasure Island Media's *Plantin' Seed* and *Slammed*. *Sexualities, 18*(1–2), 210–223.

Sedgwick, E. K. (1989). Tide and trust. *Critical Inquiry, 15*(4), 745–757.

Shamoon, D. (2004). Office sluts and rebel flowers: The pleasures of Japanese pornographic comics for women. In L. Williams (Ed.), *Porn studies* (pp. 80–103). London: Duke University Press.

Sherman, J. G. (1995). Love speech: The social utility of pornography. *Stanford Law Review, 47*, 661–703.

Smith, C. (2007). *One for the girls!: The pleasures and practices of reading women's porn*. Bristol, UK: Intellect Books.

Steuernagel, T. (1986). Contemporary homosexual fiction and the gay rights movement. *Journal of Popular Culture, 20*(3), 125–134.

Thomas, J. A. (1999). Notes on the new camp: Gay video pornography. In J. Elias, V. D. Elias, V. L. Bullough, G. Brewer, J. J. Douglas, & W. Jarvis (Eds.), *Porn 101: Eroticism, pornography, and the first amendment* (pp. 465–472). Amherst, NY: Prometheus Books.

Thorn, M. (2004). Girls and women getting out of hand: The pleasures and politics of Japan's auteur comics community. In W. W. Kelly (Ed.), *Fanning the flames: Fans and consumer culture in contemporary Japan* (pp. 169–186). New York: State University of New York Press.

Thrupkaew, N. (2003). Fan/tastic voyage: A journey into the wild, wild world of slash fiction. *Bitch Magazine*. Retrieved from http://bitchmagazine.org/article/fan-tastic-voyage

Tibbals, C. (2015). *Exposure: A sociologist explores sex, society, and adult entertainment*. Austin, TX: Greenleaf Book Group Press.

Trostle, L. C. (1993). Pornography as a source of sex information for university students: Some consistent findings. *Psychological Reports, 72*(2), 407–412.

Tucker, S. (1990). Radical feminism and gay male porn. In M. Kimmel (Ed.), *Men confront pornography* (pp. 263–276). New York: Crown.

Waldby, C. (1995). Boundary erotics and refigurations of the heterosexual male body. In E. A. Grosz & E. Probyn (Eds.), *Sexy bodies: The strange carnalities of feminism* (pp. 266–277). London: Psychology Press.

Walters, S. D. (1996). From here to queer: Radical feminism, postmodernism and the lesbian menace (or, why can't a woman be more like a fag?). *Signs: Journal of Women in Culture and Society, 21*(4), 830–869.

Ward, J. (2013). Queer feminist pigs: A spectator's manifesto. In T. Taormino, C. Penley, C. Shimizu, & M. Miller-Young (Eds.), *The feminist porn book* (pp. 130–139). New York: The Feminist Press.

Ward, J. (2015). *Not gay: Sex between straight white men.* New York: University of New York Press.

Waugh, T. (1996). *Hard to imagine: Gay male eroticism in photography and film from their beginnings to Stonewall.* New York: Columbia University Press.

Weinstein, M. (2006). Slash writers and guinea pigs as models for a scientific multiliteracy. *Educational Philosophy and Theory, 38*(5), 607–623.

Welsh, K. (2014, August 25). 'Watching two handsome guys? There's nothing better.' How women fell for gay porn. *The Telegraph.* Retrieved from http://www.telegraph.co.uk/women/sex/11051140/Why-women-watch-gay-porn-more-than-ever-before.html

Woledge, E. (2006). Intimatopia: Genre intersections between slash and the mainstream. In K. Hellekson & K. Busse (Eds.), *Fan fiction and fan communities in the age of the internet* (pp. 97–114). London: McFarland.

9

'The Times, They Are a Changin'

We're beginning to claim our own sexuality. We're beginning to stand up and refute the madonna/whore dichotomy. We can be women, wives, mothers, sisters, teachers, scientists, etc., and yet we can still like sex or porn.
(American, 35–44, married, heterosexual)

The internet has revolutionised SEM, particularly for women. Attwood (2010a, p. 2) observes that the internet has 'domesticated porn', bringing it in to the home and allowing women to interact with it on their own terms, thus freeing women's porn use from much of the stigma that has historically dogged it. One of my participants explains, 'obviously we always *wanted* to look at porn, but probably were too embarrassed to buy magazines, and most of them didn't appeal to us anyway. Now there's the internet, there is niche porn which can appeal to more types of people, including women who were historically left out. Also, we can view it without anyone knowing, which makes it much easier, safer, and less "shameful"' (American, 25–34, in a relationship, heterosexual). This does not mean that there is not still the potential for shame—one woman laments that while porn is now 'easier to get privately, so that's great' she 'hate[s] it when Amazon pops up and recommends porn for me! My

© The Author(s) 2018
L. Neville, *Girls Who Like Boys Who Like Boys*,
https://doi.org/10.1007/978-3-319-69134-3_9

daughter has a field day with that' (American, 45–54, divorced, heterosexual)—it has certainly made it exponentially easier for women to consume SEM without fear of social condemnation. The internet has also taken a lot of the work out of accessing SEM—both emotionally and, to a lesser extent, physically. As one participant jokes, 'I'm betting [my daughter] will grow up viewing porn differently than I did. In my day, we had to go to an actual dirty video store! Uphill! Both ways! In the snow!' (American, 35–44, single, heterosexual).

Not only can the internet provide women with unprecedented opportunities for accessing SEM, it can also provide them with space to engage with their sexuality and sexual identity in new and dynamic ways. These two aspects are often linked. Accessing SEM can potentially provide a catalyst for changes in how women view sexuality, and the growing visibility of women's perspectives on sexually explicit representation can change how we think about women's desire. As Milne (2005, p. xiii) observes, women's involvement in SEM is often seen as 'helping shape and change society's views on sexuality'. One participant observes,

> I think the internet has particularly opened things up for women. I think men are culturally expected to consume pornography from a relatively young age. "Finding the *Playboys* under his bed" is a cliché, and we don't have an equivalent cultural-norm cliché yet for girls. It isn't generally considered to be a rite of passage, in the same way it is with men, for a girl to get her first piece of porn. And there's still lot of bullshit cultural baggage in the way the media discusses women's porn usage. Ugh, if I never again hear the condescending term "mommy porn" in relation to the *Fifty Shades* phenomenon… (American, 35–44, single, heterosexual).

McNair (2002, 2013) builds on these ideas, maintaining that sexual liberation in general, and acceptance of feminism and gay rights in particular, has generated a societal demand for more sexual culture, and for forms of sexual culture that deviate in various ways from those associated with established or traditional patriarchy. He believes that the expansion of what he refers to as 'the pornosphere'—'the space in which explicit sexual discourse is circulated' (McNair, 2013, pp. 14–15)—has led to a greater democratisation of desire, and the entry of traditionally excluded or marginalised groups into sexual citizenship. The internet, then, is 'the single most important influence on the structure of the pornosphere since the invention of pornography' (McNair, 2013, p. 28). Not only can it provide a storehouse for a depth and breadth of sexually explicit material, but it can also play a number of roles with regards to SEM: introducer, connector, provider, instructor. In 1990 Linda Williams suggested that 'pornography produced by, and featuring, sexual minorities, could provide a political response to the misogynistic and aggressive pornography of the mainstream market, offering a platform for the discussion of non-oppressive sexual practices and identities' (Williams, 1990, p. 64). Thanks to the advent of the world wide web 'traditional' heterosexist male-orientated pornography has now been joined in an ever more segmented marketplace by a diversity of pornographies, catering to all sorts of tastes and desires. As Katrien Jacobs (2011, p. 186) notes, 'digital media networks have allowed women and queer groups to develop and distribute their own types of sexually explicit media and to create niche industries', providing a medium for non-traditional SEM consumer groups to define their sexual selves. As Williams envisioned, the internet has not only provided access to diverse types of SEM, it has also offered a medium for discussion and dispersion of pornographic material, meaning that 'alternative' SEM is both more visible and more public. As one of the women in my study points out, SEM 'is becoming more open and mainstream. There is the potential for it to be a driving force in changing public opinions about sexuality' (Australian, 18–24, single, bisexual). In virtual space, consumption of SEM has become routine, almost mundane, part of a multitasking mode as users move between 'socialising, buying commodities, and searching information … chatting, peeping, cruising, masturbating, and maintaining friendships' (Jacobs, 2004, p. 73). Attwood (2010a) observes that porn then becomes part of a wider repertoire of interests and interactions that are simultaneously more public and more private than before. It is this public element that I wish to focus on in this final chapter.

The internet has also radically altered the dynamics and size of slash fandom. At the time Jenkins (1992) and Bacon-Smith (1992) were writing about slash, fandom was a place where introduction by a mentor was common, with tight-knit conferences and zines shared among friends or sent out to membership lists in the post being the norm. Now one need not come to a fandom via love of the original media text, then find fan fic, and then slash (the route suggested by Bacon-Smith), but instead can stumble over slash quite by accident when searching on Google for material related to a particular movie or TV show. One of my participants explains that she was 'looking for additional material about *A Knight's Tale*, at the tender age of thirteen I believe, and stumbled across [slash]' (American, 18–24, single, bisexual). As Collier (2015, p. 115) points out, 'gone are the days when potential slash fans had to be vetted and tested before being told about or offered slash'. One of my participants discusses slash in the 'time before internet': 'fandom was hard to find and slash fandom even more so—fic was insanely expensive photocopied zines, and, later, through *Professionals Circuit* archive, *if* you managed to find someone who had the goods and was able [and] willing to copy them. Bear in mind when I first found out about slash … most houses didn't even have a PC, let alone a printer or a scanner' (Australian, 45–54, single bisexual). For a small minority of my participants, the explosion of slash fandom in the digital age is seen as a bad thing, with one explaining,

> for me, and many like me who've been in fandom a very long time, it has changed to the point where the sense of community has changed. That sense of sisterhood that once existed between all fan fiction writers and readers has been lost, or at the very least stretched to breaking point. A different kind of bond exists with online writers than that which existed for those of us who wrote before the internet. In the old days, to exchange ideas we needed to either write a letter or go to the trouble of travelling to a fan convention. Now it's very impersonal, cold (American, 45–54, single, bisexual).

However, the vast majority find the availability of explicit slash and slash fandom communities on the internet a source for positive change, noting that it has 'allowed women to own their sexuality in a generally female-positive, woman-powered, safe and encouraging environment' (American, 25–34, single, lesbian). They comment that, historically, fandom was the prerogative of those who were wealthy and/or well-connected enough to be able to have access to expensive zines and to afford to travel to fan conventions, which was not easy for a number of women. While the internet is not a magic panacea for issues of access and inclusion (e.g. see Fazekas, 2014 for more on slash's race problem), it has vastly increased the availability of slash, and opportunity for discussion within the slash community. One woman in my study talks about how if you look at the recent past—say, the Victorian era through the Second World war—I think it was very hard for many reasons for women to congregate together, either physically or through print media, to create things such as slash. I'm sure they did throughout time. If you look at the Greek female poet Sappho from, god, 2600 years ago, it's clear that some women, always, throughout time, have succeeded in broadcasting to others—even to other women—their interior, sexual, erotic lives and fantasies. But on this scale? An almost-global—I say "almost" as many still don't have access or a shared language—scale? No. This is a new frontier, and an exciting one (American, 25–34, married, heterosexual).

The internet has proved pivotal in how consumers and producers of m/m SEM engage with one another, the formation and maintenance of m/m fan communities, and the demonstration of fan activities. It has also radically altered the production–consumption dichotomy, from disrupting it entirely, to allowing traditional producers to further control consumption by co-opting fan activity (Deuze, 2007; Reinhard & Dervin, 2012). The women I spoke with are aware of the potential for this, with one complaining 'we've been writing porny slash since 1974. It ain't new. What's new is that the mainstream is realising that we've been writing our own porn on our own terms with *Fifty Shades of Grey*. And now they want to monetise it' (American, 18–24, single, queer).

Indeed, Germaine Greer (2000) argues that the 'cool, post-liberal consensus' on porn misses the point. Greer maintains that porn has nothing to do with freedom of expression: it is primarily a business, a ruthless impersonal industry. However, a lot of the types of SEM discussed by the women I spoke to do not fit within the 'classic' porn industry model. One would be hard pushed to describe slash fandom, community writing forums such as Literotica, pornographic micro-blogs on Tumblr, user generated or amateur porn, or even much gay porn which—while commercial—has perhaps always had a wider social and cultural purpose (Mercer, 2017), as ruthless or impersonal. The sharing market we see in slash and BL (and, increasingly, in some of the DIY porn that women in this study express a preference for) is not only resistant to commercial and capitalist industries, it also demonstrates 'subcultural resistance to heterosexist regimes that attempt to enforce their notions of normativity and limit or cut off access to queer

media' (Wood, 2013, p. 51). As discussed in Chap. 3, amateur pornography—films, texts, and images—has come to connote a 'better kind of
porn' (Paasonen, 2010) that is ethical in its principles of production, and
somehow more real, raw, and innovative than products of the mainstream
porn industry (Dery, 2007). DIY porn sites such as *Sharing is Sexy*, an
open source 'sex positive collective' of polyamorous, queer, and transgender people who make porn 'for love rather than money' have been praised
for their innovation in bringing experimental porn 'up to date with the
latest ideas about everything from intellectual property and social net-
working to collaborative online creation' (Penley, in Attwood, 2010b,
p. 93). Many of the women I spoke to welcome the availability of these
'new' types of pornographies. While they recognise that the 'mainstream'
porn industry does not cater for them particularly well—'when having a
look at the covers of the porn DVDs in the local video store I still don't
feel addressed' (German, 45–54, single, bisexual)—the opportunity the
internet has given women to both produce and consume the type of SEM
they want is widely praised. 'I think women have taken charge of their
own [SEM],' one participant comments, 'we are producers, not passive
consumers. It's awesome' (American, 35–44, married, heterosexual).
Another adds, 'the internet has allowed women to gather and produced
porn [and] erotica by themselves and for themselves. This porn [or] erotica can also be distributed entirely without outside intervention or mon-
etary exchange. That's pretty much unprecedented' (French, 18–24,
single, bisexual).

Attwood (2010b) argues that the 'gift economy' and amateur origins
of much new porn production also provide a different context for understanding porn labour, part of a broader shift from cultural production
and consumption to usage and active engagement in participatory cultures such as that which has always existed in slash fiction (see Jenkins,
2006). Obviously not all DIY porn is an example of ethical, liberal and
guilt-free sexual representation, but the loss of elite control over sexual
discourse is arguably a positive, progressive trend (McNair, 2013).
Amateur porn makers often talk about how they want to 'give back to the
community' (McKee, Albury, & Lumby, 2008, p. 131). They see themselves as part of 'a community of fans and connoisseurs', where they are
not just producers but also ideal spectators (McKee et al., 2008, p. 131).

It is these more home-grown and community- based types of erotic content that seem to appeal to the women in my study, as discussed in Chap. 3. Often the sense of community and creative sharing they have found in their slash consumption (for the 84 per cent of the sample involved in slash) has informed their use of porn more generally. Mowlabocus (2010) has observed that the current set-up of many porn websites often engenders a sense of community, where individuals are able to express themselves in non-hierarchical and non-institutional spaces. XTube, for example, encourages users to engage with consumers and producers via their profiles and comments. The ability to comment on a video posted to the site—and 'track-back' and identify the author of that comment—suggests to Mowlabocus (2010, p. 72) that 'the video is not experienced on its own, but is embedded within the community that consumes it. These responses are sometimes, but not always, complementary and inclusive'.

The internet has smudged the boundaries between producer, performer, distributor and consumer for many types of SEM. Using the internet for distribution has 'changed the relationships between producers and consumers' (Kibby & Costello, 2001, p. 359) and complicated 'established ways of viewing cultural production and consumption as a linear process where ordinary people "receive" media and other products from media professionals' (Attwood, 2007, p. 442). This can help to alleviate the stigma of both porn production and consumption, as one of my participants notes:

> I think the stigma that porn is for men and women must be disgusted [or] threatened by it is weakening under the cheap means of production and distribution of the internet—it's now so easy to make and find the kind of porn you like, whatever kind that is, that the previous choke points of producers and wholesale buyers who kept the porn industry focused on a particular heterosexual male viewpoint are losing their grip. Plus, as the producer/consumer distinction erodes, the stigma on appearing in porn is weakening too, though not as quickly when it's a question of getting paid. From sexting selfies to your boyfriend, to high end 'boudoir photography' shoots, to pole dancing and strip teasing fitness classes, the sex life of 'good girls' is getting pornified. I know a lot of people hate that but on balance I

think it's a good thing... I just wish we could go a bit further in the direction of men being allowed and encouraged to want to be sexual objects—
consensually, and not exclusively—to women, not just to other men.
(American, 35–44, in a relationship, bisexual)

Patterson (2004, p. 211) believes that the participatory nature of
today's online porn consumption offers 'a sense of interactivity, which
brings with it a sense of shared space and a collapse or disavowal of distance'. There is now a sense of 'being there' when consuming porn, rather
than simply watching, as there 'is a sense of participation with the performer's life' (Patterson, 2004, p. 119). Likewise, many sites that focus on
written SEM, such as Literotica, also provide a creative community
detached from the institutions of publishing and literary critique. The
community is inhabited by dedicated and enthusiastic contributors, who
don't write for money, but instead for 'the love of it' (Leadbeater & Miller,
2004, p. 20). It is these sorts of virtual public sex sites which have the
potential to bring about social and political change—something I will
return to later in this chapter.

Dirty Little Secret: 'Coming Out' of the m/m Closet

While the stigma of women's SEM production and consumption may
have lessened in the digital age, I do not mean to imply that it has disappeared entirely. Talking about how she never discusses her use of m/m
SEM, one woman spoke about how she harbours a great deal of 'internalised shame—I come from an era where pornography was dirty, dirty,
dirty and no respectable woman would *ever* admit she used and enjoyed it'
(Australian, 45–54, single, bisexual). Others feel it is pragmatic not to
discuss their SEM consumption, particularly given the 'taboo' nature of
women engaging with m/m content: 'my porn use rests squarely in the
"known to self/ unknown to others" square of my Johari's window. I do
not think it would be appropriate within my social circles and it would
definitely adversely affect [people's] perception of me if they knew I
watched gay porn on a regular basis' (Singaporean, 25–34, single,

heterosexual). However, over two-thirds (68 per cent) of the women in my sample say that they *do* discuss their SEM use and preferences more generally with people. Often this is a conscious choice, informed by the fact that they actively want to remove some of the stigma around women engaging with SEM. One woman states, 'I'm very open about watching and enjoying porn, because I think it is important for women to speak up and acknowledge they enjoy sexual fantasies without shame' (American, 25–34, single, lesbian). Discussing porn is also seen as a way of helping other women to explore their sexuality and the potential of SEM to excite them. 'I have become much more vocal about [my porn use] recently', explains one woman. 'I'm tired of this idea that women can't enjoy porn. And when women tell me they find porn distasteful, it *always* turns out that they're talking about het porn, in which case I encourage them to check out gay porn' (American, 35–44, married, heterosexual). For some, the assertion of their enjoyment of m/m SEM is something they enjoy *because* it can be provocative: 'bigots just looooove being uncomfortable, and since they think about gay sex more than anyone else, who am I to deny them their pleasure?' (Greek, 18–24, single, demisexual lesbian). However, there is still wariness about having these discussions in front of certain people. As one woman explains, 'I love dishing on what I find appealing versus what others find appealing. Unfortunately, I've found straight guys can really tend to get the wrong impression about women who speak candidly about their porn use [and] preferences. They can often take it as "hey, she likes sex, she must want to fuck me", and then get all douchey about it' (American, 25–44, single, heterosexual).

However, while the majority of consumers are happy to discuss their SEM preferences, producers tend to be slightly more circumspect. While 83 per cent of participants who produce m/m SEM discuss their production with friends, only 33 per cent feel comfortable doing so with family. As one participant notes, 'there are some things a daddy should not know about his baby girl. It would distress certain of my family members if they knew anything about my activities' (Zimbabwean, 25–34, single, asexual/omnisexual). It has long been noted that many m/m SEM writers feel safer behind anonymous screen names (Morrissey, 2008). As Cumberland (2003, p. 263) points out, pseudonyms 'allow writers to avoid the real world "crap" that many of the women who write … erotica would face if their work was published under their legal names, or in the print media'. Cumberland (2003, p. 264) credits the internet for allowing writers to produce m/m SEM in a safe environment, noting 'in the past, the desire or need for privacy would have either limited the author's access to the audience or would have placed the author at risk of discovery'. In cyberspace, however, the audience for m/m SEM is potentially very large, since people can access it and read it in the privacy of their homes. While this means that writing non-heteronormative erotica has 'lost its undercurrent of seediness and danger' (Cumberland, 2003, p. 273), it is clear that a certain stigma still remains—hence the continuing need for anonymity among a minority of my sample.

However, the fact that comparatively few women in my sample (17 per cent) felt the need to keep their production of m/m SEM secret from *everyone* suggests that the stigma associated with women's porn use, even their m/m porn use, is lessening. In Boyd's (2001) study (n = 210), 90 per cent of slash writers maintained at least a small level of secrecy about their writing, showing a 'certain cautiousness and understanding of their environment' (Boyd, 2001, p. 99). Two major factors influencing nondisclosure were employment and their community's view on homosexuality, and these continue to be significant factors within my data. One woman in my study notes, 'I am very, very careful who knows about what I write. Writing male/male erotica can get you fired, lose your kids in a divorce hearing, etc. Most people are pretty apt to dump you in the same box as a paedophile' (American, 45–54, single, heterosexual). Another adds, 'I can't afford the consequences of someone in real life discovering what I write and then being able to use that as a tool of leverage to control me or negatively affect my ability to hold down a job, pay my mortgage, etc.' (American, 45–54, single, bisexual). However, more recent surveys suggest a similar lessening of the need for anonymity as found in my data. In Hinton's (2006) study (n = 365), only 17 per cent of her sample kept their slash writing secret from everyone.

Of course, for the 86 per cent of my sample who are involved in slash fandom, as well as other forms of SEM consumption, reasons for anonymity can be more complex. Seeking to explain the desire of some slash fans to remain anonymous, Lee (2003, p. 73), a slasher herself, uses *Star Trek* fandom to describe the slash fan as 'a double taboo', stating 'it's one thing for your co-workers, domestic partners, or children to know you're a "Trekkie", it's another to know you're a producer of pornography with gay overtones'. Bury (2005, p. 94) notes that 'slash evokes the discourse of the closet and one's relative position in it in terms of "in" and "out"'. However, not all of those in her study experienced the closet negatively, some enjoyed the secrecy and elicit thrill it entailed. Jenkins (2006, p. 1) has also reflected on how many fans have been reluctant to 'open the closet doors' to fandom. Brennan (2014, p. 373) believes that there is a 'shared commitment in the fan community to maintain the underground status of slash', and that many fans relish and actively maintain the secretive and taboo nature of slash.

Anonymity can, however, lead to problems. Brennan (2014, p. 368) argues that, in the context of slash, online communities have 'as much potential for prejudice and narrow-mindedness as real-world communities, perhaps an even greater potential given cultures of anonymity'. He believes that netiquette governing how people should behave in online fandoms is routinely ignored, and that 'cultures of nastiness and encouraged ridicule within online fan communities have free rein' (Brennan, 2014, p. 369). To a certain extent, Davies (2005, p. 201) agrees, noting that the 'intense world of slashers' can feel 'intimidating' to men, and that gay and bi male readers remain very quiet, seldom acknowledging that they read slash. A small minority of writers in my study also spoke negatively about the political aspects of the genre, discussing times when they had been called homophobic or insensitive because of their writing, with one lamenting the 'hatred and venom toward straight women' in the community (American, 35–44, heterosexual, married). However, this is a small group of respondents, and most add that they have seen a marked improvement—both in terms of the portrayal of m/m sex in fics, and in terms of community behaviour—over the course of their involvement with slash. It should be noted that this research did not specifically address negative experiences participants might have experienced in fandom spaces (arguments, flame wars etc.) and so should not be taken as an indication that slash fandom is free from unpleasant and upsetting interactions (see, e.g., Brennan, 2014). However, the vast majority of respondents spoke extremely positively of the impact their involvement has had on their social and political awareness around issues relating to gender and sexuality, and of their dedication to bringing about real-world change with regards to both homophobia and dismissal of women's sexual agency. Jenkins (1992, p. 221) agrees, noting that slash has 'established channels of communication between lesbian, bisexual, and straight women', providing them with 'common terms within which a dialogue about the politics of sexuality may be conducted'.

Fifty Shades of Change: Women and Porn in a Post *Grey* World

McNair (2013, p. 92) sees the demand for more and better porn for women that is prevalent in my study as 'an *achievement* of feminism rather than its betrayal, in that it is both a consequence and a reflection of enhanced women's rights'. The overwhelming majority of women I spoke to welcome this shift, with many pointing to the phenomenal success of *Fifty Shades of Grey* as bringing about a sea change in how women and SEM are viewed.

> This fucking book, *Fifty Shades of Grey*, right? Which gets on everyone's tits, we know, we all know our reasons, as writers, it's shit, but one wholly wonderful thing about it is that women are coming out of the woodwork *everywhere* and talking about the fact that they love porn. I was at the swimming pool, in the changing room at the swimming pool and behind the door I heard: 'Oooo, have you read *that* book?' I've heard people on the plane saying, 'Oh, I've got that, and I bought one for my mother in law'— I'm sorry, can you imagine giving your mother-in-law one of our stories? But perhaps we will be able to soon, and that's just wonderful. (British-Italian, 45–54, married, heterosexual)

Many hope that the success of *Fifty Shades of Grey* will open the door for more diverse types of SEM aimed at women, and a more frank discussion of women's wants and desires. As one participant notes:

> *Fifty Shades of Grey* is the go-to example of how even mainstream women really crave explicit erotica. And they don't care about quality. They're like

the 14-year-old who has just discovered restrictedsection.org and will consume *any* written porn they can find because it is brand-new and exciting. I'm hoping the climate will continue to evolve to where quality explicit erotica has a place in mainstream culture. Women want it and are becoming comfortable asking for it and talking about it, and that is fantastic. (American, 18–24, in a relationship, heterosexual)

The significance of this move from private to public, from subculture to mainstream, from the closet to the high street, should not be underestimated. DeVoss (2002, p. 75) argues that the 'historically significant but superficial divide between public and private spaces and identities has shaped women's lives, subjectivities, and sexualities'. As Nancy Duncan (1996, p. 128) observes, 'the public/private dichotomy (both the political and spatial dimensions) is frequently employed to construct, control, discipline, confine, exclude, and suppress gender'. As the internet starts to erode these divides, we can see a shift in the perception of women and SEM.

Additionally, cyberspace provides women with both space and place to create and reflect on the kinds of changes they would like to see. Brown (1994, pp. 32, 37) has previously noted that as women are a disenfranchised group, their talk is empowering because it 'contains information contrary to ideas validated in dominant or hegemonic culture', and that women-focused forms of fandom can therefore provide a 'space for women to construct their world in their own terms'. Their talk appears to 'produce, circulate, and validate feminine meanings and pleasures' (Brown, 1994, p. 32). Welker (2006, p. 866) describes how online slash communities not only give women access to SEM they enjoy, but can serve to provide such a 'narrative safe haven' where women 'can experiment with identity, find affirmation, and develop the strength necessary to find others like themselves and a sense of belonging'. Writing in *The New Statesman* Elizabeth Minkel (2014) describes slash fandom as a 'deeply supportive space for women and girls', one which 'can honestly make a life-changing difference for a person hovering on the margins'. Slash community spaces are not just about m/m sex, they are about women having a space free of heteronormative conditionings in which to chat and share meaning, and reflect on life, politics, the world (Bury,

2005). In addition, because these spaces are queered (as discussed in Chap. 7), they are (for some) 'safer spaces of connection and reflection' (Rambukkana, 2007, p. 77). One woman explains how what she loves about online slash fandom is that 'women are engaging with each other with curiosity and without judgement, and I think that's diametrically opposed to who we're taught to be to each other, i.e., we're supposed to be competitive and critical and judgemental, and I think that's bullshit, frankly' (British, 25–34, in a relationship, pansexual).

To this extent, online forums that provide space for women to engage with and discuss m/m SEM, such as online slash fandom, can be viewed as inherently transgressive, as they provide a space for going against current restrictive social norms (Neville, 2018). If women writing about sex is still seen as transgressive, then women writing about sex using the male body and inviting other women to enjoy these stories is doubly transgressive (Jung, 2004; Neville, 2015; Stanley, 2010). As a practice, it challenges the heteronormative metanarrative that informs much social discourse about sexuality and gender, 'thumb[ing] its nose at the insidious heterosexism underpinning most forms of literary expression' and 'celebrating sexualities that fly in the face of traditional heterosexist discourses' (Hayes & Ball, 2009, p. 223). Some academics have therefore viewed online slash communities as providing a space for exploring gender performance and sexuality in a way that constitutes Foucault's vision of 'creative practice' as a form of political dissent (Hayes & Ball, 2009; see also Bury, 2005; Shave, 2004). Others have regarded slash communities as a type of heterotopia, which Foucault (1986, p. 24) describes as 'real places … which are something like counter-sites, a kind of collectively enacted utopia in which the real sites, all the other real sites which can be found within the culture, are simultaneously represented, contested, and inverted'. Rambukkana (2007, p. 73, emphasis added) highlights the importance of heterotopias being actual spaces (unlike utopias which are simply romantic ideals)—it is the realness of heterotopias that means 'they have a substantive place in politics as spaces where *actual* things can happen'. To this extent online slash communities can be viewed as a type of digital counterpublic—a space in the public sphere where alternative identities can be reflected and where subordinated social groups can find support and collective resistance (Fraser, 1992; Warner, 1999). Indeed,

Lackner, Lucas, and Reid (2006, p. 192) describe slash forums as 'counterpublics … complex and multiple constructions of queer female spaces in an easily accessible public venue'. Martin (2012, p. 365) emphasises that BL online spaces are not 'feminist utopia[s]' nor 'zone[s] of unilateral sexual-political progressiveness', but argues that it is nevertheless noteworthy that they exist—participatory spaces, that, in Mizoguchi's (2011, p. 164) words, can act as 'unprecedented, effective political arena[s] for women' with the potential for feminist and/or queer activism. Relatedly, D. Wilson (2012) rejects the idea that slash fandom is space simply of the mind: fantasy, postmodern, implied. For them, 'online fantasy space overlaps, engages, changes, and is changed by embodied space every day' (Wilson, 2012, p. 4.4).

Somewhere over the Rainbow: Que(e)rying the Future of Porn

As well as providing space for the expression of female desire, online m/m SEM forums can provide space for the expression of *queer* desire. In Martin's (2012) study of BL, some women linked use of m/m with their generation's liberal attitudes towards sexual diversity, either citing m/m as a catalyst for the liberalisation of their thinking, or vice versa, citing generational change as the reason they were relatively receptive to m/m material in the first place. Martin (2012, p. 372) notes that themes such as gay rights, gay normalisation, and the triviality of gender as a deciding factor in romantic love 'carry strong echoes of gay-friendly rhetoric since the 1990s in the broader culture', adding 'this is a generation who has come of age with these rhetorics (if not generally their effective implementation) looming large in the public arena'. While this might be the case, it would still be accurate to describe our culture as heteronormative. As Johnson (2005, p. 56) observes, 'we call what we see in the world "marriage", "the family", "reproduction", "relationships", but we rarely prefix any of these things with the word "heterosexual". Far more visible, in relation to sexuality, is homosexuality'. Berlant and Warner's (1998, p. 548) assertion that the heterosexual couple is 'the referent or the privileged example of sexual culture' still holds true. Slash fandom (and other interactive homosexual porn sites) may be one of the few spaces inhabited by heterosexual people where this is *not* the case. Acadafan Jung (2004, p. 14) recounts a personal anecdote of a moment when, fully immersed in the fictional universe she was writing where same-sex relations were completely normalised, she spotted a heterosexual couple kissing at a bus stop, and thought 'how strange they look! A man and a woman', adding that 'a couple consisting of two men or two women would [at] that moment have felt more natural'. She explains that she is recounting this story not to argue for the primacy of homosexuality over heterosexuality, but in an attempt to describe how up to that point, and without her even being aware of it, compulsory heterosexuality must have been constantly at the back of her mind, that feeling of being 'a copy, an imitation, a derivate example, a shadow of the real' (Butler, 1991, p. 20). 'Only by its absence did I realise its otherwise constant presence', Jung (2004, p. 14) concludes. She states that one of her hopes as a writer is that 'some of that feeling of having truly been in a land "somewhere over the rainbow" for a while will also communicate itself to the reader, regardless of gender or sexuality' (Jung, 2004, p. 14). One of my participants similarly discusses how she rarely reads m/f erotica because 'heterosexuals having sex has to be about the characters. Sometimes I forget heterosexuals actually have sex in the real world. I'll think about it and become confused: "...oh, but not *really*... Really?"' (American, 25–34, in a relationship, lesbian).

Many of the women in my sample maintain that by speaking about their preference for m/m SEM—both semi-privately on m/m porn sites or slash fandom forums, and publicly with friends and acquaintances—they can effect some kind of real-world change. Elizabeth Wilson (1997) is sceptical of these sorts of arguments, and maintains that this sort of experimentation with sexual practices and roles does not mean social change. Transgression is limited in its effects. It may be personally liberating, and may indeed make an important ideological statement, but whether we can do anything more seems uncertain: transgression 'is a word of weakness ... we can shake our fist at society or piss on it, but that is all' (Wilson, 1997, p. 169). However, other writers have refuted this. In saying this, Wilson is suggesting that sexual activities are merely personal/private and do not amount to politics; that they cannot be productive in terms of social change. Beasley (2011, p. 27) disagrees, stating that the personal/private cannot be set apart from the political, and likewise that sexuality cannot be distanced from 'the terrain of social change'. Indeed, there is a long-standing assumption that what has been deemed private, including sex, does have political implications (Corber & Valocchi, 2003), something I touched on in Chap. 3 when I looked at Penley and DeVoss's arguments for the political impacts of slash.

Zizek, for example, argues that desire is constituted through fantasy, it is through fantasy that 'we learn how to desire' (Zizek, 1990, p. 118). If fantasies have no effect whatsoever on practices and identities, then the whole project of producing feminist sexual imagery to displace sexist sexual imagery, as pioneered by filmmakers such as Erika Lust and Louise Lush would be in vain—simply an interesting and amusing novelty rather than an intensely political intervention. However, a gay man quoted in Giddens' (1992, p. 123) *The Transformation of Intimacy* argues that 'sexual fantasies, when consciously employed, can create a counter-order, a kind of subversion, and a little space into which we can escape, especially when they scramble all those neat and oppressive distinctions between active and passive, masculine and feminine, dominant and submissive'. Among my sample of women there is great enthusiasm for the idea of online m/m SEM fandom spaces, particularly online slash fandom spaces, as heterotopias, counterpublics, spaces that are radical and have the potential to be genuinely transformative (Neville, 2018).

In his discussion of slash and heterotopias, Rambukkana (2007) draws on Warner's (1999) observation that restrictive zoning laws in real space which limit the number, size, and proximity of sex-related businesses in areas that also contain residences can threaten gay areas of a city. In this sense, non-conventional sexuality is constrained to the margins, to liminal spaces where no one lives, places which are 'out of site and out of mind' (Rambukkana, 2007, p. 78). If explicit m/m sites serve merely as idealised fantasy spaces for women interested in getting off on gay sex they would not have any impact on mainstream space, place, or culture. However, the change in knowledge, attitudes, and behaviours expressed by the women I talked to shows how participation in such a counterpublic can interrogate and overturn hegemonic codes governing the public expression of gender and sexuality, meaning that explicit m/m fandom 'can work to elaborate new worlds of culture and social relations … including forms of intimate association, vocabularies of affect, styles of embodiment' (Warner, 2002, p. 57).

For many respondents, participation in such online fandom spaces encourages them to talk more openly about queer sex—to demystify it, to challenge prejudiced 'jokes', to correct misinformation when they find it in the public sphere. Berlant and Warner (1998, p. 562) argue that the potential to change our social system lies in freeing sex and intimacy from their 'obnoxiously cramped' position within private space; by having 'public sex'. By 'public' sex, Berlant and Warner do not mean sex that is happening out in the open, but rather sexual relationships that do not pretend they have no connection to any social context, that can instead be a foundation for new communities that may then become dissenting political bodies—'public in the sense of accessible, available to memory, and sustained through collective activity' (Warner, 2002, p. 203). Many of the women in this study maintain that their involvement with m/m fan spaces *is* political, and we can read this through the lens of 'public sex'—m/m fandom can serve to decouple sexuality and intimacy from the private, and resituate them in the public. Sexuality is thus rendered a more public activity, not just because of its setting, but also in its cultivation of important dimensions of performance and collective witnessing. As Abrams (2012, p. 32) describes, sexual cultures such as explicit m/m fandom can foster forms of intimacy and trust that create a context for stranger sociality—'for casual contact or intense, shared observation that forge new forms of collective bonds between people with no prior acquaintance'. Explicit slash sites can help freer circulation of sex-radical discourse and change the dynamic relation between sexual subcultures and the mainstream public sphere, as well as asking that queer sexuality and relationships be publicly celebrated (Levin Russo, 2002; Neville, 2018).

Maddison (2010) describes how responses to the proliferation of pornographies online have worked to intensify views of porn as frighteningly pervasive and oppressive, or wonderfully liberatingly abundant, with both views working to mythologise porn. The aim of this book is not to say that women engaging with m/m SEM is a universal force for good, but rather that engaging with m/m SEM has had a positive impact on many of these women's lives and, arguably, an effect on their politics. As one participant argues, 'I think it's all contributing to the social acceptance of the idea that women can have sexual identities and desires of their own, independently of a man, and it doesn't make them weird [or] sluts, just human' (Scottish, 25–34, single, grey-a [demisexual]). This does not mean that women's choice of SEM is *consciously* political or that this is a primary reason for their engagement with it—as laid out in this work, women's motivations for engaging with m/m SEM are complex, multifaceted, and sometimes contradictory. Fathallah (2010, p. 3.7) notes that attempting to theorise why people like certain kinds of media is essentially problematic, inasmuch as media effects need to be interpreted through 'social/personal histories, parts of which must necessarily escape us'. She continues, 'we can theorise its potential and effects; we can describe our experience of it to each other, look for more or less frequently recurring patterns in its pleasures and problems, and try to understand what that tells us about ourselves and our communities in the context in which we live. But the attempt to say … why people like it will only lead us back to the exhausted, self-consuming mystery of an individual human nature detached from politics' (Fathallah, 2010, p. 3.7). So it is with women and m/m SEM—not to mention that some women *don't* like m/m SEM at all. However, the 'right' answer as to why women like this kind of SEM is arguably less important than the fact that women are finally having their voices heard. Not only that, but online fan spaces from within slash fic and BL afford women the opportunity to share the process of collectively thinking through these reasons in an inclusive and woman-dominated cultural space.

As Angela Carter (2000, p. 527) so eloquently wrote, 'pornographers are the enemies of women only because our contemporary ideology of pornography does not encompass the possibility of change, as if we were the slaves of history and not its makers, as if sexual relations were not necessarily an expression of social relations, as if sex itself were an external fact, one as immutable as the weather, creating human practice but never a part of it'. The women in this study show this need not be the case. Women *can* be the makers of history, and they *can* be the makers of porn. Through engaging with non-conventional SEM women also have the potential to change social practice. While m/m porn does not eradicate all of the problems posed by m/f porn, it does seem to offer women a space where they can positively engage with sexuality free from much of the concern and guilt which plagues their m/f SEM consumption. For, as Tom Waugh (1985) has noted, m/m porn subverts the patriarchal order by challenging masculinist values, providing a protected space for non-conformist, non-reproductive, and non-familial sexuality, and encouraging many sex-positive values. Is it any wonder so many women like it?

References

Abrams, K. (2012). Disenchanting the public/private distinction. In A. Sarat et al. (Eds.), *Imagining new legalities*. Stanford, CA: SUP.

Attwood, F. (2007). No money shot? Commerce, pornography, and new sex taste cultures. *Sexualities, 10*(4), 441–456.

Attwood, F. (2010a). Porn studies: From social problem to cultural practice. In F. Attwood (Ed.), *Porn.com* (pp. 1–13). New York: Peter Lang.

Attwood, F. (2010b). 'Younger, paler, decided less straight': The new porn professionals. In F. Attwood (Ed.), *Porn.com* (pp. 88–104). New York: Peter Lang.

Bacon-Smith, C. (1992). *'Enterprising women': Television fandom and the creation of popular myth*. Philadelphia: University of Pennsylvania Press.

Beasley, C. (2011). Libidinous politics: Heterosex, 'transgression', and social change. *Australian Feminist Studies, 26*(67), 25–40.

Berlant, L., & Warner, M. (1998). Sex in public. *Critical Inquiry, 24*(2), 547–466.

Boyd, K. S. (2001). *'One finger on the mouse scroll bar and the other on my clit': Slash writers views on pornography, censorship, feminism and risk*. Unpublished PhD dissertation, Simon Fraser University. Retrieved from http://summit.sfu.ca/item/7501

Brennan, J. (2014). 'Fandom is full of pearl clutching old ladies': Nonnies in the online slash closet. *International Journal of Cultural Studies, 17*(4), 363–380.

Brown, M. E. (1994). *Soap opera and women's talk: The pleasure of resistance*. Thousand Oaks, CA: Sage.

Bury, R. (2005). *Cyberspaces of their own: Female fandoms online*. New York: Peter Lang.

Butler, J. (1991). Imitation and gender insubordination. In D. Fuss (Ed.), *Inside/out: Lesbian theories, gay theories* (pp. 13–31). New York: Routledge.

Carter, A. (2000). Polemical preface: Pornography in the service of women. In D. Cornell (Ed.), *Feminism and pornography* (pp. 527–539). Oxford: Oxford University Press.

Collier, C. M. (2015). *The love that refuses to speak its name: Examining queer-baiting and fan-producer interactions in fan cultures.* Thesis submitted to The University of Louisville. Retrieved from http://ir.library.louisville.edu/cgi/viewcontent.cgi?article=3268&context=etd

Corber, R. J., & Valocchi, S. (Eds.). (2003). *Queer studies: An interdisciplinary reader.* Malden, MA: Blackwell.

Cumberland, S. (2003). Private uses of cyberspace: Women, desire and fan culture. In D. Thorburn & H. Jenkins (Eds.), *Rethinking media change: The aesthetics of transition* (pp. 261–279). Cambridge, MA: The MIT Press.

Davies, R. (2005). The slash fanfiction connection to bi men. *Journal of Bisexuality, 5*(2–3), 195–202.

Dery, M. (2007). Naked lunch: Talking realcore with Sergio Messina. In K. Jacobs, M. Hanssen, & M. Pasquinelli (Eds.), *C'lick me: A netporn studies reader* (pp. 17–30). Amsterdam: Institute of Network Cultures.

Deuze, M. (2007). *Media work.* Cambridge: Polity.

DeVoss, D. (2002). Women's porn sites—Spaces of fissure and eruption or 'I'm a little bit of everything'. *Sexuality & Culture, 6*(3), 75–94.

Duncan, N. (1996). Renegotiating gender and sexuality in public and private spaces. In N. Duncan (Ed.), *Bodyspace* (pp. 127–145). New York: Routledge.

Fathallah, J. M. (2010). H/C and me: An autoethnographic account of a troubled love affair *Transformative Works and Cultures, 7*. Retrieved from http://testjournal.transformativeworks.org/index.php/twc/article/view/252/206

Fazekas, A. (2014). *Queer and unusual space: White supremacy in slash fanfiction.* MA dissertation, Queen's University. Canada. Retrieved from https://qspace.library.queensu.ca/bitstream/handle/1974/12609/Fazekas_Angela_M_201411_MA.pdf?sequence=1

Foucault, M. (1986). Of other spaces. *Diacritics, 16*, 22–27.

Fraser, N. (1992). Rethinking the public sphere: A contribution to the critique of actually existing democracy. In C. Calhoun (Ed.), *Habermas and the public sphere* (pp. 109–142). Boston: MIT Press.

Giddens, A. (1992). *The transformation of intimacy: Sexuality, love and eroticism in modern societies.* New Jersey: Wiley.

Greer, G. (2000, September 24). Gluttons for porn. *The Observer.* Retrieved from http://www.theguardian.com/books/2000/sep/24/society

Hayes, S., & Ball, M. (2009). Queering cyberspace: Fan fiction communities as spaces for expressing and exploring sexuality. In B. Scherer (Ed.), *Queering paradigms* (pp. 219–239). Oxford: Peter Lang.

Hinton, L. (2006). *Women and slash fiction.* Unpublished dissertation, James Madison University. Retrieved from http://www.jmu.edu/mwa/docs/2006/Hinton.pdf

Jacobs, K. (2004). Pornography in small spaces and other spaces. *Journal of Cultural Studies, 18*(1), 67–83.

Jacobs, K. (2011). *People's pornography: Sex and surveillance on the Chinese internet.* London: Intellect.

Jenkins, H. (1992). *Textual poachers: Television fans and participatory culture.* New York: Routledge.

Jenkins, H. (2006). *Fans, bloggers, and gamers: Exploring participatory culture.* New York: New York University Press.

Johnson, P. J. (2005). *Love, heterosexuality, and society.* London: Routledge.

Jung, S. (2004). Queering popular culture: Female spectators and the appeal of writing slash fan fiction. *Gender Queeries, 8.* Retrieved from http://www.genderforum.org/fileadmin/archiv/genderforum/queer/jung.html

Kibby, M. & Costello, B. (2001). Between the image and the act: Interactive sex entertainment on the internet. *Sexualities, 4*(3), 353–369.

Lackner, E., Lucas, B. L., & Reid, R. A. (2006). Cunning linguists: The bisexual erotics of words/silence/flesh. In K. Hellekson & K. Busse (Eds.), *Fan fiction and fan communities in the age of the internet* (pp. 189–206). London: McFarland.

Leadbeater, C., & Miller, P. (2004). *The pro-Am revolution: How enthusiasts are changing our economy and society.* London: Demos.

Lee, K. (2003). Confronting *Enterprise* slash fan fiction. *Extrapolation, 44,* 69–82.

Levin Russo, J. (2002, August). 'NEW VOY 'cyborg sex' J/7 [NC-17]': New methodologies, new fantasies. *The Slash Reader.* Retrieved from http://j-l-r.org/asmic/fanfic/print/jlr-cyborgsex.pdf

Maddison, S. (2010). Online obscenity and myths of freedom: Dangerous images, child porn, and neoliberalism. In F. Attwood (Ed.), *Porn.com* (pp. 17–33). New York: Peter Lang.

Martin, F. (2012). Girls who love boys' love: Japanese homoerotic manga as trans-national Taiwan culture. *Inter-Asia Cultural Studies, 13*(3), 365–383.

McKee, A., Albury, K., & Lumby, C. (2008). *The porn report.* Melbourne: Melbourne University Press.

McNair, B. (2002). *Striptease culture: Sex, media, and the democratisation of desire*. London: Routledge.

McNair, B. (2013). *Porno? Chic!* London: Routledge.

Mercer, J. (2017). *Gay pornography: Representations of sexuality and masculinity*. London: IB Tauris.

Milne, C. (Ed.). (2005). *Naked ambition: Women who are changing porn*. New York: Carroll & Graf.

Minkel, E. (2014, October 17). Why it doesn't matter what Benedict Cumberbatch thinks of Sherlock fan fiction. *New Statesman*. Retrieved from http://www.newstatesman.com/culture/2014/10/why-it-doesn-t-matter-what-benedict-cumberbatch-thinks-sherlock-fan-fiction

Mizoguchi, A. (2011). Theorizing comics/manga genre as a productive form: Yaoi and beyond. In J. Berndt (Ed.), *Comics worlds and the worlds of comics: Towards scholarship on a global scale* (pp. 143–168). Kyoto: International Manga Research Centre, Kyoto Seika University.

Morrissey, K. (2008). *Fanning the flames of romance: An exploration of fan fiction and the romance novel*. MA dissertation, Georgetown University. Retrieved from https://repository.library.georgetown.edu/bitstream/handle/10822/551540/17_etd_kem82.pdf

Mowlabocus, S. (2010). Porn 2.0? Technology, social practice, and the new online porn industry. In F. Attwood (Ed.), *Porn.com* (pp. 69–87). New York: Peter Lang.

Neville, L. (2015). Male gays in the female gaze: Women who watch m/m pornography. *Porn Studies, 2*(2–3), 192–207.

Neville, L. (2018). 'The tent's big enough for everyone': Online slash fiction as a site for activism and change. *Gender, Place and Culture*. Online first http://dx.doi.org/10.1080/0966369X.2017.1420633

Paasonen, S. (2010). Good amateurs: Erotica writing and notions of quality. In F. Attwood (Ed.), *Porn.com* (pp. 138–154). New York: Peter Lang.

Patterson, Z. (2004). Going on-line: Consuming pornography in the digital era. In L. Williams (Ed.), *Porn studies* (pp. 105–123). Durham, NC: Duke University Press.

Rambukkana, N. (2007). Is slash an alternative medium? 'Queer' heterotopias and the role of autonomous media spaces in radical world building. *Affinities: A Journal of Radical Theory, Culture, and Action, 1*(1), 69–85.

Reinhard, C. D., & Dervin, B. (2012). Studying audiences with sense-making methodology. *The International Encyclopaedia of Media Studies, 4*(1), 3.

Shave, R. (2004). Slash fandom on the internet, or, is the carnival over? *Refractory, 6*. Retrieved from http://refractory.unimelb.edu.au/2004/06/17/slash-fandom-on-the-internet-or-is-the-carnival-over-rachel-shave/

Stanley, M. (2010). 101 uses for boys: Communing with the reader in yaoi and slash. In A. Levi, M. McHarry, & D. Pagliassotti (Eds.), *Boys' love manga: Essays on the sexual ambiguity and cross-cultural fandom of the genre* (pp. 99–109). Jefferson, NC: McFarland & Company, Inc.

Warner, M. (1999). *The trouble with normal: Sex, politics, and the ethics of queer life*. Cambridge, MA: Harvard University Press.

Warner, M. (2002). *Publics and counterpublics*. New York: Zone Books.

Waugh, T. (1985). Men's pornography: Gay vs. straight. *Jump Cut, 30*, 30–35.

Welker, J. (2006). Beautiful, borrowed, and bent: Boys' love as girls' love in *shojo* manga. *Signs: Journal of Women and Culture in Society, 31*(3), 841–870.

Williams, L. (1990). *Hard core: Power, pleasure and the 'frenzy of the visible'*. Los Angeles, CA: University of California Press.

Wilson, D. (2012). Queer bandom: A research journey in eight parts. *Transformative Works and Cultures, 11*. Retrieved from http://journal.transformativeworks.org/index.php/twc/article/view/426/344

Wilson, E. (1997). Is transgression transgressive? In S. Kemp & J. Squires (Eds.), *Feminisms* (pp. 368–370). Oxford: Oxford University Press.

Wood, A. (2013). Boys' Love anime and queer desires in convergence culture: Transnational fandom, censorship and resistance. *Journal of Graphic Novels & Comics, 4*(1), 44–63.

Zizek, S. (1990). *The sublime object of ideology*. London: Verso.

Index[1]

---

[1]Note: Page numbers followed by 'n' refer to notes.

© The Author(s) 2018
L. Neville, *Girls Who Like Boys Who Like Boys*,
https://doi.org/10.1007/978-3-319-69134-3

CPI Antony Rowe
Eastbourne, UK
January 11, 2019